D1564332

FLIGHT OF FANTASY

FLIGHT OF FANTASY

New Perspectives on *Inner Emigration* in
German Literature, 1933–1945

Edited by

Neil H. Donahue

and

Doris Kirchner

Berghahn Books
NEW YORK • OXFORD

Published in 2003 by
Berghahn Books

www.berghahnbooks.com

Library of Congress Cataloging-in-Publication Data

Flight of fantasy : new perspectives on inner emigration in German literature,
1933–1945 / edited by Neil H. Donahue and Doris Kirchner.
    p. cm.
Papers presented at a symposium held at Hofstra University.
Includes bibliographical references and index.
ISBN 1-57181-001-3 (alk. paper)
    1. German literature—20th century—History and criticism—Congresses 2. Authors, German—20th century—Political and social views—Congresses. 3. National socialism and literature—Congresses. 4. Germany—Politics and government—20th century—Congresses.
I. Donahue, Neil H. II. Kirchner, Doris.

PT405.F54 2003
830.9'00912—dc21

                                              2002043678

British Library Cataloguing in Publication Data

A catalogue record for this book is available from
the British Library.

Printed in the United States on acid-free paper

CONTENTS

New Perspectives: Case Studies

The Turn Inward Outside of Literature

History

Film

ACKNOWLEDGMENTS

This volume grew out of a symposium organized at Hofstra University by the Hofstra Cultural Center in cooperation with the University of Rhode Island and with the support of the German Academic Exchange Service (DAAD). We would like to thank those institutions for their generous support of that event, and in particular we extend our gratitude to Deborah Lom of the Hofstra Cultural Center, who was the symposium coordinator, along with Natalie Datlof, Rich Pioreck, Athelene A. Collins-Prince, Joanne Flood, and Jo Ellen Ryan, all of whom worked hard to help us realize this event and assure its smooth operation at all stages. The competence of professionals in knowing and doing what needs to be done for a successful conference is invaluable and rare, and we appreciate immensely their assistance. We would also like to thank Barbara Motyka of the German Academic Exchange Service for her support of the project. In addition, University Provost Herman Berliner made time to welcome participants to Hofstra in person and in German, which set the tone for amiable discourse in both languages throughout and added another dimension to Hofstra's hospitality to people and ideas. The graphic artists in Hofstra's Publications Services department were patient and innovative in helping me realize my concept for the program design, and I would like to thank them for their crucial help. We thank Frank Trommler and Wulf Koepke for encouraging us, after a panel discussion on *Inner Emigration* at a German Studies Association conference, to pursue this volume by remarking on the need for such an introduction of the topic to an English-speaking audience.

Finally, the authors deserve our thanks for patiently and repeatedly responding to our queries and requests in developing the final versions of their essays. The contact with them at all stages of this dialogue was a privilege and a pleasure. Our translators, beside myself, were Professors Stephen Brockmann (Carnegie Mellon), Renata H. Lefcourt (SUNY-Fredonia), Larson Powell (Texas A & M), and Damon Rarick (University of Rhode Island): they deserve special gratitude for their hard labor, which provided crucial help in putting together the volume. Of course, we would also like to mention our appreciation of Marion Berghahn's abiding interest and steady support through all of the stages of this volume's preparation.

* * * *

We would like to thank the following publishers for permissions to quote: Suhrkamp Verlag in Frankfurt am Main for poems quoted by Leonard Olschner, and, also in Leonard Olschner's essay, the Anvil Press in London for the translation by Michael Hamburger of Paul Celan's "Corona" from *Poems of Paul Celan* (London: Anvil Press, 1995): 61.

Likewise, the authors and editors wish to thank the following publishers for their generous permission to reprint the following materials: a shorter version of David Bathrick's essay that appeared in *Cultural History through a National Socialist Lens: Essays on the Cinema of the Third Reich,* ed. Robert C. Reimer (Rochester, NY: Camden House, 2000): 1–10; and Hans-Dieter Schäfer's essay "Die nichtnationalsozialistische Literatur der jungen Generation im Dritten Reich," which appeared originally in *Das gespaltene Bewußtsein: Deutsche Kultur und Lebenswirklichkeit 1933– 1945* (Munich and Vienna: Carl Hanser Verlag, 1983).

For Hans Dieter Schäfer's "Culture as Simulation: The Third Reich and Postmodernity" (originally published in longer form in *Literatur in der Diktatur: Schreiben im Nationalsozialismus und DDR-Sozialismus* [Paderborn: Ferdinand Schöningh, 1997]: 215–45) and for Reinhold Grimm's "In the Thicket of *Inner Emigration*" (originally published in this version in *Die deutsche Literatur im Dritten Reich: Themen, Traditionen, Wirkungen,* ed. Horst Denkler and Karl Prümm [Stuttgart: Reclam, 1976]: 406–26), the rights are with the authors, who have granted their permission to reprint.

CONTRIBUTORS

DAVID BASKER, B.A. (Manchester), Ph.D. (Wales), is Senior Lecturer in German at University of Wales Swansea. His publications cover various aspects of Wolfgang Koeppen's literary career and include the volume *Chaos, Control and Consistency: The Narrative Vision of Wolfgang Koeppen* (1993). His research interests also include contemporary German literature; he has edited volumes in the University of Wales Press *Contemporary German Writers* series on Uwe Timm, Sarah Kirsch, and Hermann Peter Piwitt.

DAVID BATHRICK is the Jacob Gould Schurman Professor and Chair of Theater, Film, and Dance and Professor of German Studies at Cornell University. His publications include *The Dialectic and the Early Brecht* (1976), *Modernity and the Text* (1989, co-edited with Andreas Huyssen), *The Powers of Speech: The Politics of Culture in the GDR* (1995), for which he was awarded the 1996 DAAD/GSA Book of the Year Prize, and numerous articles on the theory and history of twentieth century literature and cultural studies. He is a co-founder of *New German Critique* and is currently completing a book on visual culture in the Third Reich.

STEPHEN BROCKMANN is Associate Professor of German at Carnegie Mellon University, with courtesy appointments in the Departments of English and History. He is managing editor of the *Brecht Yearbook* and the author of *Literature and German Unification* (1999). He is also co-editor with James Steakley, of *Heroes and Heroism in German Culture: Essays in Honor of Jost Hermand* (2001).

GLENN R. CUOMO is Professor of German language and literature and Chair of the Division of Humanities at New College of Florida. He received his Ph.D. in German from Ohio State University. He is the author of *Career at the Cost of Compromise: Günter Eich's Life and Work in the Years 1933–1945* (1989) and editor of and contributor to *National Socialist Cultural Policy* (1995). His other publications include articles on Eich's pre-1945 radio broadcasts, Hanns Johst and the Reich Chamber of

Literature, Gottfried Benn, Heinar Kipphardt, Joseph Goebbel's diaries, Ina Seidel, and the reception of exile literature and foreign authors within the Third Reich.

VOLKER DAHM works at the *Institut für Zeitgeschichte* in Munich and Berlin and is *Wissenschaftlicher Leiter* of *Dokumentation Obersalzberg* in Berchtesgaden. His publications include *Das jüdische Buch im Dritten Reich* (1993). He is co-editor of *Die tödliche Utopie. Bilder, Texte, Dokumente, Daten zum Dritten Reich* (2002). He also produced a documentary film *Violence, Destruction, Death: Scenes from the Second World War* (2002).

NEIL H. DONAHUE is Professor of German and Comparative Literature at Hofstra University, where he has taught since 1988. His publications include *Forms of Disruption: Abstraction in Modern German Prose* (1993), *Voice and Void: The Poetry of Gerhard Falkner* (1998), and, most recently, *Karl Krolow and the Poetics of Amnesia in Postwar Germany* (2002). He has edited *Invisible Cathedrals: The Expressionist Art History of Wilhelm Worringer* (1995), and the forthcoming *Companion Volume to German Expressionism*.

GERALD FUNK is *Wissenschaftlicher Mitarbeiter* at the *Forschungsstelle Georg Büchner* in Marburg, Germany. His research focuses predominantly on German and French literature of the nineteenth and twentieth centuries. His publications include *Heinrich Schirmbeck: Die Angst des Ödipus. Zum sozialethischen Defizit der Moderne* (1996, editor), *Die Formel und die Sinnlichkeit* (1997), *Heinrich Schirmbeck: Gestalten und Perspektiven. Aufsätze, Portraits und Reflexionen aus fünf Jahrzehnten* (2000, editor), and *Georg Büchner: Dantons Tod. Erläuterungen und Dokumente* (2002). He is also co-editor with Gert Mattenklott and Michael Pauen of *Ästhetik des Ähnlichen. Zur Poetik und Kunstphilosophie der Moderne* (2001).

CATHY S. GELBIN was raised bilingually in a German-American family in East Berlin and received her Ph.D. in 1997 from Cornell University. She returned to Germany in 1995 for a three-year position as Research Associate at the *Moses Mendelssohn Zentrum für europäische Studien* at *Universität Potsdam*, where she also taught in the Jewish Studies Program. In 1998, she became Director of Research and Educational Programmes at the Centre for German-Jewish Studies at the University of Sussex (UK), and has been a full-time Lecturer in the Department of German Studies at the University of Manchester since September 2000. Selected publications include: *An Indelible Seal: Race, Hybridity and Identity in Elisabeth Langgässer's Writings* (2000); *AufBrüche: Kulturelle Produktionen von Migrantinnen, Schwarzen und jüdischen Frauen in Deutschland* (1999, co-editor); *Archiv der Erinnerung: Interviews mit Überlebenden der Shoah. Videographierte Lebenserzählungen und ihre Interpretationen* (1998, co-editor).

REINHOLD GRIMM was born in Nuremberg (Germany) in 1931. He studied at the University of Erlangen-Nürnberg and the University of Colorado-Boulder. He taught at the University of Erlangen-Nürnberg and the Goethe University in Frankfurt. He was the Alexander Hohlfeld Professor of German and Vilas Research Professor of Comparative Literature and German at the University of Wisconsin-Madison; he is presently Distinguished Professor at the University of California-Riverside. He has published 16 books, over 40 editions and co-editions, and about 140 scholarly articles and essays.

DORIS KIRCHNER is Associate Professor of German at the University of Rhode Island with an affiliate appointment in Women's Studies. She has taught at Columbia University and the Huazhong University of Science and Technology in China. She has published articles on twentieth-century German literature and is the author of *Doppelbödige Wirklichkeit. Magischer Realismus und nicht-faschistische Literatur* (1993).

WULF KOEPKE is Distinguished Professor Emeritus at Texas A&M University. He has held teaching and administrative positions in Singapore, Munich, the University of Illinois, Chicago, Rice University, and Texas A&M University. He has written and edited books on Jean Paul Richter, J. G. Herder, Exile Literature, Lion Feuchtwanger, and Max Frisch. He has published more than one hundred articles and book chapters on Herder, J. P. Richter, Heinrich Mann, Alfred Döblin, Lion Feuchtwanger, Max Frisch, Wolfgang Borchert, H. M. Enzensberger, eighteenth-century novels, aesthetics, exile literature, Inner Emigration, and postwar literature. He is also co-editor of the yearbook *Exilforschung* and the *Herder Yearbook*.

LEONARD OLSCHNER received his Dr. Phil. at the University of Freiburg in Germany. He taught briefly at the Universities of Mannheim and Illinois, joined the German faculty at Cornell University in 1985, and became Professor of German at Queen Mary, University of London, in 1995. He has worked extensively on poetry of the twentieth century, especially that of Paul Celan in various contexts. Other research areas include Adorno, translation theory, and more recently Goethe and Lichtenberg. He is presently working on monographs on Paul Celan and on temporality in German poetry from the early to mid twentieth century.

DIANA ORENDI is Associate Professor of German at Cleveland State University. A native of Frankfurt, Germany, she received her undergraduate training at the Universities of Heidelberg and Munich. She holds M.A. and Ph.D. degrees in German from Washington University, St. Louis. She teaches German language and literature and European and Non-Western Literature in Translation. Orendi's field of specialization is Holocaust literature, specifically German-Jewish literature in postwar Germany. Her most recent publication is a book she co-edited entitled *Evolving Jewish Identities in German Culture* (2001).

COLIN RIORDAN has been Professor of German at the University of Newcastle upon Tyne, England, since 1998. He has published widely on postwar German literature, with a particular interest in the legacy of National Socialism in the works of Uwe Johnson and Peter Schneider.

HANS DIETER SCHÄFER teaches German literature at the University of Regensburg in Germany. His works *Das gespaltene Bewusstsein: Über deutsche Kultur und Lebenswirklichkeit 1933–1945* (1981) and *Berlin im Zweiten Weltkrieg* (1985) have generated much discussion and further research into German life and literature in the 1930s and 1940s. He has published poetry—*Dem Leben ganz nah* (1982)—and the autobiographical text *Auf der Flucht. Meine Kindheit in Bildern* (1999). Two new volumes of poetry have appeared recently: *Spät am Leben* (2001) and *Final Cut* (2002, with illustrations by Christoph Meckel). He is also a member of the Mainzer Akademie der Wissenschaften und Literatur.

KARL HEINZ SCHOEPS was educated at universities in Germany, Austria, Great Britain, and the US and is Professor of German Emeritus at the University of Illinois at Urbana-Champaign. His areas of research include twentieth-century German literature and culture, East German literature, literature during the Third Reich, and Bertolt Brecht. His major book publications include *Bertolt Brecht und Bernard Shaw* (1974), *Bertolt Brecht* (1977), *Bertolt Brecht: Life, Work, and Criticism* (1989), and *Literatur im Dritten Reich* (1992). He has written numerous articles and book chapters on the East German novel, German writers in American POW camps, *völkisch*-national conservative literature, Heiner Mueller, Stephan Hermlin, Guenter Kunert, Wolf Biermann, Christa Wolf, and Hans Joachim Schaedlich.

AMY R. SIMS is Adjunct Professor of History at California College of Arts in San Francisco. She taught previously at Golden Gate University, Stanford University, and Boston College, and was a teaching fellow at Harvard University. Her specialty is Modern German History, and she is the author of several papers and articles on the German academic community during the Nazi period. Presently, she is working on a book about German historians during the Third Reich. She has participated in the faculty seminar at the Center for Advanced Holocaust Studies at the United States Holocaust Museum and has been a Fellow at Northwestern University's Sixth Annual Institute on the Holocaust and Jewish Civilization.

GUY STERN has been a Distinguished Professor of German at Wayne State University in Detroit, Michigan, since 1981. He is the author of numerous books and articles, including, recently, *Literarische Kultur im Exil* (1998), a collection of his essays on exile literature. He is a co-founder of the Society for Exile Studies and of the Lessing Society, and his scholarship has bridged the gap between German traditions of enlightenment and tolerance, and the German-Jewish experience of intolerance, exile and the Holocaust. He is the recipient of numerous awards, including, from the Federal Republic of Germany, the Order of Merit, First Class (in 1972) and the Grand Order of Merit (in 1987), and the Goethe Medal (in 1989).

FRANK TROMMLER is Professor of German and Comparative Literature at the University of Pennsylvania in Philadelphia. Since 1995 he has been Director of the Humanities Program at the American Institute for Contemporary German Studies in Washington, D.C. He has published widely in the areas of nineteenth-and-twentieth century German literature, theater, and culture as well as German-American cultural relations. Modernism, Weimar Culture, and literary developments before and after 1945 have been areas of special interest. Recently he co-edited *The German-American Encounter: Conflict and Cooperation between Two Cultures, 1800–2000* (2001).

RHYS W. WILLIAMS is Professor of German at the University of Wales, Swansea. He has published on German Expressionism (Sternheim, Benn, Einstein, Kaiser, and Toller), and on postwar literature (Andersch, Böll, Siegfried Lenz, Hans Werner Richter, and Martin Walser). More recently he has been General Editor of the Contemporary German Writers series published by the University of Wales Press, and has written articles for the volumes on Sarah Kirsch, Peter Schneider, Jurek Becker, Uwe Timm, and Hermann-Peter Piwitt.

INTRODUCTION

"Coming to Terms" with the German Past

Neil H. Donahue

At the end of World War II, the term *inner emigration* gained currency in Germany as a way to describe the plight of writers who were not forced into exile after 1933 when Adolf Hitler came to power, but rather were able to remain in Germany during the Nazi period. The term suggested, after the war, that these writers had in fact 'emigrated' in spirit, if not in body, by turning inward, away from the enforced or coerced beliefs of National Socialist ideology that surrounded them, in order to survive oppression and war with their own humane values intact. But could one continue to publish works of fiction or commentary under the Nazis that might amount to aesthetic resistance to fascism? Or could one even remain pointedly neutral? If so, how? Was it at all possible to stay in Germany and avoid collaboration, compromise, and complicity in the ideological apparatus of the Nazi state? If so, how? Even before 1945, and certainly ever since then, the term *inner emigration* has been at the center of debates about the period of National Socialism in Germany, and the term has continually posed questions about what exactly a given writer (or artist or scholar, etc.) did during the twelve-year period from 1933 to 1945, and about how specific actions and specific texts are to be evaluated. This volume raises issues of historical and literary interpretation with respect to a morally complex situation. In the last decade, new research and information have forced a reassessment of individual writers, which in turn has forced a reassessment of the period as a whole, and given new urgency to questions surrounding *inner emigration*.

In the wake of German reunification during the 1990s, developments in research related to literary life and work under the Nazis and its relation to postwar German literature seemed constantly to overtake the ability of scholars to maintain an overview of the period: the ground of discussion in this area was constantly unsettled by volcanic eruptions of new knowledge and seismic rumblings and aftershocks of reinterpretation and debate, all of which form a new basis for a comprehensive portrayal of the period. In fact, however, an organized understanding of the phenomenon of *inner emigration* has always been confounded by disputes over the term itself, though the issue is ultimately not a matter of nomenclature, but rather of more far-reaching concerns about literary evaluation, moral discernment, and the writing of history. This volume brings together scholars who have participated in either of the *two* most recent of *four* phases in the reception of *inner emigration* that I would like now to summarize briefly.

(1) In the early 1930s, the term *inner emigrant* (or a close variant) began to appear in scattered utterances with a plainly positive meaning, referring sympathetically to someone, either liberal or conservative, who no longer felt at home in Germany but who remained there anyway under adverse and increasingly dire circumstances and who retained strong critical and anti-Nazi convictions, turning inward out of necessity in order to ensure the survival of an opposition in Germany—active in spirit if not in deed. In 1935 the surprise appearance of a man in a mask at the Writers' Congress in Paris—a faceless emissary from Germany representing an underground of German antifascist writers—provides the emblematic scenario for this heroic view of *inner emigration* in brave but anonymous solidarity with the world against Hitler and his thugs and minions. German writers in exile and in *inner emigration* seemed to share a common plight and hope, despite very different circumstances. Yet after that symbolic moment at center stage as the object of international admiration and moral support, the writer of *inner emigration* in Germany was lost to view: the ensuing decade of menace and persecution, isolation and estrangement, terror and coercion, hardship and violence, propaganda and war, made such a posture of spirited defiance increasingly difficult or perhaps even impossible to maintain within Germany, as the pressures grew to conform and to collaborate in the ideological apparatus of the Nazi state. The exact nature of those pressures and how they affected the daily reality and literary production of writers in—but perhaps not of—the Third Reich still requires elucidation.

This volume aims to focus attention on writers and, to a lesser degree, other artists and intellectuals in this period, both individually and collectively. The goal of the volume is twofold: to take another step in broadening the basis of historical specificity in evaluating this literature in this period, and to open up and introduce the complex phenomenon of German literary and cultural history in this century to an English-speaking public through essays that view the phenomenon from different general perspectives, and through individual case studies. Such historical specificity allows for finer discrimination of guilt—not necessarily for exoneration—and greater understanding of the range of complicity, integrity, or ambiguity in its fine gradations in the work and in the person. Thus, the emphasis of the volume is historical and literary, and the link is necessarily biographical. Unlike older New Criticism or more recent poststructural-ist discourse, this volume brings the author's life back into immediate juxtaposition with, and integration into, the literary work to order to locate the points of interpenetration.

(2) After the war, however, German society in general, West and East, was not interested in looking critically into the recent past, but solely, even blindly, toward the future: a monolithic view of the totalitarian dark ages blocked further inquiry into the texture of everyday life in that period, and into the actual activities, literary and otherwise, of writers under the Nazi regime. The heroic *inner emigrant* seemed at first to have vanished from the stage of history—except that, right away in 1945, the novelist Frank Thieß invoked again that heroic image of a defiant underground of *inner emigrants* in an intemperate and accusatory exchange with Thomas Mann, the most famous of all German writers in exile. Thieß asserted the once positive connotations of the term for polemical and self-aggrandiz-ing purposes: he staked out a clear but untenable position, claiming the moral superiority of writers in *inner emigration*, who had experienced the German tragedy on location, rather than as spectators from the balcony seats of exile, as he phrased it. Such provocations were acts of preemptive obscurantism, designed to impose a simplistic and favorable interpreta-tion onto an intellectually, morally, and emotionally complex situation. Thomas Mann was goaded into the following harsh response: "In my eyes, the books that could even get into print in Germany from 1933 to 1945 are less than worthless and not to be touched. A stench of blood and criminality clings to them. They should all be pulped." Their rude exchange polarized German literature into two camps, that of *inner emigration* and that of exile. Thieß's disingenuous asseverations of a "deep inner bond" between writers in exile and those in *inner emigration* in effect actually severed any such bond. As a result, that term *inner emigration* has been fraught ever since with connotations of spurious and exculpatory self-stylization that raise questions about one's specific actions and meanings (for that reason, we have chosen to highlight the term with italics through-out the volume). Frank Thieß only managed, in fact, to attach to the term a penumbra of suspicion, to polarize writers and to impose upon further discussion a tense, even bitter dichotomy between the writers in exile and those who remained in Germany. Subsequent scholarship has had to wrest the discussion from the grips of that antithesis.

In this volume, Stephen Brockmann's essay examines in detail that cru-cial moment in German social and literary history of the initial debate about *inner emigration* ignited by Thieß with his provocation of Thomas Mann, which serves as a sort of "primal scene" for all later discussions of the term, and concept as well as for the individual responses. This clash of ideas about *inner emigration* also serves as a prototype (in its vitriolic and vituperative intensity) for future literary debates that actually rehearse much larger issues surrounding Germany's relation in the postwar and postreunification period to its past and its identity as a nation [*Staat*] or at least, on another level, as a common culture [*Kulturnation*].[1] This debate was the touchstone for discussions of *inner emigration* over the years, and is as well for the other essays in this volume.

(3) In the early 1970s, in the landmark proceedings of two linked conferences at the University of Wisconsin in Madison and at Washington University in St. Louis, published in two volumes with the title *Exile and Inner Emigration*, scholars set to work to move the discussion beyond the gulf that had divided those two camps for almost three decades: essays by, among others, Reinhold Grimm, Jost Hermand, Guy Stern, Frank Trommler, Charles Hoffmann, and David Bathrick, some of whom have now also contributed to his volume, laid the groundwork at the time for further, more detailed consideration of the period. For example, in refuting the popular notion of a *Zero Hour* in German history on 8 May 1945, Frank Trommler highlighted the continuity of German literary traditions, within Germany *and* in exile, from the 1920s through the 1930s and the Third Reich, and into the postwar period. Subsequent studies of the literary journals that provided points of cohesion and identification (such as Marion Mallmann's and Horst Denkler's separate studies of *Das Innere Reich* or Joseph Dolan's study of the *Die Kolonne*) for aesthetically—if not always politically—conservative writers in the late Weimar and early National Socialist period reinforced our understanding of the continuities in Germany from the Weimar years *through the Nazi period* into the postwar period. More recent work on international literary trends, such as Doris Kirchner's examination of "magic realism" in this period, which brings that term back from its later and more famous Latin American variants to its origin in German aesthetic discourse of the Weimar years, has also served to underscore the broad continuities at work in German literature in the mid-twentieth century. Yet the focus ultimately in that broadening scope of analysis has to remain on individual writers and their work in its relation to the reigning ideology of National Socialism. The question of continuities now turns away from historical overviews and toward the specific (in)actions, literary or otherwise, of individuals.

Reinhold Grimm, in his "In the Thicket of Inner Emigration" (1972; 1976), called for "a sliding scale ... from active opposition to passive resistance" in order to allow more finely differentiated historical analysis of individual cases. Charles Hoffmann also directed attention, even more broadly, to the range of subtle gradations between the opposite poles of antifascist and propagandistic literature. These essays provided at the time the necessary framework for historical contextualization, though without having then discovered new sources and materials, as the editors (Grimm and Hermand) also noted. Scholars such as Karl Heinz Schoeps and Hans Dieter Schäfer began the process of close critical examination of the nexus between life and work in the case of individual writers in this period. In line with contemporaneous developments in *Alltagsgeschichte* (the "school" of historiography in Germany devoted to exploring for their collective significance the unassuming manifestations of daily life), Schäfer's essay and his notion of a nonfascist literature, as distinct from an actively antifascist literature, provided a necessary tool for this scholarly labor by breaking away from prevailing notions of a unified historical experience under totalitarianism (and the strict dichotomy of fascist or antifascist literature) in order to investigate more closely the actual relations, risks, options, and actions available to individuals and publications at that time. His ground-breaking essay, packed with historical detail on the niches of "high" modernist and popular culture (here abridged for an English-speaking audience without access to all of his sources), demonstrated how a "split consciousness" permeated this generation of artists and intellectuals under Nazism. If these essays taken together (by Trommler, Grimm, and Schäfer, among others) were foundational for subsequent analysis of the period, Schäfer's continuous work in particular on this period constitutes the ground floor of that edifice.

Hans Dieter Schäfer's first essay gave fresh impetus to the examination of this period in literary history, and his investigations of this period have figured as a line of continuity for subsequent scholarship; he is, therefore, represented in this volume by two essays. In his second essay, he provocatively calls into question some of the presuppositions of his first essay, and considers Germany during the Third Reich from the perspective of modernity at large and how the Nazi culture of spectacle anticipates developments in postwar Germany and of postmodernity. With Schäfer, under the rubric of "New Perspectives: Synoptic Studies," this volume presents new, revisionary approaches to the literature of *inner emigration* as a collective phenomenon. Like Schäfer, Frank Trommler's work in the field was foundational and has also figured prominently in the latter two phases of the reception of *inner emigration*. His new essay, drawing upon theories of reader reception, approaches the phenomenon from the sociohistorical perspective of Nazi policies on reading and book production, and illuminates the participation by *inner emigrants* in a sort of semipublic sphere of literary activity, where they hovered (or tried to hover) between independent creation and ideological cooptation. Volker Dahm's essay goes a step further in that same direction to examine the precise contours of the niche for writers in the Third Reich, the bureaucratic interstice between jurisdictions and official policies that a writer, if bold enough, could try to exploit, though at considerable risk. The nexus between literature and ideology, or poetry and politics, emerges also in the essays by Leonard Olschner and Colin Riordan that demonstrate, in turn, how poets responded or reacted to their political environment by adopting a notion of time that transported them out of the historical context, a metaphysics of flight, as it were, or contrarily, by attempting in prose fiction to confront the situation in some manner by developing, or at least speculating upon, a political theory, a theory of state, set in another age but standing in (critical) relation to the historical present of National Socialism.

(4) Since those earlier foundational essays, the task of later literary-historical research has been to work within that framework by discovering and interpreting the details of writers' lives and their literature, with all due wariness of their own self-stylizations. In the recent debate about Günter Eich, Schäfer referred to this act of painstaking historical research and often contentious literary-critical inquiry as an "archaeology of the truth" (Karst, 87). The figure of the scholar resembles less an archeologist at times than a detective, and it is probably not entirely a coincidence that these decades of scholarly research into daily life under the Nazis (literary and otherwise) have given rise in Philip Kerr's trilogy *Berlin Noir* (1993) to precisely the sort of morally ambiguous detective figure (Bernie Gunther) that characterizes the hard-boiled genre in general to be sure but also seems very much at home embedded in the circumstances of the Third Reich, where he operates on his own, trying to negotiate a space of relative independence between the Party and his conscience. Such a figure captures both the predicament of inner emigrants and the challenge to later scholars to sort through the literary and historical evidence in order to try to achieve clarity of interpretation and evaluation.

Under the rubric of "New Perspectives: Case Studies," this volume presents essays on leading literary figures of the period with an eye toward the particularity of their situation, focusing on the ambiguities in their works and in their accounts of their lives, or on the simple discrepancies, or flat contradictions. Here, aside from the inevitability of some degree of self-stylization in each case, generalization has to give way to the specificity of detail and the implications of individual action in life, or specific wording in literature: what emerges is a mosaic of circumstances and individuals trying "to come to terms" first with their present in the Third Reich, and then ever after with the German collective past, and indeed with their own private pasts. From the despairing arch-conservative Reck-Malleczewen (in the essay by Karl-Heinz Schoeps) to the well-known and popular Erich Kästner (in the essay by Guy Stern), these essays show a range of uncomfortable attitudes or postures with regard to the regime. That range could of course be extended to include many other figures, who cannot all be included here.[2] Of greatest interest perhaps is how each essay illuminates the individual as an agent in public and private history. Each case is in fact a window on the making of collective history by individuals and provides a stark sense of how what we do stays with us and adds up to the historical record of our world, then and now.

But even if we approach our subjects as an archeologist, rather than as a detective (or most likely a combination of the two), it deserves emphasis that the excavation, the sleuthing, the research we perform, does not burrow into a distant past, but rather uncovers the foundation of German society and literature in the present. The award of the Nobel Prize to Günter Grass, and the fifty-year anniversary of the Federal Republic of Germany in 1999, remind us of the "presentness" of the past (that is, the Nazi past) in Germany. In fact, in the last decade, this task, far from becoming an antiquarian pastime, has gained new impetus and even public urgency: scholarly inquiry into the history and literature of the Nazi years and the immediate postwar period has been successively galvanized in turn by access to new archival materials after Reunification; by the anniversaries of the war and postwar events that invited reconsideration of the period; by the passing away of the generations that lived through that period; by the parallel questions about the relations between writer and State in the former German Democratic Republic; and, in the realm of ahistorical literary theory, by the revelations, for example, of Paul de Man's real historical collaborationist activities (see Lehmann); or, for further example in the arts, by the recurring discussion of Leni Riefenstahl, or in the field of German Studies by the surprising case of Hans Schwerte, a.k.a. Hans Ernst Schneider, who until 1996 pursued a prominent postwar career as a scholar and university administrator under a pseudonym, hiding his past service in the Nazi SS (see König, Kuhlmann, and Schwabe); or by the case of Elisabeth Noelle-Neuman, the best known German opinion pollster, whose early training was in the service of Nazi propaganda (see Pöttker); or in the natural sciences, by ongoing debates about Werner Heisenberg's role in the (non-?) development of a German atomic bomb (as brought out of the realm of scholarship and into broad public consciousness by Michael Freyn's play *Copenhagen*, about Heisenberg's inscrutable visit to Niels Bohr in Denmark).[3] The list could go on and extend even farther outside of literature into all realms of German society and intellectual or artistic disciplines. In this volume, the essay by Amy Sims demonstrates the responses of historians, as the historical conscience of the nation or culture, and how they failed to act and hid in their studies of the past. The essay by David Bathrick turns to the artistic genre perhaps most reliant on state funding and policy to show how some films, despite the pressure for political propaganda in such a mass medium, could develop cinematic codes of ambiguity and modes of (highly abstract and modest) resistance. Yet however far one pursues the notion of *inner emigration* through German society in the 1930s and 1940s, the topic would return to the context of German literature, where that debate has figured most prominently and most representatively. Literature provides here the locus of best advantage for an inquiry into the phenomenon of artistic and intellectual *inner emigration*, which only underscores the historical embeddedness of literature.

* * * *

The terms of the debate in literary circles and literary scholarship extend even beyond literature and intellectual or artistic disciplines. Whereas Ralf Schnell aptly suggests that writers in the Third Reich had a *Schattendasein* (a shadow existence), caught between conscience and compromise, they in fact shared that dilemma, though perhaps more acutely felt, pondered, and formulated, with all citizens. The historian Detlev Peukert defined it as: "the multiple everyday ambiguities of 'ordinary people' making their choices among the varying greys of active consent, accommodation and nonconformity" (243). In fact, the surprise publication in 1995 of Victor Klemperer's diaries of the period from 1933 to 1945 illuminated most starkly the lives of ordinary people in those years in Dresden and provided an uncommonly vivid, precise, poignant, and microscopic view of daily life under the Nazis from the vantage point of a German Jewish intellectual (Jewish by descent, Protestant by confession) in forced residence in a so-called Jews' House and in forced labor, who with his wife managed against the odds to survive the long nightmare of Nazi persecution leading to the Holocaust and the Dresden firebombing.

Those diaries became bestsellers in postreunification Germany and showed the need to understand—for the sake of "coming to terms" with Germany's past and Germany's future—the paradoxes and ambiguities of daily life in Germany during the Third Reich. As a German Jew who refused to emigrate abroad and leave Germany, Klemperer was forced into the position of *inner emigration* that others chose, though an *inner emigration* of much greater severity than anything endured by "Aryan" inner emigrants. In short, Klemperer's diaries provide an immediate insider's view of *inner emigration* from the perspective of a victim of active persecution, rather than of ideological intimidation (one might compare, for example, the real anguish in the diaries of Oskar Loerke as he continued to work as an editor). Diaries such as Klemperer's in particular (or Loerke's or numerous others) show the long, slow, corrosive, self-protective process of turning inward as either critical or capitulatory encapsulation, or both.

The scholar-critic has to follow that turn inward, trace its trajectory and its contexts, focus in on all the ordinary, the all-too-ordinary, ambiguities in this period, and examine all the more intently the shades of meaning in each work (whether literary, or artistic, or scientific, etc.) in order to isolate and elucidate its historical agency, and bring the author's life and literature out of history's shadows—some for the better and some for the worse.

Notes

1. Stephen Brockmann's book on *Literature and German Reunification* (Cambridge University Press, 2000) explores the issues in the full context of postwar German culture.
2. See, for example, my study of Karl Krolow, who never counted himself among representatives of an *inner emigration*, but whose biography and literary work reveal common traits with others of his generation in this regard.
3. See David C. Cassidy's biography of Heisenberg, a model of the scholarly integration of life and work that this area of inquiry requires (along with his subsequent essays on German science during the Third Reich, and his review of Thomas Powers's book, which summarizes the debate about Heisenberg). See also Beyerchen's invaluable study.

Works Cited

Beyerchen, Alan D. *Scientists under Hitler: Politics and the Physics Community in the Third Reich*. New Haven and London: Yale University Press, 1977.

Brockmann, Stephen. *Literature and German Reunification*. Cambridge: Cambridge University Press, 2000.

Cassidy, David C. *Uncertainty: The Life and Science of Werner Heisenberg*. New York: Freeman, 1992.

———. "German Scientists and the Nazi Atomic Bomb." Special Issue on The Empire of Technology: Science and the Third Reich *Dimensions: A Journal of Holocaust Studies* 10, 2 (1996): 15–22.

———. "Heisenberg, German Science and the Third Reich." *Social Research* 59, 3 (1992): 643–61.

———. Review of Thomas Powers, *Heisenberg's War: The Secret History of the German Bomb* (New York: Knopf, 1993). *Nature* 363 (27 May 1993): 311–12.

Denkler, Horst. "Janusköpfig: Zur ideologischen Physiognomie der Zeitschrift *Das Innere Reich* 1934–1944." In *Die deutsche Literatur im Dritten Reich: Themen, Traditionen, Wirkungen*, ed. H. Denkler and K. Prümm. Stuttgart: Reclam, 1976.

Donahue, Neil H. *Karl Krolow and the Poetics of Amnesia in Postwar Germany*. Rochester, N.Y.: Camden House/Boydell & Brewer, 2002.

———. "At the Heart of the Matter: Deliberations on Crisis in the Diaries of Victor Klemperer, 1933–1945." In *Literarisches Krisenbewußtsein. Ein Perzeptions- und Produktionsmuster im 20. Jahrhundert*, ed. Keith Bullivant and Bernhard Spies, 105–127. Munich: Iudicium, 2001.

Karst, Karl, ed. *Günter Eich: Rebellion in der Goldstadt. Texttranskript und Materialien*. Frankfurt am Main: Suhrkamp, 1997.

Kerr, Philip. *Berlin Noir*. London: Penguin, 1993.

Kirchner, Doris. *Doppelbödige Wirklichkeit. Magischer Realismus und nicht-faschistische Literatur*. Tübingen: Stauffenburg, 1993.

König, Helmut, Wolfgang Kuhlmann, and Klaus Schwabe. *Vertusche Vergangenheit: Der Fall Schwerte und die NS-Vergangenheit der deutschen Hochschulen*. Munich: Beck, 1997.

Lehmann, David. *Signs of the Times: Deconstruction and the Fall of Paul De Man*. New York: Poseidon Press, 1991.

Loerke, Oskar. *Tagebücher, 1903–1939*. Ed. Hermann Kasack. Deutsche Akademie für Sprache und Dichtung. Heidelberg and Darmstadt: Lambert Schneider, 1955.

Mallman, Marion. *Das Innere Reich: Analyse einer konservativen Kulturzeitschrift im Dritten Reich*. Bonn: Bouvier, 1978.

Peukert, Detlev. *Inside Nazi Germany: Conformity, Opposition, and Racism in Everyday Life*. New Haven and London: Yale University Press, 1987.

Pöttker, Horst. "Mitgemacht, weitergemacht, zugemacht: Zum NS-Erbe der Kommunikationswissenschaft in Deutschland." *Aviso* 28 (January 2001): 4–7. Also: www.dgpuk.de/aktuell/poettker/poettker_text.htm.

Schnell, Ralf. *Literarische Innere Emigration, 1933–1945*. Stuttgart: Metzler, 1976.

Chapter 1

INNER EMIGRATION
The Term and Its Origins in Postwar Debates

Stephen Brockmann

The debate about *inner emigration* that broke out in Germany in the second half of 1945 was to prove paradigmatic for subsequent debates in postwar German literary culture. The influence of the debate continued half a century later, in the 1990s, during the various literary debates that have followed the collapse of the German Democratic Republic in 1989 and the reunification of Germany in 1990. Since 1945, scholars of literary history have devoted considerable energy to defining the precise nature of *inner emigration* itself as a general phenomenon and to the specific roles played by individual writers who might fall into that category. Research has developed, quite rightly, away from the initial dispute that gave rise to that line of inquiry in the first place. But because of the enduring significance of the 1945 debate on *inner emigration*, precisely as a paradigm, it is necessary to establish exactly what transpired in the immediate postwar era in this debate. Beyond the relative merit of various claims in the debate, the debate itself defined, to a considerable degree, the terms of postwar German literary discussions and literary history; therefore, any new consideration of the period or of that phenomenon requires a detailed picture of how that discussion began, how it evolved, and how it increased in intensity and scope.

Due to his prominence and his rigorous views on the hotly debated problem of German collective responsibility, the writer Thomas Mann soon became not only the most-discussed but also the most controversial exile in the postwar German press. The question that hung in the air after the defeat of the German Reich in May 1945 was whether exiles like Mann, who had left Germany because of Hitler's rise to power, would now return to Germany after Hitler's defeat. The debate surrounding Mann's possible return to Germany started harmlessly enough. Three months after the war's end, in the first half of August 1945, Walter von Molo, one of the founders of the German PEN Club and the author of numerous historical novels about such figures as King Frederick the Great of Prussia, published an open letter to Mann in a number of newspapers put out by the American army for the German population, including the *Münchner Zeitung*, the *Stuttgarter Stimme*, and the *Hessische Post*.[1] Von Molo's letter also appeared in newspapers in the United States, England, Sweden, and South America (Hermand, 23). In this letter von Molo, who had largely withdrawn from political life during the years of the Nazi dictatorship, begged Mann to return to Germany and help in the reconstruction of his homeland, assuring Mann that most Germans had remained in Germany during the years of the Third Reich not because they agreed with or even supported Hitler but because they had nowhere else to go. By describing the physical Germany as a "huge concentration camp," von Molo insinuated that the vast majority of ordinary Germans, far from being criminals, had themselves been victims of the Nazis:

> Please come soon, look into the faces furrowed by sorrow, observe the unspeakable suffering in the eyes of the many who did not participate in the glorification of our darker sides, who could not leave their home, because they were many millions of people for whom there was no other place than home, in the gradually developing huge concentration camp, in which there were soon only various degrees of guards and the guarded. ("Offener Brief," 334)

Such wording seemed to suggest that exile from Germany had been a privilege of the particularly fortunate. Implying that Mann had no reason either to hate or to fear his own people and therefore no reason not to return to Germany, von Molo declared that, in spite of insidious Nazi hate propaganda, the German people were not guilty of the hatred and evil represented by the Third Reich. Indeed, the German people were constitutionally incapable of hatred, he asserted: "In spite of many vigorous demands from early in the morning to late at night, the German people did not hate before the war or during the war, and it does not hate now, because it is not capable of hatred, because it truly has earned and still deserves its great men and masters, whom the world loves and honors" (335). Von Molo's invocation of Germany's "great men and masters" was a reminder that the *Kulturnation*—the cultural nation—was not identical with the *Staatsnation*—the political nation—and a plea for Mann to understand that the supposedly unblemished *Kulturnation* still represented the "real" Germany. Stressing the suffering and victimization of the German people, von Molo insisted on an absolute separation between the evil of the Nazis and the essential goodness of their fellow countrymen, whom von Molo specifically identified with Mann by using the second person possessive pronoun: "In its innermost core, your people, which has now been starving and suffering for a third of a century, has nothing in common with the misdeeds and crimes, the shameful horrors and lies, the fearsome aberrations of the diseased, who therefore trumpeted so much about their health and perfection" (335).

Given Mann's oft expressed contrary conviction that there were not two Germanys but only one Germany in which evil and good were intertwined, such sentiments were destined to elicit the writer's ire. In many respects, however, von Molo's sentiments were not foreign to Mann, even though the latter wrote privately that von Molo's invitation was "stale and bad" (*Tagebücher*, 244). In a radio speech to the German people broadcast on 8 May 1945, the day of German surrender—von Molo had read the speech in its published form, and hence it was probably this speech that induced him to address an open letter to Mann[2]—Mann had also spoken of the German people as a "basically good people that loves civilization and law" ("Die Lager," 952), and two years earlier he had asserted "that the Hitler Party came to absolute power only through terror and intrigue, through a coup d'état" ("Schicksal und Aufgabe," 928), implying that the German people bore little or no responsibility for Hitler's rise to power. Nevertheless, von Molo's seemingly harmless letter already contained several exculpatory assertions and one glaring omission with which Mann, who had specifically stated in his 8 May radio speech that "everything German, everyone who speaks German, writes German, has lived in German, is affected" by Nazi crimes, was bound to take issue.

What von Molo had neglected to take into account in his letter to Mann was the physical, psychological, and spiritual suffering of German exiles. The only people about whom von Molo wrote as victims were the citizens of Germany who had remained in Germany—as if Germans who had left Germany, far from suffering, had somehow escaped the suffering reserved for their fatherland. Von Molo's positive assertions were threefold: (1) that the German people had in their vast majority remained virtuous during the years of the Third Reich; (2) that they were therefore absolutely separated from the Nazi regime that had claimed not only to represent them but to be the statist embodiment of their innermost desires; and (3) that the German people were therefore themselves Hitler's first innocent victim. Mann himself was not completely immune to these ideas, but his position was far more ambivalent and critical than that of von Molo, whose letter contained a clear rejection of the concept of German "collective guilt"—a concept widely discussed and debated both inside and outside Germany toward the end of World War II, and one to which Mann himself was attracted. As Mann had written earlier, the very concept of Germany as a unified nation implied at least a certain collective responsibility, if not a collective guilt: "[I]f Germany exists as a historical structure, as a collective personality, then there is also this: responsibility." Mann had stressed that criminals such as Hitler and Himmler would have been complete nonentities "if manly German power and blind knightly faithfulness were not, with unholy, leonine courage, fighting and dying to the present date for these villains" ("Das Ende," 946). The problem of collective responsibility, if not collective guilt, was thus at the core of the debate that subsequently emerged between Mann and intellectuals who had, like von Molo, remained in Germany during the years of the Third Reich.

Before Mann's response to von Molo was published in Germany, the latter's statement was followed by yet another from Frank Thieß, a respected author of historical and erotic novels who had, like von Molo, for the most part kept his distance from the Nazis during the years of the Third Reich. In his response to von Molo's invitation to Mann, Thieß used the term *inner emigration* to refer to writers who had remained in Germany but distanced themselves from the Nazi regime. Since the 1930s, this term, and terms similar to it, had been used by Germans both at home and abroad to refer to Germans who remained in their homeland but nevertheless felt themselves alienated from the Nazi regime. As a result of Thieß's prominent use of the term in his 1945 debate with Mann, some subsequent scholars made the mistake of assuming that the idea of separating out two emigrations, an "inner" emigration and an "outer" emigration, had originated with Thieß.[3]

Mann himself had used the term *inner emigration* as early as 1933, when he had considered himself to be one of the German writers so described; and ten years later Mann had invoked an *inner emigration* in a 1943 speech given at the Library of Congress in Washington.[4] Describing the uprooted situation of emigrants like himself, the exiled literary statesman had compared his own alienation from Germany to a similar alienation faced by anti-Nazi Germans who had remained in Germany:

> What an abnormal, pathological condition, abnormal and pathological for everyone, but especially for the writer, the bearer of a cultural tradition, when one's own country is transformed into the deepest and most hostile foreign territory! And now I do not want to think just about us here on the outside, us emigrants; I want finally to remember the people on the inside, the German masses themselves, and the horrible predicament into which fate has pushed the German soul. Believe me: for many there Germany has become just as foreign as it is for us; an "inner emigration" with numbers in the millions there is waiting for the end, just as we are waiting. ("Schicksal und Aufgabe," 922–23)

As this passage makes clear, Mann in 1943 was more than willing to accept the concept of an *inner emigration*, with its implication that many Germans who had remained in Germany were just as alienated from the Nazi government as exiles like himself.

The concept of *inner emigration* brings together two elements that directly contradict each other: "emigration," which specifically means departure from a country, in this case German writers' homeland, Germany; and "inner," which implies precisely the opposite: staying "inside" Germany. The term implies that it is possible to "leave" Germany while nevertheless staying "inside" Germany. This apparent contradiction is resolved by the idealistic concept of *Kultur*: Mann in 1943 and Thieß in 1945 were both suggesting that it was possible to "emigrate" from the evil, Nazi Germany spiritually while remaining inside it physically. The concept suggested that there were two kinds of intellectual "emigrants" from Nazi Germany: the "outer" or physical emigrants, who had physically removed themselves from the geographical entity Germany; and the "inner" or spiritual emigrants, who had removed themselves on the level of ideals and *Geist* from the morally repugnant Germany while remaining physically inside German borders. Mann's 1943 use of the term had made no attempt to distinguish the moral worth of the two "emigrations." But in his 1945 response to von Molo's invitation, Thieß went so far as to imply that the second, idealistic "emigration" was more honest and patriotic than the first, purely physical kind. Thieß's self-justifying preference for "inner emigration" was to prove typical of many writers like himself who sought to justify their actions or non-action during the Third Reich. His arguments corresponded to a widespread vituperation against not only Mann himself but also the entire German exile community.

The vituperation against exiles that emerged in 1945 can at least in part be explained psychologically by two factors, one of which the literary scholar Hans Mayer, himself an "outer emigrant" during the years of the Third Reich, has identified as the simple fact of Germany's military defeat. As a result of that defeat, all Germans living in Germany, whether Nazi, non-Nazi, or anti-Nazi, were considered defeated, not just Germans who had supported Hitler. The victorious Allies defeated Germany, not just Nazis; therefore even anti-Nazi Germans might potentially view themselves as defeated. The clearest case in point is the German *Wehrmacht*, which was home to a large number of aristocratic conservatives, some of whom had taken part in the 20 July 1944 attempt to assassinate Hitler. Gottfried Benn, who had vilified outer emigrants in 1933 and then served in the *Wehrmacht* himself, snobbishly referred to the *Wehrmacht* as the "aristocratic form of emigration" (Grimm, 37), as if only proletarian low-lifes had actually left Germany during the Nazi regime. But whether aristocratic or not, opposed to the Nazis or not, the German *Wehrmacht* was decisively defeated in 1945, and with it Germany itself as a nation-state was defeated. Conversely all German emigrants, since they had spent the years of the war outside the country and had frequently supported the war against the Nazis, could be viewed as victors. As Mayer puts it, "all emigrants seemed suddenly to have triumphed together with the victors," whereas anyone who had remained inside Germany, conformist or not, "had been defeated along with the other losers" (83). The narrator of Mann's 1947 novel *Doktor Faustus*, Serenus Zeitblom, himself a kind of inner emigrant, expresses the same thought in a different way: "we are lost. Which means: the war is lost, but that signifies more than the lost campaign, it actually means that *we* are lost, lost: our cause, our soul, our faith and our history" (234). The defeat of the Nazis implicates all of Germany. As Bertolt Brecht put it in a note written on 3 August 1945, during the Potsdam conference, "Of course we, who would not have triumphed with Hitler, have been defeated with him" (228).

16

Connected to the sense of having been defeated was the strong psychological sense of collective guilt for Nazi atrocities. In light of these atrocities, many Germans felt their claim to be a civilized, moral nation was weakened. It was not just the victorious allies who bandied about notions of collective guilt in the postwar period. Many Germans themselves, brought up in a culture that had traditionally placed great emphasis on personal responsibility, felt themselves to be guilty. Describing how, after the liberation of the Buchenwald concentration camp the citizens of Weimar had been declared participants in guilt "for the now revealed horrors" and forced by American occupation authorities to observe the remains of the camp, Mann's narrator Serenus Zeitblom acknowledges:

> The thick-walled torture cell into which a worthless regime, dedicated from the beginning to nothingness, had transformed Germany, is now thrown open, and our disgrace lies open to the eyes of the world, of the foreign commissions, to whom these unbelievable pictures are now being shown everywhere, and who report at home: what they have seen in all its hideousness goes beyond anything that the human imagination is capable of picturing. I say: our disgrace. (634–35)

Zeitblom's insistence on the pronoun "unser" [our] is an open acknowledgement that he is including himself in the condemnation of what is German. At the same time his description of Germany as a thick-walled torture cell recalls von Molo's description of Germany as a concentration camp; but in Zeitblom's description it is clear that many Germans are on the side of the torturers, not on the side of the victims—hence the term "our disgrace."

The concept of *inner emigration* was an important way for postwar Germans to fend off both outward and inner accusations of collective guilt, because a German who had spiritually "emigrated" from Germany could dissociate himself from guilt for what had happened there. As Karl Paetel put it explicitly in the first collection of documents on the *inner emigration* published after the war: "Now National Socialism is defeated. Germany is to become democratic. But even today most of the 'German experts' in the great democracies cling to the conception that all Germans share responsibility for Hitler's predatory war, and that in essence all Germans are National Socialists" (33). The existence of an *inner emigration* was therefore supposed to disprove the concept of "collective guilt." As Paetel pointed out in discussing the role of Frank Thieß, his essay on the *inner emigration* was "typical for the position and thinking of thousands of German intellectuals who did not leave the Reich" (93). Criticizing what they see as Germans' reluctance to identify themselves with emigrants— "we recognize our past better in the bearer of the Iron Cross than in the German emigrant"—Alexander and Margarete Mitscherlich later sought to explain Germans' postwar vituperation against exiles such as Mann and Willy Brandt by suggesting that such exiles excited an "envy of greater guiltlessness" by proving that there "was an alternative to the force of the dictatorship." In order to repress this guilt, Germans claimed that "emigration was cowardice; desertion is inexcusable, etc." (68). Such arguments tend to overlook the fact that Mann in particular was perfectly willing to include himself in the concept of collective guilt and thus made no absolute distinction in this regard between "inner" and "outer" emigration. At the same time, however, it was precisely Mann's willingness to entertain notions of German collective guilt that made him so controversial in postwar Germany.

The first part of Thieß's argument was to establish a distinction between two kinds of writers who had remained in Germany: those who supported or conformed to the Nazi regime and those who did not support or even opposed it. Suggesting that "inner emigrants," as "suspicious" intellectuals in the eyes of the regime, were subject to persecution, Thieß wrote that during the years of the Nazi Reich "there developed a very clearly observable split between conformists and the so-called suspicious ones, and the consequences of this split were soon felt painfully by the latter" ("Die innere Emigration," 336). Making an implied parallel between the asserted freedom and goodness of "inner emigrants" and the essential goodness of the German people that von Molo had previously claimed, Thieß insisted that "the world on which we inner-German emigrants supported ourselves was an interior space which Hitler was unable to conquer, in spite of all his efforts" (337). This claim was essentially similar to the claims of Klaus and Erika Mann—Thomas Mann's children and forceful representatives of the German exile community abroad—for the spiritual existence of an "other" Germany; but for Thieß that "other" Germany had been fully capable of existing physically within Hitler's evil and false Germany.

It is possible that if Thieß had contented himself simply with asserting the existence of an intellectual *inner emigration* that remained essentially uninfected by Hitler's barbarity, Thomas Mann would not have felt directly attacked. After all, in spite of Thieß's claim that "even such a keen and intelligent observer of German affairs as Thomas Mann" had not understood the *inner emigration* (336), Mann himself had indeed previously acknowledged and shown sympathy for the problems of an *inner emigration*. But Thieß did not stop at such a seemingly harmless assertion. Instead, he went on to vent what Kurt Sontheimer has called "a series of nasty remarks which were above all especially tailored for Thomas Mann himself as the representative spokesman for the outer emigration" (146). Directly contradicting Mann's convictions about the portability of German *Kultur*, Thieß declared that a German writer needed "German space, German earth, and the echo of German people"—an assertion that came uncomfortably close to National Socialist "blood and earth" (*Blut und Boden*) rhetoric and condemnations of rootless cosmopolitanism and as such directly contradicted the idealistic separation between *Kulturnation* and *Staatsnation* implicit not only in the self-understanding of "outer" emigrants like Mann but also in the concept of an *inner emigration* (337).[5] Moreover, Thieß implied that it was the "inner emigrants" who had been the true German patriots because they had shared in the suffering of the German people, while the "outer" emigrants had conveniently managed to escape an endangered Germany. In making this assertion, Thieß transformed von Molo's sin of omission into a sin of commission. Where von Molo had simply failed to take into account the suffering of German emigrants, Thieß actually denied it. Indeed, Thieß went so far as to imply that German emigrants had been able to enjoy the suffering of their native country as uninvolved consumers of a theatrical spectacle. In a Nietzschean assertion of the dignity and essential worth of suffering, Thieß claimed that remaining in Germany had been a difficult and painful task that nevertheless strengthened and improved the individual. Those who had remained in a suffering Germany knew and felt more than those who had escaped in time. Thieß's words drew a firm line between the inner and the outer emigration, directly valuing the former over the latter:

> I too have frequently been asked why I did not emigrate, and I could always answer only in the following way: if I were to succeed in surviving this horrible epoch, I would have won so much for my spiritual and human development that I would emerge richer in knowledge and experience than if I had observed the German tragedy from the balcony and orchestra seats of foreign countries. It makes a difference whether I experience the burning of my home myself or watch it in the weekly newsreel, whether I am hungry myself or simply read about starvation in the newspapers, whether I survive the hail of bombs on German cities myself or have people give me reports about it, whether I diagnose the unprecedented decline of a people directly in a hundred individual cases or simply register it as a historical fact. (337)

Such images carry von Molo's invocation of German emigrants as a privileged elite to a vindictive extreme, insisting in a self-pitying way on the recognition of German victimization. Thieß's words betray a refusal to understand the real suffering of German emigrants: loss of family, property, prestige, homeland, and all too frequently life itself; financial danger; homesickness; difficulties with foreign languages, foreign customs, and foreign state authorities. Anyone who could speak of "the balcony and orchestra seats of foreign countries" obviously knew nothing of the suicides of Walter Benjamin, Stefan Zweig, and Ernst Toller, for instance, and clearly had not read Bertolt Brecht's moving poem "To Those Born Afterward," in which Brecht conjures up the image of German exiles changing countries more often than they change their shoes (Brecht, 725).

Referring implicitly to Thomas Mann's radio messages to "German listeners," Thieß declared: "I believe it was more difficult to keep one's personality here than to send messages to the German people from over there" (338). Thieß compared inner emigrants to soldiers remaining at their post in the thick of battle, thus implying that physical emigrants like Mann were guilty of dereliction of duty. Inner emigrants, he suggested, were filled with "the certainty that as German writers we belonged in Germany and should hold out at our posts, no matter what happened" (337)—as if a writer like Mann had not been certain about his own belonging to Germany and had at any rate chosen to desert his country in its time of need. But, Thieß declared in a gesture of extraordinarily arrogant magnanimity, "We do not expect any reward for not having deserted Germany" (338).

Three years after the exchange between Mann and Thieß, Hans-Joachim Lang suggested that Thieß had cleverly played upon ordinary Germans' "most secret desires for self-justification," thus creating the so-called "case of Thomas Mann." Lang called this "an unparalleled trick" (367). In hindsight it is possible to read into Thieß's arrogance and lack of self-aware ness a simultaneous defensiveness and aggression that might imply at least a repressed consciousness of personal guilt or responsibility. The very vehemence of Thieß's gratuitous insults suggests that Thieß was not as confident of his own position as he appeared.

Whatever Thieß's conscious or unconscious motivation, however, the ideas he had expressed, and the implied accusations against Thomas Mann, infuriated the exiled writer, who nevertheless refrained from responding to the article directly. When he read Thieß's thoughts on 18 September 1945, Mann wrote in his journal that the article was "distorted and provocative," and added: "Here as there—*une race maudite* [an accursed race]" (*Tagebücher*, 254). In a letter written during the middle of October, Mann declared: "If Frank Thieß had intended to widen the gap between inside and outside irreparably, he could not have written in any other way" (ibid., 704–5).

Meanwhile, at the beginning of September, even before he had read Thieß's article, Mann had written a reply to von Molo for New York's German-language exile newspaper *Aufbau* entitled "Why I Am Not Returning to Germany." Published on 28 September in New York, the reply later found its way into many German newspapers and, because of the delay in its publication, created the impression that it was also a response to Thieß's article on the *inner emigration*. In this open letter to von Molo, Mann explicitly focused on the suffering of German exiles, making a clear distinction between it and the problems experienced by Germans in Germany. Referring to his own experiences after the Nazis' rise to power, he wrote: "In the year 1933 the shock of the loss of my customary livelihood was difficult enough, made my breath come harder: the loss of home and country, books, special objects and wealth, accompanied by pitiful actions at home, being kicked out, turned down." Equally difficult for Mann had, subsequently, been "the life of a wanderer from country to country, passport difficulties, hotel existence" (*GW*, 12: 954). Such experiences were not shared by the *inner emigration*, Mann insisted: "You all never went through that, you who swore allegiance to the 'charismatic *Führer*' and operated culture under Goebbels" (12: 954–55).

Mann's suggestion that any writer who had stayed in Germany during the Third Reich had sworn allegiance to Hitler was without doubt unfair. He went on to deny explicitly the very possibility of a pristine *inner emigration*, which he had celebrated only two years earlier. Declaring that

Nazi totalitarianism had affected all cultural production in the Third Reich, and that even supposedly independent culture had helped to stabilize and legitimate the Nazi regime, Mann wrote: "It was not allowed, it was impossible to make 'culture' in Germany while all around one we know what was happening: it meant to beautify depravity, to prettify crime" (12: 957). Mann illustrated his point that artistic innocence had been impossible during the Third Reich by suggesting that even a seemingly harmless production of Beethoven's opera *Fidelio* played into the hands of the Nazis by creating the impression that culture in Germany was as it should be and that nothing fundamental had changed. Referring to the twelve years of Nazi rule, Mann asked:

> How is it possible that Beethoven's *Fidelio*, this festive opera predestined for the day of German self-liberation, was *not* banned in the Germany of the twelve years? It was a scandal that it was not banned, and that indeed there were highly cultivated performances of it—that it was possible to find singers to sing it, musicians to play it, and an audience to listen to it. What kind of soullessness it took to listen to *Fidelio* in Himmler's Germany without covering one's face with one's hands and rushing out of the opera hall! (12: 958)

Mann's rhetorical question implied that producers of culture have a specific political responsibility that cannot be evaded by taking recourse to a realm of cultural freedom independent of the political realm. This meant that the concept of *inner emigration* was bankrupt. Mann made this point explicit by condemning all literature produced in Germany between 1933 and 1945: "It may be superstition, but in my eyes books that could be printed at all in Germany from 1933 to 1945 are less than worthless and ought not to be touched. They are impregnated with the smell of blood and disgrace. They ought all to be pulped" (12: 957).

In making such a blanket condemnation of all literature published in Germany during the Third Reich, Mann was clearly allowing his anger and bitterness to get the better of him. He was overlooking not only his own previous invocation of a German *inner emigration* but also numerous instances of non-Nazi and anti-Nazi literature published in Germany during the years of the Third Reich. And yet even his bitterness did not induce Mann to separate himself spiritually from the concept Germany or to deny his own participation in that concept: "I will never cease to think of myself as a German writer" (12: 959), he declared. Mann even asserted that there was a comparison between German "inner emigrants" and the most famous German literary hero, Faust, the man who makes a pact with the devil: "The pact with the devil is a deep old-German temptation, and a German novel about recent years, about suffering because of Germany, would no doubt have to have as its topic precisely this horrible promise" (12: 960–61). Since the soul of Goethe's Faust—if not of the legendary German subject on whom Goethe's play was based—is ultimately saved from the devil, Mann's Faust metaphor implied that the German soul was perhaps not irredeemably lost. And indeed, in the novel that was to appear two years later, the composer Adrian Leverkühn's final musical master-piece, "D. Fausti Weheklag," ends with a "hope beyond hopelessness," a "transcendence of despair" that serves as "a light in the night" (648).

In using the Faust metaphor in his response to von Molo, Mann was not only suggesting the possibility of an ultimate German redemption but also giving German newspaper readers a hint about the novel he was then working on, which had precisely such an artistic pact with the devil as its theme. Serenus Zeitblom, the narrator of *Doktor Faustus*, is precisely an inner emigrant: remaining in Germany during the years of the Third Reich, he begins his composition on 23 May 1943 and ends it when the war itself has come to an end. In this sense *Doktor Faustus* is the majestic attempt of Germany's most famous "outer" emigrant to imagine the literary situation of a humanist "inner emigrant." Mann's sympathies are clearly with his narrator Zeitblom, who is presented as loving his homeland painfully but also welcoming the defeat of its tyrannical rulers. As Zeitblom muses,

> The unavoidable recognition of unholiness is not the same thing as the denial of love. I, a simple German man and scholar, have loved much that is German, yes, my very life—insignificant but capable of fascination and devotion—was dedicated to love—an often horrified and always fearful but eternally faithful love—for an outstandingly German kind of humanity and artistry, whose mysterious sinfulness and horrific departure cannot touch this love at all, which is, perhaps—who knows—only a reflection of grace. (957)

However, *Doktor Faustus* was not to be published until two years after the "debate" with von Molo and Thiess, in 1947, and Mann's German audience did not pick up on this hint in 1945. Even in his reply to von Molo, Mann referred explicitly to the dialectical image of Germany he had frequently presented to audiences in the United States: "The evil Germany is the good that has lost its way, the good in unhappiness, in guilt, and in decline" ("Warum," 960). For Mann there were no two Germanys, but only one, indivisible in both good and evil. But in *Doktor Faustus* and in his American speeches, Mann presented a picture of German culture that was far more complex and nuanced than the blanket condemnation of September 1945.

After the publication of Mann's letter to von Molo in Germany in October 1945, the literary debate initiated by von Molo and Thieß and then carried further by the publication of Mann's open letter in German newspapers continued to dominate German cultural discussion well into the following year. Indeed, the repercussions of the debate continued to be felt four years later, when two new German states were to emerge out of the postwar chaos. Most of the German participants sided with Thieß and condemned Mann for betraying his fatherland, and the postwar West German tendency to reject the experiences of emigrants and to embrace the *inner emigration* was to make a powerful mark on German cultural politics in the coming decades, weakening Mann's emigrant invocation of the

German *Kulturnation* at precisely the time when a divided Germany desperately needed such antipolitical confirmation. As a result, the complex divisions between exiles and non-exiles and between *Kulturnation* and *Staatsnation* that had prevailed during the years of the Third Reich were dissolved into a more simplistic split between a largely apolitical literature in the German West and a politicized literature in the German East during the first decade and a half after the end of World War II. The first victim of this simplistic division was the concept of a *Kulturnation* that transcended the realm of politics. Hence the postwar triumph of the supposedly apolitical concept of *inner emigration* actually contributed to the Cold War politicization of German literature and weakened any invocations of a "better" Germany that could overcome the split between East and West. Likewise the unfair generalizations of both Thieß and Mann about "inner" and "outer" emigration made it necessary for subsequent scholars to embark on the arduous task of actually unpacking the difficulties and nuances of each individual case—and we will explore some of the fruits of that work in this volume.

As much as Mann and his German opponents may have disagreed on difficult contemporary problems like collective guilt and the relative value of the "two emigrations," there was one thing that all the protagonists in the debate agreed on: the value of the *Kulturnation* itself as represented by its greatest writers and poets, especially Johann Wolfgang von Goethe. In his end-of-the-year reply to Mann, Thieß had explicitly evoked this allegiance to Goethe:

> Previously, Thomas Mann, you used to speak of Goethe's Germany, to which you were devoted with deep and always equal love. Be assured, now that the seducer [*Verführer*] has been destroyed, that we too are conscious of having no other leader [*Führer*] than Goethe, that star of German authority in the world which now shines brighter than ever. ("Der Weltdeutsche," 342)

In Thieß's play on words, Hitler the *Führer* (leader) is turned into Hitler the *Verführer* (seducer), and Goethe becomes the true *Führer* of the German people. Such a transposition allows National Socialism as a political philosophy to be negated while leaving unquestioned a problematic word—and concept—like *Führer*.

As it happened, the two hundredth anniversary of Goethe's birth occurred at the end of the immediate postwar period, on 28 August 1949, during the year in which the three western occupation zones and then the Soviet occupation zone first declared themselves to be the separate political states named the Federal Republic of Germany (on 23 May) and the German Democratic Republic (on 7 October). In honor of the Goethe anniversary, which happened to fall between those two dates, the cities of Frankfurt, where Goethe was born, and Weimar, where Goethe lived most of his life and died, once again invited Germany's greatest living representative of the *Kulturnation* to visit his homeland and give speeches in the two cities now separated by what Churchill had dubbed the Iron Curtain. Many critics noted that four years after the war's end it was more difficult for Germans to travel inside Germany than it had been for Goethe two centuries earlier, when Germany had been divided into a far greater number of principalities. In view of the Cold War tensions causing the German division, Friedrich Sieburg, literary critic and co-editor of the journal *Die Gegenwart*, suggested that the *Kulturnation* itself was being eroded. Referring to Mann's conspicuous disrespect for the meaning of the inner German border, Sieburg lamented the fact that the great writer was once again at the center of a cultural-political controversy. The split within German culture between an outer and an inner German emigration had now been replaced by a split in cultural sensibilities between the West and the East, with each part claiming to represent the true tradition of German *Kultur*, while conveniently forgetting the traditional role of the *Kulturnation* as the guarantor of a national unity that transcended political division:

> Four years after the collapse we have reached the point where it is no longer considered normal for a great German-language writer to be celebrated simultaneously in the city of Goethe's birth and in the place of his world-spanning work. From Frankfurt to Weimar—in the minute space which covers the greatest of German life paths—the world is so changed that whoever is of value to us over there can hardly be valuable here. Thus the Iron Curtain runs through the middle of the fragile world of our spiritual values. Is our Goethe no longer their Goethe? (Sieburg, 375)

Sieburg's invocation of "the fragile world of our spiritual values" suggested that in the coming Cold War the *Kulturnation* might not provide as stable and unquestioned a location for an undivided Germany as it had for Mann during the Third Reich. But Mann himself refused to acknowledge the immanent division of his homeland. In spite of the fact that Frankfurt was located in the German West and Weimar in the German East, and that the Cold War between the United States and the Soviet Union had reached a feverish intensity with the Soviet blockade of all land routes into West Berlin from 24 June 1948 until 12 May 1949, Germany's best-known living representative of the *Kulturnation* did not reject the invitations he received from East and West to return home in honor of the Goethe anniversary. In the 1945 letter to von Molo, Mann had written that he still entertained the "dream of feeling the ground of the old continent under my feet once again," and that "when the hour comes, if I am alive and the transportation situation as well as a laudable state authority allows it, then I will go over" ("Warum," 962).

In honor of Goethe, Mann made the arduous trip to his homeland in the summer of 1949, returning to Germany sixteen years after he had become an exile in the spring of 1933. The writer demonstrated his adherence to the concept of the *Kulturnation* by ignoring the newly forming political boundaries between East and West and visiting both Frankfurt and Weimar. As

Mann declared in the two cities, "Who should represent and guarantee the unity of Germany if not an independent writer, whose real home is the free German language, untouched by zones of occupation?" ("Ansprache," 488). Mann could make such a declaration only as an "outer" emigrant who had both willed and experienced the continuity of German culture abroad, and whose concept of German identity allowed no unbridgeable distinctions between good and bad or West and East. As Mann saw it, Goethe's greatness was restricted to neither the East nor the West; and his belief that German cultural unity continued even in the face of the Cold War then beginning suggested that, after so many years of exile in which the concept of the *Kulturnation* had played an important role for German emigrants, the same concept had a similar role to play in sustaining the idea of German unity during the difficult years of political division that lay ahead. Unfortunately, however, such a sovereign idea of the German *Kulturnation* remained for the most part a prerogative of "outer" emigrants; Germany's "inner emigrants," some of whom had so rudely rejected the experience of emigrants like Mann, were thus largely deprived of a powerful concept that could have helped them preserve the dream of German unity in the years ahead. The rejection of the emigrant experience was part and parcel both of National Socialist propaganda and of postwar West German culture, and it set the tone for the literary Cold War between East and West, in which the idea of a greater German *Kulturnation* was weakened.

Notes

1. On the timing of the letter, see Krenzlin, especially 12 and 23, fn. 22. In what follows, translations from German into English are my own.
2. Von Molo had already written privately to Mann some time earlier; the subsequent decision for an open letter was evidently also spurred on by Johannes Franz Gottlieb Grosser, who later edited an anthology that continues to be the standard documentation of the controversy. See Krenzlin, "Große Kontroverse oder kleiner Dialog?" 13–14; and Leonore (Schiller-)Krenzlin, "Hinter den Offenen Briefen," especially 174–175.
3. For an overview of the term and a critique of its attribution to Thieß, see Reinhold Grimm, "Innere Emigration als Lebensform," especially 42. On more recent attributions to Thieß, see Volker Wehdeking, "Zwischen Exil und 'vorgeschobenem Posten' der Nation," especially 149.
4. For documentation on Mann's 1933 usage of the term, see Wehdeking, 149.
5. Thieß was here approvingly citing a response reported many years previously by the German writer Erich Ebermayer to Mann.

Works Cited

Brecht, Bertolt. *Werke. Große kommentierte Berliner und Frankfurter Ausgabe.* Ed. Werner Hecht, Jan Knopf, Werner Mittenzwei, and Klaus-Detlef Müller. Vol. 27, *Journale* 2. Berlin, Weimar, and Frankfurt am Main: Aufbau and Suhrkamp, 1995.

———. "An die Nachgeborenen." In Bertolt Brecht, *Die Gedichte von Bertolt Brecht in einem Band.* Frankfurt am Main: Suhrkamp, 1981.

Grimm, Reinhold. "Innere Emigration als Lebensform." In *Exil und Innere Emigration,* ed. Reinhold Grimm and Jost Hermand, 31–73. Frankfurt am Main: Athenäum, 1972.

Grimm, Reinhold, and Jost Hermand, eds. *Exil und Innere Emigration.* Frankfurt am Main: Athenäum, 1972.

Hermand, Jost. "Zum Vorverständnis." In Jost Hermand and Wigand Lange, *"Wollt ihr Thomas Mann wiederhaben?" Deutschland und die Emigranten,* 7–55. Hamburg: Europäische Verlagsanstalt, 1999.

Krenzlin, Leonore. "Große Kontroverse oder kleiner Dialog? Gesprächsbemühungen und Kontaktbruchstellen zwischen 'inneren' und 'äußeren' literarischen Emigranten." *Galerie: Revue culturelle et pedagogique* 15, no. 1 (1997): 7–25.

———. (a.k.a. Schiller-Krenzlin). "Hinter den Offenen Briefen: Initialzündung und Motivationsgeflecht des Streits zwischen innerer und äußerer Emigration." In *Literatur im politischen Spannungsfeld der Nachkriegszeit: Protokoll der internationalen Konferenz anläßlich des 50. Jubiläums des 1. Deutschen Schriftstellerkongresses vom Oktober 1947,* ed. Ursula Heukenkamp and Ursula Reinhold. Berlin: Institut für deutsche Literatur, 1998.

Lang, Hans-Joachim. "Der letzte Deutsche." In *Thomas Mann im Urteil seiner Zeit. Dokumente 1891–1955,* ed. Klaus Schröter, 365–74. Hamburg: Christian Wagner, 1969.

Mann, Thomas. "Ansprache im Goethejahr 1949." In Thomas Mann, *Gesammelte Werke* [GW in text], vol. 11, 481–97.

———. "Die Lager." In Thomas Mann, *Gesammelte Werke,* vol. 12, 951–53. Frankfurt am Main: Fischer, 1960.

———. "Schicksal und Aufgabe." In Thomas Mann, *Gesammelte Werke,* vol. 12, 918–39. Frankfurt am Main: Fischer, 1960.

———. "Das Ende." In Thomas Mann, *Gesammelte Werke,* vol. 12, 944–51. Frankfurt am Main: Fischer, 1960.

———. "Warum ich nicht nach Deutschland zurückgehe." In Thomas Mann, *Gesammelte Werke,* vol. 4, 953–62. Frankfurt am Main: Fischer, 1960.

———. *Doktor Faustus: Das Leben des deutschen Tonsetzers Adrian Leverkühn, erzählt von einem Freunde.* Frankfurt am Main: Fischer, 1998 [1947].

———. *Gesammelte Werke in Zwölf Bänden,* vol. 12: *Reden und Aufsätze 4.* Frankfurt am Main: Fischer, 1960.

———. *Tagebücher 1944–1.4.1946.* Ed. Inge Jens. Frankfurt am Main: Fischer, 1986.

Mayer, Hans. "Konfrontation der inneren und äußeren Emigration: Erinnerung und Deutung." In *Exil und innere Emigration,* ed. Reinhold Grimm and Jost Hermand, 75–87. Frankfurt am Main: Athenäum, 1972.

Mitscherlich, Alexander, and Margarete Mitscherlich. *Die Unfähigkeit zu trauern: Grundlagen kollektiven Verhaltens.* Munich: Piper, 1991.

Molo, Walter von. "Offener Brief an Thomas Mann." In *Thomas Mann im Urteil seiner Zeit. Dokumente 1891–1955,* ed. Klaus Schröter, 334–36. Hamburg: Christian Wagner, 1969.

Paetel, Karl O. "Das Gesicht des innerdeutschen Widerstandes." In *Deutsche innere Emigration: Anti-Nationalsozialistische Zeugnisse aus Deutschland,* ed. Karl O. Paetel, 32–38. New York: Friedrich Krause, 1946.

———, ed. *Deutsche innere Emigration: Anti-Nationalsozialistische Zeugnisse aus Deutschland.* New York: Friedrich Krause, 1946.

Rüther, Günther, ed. *Literatur in der Diktatur: Schreiben im Nationalsozialismus und DDR-Sozialismus.* Paderborn: Schöningh, 1997.

Schiller-Krenzlin, Leonore. "Hinter den Offenen Briefen." [See Krenzlin]

Sieburg, Friedrich. "Frieden mit Thomas Mann." In *Thomas Mann im Urteil seiner Zeit. Dokumente 1891–1955,* ed. Klaus Schröter, 375–78. Hamburg: Christian Wagner, 1969.

Sontheimer, Kurt. *Thomas Mann und die Deutschen.* Munich: Nymphenburger Verlagshandlung, 1961.

Thieß, Frank. "Die innere Emigration." In *Thomas Mann im Urteil seiner Zeit. Dokumente 1891–1955,* ed. Klaus Schröter, 336–38. Hamburg: Christian Wagner, 1969.

———. "Der Weltdeutsche und die 'Innere Emigration.'" In *Thomas Mann im Urteil seiner Zeit. Dokumente 1891–1955,* ed. Klaus Schröter, 338–43. Hamburg: Christian Wagner, 1969.

Wehdeking, Volker. "Zwischen Exil und 'vorgeschobenem Posten' der Kulturnation: Thomas Mann als Projektionsfigur für die im Land gebliebenen Nichtfaschisten." In *Literatur in der Diktatur: Schreiben im Nationalsozialismus und DDR-Sozialismus,* ed. Günther Rüther, 145–62. Paderborn: Schöningh, 1997.

Chapter 2

IN THE THICKET OF *INNER EMIGRATION*

Reinhold Grimm

I would like to begin with one of Grimm's fairy tales. The text, however, is from the year 1943—(and from Munich, the "capital of the movement" as it was then known, for which reason Brecht later dubbed it the "urban grave-stone of Germany" (*Stadt der deutschen Grabsteinlegung*, Brecht, 10: 947)— and is a contemporaneous version of the tale of Little Red Riding Hood.

Little Red Riding Hood figures here as "a little BDM-girl" (*Bund deutscher Mädel*, the equivalent of Hitler Youth for girls), whose grandmother resides for purposes "of rest and recovery in a National Socialist home for mothers." The German forest smells of "blood and soil" (*Blut und Boden*), and of the bad wolf one hears: "He had brown fur, so that the child should not notice his non-Aryan intentions. The child suspected nothing, since at the time, all people detrimental to the race [*Volksschädlinge*] were sitting in concentration camps, and therefore, she believed to have in front of her a very common dog of Germanic ancestry." After a short conversation between the two, the wolf hurries to the grandmother, eats her up in his good old way, puts on her clothes and gets into her bed, whereby he doesn't omit to put on for camouflage her "woman's corps pin" (*Frauenschaftsabzeichen*). When Little Red Riding Hood arrives and unsuspectingly asks how her "dear granny" is doing, the bad wolf even knows how to imitate impeccably her "folksy voice." He explains: "Ach, my dear child, we used to do well, now we're doing better; however, it would be better, if we would only do well again!" Then there follow the normal inquiries about her big ears, her big eyes, and the big mouth, and finally, the degenerate wolf eats the BDM-girl up.

To rescue her there appears no less a figure of course than the "head hunter of the Reich" (*Reichsjägermeister*) Hermann Göring, who famously prescribed cannons for Germans instead of butter, but who now nonetheless would like to know from industry (IG-Farben) whether one "could not transform several small cannons into synthetic butter for his private use." Göring slits open the wolf's belly in short order with his "dagger of honor" (*Ehrendolch*) and finds both the grandmother and Little Red Riding Hood well preserved inside. "Wasn't that a joy! The wolf was sent to the Reich's butchery, which had not seen any fresh meat for a long time, and dispensed slice by slice to all holders of the Reich's meat ration card. Little Red Riding Hood was promoted to a leader of the BDM, and the grand-mother received as a special gift from the Führer for one week a half-liter of fresh low-fat milk. The *Reichsjägermeister* was permitted to wear an embroidered wolf on his uniform" (from Paetel, 73f.). Thus the tale.

The editor annotates it with two laconic sentences: "Only a few copies reached the reading public. The unknown author was imprisoned, the printing plates destroyed, the journal in which this parody appeared was immediately prohibited" (72f.). This satirical text outlines in exemplary clarity the problem that confronts considerations of *inner emigration*: the complexly intertwined thicket of a German literature during the Third Reich that was not "ideologically coordinated" (*gleichgeschaltet*), but rather remained apart, on the margins, or even turned against the reigning regime. The complex of questions that arises concerns the representatives of such a literature and their origins, their means and their forms, their influence and their effect. First and foremost, however, it raises the ques-tion of the very existence of such a phenomenon.

The answer to this question has been passionately debated to this day. Walter A. Berendsohn, himself an emigrant in Sweden, has categorically demanded that the concept of an *inner emigration* be once and for all "eradicated" (4). This concept only conceals, he argues, the unbridgeable "chasm" that exists between the literature of "refugees" and those who "stayed at home" (4). Elsewhere, he remarks: "A writer in the Third Reich simply could not 'emigrate inwardly'" (*Reallexikon*, 336). Also Franz Scho-nauer shares this opinion. His "polemical-didactic" representation, which dates from 1961, was composed with the declared intention to "destroy" the "myth" of the "*inner emigration*" (13).

The desire to negate the term has become absolute here, as elsewhere happens to the affirmation of common traits. The differences that are really beyond question at times get completely leveled and effaced. That was the case for a long time for Elisabeth Langgässer. Everything dis-solved for her into the poetic and into the common "relation to the word" (37). However, she was far from a general absolution. Such a step was left to a critic like Karl August Horst, who claimed that not only a part but also the totality of literature in National Socialist Germany had gone into *inner emigration*. Horst went so far as to extend retrospectively this license (*Jagdschein*) even to "State Writers" such as Blunck and Kolbenheyer (13f.). Next to such nonsense, evaluations from conservative (see Wiesner) or confessional (see Ackermann)[1] points of view seem almost harmless. That they are not harmless is, however, revealed by the popularizing *History of German Literature* by Wilhelm Kahle, whose concern it is "to lead our folk [*Volk*] back onto the path of inwardness [*Verinnerlichung*]" (414). Kahle devotes a whole chapter to *inner emigration*, but merely a few paltry sentences to exile, which is, as he patronizingly assures us, "not to be disdained" (414). Please ponder the following pronouncement, which vibrates with archconservative and even Nazi sentiments:

> While the actual emigrants were in the majority politically and philosophically devoted to the Marxist parties, or inclined toward them, the work of those resistance writers who stayed at home [in Germany] issues from a deep sense of Christianity, indeed religiosity. The context remains preserved thereby with traditions formed in antiquity and handed down through the ages in German and Western culture. (416)

One can hardly be surprised that the best study of the period thus far does not come out of West Germany, but rather from the young East German literary historian Wolfgang Brekle. We must, as he remarks by way of provisional conclusion, not reject the concept of *inner emigration* outright or qualify it solely "because it became notorious ... through its misuse" (71).

What concerns the cause of this misuse goes back a generation earlier, namely to the year 1945, the so-called "Year Zero" (see Trommler, 1970–71). The actors in this drama were Thomas Mann and Frank Thieß; other authors joined in. The debate was set in motion by an open letter to Thomas Mann from Walter von Molo, in which Mann was asked, with emotional words, to return to help heal a beaten Germany (see Grosser). This famous author, so earnestly addressed, who found that the letter sounded "quite false" (*Die Entstehung*, 119), would apparently have preferred to remain silent in response. Yet he was not left in peace. Just two weeks later another letter appeared. It bore the lapidary title *Inner Emigration*. The writer was Frank Thieß, born in Livland in 1890, who had emerged since the beginning of the 1920s chiefly as a novelist and who had lived and published under the swastika. The "odd and provocative article" by Thieß is the decisive document in which, as is stated in Mann's *The Genesis of Doktor Faustus*: "a club, called *inner emigration*, established itself with much arrogance: namely, the community of intellectuals who 'stayed true to Germany,' who 'did not leave it in the lurch,' who did not watch its fate 'from the comfortable balcony seats of foreign countries,' but rather shared that fate honestly." "They would have shared it," said Mann scornfully, "also if Hitler had won" (124).

In fact, the article by Thieß was an "incomparable stroke"—of self-promotion. For it did not content itself merely with the conscious exculpation according to which the "world" of the "Inner-German Emigrants" was an "inner space," at whose "invasion and conquest, despite all his efforts, Hitler did not succeed" (Grosser, fn. 18, 23). Rather, by sleight of hand, a virtue was made out of necessity wherein one proclaimed that from that isolation "had been gained a treasure of insight and experience" and thus, "correspondingly much had been won for one's intellectual and emotional development," that one was now "richer in knowledge and experience" than the "outer emigrants." But he would not want to blame anyone, Thieß added graciously.

In his long delayed answer to von Molo, Thomas Mann responded with the following words: "It may be superstition, but in my eyes, the books that could even be printed in Germany, from 1933 to 1945 are less than worthless and not to be touched. A smell of blood and crime clings to them. They should all be pulped" (31). That these sentences, in turn, went beyond their target, can be understood, though not condoned. The rejoinder by Otto Flake, who presented National Socialism in all seriousness as a sort of Passion play of humanity, is nonetheless completely incomprehensible. Flake wrote that one day it will be said that "the Germans were foolish enough to live through in advance the danger of the modern world that in fact threatens it: namely, measureless excess." And: "So that humanity could arrive at the most horrible of experiences, a lesson that will hopefully remain unforgotten, the Germans pulled the chestnuts out of the fire" (Grosser, fn. 18; 56). In order to complete the measure, or better, the measurelessness (of insolence), Gottfried Benn bragged later with the indication that he had coined the *bon mot* back in 1933–35, to wit: "The army is the aristocratic form of emigration" (Benn, 91). In view of these and similar "outbursts of German writers in their useless vapidity and moody obscurity," as Thomas Mann remarked, one is seized, then as now, by his "mild horror" (*Die Entstehung*, 168). Even Elisabeth Langgässer observed in 1947 that the fate of "inner" emigration was "not inferior to that, however different, of 'outer' emigration" (40). Not a few emigrants, some of whom felt that they had to justify their actions, subscribed to that sentiment.[2] "They may not return with a claim to fame. In their departure lay a bitter necessity, but no glory. Whoever flees from bloodhounds can be pitied and comforted and joined in solidarity, but he does not need to be celebrated. Only those who were in hell could perhaps be praised, but even among them many hid behind the cauldrons." Ernst Wiechert wrote these sentences, which refer most immediately to him (see his memoirs from 1949; 401), since he was himself imprisoned for months, as described in his *The Forest of the Dead: A Report* (Der Totenwald: Ein Bericht). One would have to doubt, however, whether these utterances contributed much to any reconciliation when they were published in 1949.

Unfortunately, one still encounters misconceptions that became commonplace in conjunction with this controversy. Thus it gets variously assumed that the concept of *inner emigration* first emerged after the defeat, out of a "scarcely concealed [need for] self-justification" (Hans-Joachim Lang, 366). Nobody would deny that such an intention was present often enough. The remarks I have cited are rooted in a principled aversion among many Germans to any form of exile, and state that clearly enough.[3] Nevertheless, much of what there is to read to this date about the origins of *inner emigration* is either false or at least debatable. It is indisputably clear that the concept and content of *inner emigration* do not date from 1945, but rather extend back deep into the 1930s. The substance of the distinction was clear to all concerned, inside and outside of Germany, immediately after Hitler seized power. At that point, not only the concept but also, gradually, the term began to sprout, assuming, that is, that it had not already emerged even earlier. In any case, the term *inner emigration* was around long before 1945, and indeed in the consciousness of those who remained as well as in the thinking and writing of those who left. Evidence can be found in all ideological camps.

Within Germany one should name above all Ernst Barlach and Jochen Klepper. Both very quickly felt themselves condemned to the "life of an emigrant inside the Fatherland" (Barlach, *Briefe* II, 730, also 734). As early as the summer of 1933 Klepper spoke of his "emigrant mood" and explained that he found himself "now entirely in exile" (*Unter dem Schatten*, 69, 103); and Barlach complained in 1937 that he experienced "a rejection, that [amounted to] a surrender to destruction" so that his condition was "even more miserable than that of a real emigrant" (quoted by Brekle: 68). All these attestations are clearly confirmed by diaries, letters, and other documents. The same would hold for a note of Thomas Mann's from 1934 that states: "Penzoldt and Heimeran: for life within [Germany] they use the word that came to my mind from the first: 'Occupied Territory'" (*Leiden an Deutschland*, 58). Mann, who had already confirmed in March 1933 the "anguish of spiritual homelessness" (*Leiden*, 5) common to all high-minded Germans, unmistakably built with that comment the very bridge (between opposed camps of inner and outer exile) that he did not at all want to be reminded of at the end of the war. In addition, in 1938 he had counted himself in solidarity, publicly and emphatically, with those who "within Germany ... shared [his] hurts and hopes." As stated explicitly in his work *This Peace*: "and this 'we' always means the German opposition *extra et intra muros*" (*Dieser Friede*, 9).

Other well-known emigrants, too—Heinrich Mann, Paul Tillich, Wilhelm Pieck, Kurt Kersten, F. C. Weiskopf—made similar comments (see Brekle, 68–70; Tillich, 69). Most of them availed themselves of the term *inner emigration*. The inseparable community inside and outside, as was the feeling at the time, has perhaps nowhere else received such poignant formulation as in the novel *The Volcano* by Klaus Mann. In this novel "among emigrants" (411f.) from 1939, the figure of "the angel of the dispossessed [*Heimatlose*]" has an almost touchingly sentimental affect and is also a "friend and familiar of the inner emigration." That latter group is "expatriated within the homeland" and suffers over Germany, and knows how bitter isolation is and how tired one gets "mounting long, tough resistance against a power that charms or intimidates everyone else." The end concludes unmistakably: "Two lines, two curves loaded with energy, ran parallel: the forces of inner and outer emigration now want to connect."

Yet this connection did not even need to be made in 1939. Already four years earlier at the Paris Writers' Congress, 'inner' and 'outer' emigration had joined hands in the spotlight of world attention. The congress was remarkable, according to Alfred Kantorowicz, for two high points: one, the appearance of Heinrich Mann, and the other, the appearance of an unknown person with a mask on his face who came from Germany and brought greetings from a group of antifascist writers (Kantorowicz, 47f.). Is more evidence needed? Even to the allies during the war it was no secret that a *German Home Front* (such was the title of a book printed in England in 1943) existed, in which also "the word became deed" (see Schütz and Sevin).

If one asks about the originator of the term *inner emigration*, one almost always gets the answer that it came from Frank Thieß.[4] Unfortunately, this view rests solely on the testimony of Thieß himself, whose account then wraps itself in contradictions. In his article, "The Inner Emigration," he claims to have used this concept in 1933 in a letter of protest to the Nazi big shot Hans Hinkel. Nonetheless, after his later explanation, he claims to have written the letter only in November 1934. Up to now only the amended conclusion has been drawn that one might "with some certainty accept the second half of November 1933 as the date when Frank Thieß for the first time fixed on paper the concept of *inner emigration* (cf. Wiesner, 385)." By contrast, it seems to me that a historian would only, regretfully, draw the conclusion that "many meritorious actions in the fight against tyranny" cannot be checked and confirmed. Without intending to cast aspersions, the fact is and remains that precisely this piece of evidence, in contrast to all others, cannot be checked further. As long as it cannot be indisputably documented, I see no reason to include it in the literary history of the period.

Nor does the slightest justification exist to celebrate Frank Thieß, as even Günther Weisenborn does (221), as a special early trailblazer for *inner emigration*. Admittedly, his historical work *The Realm of Demons* (Das Reich der Dämonen) contains some critical allusions, although most, as I have been able to determine in the meantime, were added subsequently.[5] His other related writings are, however, either completely inconsequential in this regard or rather the opposite of what one usually calls *inner emigration*. If, among these writings, a certain political inconclusiveness obtains, one can, nonetheless, hardly speak of an "implacable" independence of mind. That Thieß "compromised himself most gravely through the publication of an interview from 1933 in which he claims enthusiastic allegiance to Hitler," as Thomas Mann indicates (*Entstehung*, 125), seems to me far more convincing. Mann's *The Genesis of Dr. Faustus* is not the only source that speaks of such an unmasking. But that one now should therefore forgo the term and concept of an *inner emigration*, as one often hears, is not acceptable. On the contrary, I would argue that the concept rather needs to be broadened and, above all, developed in a more differentiated fashion.

That of course is more easily said than done. The discipline of history has also created confusion here. Years ago it was suggested that "the whole ideological and temperamental middle range between National Socialism and active opposition should be declared 'inner emigration' and at the same time its restricted use for intellectuals and artists dropped"

(Seier, 319f.), if such a thing is even possible. However, such a conflation of all intermediate positions would be a terrible simplification. The idea of calling everything *inner emigration* that is neither simply fascist nor antifascist, leads as far astray as the contrary position that admits no intermediate positions and thereby verges on the thesis of a literary "collective guilt." No less faulty are those views that grudgingly acknowledge such positions but then glibly equate them with "flight" or try to convince us that *The Nonviolent* (Die Gewaltlosen), as was the title of a book by Harald von Koenigswald, were the actual resistance fighters.

Just as useless is the suggestion, in and of itself very interesting, to use *inner emigration* as the umbrella concept that covers two subordinate concepts: "inner German antifascist literature" (for literary resistance) and "inner German nonfascist literature" (for all writing that held itself decisively apart). Wolfgang Brekle, who employs these terms, has himself to admit that this distinction cannot "always clearly" be drawn (71). Therefore, it seems to me compelling that the phenomenon as such does not allow any sharp conceptual discrimination. If anywhere, then here, in the consideration of *inner emigration*, one has to free oneself from that sort of compartmentalized thinking and instead keep in mind a sliding scale that extends from active resistance to passive refusal. The former culminates in open action, while the latter culminates in mute silence. Even in silence, however, the essential feature has to be its unmistakable, even demonstrative quality. Whoever simply remained silent and turned away did not mount resistance of any kind; and whoever did not write in a fascist manner did not therefore write in an antifascist or nonfascist way. Only a recognizable posture of opposition deserves the name *inner emigration*.

Ricarda Huch provides the best example of such a recognizable posture. I do not refer only to her resignation from the Prussian Academy of Arts, which this courageous woman tendered immediately and voluntarily in 1933. In addition, Huch, who was over eighty years old at the end of the war, made no attempt during the Third Reich to conceal her convictions. She helped where she could, published what little she chose to publish with Swiss publishing houses, and secretly collected on the side materials about the resistance movement. The attitude of this woman was and remained unambiguous. Ricarda Huch did decisively more than the, at the outset, rather lax Thomas Mann, who wrote in 1934: "Getting through it and maintaining one's own personal dignity and liberty is everything" (*Leiden an Deutschland*, 73).

A diary entry of Ernst Jünger's sounds like an echo of that statement: "In simple survival there resides these days great merit" (*Gärten*, 75). The difference to Thomas Mann is nonetheless most revealing, since what falls away for Jünger is the "dignity and freedom." A further problem of definition, as is so characteristic of *inner emigration*, arises here unacknowledged: namely that of the necessary compromises or concessions. When was one permitted, faced with the pressures of the reigning ideological system, to yield without discrediting oneself? As is well known, these pressures rose to the point of claiming total control over even the most private utterances, especially of those most intellectually active. Already their much-scorned retreat into themselves, that is, their pure passivity, was seen as an affront. One might compare in this vein how Hanns Johst berated such individuals:

> Still there are writers who ask what that means: the Party, the Movement, the State? I say to these senile remnants of yesterday: We can do wonderfully without you. We whistle at the arrogance of so-called poets, who believe that they, by the detour of inwardness and the phrases of eternal values, can get around the necessity of a clear, proper, unambiguous declaration of loyalty to National Socialism and the fact of the Third Reich. (quoted by Klieneberger, *Christian Writers*, 197)

Wiechert's report *The Forest of the Dead* (Der Totenwald) notes here with comprehensive correctness: "In that state of mind lay already the guilt, the sin, the crime."

Ernst Wiechert's story instructs like no other, so that one has to guard oneself as a critic from any simple conclusions, since in this realm of coerced compromises, the boundaries are blurred more than ever. Prior attempts to clarify prompt even greater care in this matter. The claim, for example, that "all *inner emigration*" had "a collaborative and an oppositional side," is in such a general formulation certainly wrong (Seier, 321). Rather, what is correct, at least for some, is what the historian Hans Rothfels ascertained: "While they made the minimum of unavoidable concessions, they also remained morally untouched" (38). Werner Bergengruen offers the typical example: we possess a "summary judgment" (*Gesamturteil*) about him that was called for by the regional Party administration (*Gauleitung*) for Munich-Upper Bavaria, which states: "Bergengruen is probably not politically reliable." He displays, to be sure, "the swastika-flag at his window" and donates "always and gladly at collections," yet he receives apparently no "NS-publications" and he no more belongs to a "branch" of the Party than do his wife and children, and "the German greeting 'Heil Hitler' is not used by either him or his family, even though he raises up the arm a bit now and then" (Wulf, 519f.).

This reluctant raising of the hand "now and then" does not lack, indeed, traits of a certain bitter comedy. One should not forget that Bergengruen, on the one hand, was barred from the ministry of letters (Reichsschrifttumskammer, or Reich Chamber of Letters; see Strothmann, 95), and, on the other hand, as he credibly confirms, performed concrete illegal work. Along with his wife, he distributed, as he tells it, flyers for the White Rose as well as the rebellious sermons of the bishop of Münster that he himself copied to boot (*Desk-Memories*, 201). In addition, his volume of poems *The Eternal Kaiser* appeared anonymously outside Germany. This and other actions link the convert to Catholicism even, to choose an extreme example, to the active cells of the leftist underground movement in Berlin. Yet whom would that surprise? The front of *inner emigration* cut across, right up to the end of the war, the full breadth of different ideological and political camps. Also, it comprised not just the Christians of both confessions and the communist resistance fighters: writers such as Reinhold Schneider, Rudolf Alexander Schröder, or Jan Petersen, who was that man with the mask who caused such an uproar in Paris. *Inner emigration* is rather characterized precisely by the fact that it brought together representatives of the most varied tendencies. Liberals such as Rudolf Pechel, the brave editor of *Deutsche Rundschau,* and archconservatives such as Friedrich Percyval Reck-Malleczewen, the author of the vehement *Diary of a Desperate Man* (Tagebuch eines Verzweifelten, first published in 1947), stood alongside the National Bolshevist Ernst Niekisch, the switchcoat shock troop leader Ernst Jünger and the, for a time, fellow traveler or foolish follower of fascism, Gottfried Benn. Not at all coincidentally were there such mixed oppositional groups as the "progressive-bourgeois" (Brekle, 77) of the *Rote Kapelle* (Red Orchestra) with Adam Kuckhoff. Even writers such as Albrecht Haushofer, who found himself, so to speak, within the 'brown' exclusionary zone, joined the ranks at the front of *inner emigration.*

This heterogeneous crowd (cf. Brekle, 72f.), which was in effect a lost and forlorn crowd, was threatened not only by aspersions and repressions, but also by, in many cases, persecution, prison, concentration camp, and death. Its literary means and possibilities therefore remained, even when no explicit interdiction on publishing obtained, understandably limited. Much was not even intended for immediate publication (cf. Hoffmann, 3f.). Manuscripts were stuffed into the back drawer or buried in the ground. To these secret texts of *inner emigration* belong the notebooks of Jochen Klepper, the *Day and Night Books, 1939–1945* (1948) of Theodor Haecker, Wiechert's famous report, the angry diatribes of Benn (such as "Art and the Third Reich" [1941]), and the diary pages of Reck-Malleczewen. Even behind bars and in chains, such texts emerged, as evidenced by the *Moabit Sonnets* (1946) of Albrecht Haushofer and the allegorical-satirical novel *PLN (PLN: The Passions of the Halyconian* [sic] *Soul,* 1946) by the professor of Romance languages Werner Krauss. None of these documents became known during the years of Nazi rule.

Nonetheless, whoever wanted to reach his contemporaries had at that time, strictly speaking, only two options: either to employ illegal means inside or outside of Germany, or to employ the language of subversive servitude (*Sklavensprache*). Within Germany, there circulated, above all, apart from flyers and other means of spreading information, poems such as those by Reinhold Schneider: dozens of them went, hand-copied, from hand to hand. As for their circulation outside of Germany, it had to happen anonymously or under a pseudonym. That has already been touched upon with regard to the volume *The Eternal Kaiser,* which appeared in Austria in 1937. Bergengruen could luckily say that his authorship was not discovered due to the so-called "annexation." Much less felicitous was the case of Ernst Niekisch, who likewise had had the intention of publishing a work outside Germany (*Gewagtes Leben*, 285). He was arrested, and his uncompromising account, *The Realm of the Lowly Demons* (written 1935–36; published 1953), was confiscated by the Gestapo. That the text survived seems almost a miracle. The novelistic but factual account *Our Street: A Chronicle. Written in the Heart of Fascist Germany, 1933–34* (1958) by Jan Petersen also had an adventuresome history. The manuscript, baked into two cakes, was smuggled over the border by the author himself. Petersen's *Our Street: A Chronicle,* which describes the proletarian resistance struggle in the Charlottenburg Wallstraße (9), was the only real "anti-Nazi" book to arrive from Nazi Germany onto the foreign book market.

On the other hand, it was a suicidal, nearly impossible enterprise to publish the unvarnished truth. Here again, Bergengruen can speak. What would have happened, he asks, "if someone had attempted, at that time, to write the plain truth? ... Could one have expected a publisher to publish articles that, at the moment of publication, without having reached a single reader, would have been confiscated, robbed of any other effect than to have as a consequence the persecution, imprisonment and death sentence of the author?" (199). Bergengruen is doubtlessly correct. We need only remember the satirical fairy tale with which I began. But the best proof by example is the fate of Ernst Wiechert. He whose contradictory development runs from the noble Teutonism of his *Totenwolf* (1924) to the horrifying concentration-camp realism of his *Totenwald* (written 1939) dared, and was one of very few to do so, to stand up to the Nazis. In two public speeches at the University of Munich, Wiechert pilloried the contemporary situation in an increasingly undisguised manner, while at the same time denying any possibility of cooperation (cf. Kirschner, 38f.). He spoke literally of "wild renewers of the Volk" and exhorted his listeners not to "be seduced" by them and their glorification of brutality and barbarism, their "ethos of the boxing ring" and their "gladiator glory."

Wiechert was dragged off to the concentration camp in Buchenwald (which Goebbels only allowed him to leave with the threat of "physical destruction" if he undertook the slightest further action against the regime [cf. *Totenwald,* 192]) for other reasons as well, such as his courageous defense of Martin Niemöller; another of them was the printing of his remarks in the Moscow German emigrant journal *Das Wort*; another was the story *The White Buffalo or Of Great Justice* (Der weiße Büffel oder Von der großen Gerechtigkeit), against which the police stepped in directly at a public reading. In fact, this text, which appears set in a legendary India, indicts in truth the Nazi terror, as one of the boldest and most characteristic documents of what would count as an Aesopian manner of writing or as the 'language of slaves' of *inner emigration.*

The actual allusions are often of unnerving clarity: not only does this work describe the reign of terror by a Northern master race that acknowledges proudly: "We wanted to ride and see blood on the blade of our swords," but it also shows specific scenes of horror, such as torture and imprisonment by kin (*Sippenhaftung*); and also the idolatry of the omnipotent ruler, leader, and murderer Murduk is completely unmistakable. What concerned Wiechert was "legible." He could also count, without further ado, on the sharpened eye and "acute hearing of the subjugated." Many relied on those sensitivities;[6] even Petersen remarks: "We have the habit of reading between the lines" (*Our Street*, 158). Thus, the form of the legend used by Wiechert represents only one possibility, quite a rare one at that, of the language of slaves. There were still many other means by which to overcome those famous "Difficulties of Writing the Truth" (Brecht). Allegory or parable and historical parallels were probably the most popular. Besides Krauss, authors such as Bergengruen and Ernst Jünger also made use of these means, while this sort of historical disguise called forth an astonishing variety of forms that stretched from the essay to nonfiction to the panoramic novel. Such historical novels or stories include *El Greco Paints the Grand Inquisitor* (1936) by Stefan Andres, *The Father* (1937) by Jochen Klepper, *Las Casas before Charles V* by Reinhold Schneider, and the *Magdeburg Wedding* by Gertrud von Le Fort (both 1938), as well as *In Heaven as on Earth* (1940) by Bergengruen. All of these works mirror the present in the past.

From their titles alone it becomes clear that what is involved is not necessarily limited to warnings or even polemical-satirical caricatures. The reflection of history could be achieved through positive contrasts instead of only negative parallels. One tried, as Bergengruen later wrote, "to establish a counter-image" (*Desk-Memories*, 176). Rudolf Pechel, whose *Deutsche Rundschau* constitutes a veritable quarry for the 'language of slavery,' had made this double insight into a maxim from the beginning. The struggle in the public forum of a journal was, as he put it in his book *German Resistance* (*Deutscher Widerstand* [1947], 287), possible "only in two ways": first, through the selection of monitory examples from all times and places, and second, in that "the reality in Germany would be constantly confronted by circumstances and conditions" in which "first principles of justice and morality" obtained. "Criticism of dictators and injustice" and the honoring of "great ideas and goals of humanity" united in order "to allow the reader to draw the right conclusions."

In all of that, however, we should not overlook one thing. The more hidden the hidden meaning of these texts of subjugated language, the greater the danger of self-contained pointlessness. Other faults accrued, all pointing to a fundamental weakness that much of the publications of *inner emigration* suffered from, and which is difficult to label. Concepts such as "ambiguity" or "esotericism" or even "misguidance" come to mind, not to mention the facile moniker of escapism, but what these comprehend is always only partial.

I shall try to illustrate this shortcoming of *inner emigration* concretely with several examples. Bergengruen opines: "The slightest allusion was understood" (*Desk-Memories*, 200). Was it really? And how, if such an allusion led the reader to false conclusions? Evidence appears in four distinct endings of different narratives that suggest the conversion, the turn toward introspection or at least to an unexpectedly humane attitude, of the tyrant or dictator. All of them–*The White Buffalo, Las Casas before Charles V, El Greco Paints the Grand Inquisitor*, and Bergengruen's *The Great Tyrant and the Judgment*–count among the most frequently named texts of the non-fascist literature of the period. Their praised function of "giving comfort and hope to their readers" (Ackermann, 176) transmogrifies into "a comforting, but unrealistic fiction" (Schonauer, 152) about the possibility of a miraculous transformation and salvation. This deception, which in fact has something "fatal" to it, appears most obviously in the case of Andres, where the Grand Inquisitor appears "always as a more than morally equal counterweight," so that in the end, contrary to the historical facts, a "reconciliation" intercedes (Jeziorkowski, 81). Hopes and expectations were raised that were from every perspective out of place, whether intentional or not. Bergengruen guarded himself against such interpretations and asked: How should he have come upon the thought that "a Hitler would be able to experience a humane conversion and, deeply shaken, bring himself before the court of his own conscience?" (*Desk-Memories*, 80). Not Hitler, but his *Völkischer Beobachter* had an illumination at the time and announced enthusiastically of Bergengruen's book: "That is *the* Führer novel of the Renaissance period!" (*Desk-Memories*, 182). The paper, which was after all the official organ of the Party, gave a similarly warm reception to the novel *Der Vater* by Klepper.

The flip side of this official support came with the same inevitability: overinterpretation from the opposite direction. Texts that were meant to be completely innocuous were taken as messages in the language of slaves and as disguised critique. Charles W. Hoffmann recognized this most clearly: "It is quite possible" he writes, "that lines intended by the author as nothing more than a simple lyric might be accepted by readers as an oppositional poem" (4). The same danger threatens self-evidently the historian and literary historian. Schonauer has every reason to remind us "that works be considered documents of resistance solely for their actual, interpretable content" (153). A later apologist goes so far as to offer the presumptuous assurance "that one could even express entirely the opposite meaning with National Socialist phrases" (von Koenigswald, 15). In 1947, Elisabeth Langgässer had already provided the appropriate response. Nonetheless, one should not lose sight of the fact that such a "juggling act," as she called it (39), is only the outermost extreme of a fundamental ambivalence. Occasionally, it could in fact disguise genuine resistance and perhaps lead to the desired result. In general, texts of *inner emigration* can be interpreted either in a good sense or in a bad sense, with the benefit of doubt or without it, if no decisively compelling evidence is on hand.

That this openness to multiple interpretations is closely related to their esoteric quality needs no further elucidation. Ernst Jünger provides the most vivid instance. His esotericism comes close to snobbism. The Hanover native explains: "I searched out a higher standpoint, from which I could observe how the bugs devour each other" (*Strahlungen*, 162). It seems to me therefore off the track to trumpet his works as the "most significant anti-nationalsocialist documents" among all others that were written during the Third Reich (Paetel, *Ernst Jünger*, 16). Jünger's war diary *Gardens and Streets* (Gärten und Straßen*)* was in no way "a determined … frontal attack" (Schütz and de Sevin, 223); on the contrary, the way in which he distanced himself remained highly obtuse and esoteric. What difference does it make or what significance can it have if an officer on the advance into France, between the bottles of Veuve Cliquot and Pommard that he "taps into," reads Psalm 73 for a change of pace? I am unable to see in that action any inordinately impressive act of resistance. The same objection arises with respect to the extravagantly overrated story *On the Marble Cliffs*. The complete wisdom of that book issues in arrogant withdrawal and the decision "to resist solely through the pure power of mind" (*Marmorklippen*, 73). The world of this book, which gets caught in the thicket of its own allegory, is not just an uninspiringly aestheticized and artificial world of "plush" (Bense, 28f.) and plastic, but rather, now as then, the undisturbed expression of that elite ideology of fire and blood that marks Ernst Jünger's entire literary production (see Schelle). The fact that Jünger, on the other hand, sharply turned down his nomination for the Academy of Arts and wrote a disdainful letter to the *Völkischer Beobachter* (the Nazi newspaper) for having printed something of his without his knowledge, does not contradict this conclusion in the least. One of the most essential traits of *inner emigration* resides precisely in such apparent contradictions.

A further contradiction that touches not just Jünger but also Gottfried Benn arises out of direct contact or temporary connection with the National Socialists. With the former of these two writers, it involves his well-known ideological commonalities; with the latter, his Nazi adventure of 1933–34. Paul Rilla described the case of Jünger most succinctly when he named him "one of the most confirmed opponents of National Socialism" who was also "a confirmed pacemaker of the Third Reich" (Rilla, 79). The same can be said *mutatis mutandis* of Benn, who was less a collaborator than, for one or two years, a mindless adherent and fellow traveler. In any case, with respect to Benn's ideological involvement as well his conception of art, so much has been written that such a discussion is not necessary here (see Wellershoff). The poetic form, in and of itself, as an act of resistance seems as tenuous as Jünger's reading of the Bible on the front. Such a formation is nothing more than a "formal" opposition in the full—that is, the double—meaning of the word.

Therefore let us dwell rather on common traits, since these do not limit themselves at all to Benn and Jünger. Ernst Wiechert and even Rudolf Pechel also share them. When Pechel described Russia as a GPU-state (Soviet Secret Police) and Stalin as a bloody tyrant, he sketched not only a cryptogram (*Vexierbild*) of Hitler and the terror of the National Socialists, but likewise branded at the same time their opponents. This double effect seems to have been not unwelcome to him. Even more powerfully, though also more naively, Ernst Wiechert pulled on the same rope as the National Socialists. This commonality expresses itself most clearly in the totality of his worldview, whose proximity to the myth of *Blood and Earth* (*Blut und Boden*) is unmistakable, and it extends beyond to leave its imprint on many particulars, for example, the "Romance of the Steel Helmet" (noted in Klieneberger, 195), from which Wiechert was unable to separate himself even after 1933.

Entirely grotesque is the effect, however, of the antimodernism extolled by this author, owing to which he aligned himself with the brown cadre of the Nazi front. For Wiechert, as for the Nazis, there existed a "degenerate art" that had to be fought; he too knew who was meant and affected by that term, and carried the fight out with purpose nonetheless. He issued polemics, completely in the vein of Rosenberg and his cultural administrators, against the "literary types of this degraded epoch" (in "The Poet and Youth") not only after 1933, but also in his 1948 memoirs. What Wiechert has to say there is more than embarrassing: it is dangerous nonsense. The fatal separation of poets and writers, art and literature, is carried so far with confused argumentation that ultimately the experimental impulse of modern art and science collapses and falls in together with the experiments on humans, and even the genocide, practiced by the National Socialists (*Jahre und Zeiten*, 282f.). I need only add to that the following lines:

> God gave the ancient Jews the right to conquer Palestine and to annihilate whole peoples or deprive them of their rights. We can be permitted to assume that these peoples were degenerate and had misused their rights. We can be permitted to assume the same of the Incas in Mexico [*sic*] or even of Carthage or the Abyssinians of today.

Written on 1 May 1940, does it not sound like a perverse proclamation by Himmler or Eichmann? The quotation comes, however, from neither of them nor from Wiechert, but from the Catholic Theodor Haecker (*Tag- und Nachtbücher*, 77). One was so deluded even on the Christian branch of *inner emigration*, even especially there; one no longer noticed in what close and frightful proximity one had arrived.

More telling, nonetheless, is the conclusion that is valid for the whole of *inner emigration*: the sort of fascist thinking to which Haecker had so exemplarily succumbed, contaminated even its own conscious negation. Ernst Jünger, who suffered not at all from a lack of acuity, confessed as much. He noted in his war diary *Radiances* (Strahlungen), where he uses the pseudonym Kniébolo for Hitler: "Nothing speaks more loudly for the uncommon significance that Kniébolo assigned himself than the degree to which even his strongest opponents depend on him" (497). We can pick up directly from this insight; for nothing expresses the horrifying degree of such dependence more eloquently than the images that those in *inner emigration* chose to use to condemn the National Socialists. Everywhere, with

Jünger as with Haecker, Wiechert, Bergengruen, Schneider, Niekisch, Krauss, and Reck-Malleczewen, one encounters the comparison, even the equation, of Hitler with the Antichrist, of the Third Reich with a "Satanocracy," and its history with the Apocalypse. This theological elevation of historical events appears in Reinhold Schneider in an especially crass manner; it even overtakes itself in the macabre interpretation that we found at the outset in Otto Flake, though in a secularized and trivial form. That such images are utterly indebted to the historical view and understanding of the National Socialists, which they simply reverse and reverse again, is a palpable fact. They, too, perpetuate the ideology of a "providence" that sent Hitler, only with a negative accent.

Just as the history of salvation was pressed into metaphorical service, so too was the universe. Above all, Reck-Malleczewen, who apostrophizes Hitler repeatedly as "Satan," speaks of a "frightful and incalculable cosmic rotation" that is taking place (*Tagebuch*, 24). From this point to the dissolution of German guilt into the guilt of all humanity, it was only a short step. Werner Bergengruen, with his poem "To the Peoples of the Earth," took that step. As an antifascist, he had to repress as much as he had as a convert, so as to evaluate Hitler's apocalyptic scenario. Hadn't the Holy See back in 1933 entered into an agreement with this antichrist and thereby given politically, so to speak, its blessing to Hitler's Germany? No, I know of only one single kind of generalization that is allowed, or even called for, in this area. It is the question of *inner emigration* as a way of life.

Of course, there was then a comparable situation in Mussolini's Italy, and elsewhere it obtains even today. Yet nowhere but in Germany was there and is there still a corresponding tradition. This tradition of "mystical authority" (Klepper, *Schatten*, 756) and excessive "inwardness" (Wiechert, *Jahre und Zeiten*, 430), and the model of existence captured in Gottfried Benn's title *Double Life* (*Doppelleben*, 1950) that results from both, make this question legitimate. In contrast to the widespread view that Benn only lived and espoused such a "double life" as a reaction to his fascist escapade in the early 1930s (see Wellershoff, *Fieberkurve*, 35f.; and Schonauer, 143), such a model, in fact, determined his behavior from the beginning. He had already fully realized such a model in Brussels during World War I—just as he later did in the chaos of World War II, when he lived in "Block II, Room 66" of a barracks in Landsberg. The aphoristic coinages of this model, such as *Der Ptolemäer* (1949) or his posthumous *Radar Thinker*, are anticipated by his earlier texts, such as *Alexandrian Campaigns by Means of Flushes* (Alexanderzüge mittels Wallungen).[7]

Gottfried Benn was in no way alone in this respect. Ernst Jünger had given shape to entirely similar ideas in his story *On the Marble Cliffs*. Not only does the so-called "rue [medicinal herb] retreat" (*Rauten-Klause*) fall into this category, but also the image of the "untouched stillness" at the "center of the cyclone" (9, 31) This image of the calm at the center of the storm might express in general a sort of primal experience of *inner emigration*. It is even present in Ernst Wiechert's favorite concept, the island (see Jetter). Wiechert called his 1939 novel *The Simple Life*, which is dominated by this basic motif: on the one hand, "the Island of the Blissful," and on the other, "the asylum, in which one can find refuge from the world of loudspeakers, processions, informers and barbed wire" (*Jahre und Zeiten*, 346). That refers to the act of writing as well as to the book, to art as well as to life. Both become for Wiechert a "calm corner" (302) around which the tornado of history rages and the "the horrible wagon of Juggernaut," as it is elsewhere dubbed, leaves its "bloody tracks" (40).

We all know that this German path into interiority or inwardness did not just begin yesterday. It extends back decades and centuries. Not for nothing does Wiechert appeal so often to Wilhelm Raabe (*Jahre und Zeiten*, 396; 428 passim), who provided in a work like *Stuff-Cake* (Stopfkuchen, 1891) a classical paradigm for Benn's model of existence. But does not Ludwig Tieck's *On Life's Superabundance* (Des Lebens Überfluß) also belong in this context? Shouldn't his idyll of the attic room under the eaves of 1837 be viewed as a variant from the Biedermeier period, just as Raabe's *Rote Schanze* would figure as a variant from the Wilhelmian period? *Inner emigration*, like exile, has a long history in German letters.

At its origin, I should like to add in conclusion, stands none other than Martin Luther. His exegesis of Romans and the lesson of the two realms that develops out of that interpretation provides the ideological basis of *inner emigration*. Unlike Calvinist or Jesuit moral theology, Lutheran morality knows no right to resist; rather it exerts, precisely in this respect, a paralyzing effect (Rothfels, 51). The key document for that effect is provided, once again, by Jochen Klepper, who wrote on 6 August 1937: "I remain with Romans 13, obedient to an authority even to which I am so opposed" (*Unter dem Schatten deiner Flügel*, 479). This sentence stands in absolute harmony with church teaching; even a tyranny would constitute such an authority.

For the last time, *inner emigration* and outer emigration, or exile, converge here. Thomas Mann in his text *Germany and the Germans* circles around the question; he, too, cites Romans and connects German inwardness or interiority (*Innerlichkeit*) with Luther's authoritarianism. Indeed, in doing so he draws the fatefully wrong conclusion when he opines: "The great historical deed of German inwardness was Luther's Reformation" (31). Was it not rather the other way around? Doesn't one run the risk of hypostasizing this inwardness and mythologizing history? The actual history of a people emerges from its historical experience, not some ensemble of essential traits. Even if *inner emigration* does constitute for Germans a way of life from the past, it does not therefore need to be one for the future.

Translated by Neil H. Donahue

Notes

1. Ackermann notes on *Inner Emigration*: "One understands by that term an intellectual posture that preserves the continuity of its thought through its conscious abstraction away from daily politics, an attitude that finds itself bound to the realm of the spirit and of intellectual order in a world that has fallen away from those values" (38).
2. See the editions *Werk und Dichter* by Thieß (215f. and 252f.) and *Deutsche Schriftsteller im Exil* by Kantorowicz (42f.).
3. The posture of Ernst Niekisch is characteristic; he had to reckon at any moment with "Hitler's henchmen walking in" and had repeated opportunity to go into exile: "But I declined to leave Germany: I didn't want to be an emigrant" (Niekisch, 239). In Ernst Jünger's *Strahlungen*: "The step into emigration always leads into a weaker element" (550).
4. Cf. Wiesner, fn. 11, 384; also, Klieneberger, *Christian Writers*, 9; and his article "The 'inner emigration,'" 171.
5. It is especially embarrassing that hardly any of the brave moments that Wiesner highlights are found in the first printing (1–10 thousand copies) or even in the second (10–31 thousand copies), but rather only in the new editions after the war that in fact truly earn the rubric of "corrected" edition.
6. Most clearly, Karl Barth, who had already made in 1934 "Between the Lines" the "invisible subtitle" of his series "Theological Existence Today." Cf. Ackermann, 40.
7. For more details, see Reinhold Grimm, "Brussels 1916: Gottfried Benn's *Urerlebnis.*"

Works Cited

Ackermann, Konrad. *Der Widerstand der Monatsschrift Hochland gegen den Nationalsozialismus.* Munich: Kosel, 1965.

Barlach, Ernst. *Briefe II (1925–1938).* Ed. F. Dross. Munich: Piper, 1969.

Benn, Gottfried. *Gesammelte Werke.* Ed. Dieter Wellershoff. Wiesbaden: Limes, 1958–61.

Bense, Max. *Ptolemäer und Mauretanier oder die theologische Emigration der deutschen Literatur.* Cologne and Berlin: F. Krause, 1950.

Berendsohn, Walter A. "Emigrantenliteratur 1933–47." In *Reallexikon der deutschen Literaturgeschichte,* vol. 1, 336–43. Berlin: de Gruyter, 1958.

Bergengruen, Werner. *Schreibtischerinnerungen.* Munich: Nymphenburger, 1961.

Brecht, Bertolt. *Gesammelte Werke.* Vol. 10. Frankfurt am Main: Suhrkamp, 1967.

Brekle, Wolfgang. "Die antifaschistische Literatur in Deutschland (1933–1945). Probleme der inneren Emigration am Beispiel deutscher Erzähler (Krauss, Kuckhoff, Petersen, Huch, Barlach, Wiechert u.a.)." *Weimarer Beiträge* 16, no. 6 (1970): 67ff.

Grimm, Reinhold. "Brussels 1916: Gottfried Benn's *Urerlebnis.*" In *The Ideological Crisis of Expressionism: The Literary and Artistic German War Colony in Belgium 1914–1918,* ed. Rainer Rumold and O. K. Werckmeister, 133–49. Columbia, S.C.: Camden House, 1990.

Grimm, Reinhold, and Jost Hermand, eds. *Exil und Innere Emigration. Third Wisconsin Workshop.* Frankfurt am Main: Athenäum, 1972.

Grosser, J. F. G. *Die große Kontroverse: Ein Briefwechsel um Deutschland.* Hamburg, Geneva, and Paris: Nagel, 1963.

Haecker, Theodor. *Tag- und Nachtbücher 1939–1945.* Olten: Hegner/Summa, 1948.

Hoffmann, Charles W. *Opposition Poetry in Nazi Germany.* Berkeley and Los Angeles: University of California Press, 1962.

Hohendahl, Peter Uwe, and Egon Schwarz. *Exil und innere Emigration II: Internationale Tagung in St. Louis.* Frankfurt am Main: Athenäum, 1973.

Horst, Karl August. *Die deutsche Literatur der Gegenwart.* Munich: Nymphenburger, 1957.

Jetter, Marianne R. *The "Island Motif" in the Prose Works of Ernst Wiechert*. Vancouver, B.C.: Continental Book Centre, 1957.

Jeziorkowski, Klaus. "El Greco malt den Großinquisitor." In *Interpretationen zu Stefan Andres*. Munich: Oldenbourg, 1969.

Jünger, Ernst. *Auf den Marmorklippen*. Hamburg: Hanseatische Verlags-Anstalt, 1939.

———. *Gärten und Straßen. Aus den Tagebüchern von 1939 und 1940*. Berlin: Mittler & Sohn, 1942.

———. *Strahlungen*. Tübingen: Klett, 1959.

Kahle, Wilhelm. *Geschichte der deutschen Dichtung*. Münster: Regensberg, 1964.

Kantorowicz, Alfred. "Deutsche Schriftsteller im Exil." *Ost und West* 1, no. 4 (1947): 42ff.

Kirschner, Sumner. "Some Documents Relating to Ernst Wiechert's 'Inward Emigration.'" *German Quarterly* 38 (1965): 38–43.

Klieneberger, H. R. "The 'Innere Emigration': A Disputed Issue in Twentieth-Century German Literature." *Monatshefte* 57 (1965): 171ff.

———. *The Christian Writers of the Inner Emigration*. Den Haag and Paris: Mouton, 1968.

Koenigswald, Harald von. *Die Gewaltlosen: Dichtung im Widerstand gegen den Nationalsozialismus*. Herborn: Oranien, 1962.

Klepper, Jochen. *Unter dem Schatten deiner Flügel: Aus den Tagebüchern der Jahre 1932–1942*. Stuttgart: Deutsche Verlags-Anstalt, 1955.

Lang, Hans-Joachim. In *Thomas Mann im Urteil seiner Zeit. Dokumente 1891–1955*, ed. Klaus Schröter, 365–74. Hamburg: Christian Wagner, 1969.

Langgässer, Elisabeth. "Schriftsteller unter der Hitler-Diktatur." *Ost und West* 1, no. 4 (1947): 36ff.

Loewy, Ernst. *Literatur unterm Hakenkreuz. Das Dritte Reich und seine Dichtung*. Frankfurt am Main: Europäische Verlagsanstalt, 1966.

Mann, Klaus. *Der Vulkan. Roman unter Emigranten*. Orig. Amsterdam: Querido, 1939; Frankfurt am Main: Fischer, 1956.

Mann, Thomas. *Die Entstehung des Dr. Faustus. Roman eines Romans*. Amsterdam: Bermann-Fischer, 1949.

———. *Dieser Friede*. Stockholm: Bermann-Fischer, 1938.

———. *Leiden an Deutschland: Tagebuchblätter aus den Jahren 1933 und 1934*. Los Angeles: Privatdruck der Pazifischen Presse, 1946.

Niekisch, Ernst. *Gewagtes Leben. Begegnungen und Begebnisse*. Cologne and Berlin: Kiepenheuer & Witsch, 1958.

Paetel, Karl O., ed. *Deutsche Innere Emigration. Antinationalsozialistische Zeugnisse aus Deutschland*. New York: F. Krause, 1946.

Pechel, Rudolf. *Deutscher Widerstand*. Erlenbach-Zurich: Rentsch, 1947.

Petersen, Jan. *Unsere Straße: Eine Chronik, 1933–34*. Berlin: Dietz, 1947.

Reck-Malleczewen, Percival. *Tagebuch eines Verzweifelten*. Stuttgart: Goverts, 1966.

Rilla, Paul. "Der Fall Jünger." *Die Weltbühne* 3 (1946).

Rothfels, Hans. *Deutsche Opposition gegen Hitler. Eine Würdigung*. Krefeld: Scherpe, 1951.

Schelle, Hansjörg. *Ernst Jüngers Marmor-Klippen. Eine kritische Interpretation*. Leiden: Brill, 1970.

Schonauer, Franz. *Deutsche Literatur im Dritten Reich. Versuch einer Darstellung in polemisch-didaktischer Absicht*. Olten und Freiburg im Breisgau: Walter, 1961.

Schröter, Klaus, ed. *Thomas Mann im Urteil seiner Zeit: Dokumente 1891–1955*. Hamburg: Wegner, 1969.

Schütz, W. W., and B. de Sevin. *German Home Front*. London: Gollancz, 1961.

Seier, Helmut. "Kollaborative und oppositionelle Momente der inneren Emigration Jochen Kleppers." *Jahrbuch für die Geschichte Mittel- und Ostdeutschlands* 8 (1959): 319ff.

Strothmann, Dietrich. *Nationalsozialistische Literaturpolitik. Ein Beitrag zur Publizistik im Dritten Reich*. Bonn: Bouvier, 1968.

Tillich, Paul. *The Interpretation of History*. New York and London: Scribner, 1936.

Trommler, Frank. "Der 'Nullpunkt 1945' und seine Verbindlichkeit für die Literaturgeschichte." *Basis* 1 (1970): 9–25.

————. "Der zögernde Nachwuchs: Entwicklungsprobleme der Nachkriegsliteratur in Ost und West." In *Tendenzen der deutschen Literatur seit 1945,* ed. Thomas Koebner, 1–116. Stuttgart: Kröner, 1971.

Weisenborn, Günther, ed. *Der lautlose Widerstand. Bericht über die Widerstandsbewegung des deutschen Volkes 1933–1945.* Hamburg: Rowohlt, 1953.

Wellershof, Dieter. "Fieberkurve des deutschen Geistes: Über Gottfried Benns Verhältnis zur Zeitgeschichte. In *Die Kunst im Schatten des Gottes. Für und wider Gottfried Benn,* ed. Reinhold Grimm and Wolf-Dieter Marsch, 11–39. Göttingen: Sachse and Pohl, 1962.

————. *Gottfried Benn – Phänotyp dieser Stunde. Eine Studie über den Problemgehalt seines Werkes.* Cologne and Berlin: Kiepenheuer & Witsch, 1958.

Wicchert, Ernst. *Jahre und Zeiten. Erinnerungen.* Erlenbach-Zürich: Rentsch, 1949.

————. *Der Totenwald. Ein Bericht.* Munich: Desch, 1946.

Wiesner, Herbert. "'Innere Emigration': Die innerdeutsche Literatur im Widerstand 1933–1945." In *Handbuch der deutschen Gegenwartsliteratur,* vol. 2, ed. Hermann Kunisch, 383–408. Munich: Nymphenburger, 1970.

Wulf, Joseph. *Literatur und Dichtung im Dritten Reich. Eine Dokumentation.* Gütersloh: Sigbert Mohn, 1966.

Chapter 3

THE YOUNG GENERATION'S NON-NATIONAL SOCIALIST LITERATURE DURING THE THIRD REICH

Hans Dieter Schäfer

In recent years, we have come to know more about Nazi literature and exile authors, as well as about religious confessional writing, than about the group of young authors who began to write and publish toward the end of the Weimar Republic. Our knowledge of these contexts is not improved by the fact that many of these writers were among the most famous representatives of post-1945 literature. Just as the German people, after the "collapse," demonized Hitler as something superhuman in order to avoid their own sense of responsibility, so many authors and publicists exaggerated the reactionary aesthetic policies of the Nazis while blocking out their own work, thereby making the cultural life of the Third Reich seem unreal. Again and again, the authors of the "Zero Hour" directed their attention to the regime's attempt to impose conformity (*Gleichschaltung*), to book-burnings and forced emigration. Very little was known about the fact that in Hitler's state, as in every dictatorship, spontaneous relationships could nonetheless be asserted, and even publicly. This possibility was hidden out of the need to justify and legitimize past behavior. It is beyond doubt that the Führer's state wanted to destroy the freedom that was tied up with a living culture, but at the same time this state had to encourage a depoliticized sphere in order to bind the majority of the people to it for the long term. Owing to these two goals, which were difficult to separate from each other, there did arise possibilities for younger authors to publish, even though their understanding of the aesthetic norms of the Third Reich was often highly deviant.

The tolerance for this literature in the Third Reich is connected with the readiness of a part of this generation *not* to challenge the political conditions of the Hitler regime, despite their opposition to its ideology. Already around 1930 many younger people had withdrawn hopelessly into themselves, away from the shock of the Great Depression. The result was depression and a sense of paralysis. After World War II, Oskar Splett, in his speculative essay "The Living Generation" (Die lebenden Generationen), observed a "Janus face" among those born between 1900 and 1914. "Not only their gaze is split, since it looks both ahead into the future and also back into the past. This group is systematic and intuitive, both very individualistic and also open to broad concepts" (Splett, 42). In 1930, Frank Matzke's text *Youth Confesses: This Is How We Are* (Jugend bekennt: so sind wir) had expressed this splintered quality, which was so typical of this generation. On the one hand, Matzke demanded community (*Gemeinschaft*); on the other, he adhered to individualism: "we subject ourselves silently, even when we know better and feel otherwise. But this is a subjection only in external matters, and never in the core of the soul, which is always individual and alien to the community, even if it may long for community nowadays" (Matzke, 82). Characteristic for most of these people is a peculiar oscillation between deep despair and the need to include themselves in a "field of leadership." Matzke sketched out the image of a youth who wanted to face up to reality in a "soldierly" way. "We stand fast here with clenched teeth, seeking to fill out our place, a place onto which someone—yes, who?—has set us" (Matzke, 86).

Left in such disorientation, this generation hardly protested against the irruption of Nazism, since it had already closed itself off in advance to the "environment born of mere chance" (Heist, 183). Thus it no longer had any contact with republican traditions. Democracy appeared "pale and outmoded" to them (Kaschnitz, *Places* [Orte], 92). Disappointed by the Weimar Republic—called an "interregnum" (Lange, 23)—they consented to its collapse through their own selfish attitude. Even an author like Hans Erich Nossack, who was close to the Communist Party, recognized the destructive character of the Hitler regime only after the 1934 murder of Röhm. Since any idea of making the world better was condemned by the younger generation, few could, after Hitler's seizure of power, consider the options of political resistance or exile. "It wasn't a matter of physical resistance, but of a spiritual one" Nossack explained (*Glossen*, 64). Marie Luise Kaschnitz noted in retrospect: "Better to survive, better just to be there still, be able to go on working, once the specter had passed" (Kaschnitz, *Places*, 112). The regime's acts of terror were indeed noticed with a "feeling of humiliation and shame," but horror was kept at a distance out of self-preservation. In a letter after Kristallnacht, Felix Hartlaub remarked that he had, "in the course of time, adopted a Stoicism which had something rather bestial about it" (Hartlaub, *Gesamtwerk*, 454). One made little "pinpricks" against the system: flew no flag, refused to make contributions for winter help, or listened to foreign radio and "offered a handshake now and then to a Jew on the street," but in general, people withdrew into an inner domain, for "we can today find no consolation but in ourselves" (Bussmann, 13). In almost all the notebooks and diaries of those years, discussion of political questions remained almost entirely elided: "political reality was not discussed, it was much more a question of finding means to survive as a human amidst the terror, in a defensive position" (Inge Jens, 35). When Hermann Kasack gave a reference for Günter Eich on an Allied questionnaire in 1946, he wrote: "He always rejected the Nazi ideology. He is by nature a person who stands naively and disinterestedly apart from all political questions" (Zeller, 143).

Although people bracketed contemporary political problems out of their minds, many nonetheless professed their adherence to the spirit of Europe, which admittedly "should have remained conservative, if only for its vital traditions." Students above all, who were educated by such professors as Ernst Robert Curtius, Max Kommerell, Karl Vossler, and others, felt that they had been won over "immediately and forever by the humane aura of the supra-national" (Hocke, *Europäertum*, 7). It has until now been overlooked that many authors of this generation were able to spend longer periods of time abroad, where they—above all in Fascist Italy—often came into contact with modern currents that had not been suppressed. This was true for Marie Luise Kaschnitz and Wolfgang Koeppen, as well as for Stefan Andres, Eugen Gottlob Winkler, Felix Hartlaub, Gustav René Hocke, and others. From time to time these young people felt themselves to be in exile, and yet they refused the name of emigrant. Stefan Andres explained: "Everyone knew where I stood, and every day I could have been taken and sent off wherever they wished. I wasn't even living in hiding, but simply in reclusion" (Andres, 58). Such a reclusion was hardly seen favorably by the Nazi regime. In a time when poetry was viewed as "expression of the community," as the belligerent declaration of a "renewed *Volk* which was seeking purity and thus remaining sure of its immortality," this sort of urbane subjectivism had to be seen as "disuniting" and "harmful to the *Volk*" (Böhme, 634). Nonetheless the cultural policy makers of National Socialism saw this group, which was spiritually lively and yet disinterested in daily political life, as far less dangerous than Marxist or religiously engaged writers. Thus the authors discussed here were only rarely in any conflict with the state apparatus, which might have endangered their freedom or survival. Their chances at publication must be seen as quite good, up until the outbreak of war.

Those authors who became prominent later on veiled their publications during the Third Reich, or exaggerated the difficulties with censorship, probably out of a sense of guilt. Joachim Günther belongs to the few who acknowledged truthfully: "On the whole, we suffered inwardly from a great deal less shortness of breath than it may seem today" (Marcuse, 33). Publishing houses such as Beck, Goverts, Rauch, and Fischer/Suhrkamp and significant journals such as the *Neue Rundschau*, the *Europäische Revue*, the *Deutsche Rundschau*, and *Literatur*, as well as religious organs such as *Hochland* and *Eckart*, specialized in the publication or reviewing of non-Nazi literature. Of especial significance for the continuity of modernism were above all the cultural pages of the *Berliner Tageblatt*, the *Frankfurter*

Zeitung, the *Kölnische Zeitung*, and the *Deutsche Allgemeine Zeitung*. There were for a long time possibilities of publishing in magazines such as *Die Dame, Die Neue Linie*, and *Koralle*, as well as in organs that were more open to *völkisch*-national propaganda, such as the weekly paper *Das Reich* and the periodical *Das Innere Reich*. In this last, we may find represented from our group authors such as Emil Barth, Johannes Bobrowski, Günter Eich, Albrecht Fabri, Peter Huchel, Karl Krolow, Horst Lange, Wolf von Niebelschütz, Johannes Pfeffer, and Eugen Gottlob Winkler. A completely apolitical beginner like Karl Krolow could still, just before 1945, begin a broad literary career without having trouble with censors. In the last years of the war, he published more than sixty poems and a good two dozen book reviews, and in these he had only rarely to make compromises with Nazi ideology. Max Frisch, too, made a name for himself in Germany during the Hitler dictatorship. In 1934 and 1937 he published his first volumes of prose, titled *Jürg Reinhart: A Fateful Summer Journey* (Eine sommerliche Schicksalsfahrt) and *Answer from the Silence* (Antwort aus der Stille) with the Deutsche Verlagsanstalt. These books were greeted with applause from German critics. More than a third of Günter Eich's postwar volume of poetry, *Distant Farms* (Abgelegene Gehöfte, 1948), was written during the Third Reich and partly published in journals and newspapers. The same is true for Peter Huchel, who, like almost all of those of his generation, scarcely "remained silent ... during the Hitler years" (Drews and Kantorowicz, 77). Nineteen radio dramas of his are known to have existed until 1940. Eich claimed that his numerous radio plays, which were broadcast from 1933 to 1940, were hardly noticed at the time. This is contradicted by the fact that his play, *Death at Hands* (Tod an den Händen), which dealt with the Semmelweiss material, was chosen as one of the most popular radio plays in the winter of 1938–39. The roughly hundred radio series of the *German Calendar* (Deutscher Kalender) and *Märkischer Kalendermann*, which were prepared with Martin Raschke from October 1933 up to the outbreak of war, were among the most successful broadcasts. In an official review, they were expressly credited with an "important influence ... on the mutual understanding of city and country" (Eckert, 561).

Some novels also succeeded beyond a mere *succès d'estime*. Thus Wolfgang Koeppen's novel *The Wall is Swaying* (Die Mauer schwankt, 1935) appeared four years later with the heroically colored title *The Duty* (Die Pflicht). Ernst Kreuder's short stories had a second edition, *The Night of the Prisoners* (Die Nacht der Gefangenen, 1939, 1941). So did a few works of Emil Barth, whose novel about Sappho, *The Laurel Banks* (Die Lorbeerufer, 1943), was translated into Dutch and also in part into Italian. Ernst Schnabel's novel *Nightwind* (Nachtwind) appeared in Holland in 1943; further German editions were "specially produced for Wehrmacht troops." Eich's story *Catherine* (Katharina), which, after having appeared in *Das Innere Reich*, was published by Paul List in 1943, was prepared in a military edition (1945: 23rd to 32nd thousand). Among Wolfgang Weyrauch's works, it was, along with his five belletristic works from 1934–43, the anthology *1940—Young German Prose* (1940 – Junge deutsche Prosa, 1940) and *The Berlin-Book* (Das Berlin-Buch, 1941) that were most successful. Klaus-Dieter Oelze has found in the *Kölnische Zeitung* from 1933 to 1944 alone about 320 contributions from Max Bense, who published twelve books under Hitler. In general, reception of this group was limited. In Germany, people read more of Wiechert (editions numbering 1,165,000), Hesse (481,000), and Fallada.

An article by Albert Bettex from the *Basler Nachrichten* shows that outside Germany, the literary work of the younger generation was perceived as an independent grouping. Bettex distinguished this group from the poetry of the emigration and the "state-sponsored political propaganda literature," calling it a literature "which was generally tolerated in Germany, officially very rarely praised, and more often ignored, and in which one may already see signs of supratemporal endurance and morning light" (2 October 1935). When in 1937 Karl Rauch published the essays of Eugen Gottlob Winkler, who had committed suicide, the reviews were unmistakably converted by non-Nazi reviewers into a demonstration for this younger generation's work. Among the reviewers were Max von Brück, Hans Hennecke, Gustav René Hocke, Karl Korn, Johannes Pfeffer, Walter Schmiele, Gert H. Theunissen, and Bruno E. Werner. The communications network of this "group of loners" functioned relatively well until 1939. "We knew and recognized each other," Hans Egon Holthusen noted. "Those who were like-minded gave each other signs (like beacons) in a hostile territory." In her memoirs, Oda Schaefer describes prewar Berlin, which still had about it a remnant of the glamour of the "Golden 20s." Among others, the publishers Stomps and Ledig-Rowohlt met in bars and nightclubs with jazz in the background; so did authors such as Horst Lange, Peter Huchel, and—whenever they were in Berlin—Günter Eich and Martin Raschke. They all wanted to "enjoy this remnant of a hidden freedom" (Schaefer, 267). Berlin was "wonderful then as it had been earlier" (Felix Hartlaub, *Gesamtwerk*, 452). Under the pressure of dictatorship, people were more closely bound together. Karl Korn, who was editor of the *Berliner Tageblatt* from 1934 to 1937 and then was responsible for Peter Suhrkamp's *Neue Rundschau* until 1940, observed an increase in private sociability in the capital of the Reich. "Suddenly the walls came down that had separated groups from each other. Whoever was neither a Nazi nor wanted to be one sensed an increased need for information. People got together more easily" (Korn, 251).

The younger ones tried "systematically to fill gaps" in their knowledge of literary modernity. "Read a few very powerful American novels —Green, Faulkner, Wolfe," Felix Hartlaub wrote in a letter of 16 April 1936 (*Gesamtwerk*, 457, 454). And on 17 February 1935: "I am again reading Kafka and Proust" (*Briefe*, 270). We can assume a rather broad familiarity with twentieth-century literature for almost all of this group. Even an author like Borchert, who grew up under considerably less favorable circumstances than Hartlaub, had encountered Expressionism before 1945, especially the work of Benn. There can be no talk of a spiritual quarantine by the Nazi regime, at least not for the 1930s. "Even during the war the repression was not entirely successful" (Korn, 250). Important philosophical texts of Existentialism were published and discussed at length in periodicals and newspapers. A quarantine from foreign modernism, such as was retrospectively claimed after 1945 for the whole Hitler era, never in fact existed. Our ideas of an imposed conformity (*Gleichschaltung*) are formed by book-burning and taboo lists; in reality, however, these "black lists" were only valid for public libraries. Within the Third Reich itself, the presence of foreign literature on the German book market was frequently noted. The exclusion of Jewish authors was not always consistently carried out. Thus seven books of André Maurois could be published, the last as late as 1938.

The flood of English detective and society novels, which were published, stopped only with the war. Joyce's *Ulysses* was rejected as a "literary sensation of the spiritually leaderless west European postwar period" and as a 'diseased self-dissection." However, a few periodicals such as the *Neue Rundschau* continued to celebrate the "epochal significance of the poet and artist Joyce" (1941, 120f.) and defended him against Catholic attacks. ("To let the ... aesthetic characteristics of an artwork vanish beneath and behind inartistic criteria is barbaric and widely spread" *Hochland* 1937/38, 329.) One may surmise that the Third Reich's cult of Ireland made it possible for the readers of *Literatur* and the *Deutsche Allgemeine Zeitung* to be objectively informed even as late as 1939 about the English first edition of *Finnegans Wake*.

American best-sellers such as Margaret Mitchell's *Gone with the Wind* (1937; 1941; ca. 300,000) aimed at large editions in the Hitler state. In addition, novels by Pearl S. Buck, John Erskine, George Santayana (*The Last Puritan*, 1937), and Sinclair Lewis were translated into German. After 1933–34, only a few books of Lewis appeared; a new edition of *Babbitt* (1942) was ordered by the Ministry of Propaganda and was meant to show the reader the repellent face of an "ugly America." The younger generation in Germany was fascinated above all by Thomas Wolfe and William Faulkner. Rowohlt translated Wolfe's *Look Homeward Angel* (1936), *Of Time and the River* (1936), *From Death unto Morning* (1937); and Faulkner's *Light in August* (1935), *Turning Points* (1936), and *Absalom, Absalom!* (1938). The image of both of these writers could be filled out with a few short stories and essays, which were also translated for periodicals and anthologies. In 1937, Kurt Ullrich (of the Fischer publishing house) published a volume titled *New America* (Neu Amerika), containing stories by Sherwood Anderson, William Faulkner, F. Scott Fitzgerald, Katherine Anne Porter, William Saroyan, and Thomas Wolfe. In his introduction, Ullrich especially stressed the antimaterialistic position of these authors and pointed to their modern narrative techniques. He believed that this generation had stylistically rebelled against the "absolute tyranny of minute but fantasy-less realism…. They received their decisive impetus from the works of Joyce and Proust" and from "everyday language" (Ullrich, 12). Translations of Thornton Wilder (*Heaven is my Destination*, 1935; *The Bridge of San Luis Rey*, 1940) were also admired by the younger generation, as were works by William Saroyan ("The One and the Other," 1938). None of Eugene O'Neill's plays were performed on German stages after 1933, but discussions of his work were not completely cut off. Otto Koischwitz published an introduction in 1938, and Curt Hohoff compared his work with Expressionist drama: "What became a type and an abstraction with the Germans was drawn here from unique living human character" (Hohoff, 46). Ernest Hemingway's anti-Nazi position inhibited further editions of the four books he published with Rowohlt between 1928 and 1932. But original editions were occasionally advertised, such as *Green Hills of Africa* or *For Whom the Bell Tolls*. Albatross Editions, which was founded in Hamburg in 1932, was very important for the dissemination of English-language literature. Albatross published Hemingway's *The Sun Also Rises* and *Men Without Women* in 1937. Unlike Tauchnitz, this house specialized in modern literature. It began its series with Joyce's *Dubliners* and kept going until the summer of 1939 with several hundred titles. The last volumes published were Graham Greene's *Brighton Rock* and stories of William Saroyan. Steinbeck's novel *Of Mice and Men* had a second edition in 1940, and there were reprint editions of other of his works until 1941. Even though Steinbeck's novel *The Grapes of Wrath* could still appear in German in 1943—after appearing in the *Deutsche Allgemeine Zeitung* (10 January–12 May 1943)—Anselm Schlösser described the situation in the 1940s accurately in the magazine *European Literature* (May 1944, 15) when he noted that "the American novel, which was once so modern and so much in demand, has, with a few exceptions, disappeared from the German book market as a result of the war." The *Annual Report 1940* of the Writers' Bureau (Amt für Schrifttumspflege) explicitly stated that the diminution in numbers of translations from English and French had no ideological grounds, but was "purely an effect of the war" (Jahresbericht 1940).

As late as 1937, Will Vesper complained (exaggeratedly) of a "flooding of the German book market with literature from non-German Jewish publishing houses" (*Neue Literatur* 1937, 103). Since the *Börsenblatt* could not reject advertisements on the basis of business contracts, *Neue Literatur* published lists of these businesses, for even party periodicals discussed Jews in "amicable ignorance" (1938, 45, 154). Although racially discriminated publishers in the Third Reich were requested "to publish for an exclusively Jewish readership," some titles from Schocken did reach the German book market. Four of the planned six volumes of Franz Kafka's *Collected Works* (Gesammelte Schriften) could appear officially in 1935; even after the interdict (*Verbot*) the two remaining volumes were nonetheless published. "Pro forma, Heinrich Mercy of Prag—meaning Schocken's printer—signed as publisher." Initially, the press reviews called attention not only to Kafka, but also to Hermann Broch, Elias Canetti, and Robert Musil. But such reviews were rare. This sort of literature was, unlike American literature, rejected as too intellectual. Typical of this is Wolfgang Weyrauch's review of Musil's *Posthumous Works While Living* (Nachlass zu Lebzeiten) in the *Berliner Tageblatt*: "For him, the forest is not a forest at all, but a pretty inventory of technology and trade. For Musil, wood gods are the lumber dealers and sawmills. The god of the woods however is a drunken god, and whoever does not believe this will, we hope, see his screaming procession before his own eyes and ears" (9 February 1936). Here are the foundations of the resentment with which many writers such as Ernst Kreuder would react, after 1945, to the literature of emigration. It was not only the administrative measures of the Hitler regime, but also a deep-seated enmity toward the Enlightenment, which let only a few of the émigrés' books into Germany. Thus, Wilhelm Hausenstein could comment on the controversy between Thomas Mann and Frank Thiess over *inner emigration*: "We who stayed at home did all we could during those awful years to obtain German books written abroad" (Grosser, 63). This statement was only true for a few works of Thomas Mann, which had apparently found their way into the Reich. Hausenstein refuted himself when he testified in his essay on Stefan Andres's *We Are Utopia* (Wir sind Utopia) that "I dare to doubt that anything has been written in the emigration that approaches the level of this story" (Grosser, 69). Apparently he had not read the work of Anna Seghers, Bertolt Brecht, Robert Musil, Joseph Roth, and others. Hans Erich Nossack's lapidary statement that "émigré literature was unknown to us" (Nossack, *Glossen*, 51) comes much closer to the truth.

The debate about Expressionism was, at least in the first years of the regime, still open. The attempts of Gottfried Benn, and of parts of the National Socialist Student Organization grouped around Otto Andreas Schreiber, to reconcile Futurism with the "new power" were only definitively and demonstratively defeated by traditional artistic currents with the exhibition *Degenerate Art* (Entartete Kunst) in 1937 and with Benn's banning from publication (18 March 1938). The younger generation was widely involved in this debate and tried, with the concept of "German Expressionism," to preserve a few elements of modernism as a racially typical movement (*arteigene Bewegung*). So Rudolf Ibel stated in 1936 in *Literatur*: "These [Expressionistic] phenomena are all ... dismissed as un-German, Jewish-intellectualist claptrap, in an indefensibly superficial manner. Whoever reads the poetry of that age in a thoughtful manner is astonished at the wealth of impulses of poetic art, all in a high and German sense" (Ibel, 405). Theodor Sapper expressed himself similarly; for him, it was finally time "to save the memory of the poets Trakl, Heym, Lichtenstein, Stramm, and Stadler from oblivion" and to set "Expressionism as German poetry" against "materialist objectivity" and "superficial reportage" (*Berliner Tageblatt*, 14 September 1933). It was above all the early Expressionists who were successfully defended against the many "word-distorters and dithyramb-stammerers" and the "mob of unleashed brains." Emil Barth's essay on Trakl (1937), which became so famous, was only one of a dozen commemorative articles that appeared in that year on the occasion of Trakl's fiftieth birthday and which set his poetry in the canon of classical European modernity. At this time it became habitual, as it would be during the postwar period, to group Trakl, Heym, and Stadler as poets of a muted form of Expressionism; the dissemination of their poetry was uninterrupted. While Trakl's work was distributed by Otto Müller Verlag in Salzburg, the series *The Poem: Pages for Poetry* (Das Gedicht. Blätter für die Dichtung) was put out by the Ellerman publishing house, which during the war published slender volumes of Stadler (November 1939) and Heym (April 1942). Reprints of poems in the literary sections of larger regional newspapers during the last years of the Third Reich kept alive the memory of early Expressionism.

For Expressionist painters and sculptors there were still a few protected spaces left, although they became smaller and smaller every year. While modern images had to be removed from countless museums, the Kunsthalle in Düsseldorf set up as late as 1935 a "Galerie der Neuzeit" with works of Barlach, Heckel, Hofer, Kokoschka, Macke, Marc, Nolde, Schmidt-Rottluff, and others. Most of this art was forced off into private galleries, but it is still astonishing that, in the *Berliner Tageblatt* alone, forty-three positive reviews of individual and group exhibits of "decadent artists" in Berlin were published up to the end of 1938. Despite sanctions and public appeals, modern art and sculpture were not totally cut off from the public even during the war.

When the exhibit *Degenerate Art* (*Entartete Kunst*) used a record player to reproduce Stravinsky's *Firebird* as an example of "cultural dissolution," this composer was still one of the most popular and frequently performed foreign musicians in the Third Reich. From the autumn of 1934 up to its cessation of publication on 31 January 1939, the *Berliner Tageblatt* devoted thirteen reviews to Stravinsky ballets and concerts. The record industry took over a significant function in the dissemination of modern music. However, Nazi critics did not tire of attacking Stravinsky as a "cultural Bolshevist" and denouncing his work as "soullessly formed constructivism" and as the "racially alien music of a comedian in noise who is backed by Jewish circles" (Wulf, 287). While Goebbels, in his debate with Furtwängler, succeeded in preventing the performance of Hindemith's work, other composers such as Orff, Egk, Blacher, Fortner, and von Einem were able to propagate their work unhindered, even during the war. It was probably tied up with the Nazis' need for cultural representatives that music was not only just tolerated, but also sponsored by the state. Even in the 1940s fragmentary testimonies and reports on modern literature reached the German Reich from overseas. Decisive for this press policy was, however, not any changed consciousness, but rather the propagandistic effort to portray the German Reich as a Western protective power against the "hostile will to destroy"—even when art from Rome and Paris stood in contradiction to the reactionary opinions of the Hitler state.

The literature of the younger generation participated in this disunity of development. The larger picture was so diffuse that even in 1936 Erich Pfeiffer-Belli could earnestly believe that there were people in key state positions "who cared about a free and progressive German art" (*Berliner Tageblatt*, 17 March 1936). But with Hitler's two programmatic speeches in Munich and Nuremberg in 1937, in which he announced his "inalterable decision" to "put an end now to the hollow phrases in the cultural domain just as to the confusion in politics," the possibilities of diffusing modernism became even further reduced (*Berliner Tageblatt*, 20 July and 9 September 1937). In 1938–39 literary periodicals and publishers were put under stricter control; a second wave of emigrations began after Kristallnacht. The outbreak of war meant a further strangulation of cultural life. Although many authors were spared for years from any immediate duty on the front, service in the barracks reduced the freedom necessary for writing. Those who had stayed home felt themselves subjected to an incessantly increasing pressure: "Everyone began to be afraid of everyone else. Even in the Fischer house ... people began to be suspicious of this or that colleague," as Karl Korn recalled (295). The publishers and editorial boards scrupulously avoided offending anyone in an official position, and repeatedly requested that authors revise their work. Heinrich Schirmbeck noted, with regard to the story of the origin of his novella *Scale Chain and Horsehair Bush* (Schuppenkette und Rosshaarbusch): "Peter Suhrkamp told me that my story had been rejected by the Propaganda Ministry, since a love affair between a German cavalry officer and a Belgian woman was unacceptable to the *völkisch* concepts of honor of the time. I had to rewrite the story, set it back in the time of the French Revolution, and change the German officer into a Frenchman, and then it was all right."

The censor's definitions became ever more narrow. In a secret communiqué of the Writers' Bureau from 1940–41, an appeal was made for increased vigilance with regard to the authors of our group. The report accuses them of, among other things, "showing more relations with literature before 1933 than with the popular (*volkhaft*) poetry of our time," and stresses "that a literary clique is here arising which already makes claims to be dominant and has increasing interest among readers." Along with individual writers such as Horst Lange and Stefan Andres, the article mentions Wolfgang Weyrauch's anthology *1940—Young German Prose* (1940 – Junge deutsche Prosa) as well as the collections of the *New Line* (Neue Linie) edited by Bruno E. Werner. It was especially criticized that the works of these "authors between the realms" (*Zwischenreichautoren*) had unfortunately also found "praise and recognition ... in National Socialist newspapers" (*Jahresbericht 1940*). Books that had been previously discussed with approval were now more frequently attacked in accordance with this official recommendation, such as, for instance, Lange's novel *Black Willow* (Schwarze Weide), which had been praised as an "event" when it appeared in 1937. The periodical *Die Weltliteratur* now faulted the work's deep pessimism and called the novel, doubtlessly the most significant one produced by the writers who did not emigrate, a "distorted image of Silesia," although this attack did not cause the author any disadvantages (1941, 80).

Air war destroyed a great many publishing enterprises and book stocks. The bombing of Leipzig in 1943 led especially to an interruption of production from which German publishers would not recover until the war's end. As Horst Lange noted then, "books will become as much of a rarity for us as cigarettes or alcohol." The editions of books published during the war remained still relatively large, at around 5,000 copies, of which however only a part reached the open book market. Publishers were asked to "divert stocks for the bomb-damaged, for the front and for hospitals." On the other side, the Ministry of Propaganda made the allotment of paper increasingly difficult as the war went on. A letter of Peter Suhrkamp's from 22 November 1943 reads: "The paper allotment for books has again been substantially reduced. Thus we have been requested to answer only requests for matters important to the war effort. After this I certainly expect a further reducing of production. This is also indicated by the fact that I just learned of in the Ministry, namely that in the course of this December, a series of large printers and binderies will be closed or used for other forms of production." Because of this, the printing of certain works was delayed or blocked. Despite repeated requests, Suhrkamp could obtain no paper for Nossack's poetry. But these measures should not be equated with political sanctions, as was later done in hindsight. They were rather a matter of a real paper shortage and corresponded to the regime's desire to be sure at least of the publication of the literature it saw as important. For a long time it was overlooked that the stopping of the *Frankfurter Zeitung* and the *Neue Rundschau* in 1943–44 coincided with a general wartime concentration of the press that also affected Nazi organs of publication.

Our knowledge of the unity of the epoch is substantially less than that of the sense of life of non-Nazi authors, or of their conditions of work and publication. Before any larger interpretations are attempted, it is more urgent to set up the literary-historical preconditions for such a view. Bernard Diebold wrote in a preface to Frank Matzke's *Youth Confesses: This Is How We Are* (Jugend bekennt: so sind wir, 1930): "The large forms stand ready to be filled with new life. Form is waiting for life." For Diebold, classicism was the "opposite style to that of every latest form of Romanticism, which in our time was called Expressionism" (Matzke, 3). Elisabeth Langgässer wrote in similar terms in the *Berliner Tageblatt* in 1934: "Once again, as in earlier times, the Germans were faced with the demand for antique form, measure, moderation and clarity, fullness and ripeness on a volcanic spiritual foundation" (21 October 1934). Young writers, painters, and composers sought a synthesis. The "adherence to Expressionism" (Benn) that was repeatedly set forth in the 1930s was not meant to signify any renewal of radical attempts at liberation, but rather the recasting of what had once been revolutionary into a formal fulfillment in order to "open up deeper levels of reality." The notion of form gained a metaphysical and utopian significance; it represented an articulated world, which was opposed to that of everyday aims, "floating in a blessed realm (*Reich*) of the middle between the everyday and complete distantiation" (Matzke, 132). Consequentially, those epochs against which Expressionism, Futurism, and Dadaism had rebelled were rediscovered. As Frank Matzke stated, "older cultures are like a lost homeland (*Heimat*) to us, where we can withdraw for a few hours in order to feel safe and have peace in our hearts" (136–37). This sort of looking backward is comprehensible only in the context of the political and economic upheavals of the world financial crisis of 1929–32. The young generation also felt itself to be depressively caught up in chaos. The articulation of older forms represented for them an order that was opposed to the current "dissolution" of their environment. If, in what follows, a presentation according to genre and stylistics has been chosen, this procedure is justified by the longing of younger people for some sort of binding obligation that would not be found in class struggle, racial theory, or, the Christian doctrine of salvation. These writers were desperately attempting to reconcile individual nonconformity with a fundamental preservation of the existing order. Since these younger writers accepted the political as unchangeable and thus could not, in their withdrawal, recognize the actual causes of their depression, they could also permit themselves, in conditions of increasing repression, a limited freedom.

The younger writers rejected the false objectivity of realistic narration; their preference for the subjectively expressive forms of modernism corresponded to their oscillating instability. They struggled—often in vain—against slick stylization, since lived reality increasingly receded with prolonged isolation from the outer world. Narrative prose may not, in its classicism, be separated from the larger works of the Nazis and the exile and religious writers. Nonetheless there are some distinctions of degree. With the exception of Gustav René Hocke and Horst Lange, authors rejected larger narrative forms and preferred short novels, novellas, or diary-like sketches; for this last genre, Ernst Jünger's collection *The Adventurous Heart* (Das abenteuerliche Herz, 1929; second version 1939) became the model. The division into short parts and the reduction to object descriptions even affected the genre of the novel. Friedo Lampe's *At the Edge of the Night* (Am Rande der Nacht, 1934) is subdivided into miniature-like chapters that flit past like the images of a magic lantern. "All light and gliding, only very loosely linked up, painterly, lyrical, strongly atmospheric" (Lampe, *Gesamtwerk*, 326). Koeppen, too, in his two novels *An Unhappy Love* (Eine unglückliche Liebe, 1934) and *The Wall Is Swaying* (Die Mauer schwankt, 1935), worked with small narrative units separated from each other by sharp cuts reminiscent of film technique. The tendency toward short form has various causes. First, they lie in the attempt to preserve through small subdivisions a maximum of the vanishing proximity to life.

A further aspect is an emphatically exemplary form of representation and finally the absence of any political or historical consciousness. This last cause is especially important for the lack of inclination to larger narrative form; social context was relegated to a small role purely in terms of material. The distaste for history was so strong that this literature, in distinction to confessional writing, even disapproved of popular biography. Thus myths of antiquity, which had for a long time been banned from German novels, were the subject of renewed interest. Attempts were made both to contrast classical humanity to the primitive vitalism of the Nazis, and also to retell traditional sagas, parallel to Jean Cocteau, Jean Giraudoux, and Jean-Paul Sartre. Marie Luise Kaschnitz's novel *Elissa* (1937) varied the Dido myth, and Hermann Stahl retold *The Return of Odysseus* (Heimkehr des Odysseus, 1940), while Emil Barth called up again the Sappho story *The Laurel Shores* (Die Lorbeerufer, 1943). Marieluise Fleisser narrated *Penelope's Awakening* (Das Erwachen der Penelope, 1936), while *The Caledonian Boar Hunt* (Die kalidonische Eberjagd) and *The Rape of Europa* (Der Raub der Europa) were told again by Friedo Lampe. After the war Ernst Kreuder in *The Sixth Chant* (Der sechste Gesang, 1956) and Walter Jens in *Odysseus' Testament* (Das Testament des Odysseus, 1957), along with other authors, continued this tradition.

The return to antiquity and mythological models, which had begun chiefly under the dictatorship, is doubtlessly tied to the desire to distance oneself from the period and from its terrors, and to a nostalgic longing for another world. Emil Barth expressed this most clearly in a diary note: "wrote a dozen pages on my reading of the *Odyssey*, which I reached for as if it were a book of fairy tales, in order to escape the devouring misery for at least a few hours" (Barth, *Lemuria*, 181). Antique myths were often made concrete through nature: the garden appears, in contradistinction to society, as an "intact world" where time stands still and where one can catch one's breath. In such a static order, the experience of plants and stones received precedence over treatment of humans and ideas. The "regression into remote domains" that Walter Benjamin observed from Paris in 1938 indeed characterizes large parts of exile novel writing as well. But while the tradition of the Enlightenment remained alive among the emigrants, so that their historical or mythical material usually served to illustrate contemporary political events, helplessness and despair were dominant among the inner emigrants. It is illuminating that these younger writers reversed the trend toward didacticism. The secularized soul-strengthening of the older non-emigrants (Bergengruen, Schneider, Wiechert, and others) apparently squared only with difficulty with the sense that all historical events were veiled in an impenetrable darkness. Thus, after the war, Günter Eich expressly criticized in Hermann Kasack's novel *The Town beyond the River* (Die Stadt hinter dem Strom) the "explicatory, even pedagogical element" (Tgahrt, 28). The fundamental metaphysical attitude demanded an antinaturalist and multilayered narrative technique. Despite their distance from didacticism, many followed a general tendency to renew dualistic forms of representation, but preferred allegory to parable—as did also some of the more conservative exile writers (Thomas Mann, Hermann Broch). This naturally does not mean that no social meaning was imported into metaphysical concepts. As with all opponents of the regime, the younger existentialists were concerned with a humane image of man, one that had been shaken by terror, and they maintained this concern even when they were conscious that they had no future ahead of them.

In the two longer novels by writers from our group, Gustav René Hocke's *The Dancing God* (Der tanzende Gott, 1943; published 1948) and Horst Lange's *Black Willow* (1937), the typological narrative form is given an especially memorable form. Hocke set his story of the seductive arts of the doctor Telys in Sybaris, a Greek colony that flourished on the Gulf of Tarento in pre-Christian times. The plague of tarantulas (which breaks out like an epidemic through autosuggestion), the exiling of dissidents, and finally the total destruction of the city through the loss of "beautiful moderation" all point to both contemporary and transcendental events. Lange's *Black Willow* is also allegorically conceived. The author had in mind the marshy landscape near Liegnitz, which lies around a river called the Willow, along with the willow of life, which he refers to with a quote from Heraclitus of Ephesus: "All that creeps is driven by the scourge of the willow" (Lange, *Weide*, 540). As in Droste-Hülshoff's swamp metaphors, Lange also always intends an ontological dimension. The "brood of the dark depths," the "mute, cold-blooded creature" (385) is a mirror of mankind cut off from salvation. But historical time is also integrated. The innkeeper and sectarian Smorczak, who plunges the peasants of the village of Kaltwasser alternately into despair and ecstasy while hypocritically concealing his own murderous deed, is fitted out with traits similar to those of Telys in Hocke's *The Dancing God* or Ramsin in Joseph Roth's *Tarabas* (1934). Lange himself called Smorczak a "throat-slasher" and "strangler," a "fattened spider" and "hell-driver, who lashed out with his whip on the backs of all who got involved with him" (267). Readers could recognize in the innkeeper's "jolly cunning" and "amphibian cold-bloodedness" a secret portrait of Hitler, but did not have to do so to understand the novel. Lange, like Broch, Canetti, and many other exile authors, saw the most pure destructiveness in the "arrogant claim of the masses to determine rank and measure" (Barth, *Works* [Werke], 485) and in the "un-spiritual proletarian element" (Winkler, 77). Smorczak's misdeeds thus stood in relation to the "huge, distorted body" of the masses (Lange, *Weide*, 442), whose power was distinguished by unaesthetic attributes. "The stench of sweat, human bodily odors, trampled horse dung, bloodthirstiness and hoarse throats would not go away" (438).

Marie Luise Kaschnitz's novel *Beginning Love* (Liebe beginnt, 1933) is not yet allegorically conceived. The problem of the masses is here treated only as a private phenomenon, not as historical and political or metaphysical one. But by the time she completed *Elissa* (1937) this author had also achieved complete mastery of the multilayered and simile-ridden style. The novel does not have, as its main theme, the education of Elissa to pity; instead, the process of purification takes place in secondary motifs that are covered over with descriptions of nature and love, along with mythological narratives. In contradistinction to Reinhold Schneider, who made a clear parallel between the extermination of the Indios and the persecution of the Jews in his *Las Casas for Karl V* (1938), Kaschnitz worked in a more esoteric fashion. Readers, who would have been accustomed by the dictatorship to constant attentiveness, are immediately confronted with the figure of a businessman who has been driven out of his house. This old man, who is driven ahead by the blows of the raging mob, finally acquires the suffering features of Ahasver: "His clothes hung raggedly upon him, his beard was disheveled and covered with blood, and a long bleeding wound ran down above his forehead" (*Elissa,* 151f.). Of Elissa it is said that she felt the sight of this persecuted man as a "painful indictment," and yet her attempt to help is thwarted by the masses who intervene between her and the Ahasver figure. The reference to the persecution of the Jews was apparently so cleverly disguised that Walter Bauer could write in *Die Literatur:* "Here there is no time, there are none of our present concerns, not a hint of the present day" (*Literatur* 1937/38, 241).

The novel *The Laurel Shores* (Lorbeerufer, 1943) by Emil Barth begins in near programmatic fashion: "It was no longer possible to ascertain the time when this story happened" (7). In Barth's work, too, the horror of the present is included in a mythic action. In the sulfur pits of the uncle, Diana finds children, "many of whom were not older than seven, small, naked, tortured-looking boys, who climbed up in panting rows out of the maw of the mine" (59). Barth was probably thinking of concentration camp inmates, whom he repeatedly observed in Düsseldorf while they were removing rubble; he writes of them also in his diary, which was first published in 1947. Wolfgang Koeppen made use of a similar topographical estrangement device in his novel *The Wall Is Swaying* (Die Mauer schwankt, 1935). "I was appalled at what was happening in Germany," he said in a 1968 interview with Horst Krüger, "and I tried to represent this horror in a veiled fashion, by letting the opening of the book take place in a Balkan country where oppression and persecution occurred" (Koch, 61). In the first sections of the book, Koeppen described the extreme brutality with which the police attacked revolutionary forces who sought to "free the people from the yoke of oppression" (99). The mistreatment of prisoners, which the architect Süde sees at first hand, was depicted by Koeppen with merciless harshness. Unlike Weisenborn, however, he made the deciphering of the acts of terror he depicted much harder. Any unambiguously humane message is obscured by the depiction of enthusiasm for World War I and by "irrationally stimulating words" such as "the voice of fate" (180f.), "the great breakthrough" (271), or "resurrection from the foundations of the *Volk*" (334). In this novel, an architect, senselessly fulfilling his duty, rebuilds a city according to its old plans, but on a ground that is undermined. It was seen by critics as a "struggle ... against weakness, disorder and dissolution," as an "education to duty," and as a "determined farewell to individualism." The title, *The Wall Is Swaying* (Die Mauer schwankt), points to the state of mind of its author and of many of his contemporaries, who felt they were standing on unsolid ground amidst a historical crisis. The "tottering" and "uncertainty" is the actual level of meaning to which the allegorical narratives of non-Nazi writers finally point, and which Koeppen programmatically formulates in his book as follows: "Did one know anything? One knew nothing. Every step was a step into the darkness. One could fall at any minute into the abyss, and even if one wanted to do good, one was even more in danger of doing injustice" (247).

The tendency to simile, the retouching of the empirical and factual, along with the "peculiar placelessness and disorientation" that Franz Schonauer has observed, were indeed heightened, but not initiated, by censorship (Schonauer, 151). It was an error to interpret non-Nazi narrative prose as a literature written under a veil. Ernst Jünger in *On the Marble Cliffs* (Marmorklippen, 1939) was not concerned with a mirror-like coming to terms with the Third Reich, but rather with an allegory of a sense of life. The contemporary tendency of readers to see an allusion to political conditions in everything often went against this general allegorical intention. Even younger writers could not escape these readerly expectations. "I recall that *Marble Cliffs* seemed to me at the time like a huge *roman à clef* about the Third Reich," Ernst Schnabel reports. Heinrich Böll remembered similar reactions: "The appearance of this book was a sensation, it was taken to be the book of the resistance." But in their own works, these authors presented themselves as much less historically conscious and confronted their sense of happiness and security only with indefinable threats and confused discomfort. It appears self-evident that the rats in Friedo Lampe's novel *At the Edge of the Night* are not a representation of the advance of Nazi barbarism. Nor are they such a symbol in Horst Lange's *Black Willow*, where the narrator can hear "their barely perceptible scurrying … under the rotting floorboards" (244), or in Hans Erich Nossack, who wrote, in his report *The End* (Der Untergang, 1943, published 1948), about "shameless fat hordes of rats" and "huge greenly-glimmering flies" that "rolled around in clumps … on the plaster" (*The End*, 52). In a similar fashion, Jean-Paul Sartre (*Nausea*, 1938; *The Flies*, 1943) and later Albert Camus (*The Plague*, 1947) wanted to use images of crass ugliness to call individuals to their senses and to moral conversion. Thus the younger generation deployed fundamental concepts of Existentialism through signals such as "physical disgust" (Lange), "revolting" (Nossack), "terror of fatal force" (Kaschnitz), "breathtaking vulnerability" (Hocke). In Horst Lange's *Ulans' Patrol* (Ulanenpatrouille, 1940; 1941: 24–29,000 copies printed), the Imperial soldiers ride as if straight out of a painting by Alfred Kubin. They "hung skewed and discontented on their horses, without the least trace of capacity to decide, with dull-witted and empty faces, with swollen eyelids." Their tackle and equipment is eaten away by rust and mildew; the patrol, which stops at the Polish border for a maneuver, has the effect of a "cavalcade of ghosts and dead men" (49). When the censor, after an advance excerpt in the *Frankfurter Zeitung* (21 January–19 March 1940), found "defeatism, destruction and mockery of the Wehrmacht" in the novel, Lange could retreat in good conscience to his soldierly creed and dispel the censor's concerns with the help of Jürgen Eggebrecht (Schaefer, 286). Independently of authorial intent, there developed under the dictatorship an antithetical model for reception. Decisive for a book's effect were reader attitudes that could be projected into vagueness. When Alexander Mitscherlich, debating with Existentialism, polemicized in the *Kölnische Zeitung* in 1944 for an overcoming of *Angst* (4 March 1944), he thereby worked to stabilize both citizens' private courage and Nazi propaganda, which energetically attacked cowardice as a vice toward the end of the war. This dilemma becomes clearest in the case of the concept of duty, which was propagated from all sides at the time. With the exception of Nazis, authors tended scrupulously to avoid clearly formulating their moral categories. Max Planck, in a leading article for the *Deutsche Allgemeine Zeitung* of 1942, asked individuals to "hold on in a spirit of patience and courage." There could be no "legal claim to happiness, success and well-being in life"; the only property people could claim was that of "pure intent," which however would find its expression in "conscientious fulfillment of duty" (27 September 1942). Since even many non-Nazi soldiers were convinced that they had to defend Europe "out of pure intentions" against Bolshevism, they could thus feel themselves to be encouraged in their murderous and senseless struggle through this article, even though Planck probably wanted only to appeal to a Christian and humanitarian attitude in daily life. The same is true of the advice of Heinrich Albertz to follow the path of one's "inner trial" instead of that of "external success." As he wrote ambivalently in *Eckart* in 1941, "the pressure of national and *völkisch* responsibilities" had constantly increased, and no one could or should evade them: "indeed, only complete thoughtlessness or resignation would want to do so" (June/July 1941, 159).

Along with the literature of despair, there arose a broad variety of the idyllic that in turn affected all genres. A poll taken by *Westermanns Monatshefte* in June 1940 was titled *Return to the Idyllic?* (Rückkehr zum Idyll? 504). Poetry of childhood, which had been a favorite point of departure for garden and domestic idylls, and which had already been characteristic of the period around 1930, reached its quantitative heights under the dictatorship, along with a not unconnected qualitative decline. As an opposing movement to *völkisch* heroism, there arose a longing for sociable and intimate literary forms, for which older expressive models were sought. In the title of her fairy tale *The Old Garden* (Der alte Garten, 1940–41, published 1974), Marie Luise Kaschnitz pointed to the work's roots in the Romantic and Biedermeier periods. However, the stronger the efforts that were made to reconnect to tradition in smaller forms, the more any specific character was lost. Reaching back to Eichendorff and Mörike, Stifter and Kleist led only to an even further thinning out of any relation to reality.

Bucolicism in a void (Ernst Wiechert, Friedrich Bischoff), an idyllic rendering of the surrounding world, including the experience of war (Curt Hohoff, Günter Böhmer), and classicizing short stories (Werner Bergengruen) were signs of the general crisis in form and content that was already recognized and lamented during the Hitler state. In 1937, the *Neue Linie* criticized in its March issue the "escape into primitivism" out of "mistrust of the problematic," which it found typical of the submissions it had received. Instead, the magazine suggested, "classical simplicity" should be "the last stage of development" and should be won "at a great expense of effort, by going through the complex." Similarly, in a letter to the *Deutsche Allgemeine Zeitung*, one reader noted a loss of the "capacity for immediate experience" among younger authors, apparently connected "to the lack of objectivity, or of love for the material" (13 April 1937). Along with Kaschnitz's garden idyll, it was, among the writers of shorter narrative prose, works of Günter Eich, Hermann Lenz and Heinrich Schirmbeck, as well as Friedo Lampe's short novels that were able to escape the fate of unreality. Their quality consists above all in their offering not merely distracting genre imagery, but rather a longing for nature of which despair is the constant source.

In his *At the Edge of the Night* (1934), Friedo Lampe succeeded, using a detailed magical realism and filmic sequences of action, in blending modernism with a revivified Biedermeier tradition. While Tumler's prose (which was not written without "agonizing over purity") was officially praised and distinguished, the sensual novel *At the Edge of the Night* was taboo on account of its frank treatment of sexual motifs. In small segments, the author reviews events happening over the course of a few hours in a port city; the characters do not seem pale and ethereal, but rather brightly colored in, much as the objective picture book figures drawn by Walter Trier at the time. Lampe sketched delicate and sharply etched images such as the "bower surrounded by great leaves" where the geography teacher Hennecke reads aloud to his sons in the evening about foreign countries, the longing horn-calls of the steamer *Adelaide* heard from the port, and the countless interior scenes. These images are nonetheless darkened by sadistic tortures, child abuse, and sexual dreams. As in Marie Luise Kaschnitz's *The Old Garden*, which lures children over the wall into its "green endlessness," there can never be any sense of an enduring idyllic happiness. A similar sense of life is found in Helmut Käutner's melancholy films *Romance in Minor* (Romanze in Moll, 1943) and *Below the Bridges* (Unter den Brücken, 1944), with their flowing traveling shots, calm transitions, and muted tones of light dissolving in the rain. A happiness that appears briefly and is yet denied at the end, along with the human heart's revealing itself in synchrony with natural events, suited well the emotions of contemporaries living under the dictatorship. Erich Jansen explicitly subtitled his book *The Green Hour* (Die grüne Stunde, 1937) "Landscape and Plant Images." Objectivity preserved itself most effectively in such pessimistic genre forms. In the stories Wolfgang Koeppen wrote for the *Berliner Tageblatt* in 1935 and 1941, which were published in slightly revised form in 1972 in the collection *Romantic Café* (Romanisches Café), there dominates a turn to the world of things that is similar to that in Lampe and Lenz. Yet the quiet, solid, clear description of objects vanishes into an increasingly precious mode of representation that recalls Rococo sensibility ("Cakes were carried, the air tasted of marzipan and soft red aspic, little plates rattled with the cups, Mrs. Keetenheuwe prepared the coffee.... In front of the netted curtains, the pale majolica of the flower-tray, and the evergreen of the plants, the fire could be seen, light and disembodied" [*Kölnische Zeitung* 1, 1 January 1941]). The eleven prose pieces that Horst Lange published in newspapers and magazines from 1936 to 1944, and Alfred Andersch's "delicate and infinitely sensitive" story of adolescence, *First Journey Out* (Erste Ausfahrt, *Kölnische Zeitung* 113, 25 April 1944), are further documents of an evanescence of all things material that is typical of the war years. Many of the younger writers, in defiance of the technical and military coldness of everyday life, set a gentle and warm harmony of feeling above the world of facts. When Heinrich Schirmbeck chose the form of the novella for his *Fencing Brothers* (Fechtbrüder, 1944), he wished to contain the sentimental idyll within a severe constructivism. Despite the tidiness of his conclusion and his precisely calculated composition, he managed to escape the empty polish of neoclassicism.

During the Weimar Republic, a turn toward the reader had taken place, in view of the upheavals of the time. This remained in effect after 1930, resulting in a new valuation of practical forms (*Gebrauchsformen*). Authors interested in tendentious literature preferred other genres to these apolitical ones. In the 1930s, this spectrum became even more splintered. While traditions from Weimar such as satire, reportage, and the pamphlet lived on in the exile writers, Nazis and religious-confessional writers within the Reich took to speeches and war reports, to sermons and legends. The authors of our group preferred instead smaller forms such as feuilleton columns, essays, travel reporting, and diaries, which best answered their need for the private sphere, for objective description and aperçus. It is surprising to see to what extent the feuilleton article, the favorite form of the 1920s, lived on and continued to attract numerous writers from Bamm, Finck, Lampe, and Kusenberg to Penzoldt, von Radecki, Weyrauch, and Count Wickenburg. In 1939 and 1941, Wilmont Haacke published the collections *The Air Swing* (Die Luftschaukel) and *The Circle Game* (Das Ringelspiel). The titles alone point more to general cheerfulness than to images of the metropolis and a "mosaic of the time." Indeed, the feuilleton article had lost some of its delicate aggressiveness and proximity to the object; the empirical discoveries that were seductively present in the works of Siegfried Kracauer, Ernst Bloch, Walter Benjamin, and Joseph Roth now vanished in favor of harmless and partially humoristic observations. All this reminds one, under the dictatorship, rather of the brightly colored "balloons" evoked by a popular song of the day, which Friedrich Luft then used as a title for his collection (1939).

While Karl Valentin was taken as a model by feuilletonists of the younger generation, the essayists of our group owed decisive impetus to Ernst Jünger and Gottfried Benn. The dominant image of the "poeta doctus, essayist and poet in one person," which Walter Jens would evoke after World War II, had already begun to affect writers earlier on. Gustav René Hocke, in his 1938 collection *The French Spirit* (Der französische Geist), called the essay "the universal literary genre of the age" (25) and gave special mention to Valéry, Gide, T. S. Eliot, Heisenberg, Jaspers, and especially Ernst Jünger with his "will to unveiled objectivity." Hocke also stressed Jünger's great influence on the younger generation, especially on Eugen Gottlob Winkler, who had committed suicide in 1936 (26). This genre reached its apogee early on in Winkler's essays on George, Platen, and the late Hölderlin; even Walter Benjamin could not resist a certain grudging respect for this nihilistic and artistic prose. Relative to the formal mastery of Winkler, the works of others can only pale. Yet the form of the Existentialist postwar essay was already fully developed in the 1930s, with Dolf Sternberger's analyses of the nineteenth century, Hans Egon Holthusen's work on Rilke and Wilder, Hans Hennecke's essays on English literature, and the essays of Gustav René Hocke, Max Bense, and Albrecht Fabri.

At a time when travel gained an extraordinary popularity and was increasingly in demand, the literature connected to it also experienced a significant upturn. The summit of the genre was reached during World War II. War reports and travel diaries were blended. Walter Bauer's *Diary Pages from France* (Tagebuchblätter aus Frankreich, 1943: 55,000) was a notable success, as was Erhart Kästner's *Greece: A Book from the War* (Griechenland. Ein Buch aus dem Kriege, 1943); in 1940 Max Frisch published his Pages from the Bread Bag (*Blätter aus dem Brotsack*) as a Swiss soldier. Ernst Jünger's *Leaves and Stones* (Blätter und Steine, 1934) and *Gardens and Stones* (Gärten und Steine, 1942) make clear the tendency to make sensual experience transparent via reflection and aperçus. However, the diary itself had no unitary shape at this time. Notes oscillated between descriptions in the sense of Nazi propaganda (Martin Raschke, Kurt Lothar Tank) to esoteric self-reflection (Ernst Jünger, Heimito von Doderer) and the secret diary. Shortly after the war, Gerhard Nebel tried to explain the reasons for the high esteem in which the diary genre was held. In the preface to his *Northern Hesperides* (Nördliche Hesperiden, 1948), he defined the diary as the "literary form of the dungeon." Under dictatorship, people had only "two means of emancipation: prayer and diary." There was neither the time nor the strength for more than "disparate notes," and thus the diary was "the last weapon remaining to the individual defending his freedom." Nebel consequently interpreted the diary as a book of existential confession and pointed to the Pietistic tradition that was revived with the diary genre (5–6). Even outside of Germany, the diary experienced a new popularity between 1930 and 1950 (Cesare Pavese, Albert Camus, Klaus Mann). The aesthetics of the fragment and of confessional subjectivity inevitably had to lead European authors of the "new world-pain" back to this genre. The widely shared retreat into privacy explains why thus fashion for the diary reached broad and nonliterary groups in Germany. But almost none of the literarily valuable diaries of those years were destined for immediate publication. Above all, they served to help orient the author; beyond that, they could signify a "dialogue with God" (Jochen Klepper), or an attempt to leave a testimonial for the next generation (Friedrich Reck-Malleczewen, Emil Barth, Theodor Haecker et al.)

Felix Hartlaub's diaries distanced themselves from this sort of religious justification and brought the genre into the lofty domain of art. His notebooks, which were first published in 1950 with the title *Seen from Below* (Von unten gesehen), depart from the then prevalent idyllic tone with their closeness to objects and their satirically demasking perspective. The only comparable works, among those written within Germany, would be Nossack's unvarnished observations in *The End* (1943) and those of Gottfried Benn in his *Block II, Room 66* (Block II, Zimmer 66, 1943–44). Hartlaub was able to further cultivate elements of the New Objectivity's empiricism and make use of them to describe the Hitler period. As a student he had published sketches of areas in the north of Berlin that were rejected by the press for their "socially critical bitterness." After earning his doctorate in history, he was sent as a soldier to battalion units in northern and western Germany and also in Rumania. In 1941, he stayed in Paris as a member of the archival commission of the German foreign service, and from 1942 to 1945 he kept the official war diaries as a corporal in close proximity to the headquarters of the Führer. His secretly written notebooks avoid all mention of the "big events." Instead, Hartlaub offered sketches of nature and industry such as "Meadows" (Wiesen) and "Industry Protection" (Industrieschutz); genre scenes in *Children* (Kinder), *The Bar at the Canal* (Die Kneipe am Kanal), and *The Jan Family* (Familie Jan); and from 1941 on, images of the Parisian metropolis: *Place Pigalle, Quartier Latin, Changing World at the Bordello* (Weltwende im Freudenhaus), *Hotel Sully*. On the edge of the war, he devoted the same attentiveness to the "long fish, stiff as a board, on the tin can" as he did to the cashier in a café-bar or an artificially puffed-up flag of a swastika before a stormy sky. His sharpness of vision is astonishing in these details. Many aspects of his technique of observation recall the painting of New Objectivity, with which Hartlaub had long been acquainted through his father. Hartlaub's writing was primarily concerned with the surface of appearances, but he too, like all of his contemporaries, wanted to represent the mysterious. "The best thing for me is to tell simply what is visible to me every day," he wrote in 1941 from Paris to Gustav Radbruch. "Perhaps that is the best way to approach the invisible, which is after all the most important thing" (*Gesamtwerk*, 458). The position from which he described things was that of the cold observer surrounded by coldness outside. "The typical climate here is Arctic," it says in the same letter. "I see so many examples of progressive inhumanity, hair-raising egotism, cold-nosed indifference." The images from the Führer's headquarters, that "wind still dead center of the typhoon," are defined by a similar attitude, which holds all events at a distance. In the course of the last two years of the war, Hartlaub became ever more self-consciously a merciless portraitist of the officer corps, which was heading as if in a trance toward the abyss. His satires became more forceful. Hartlaub's talent for extracting the characteristic features of the period from banal details is especially successful in his sketch *In Hitler's Special Train* (Im Sonderzug des Führers, 1944). The artificial world of the train, which was outfitted with beautiful blue upholstery, gleaming uniforms, and "real coffee and marmalade," contrasts with the bombed-out cities and the "downcast processional" of suffering people outside on the platforms. The train's sudden disappearance into a tunnel is heightened by Hartlaub into an existential emblem: "And what sort of an endless tunnel is this, and what sort of green lamps are they swinging? How many train engines do we have ahead of us?... And this tunnel has strange acoustics; someone is playing *Deutschland, Deutschland* on a Wurlitzer organ, or at least something similar ..." (*Gesamtwerk*, 196). Hartlaub's secret diary increasingly transformed itself into fictional literature. Christian-Hartwig Wilke has shown, after looking through the manuscripts, that the author finally combined more than he actually represented real circumstances. Apparently he intended, at the latest in the summer of 1944, to make a novel out of it. Hartlaub had no illusions about the loss of reality risked with this change of genre. In his last letter of 8 March 1945, he demanded for his project: "Only the enrichment [of the novel] with real experience must be expanded in *scope*"(*Gesamtwerk*, 466).

Hans Erich Nossack's description of the destruction of Hamburg in *The End* (Der Untergang, 1943, published in 1948) is tangent to Hartlaub's attempt "to bring the completely immeasurable suffering ... to people's consciousness, to give it form and word" (*Gesamtwerk*, 458). Both of these prose works are connected to the genre of 'useful literature' (*Gebrauchsliteratur*), bound up with the diary and the war report, and yet they work against these generic models, expanding the form into a documentation of the underworld with the help of an unprecedented fidelity to the facts and a restricted emotional vocabulary. Nossack, too, who gave his notes the title "Report," felt himself to be on the "other side of the abyss" (*Untergang*, 12). In July 1943, from the idyllic viewpoint of the Lüneburger Heide, he observed the nightly bombing attacks on Hamburg. The spotlights, which momentarily formed themselves into "geometrical figures and tent-supports," the droning of the bomber squadrons slowly approaching the city, the umbrellas of light sinking downward, and finally the mushrooms of smoke, lit up by flak tracery, had all the effect of a morbidly beautiful spectacle. This "inferno in pastel tones" (W. Boehlich) appears as senseless as the ruined city districts through which the reporter wandered days later in search of his apartment. "The abyss was right nearby, in fact perhaps even directly beneath us, and we floated above it only through some sort of grace" (35). This sentence condenses Nossack's experience of reality in paradigmatic fashion. Objects lose their functional context, and the external world acquires the character of an illusion. A woman who cleans the windows of a house that has escaped destruction amidst a desert of ruins and the people who sit peacefully drinking coffee on their terrace in a suburb that was spared, both possess the same absurd emblematic quality that Hartlaub had sought in his *Special Train*.

No genre better answered the need for subjectivity than did poetry. As a consequence, poetry should have been held in high esteem at this time. But despite the broad spectrum of production, one can hardly speak of a flowering of poetry among the younger generation; the real achievements lay in the genres of diary and narrative prose. Eich, Lange, Nossack, Kaschnitz, and Lampe rarely attained, in their poetry, the level of their other work. The fundamentally positive attitude toward poetry in the Third Reich is evident in a statement by Karl Rauch, who blamed the "eccentric objectivity of previous years" for the devaluation of poetry. "Many signs point to the fact that we are, amidst the current new concern of German man for his origin and meaning, experiencing a renaissance of poetry and a renewed sensitivity to beauty" (Rauch, 38). Poetry could hardly have been renewed only by "renewed concern for German origins" and by an affirmation of beauty, since most poets were afraid of any spiritual openness and saw in the form less the attainment of expression than refuge and salvation from chaos. One could detect a similar development in contemporary poetry in France, England, and America. Hans Hennecke rightly saw circa 1938 a "conscious will to a new classicism" in European poetry (Hennecke, 722), but both in German-language exile poetry and in the *inner emigration*, this turn backward was particularly extreme. Even such poets of the older generation as Johannes R. Becher, Gottfried Benn, Wilhelm Lehmann, and Georg Britting could not always escape an omnipresent classicism and restorative Anacreontic poetry. Rudolf Alexander Schröder, Friedrich Georg Jünger, Bernt von Heiseler, and others expressly celebrated the classical tradition. Friedo Lampe may have articulated a certain opposition to current tendencies when he judged Friedrich Georg Jünger to be "very clear, bright and cheerful, but also extremely dematerialized, lacking in content, too formal" (Lampe, *Briefe*, 112). Yet in his own poems he could only slightly resist this all-powerful urge toward a backwards-looking order.

A good source for the development of poetry within the younger generation is the yearly contest that had been held by the magazine *Die Dame* since 1934, whose participants included Günter Eich, Peter Huchel, Marie Luise Kaschnitz, Rudolf Hagelstange, and Wolf von Niebelschütz, among others. In 1935, Marie Luise Kaschnitz received first prize for her poem *The Waves* (Die Wellen), which was called "perfect in itself as a form of emotion, thought, vision and language." The last strophe is as follows (*Die Dame*, January 1935, 2):

I was overrun by many waves,
Lamed by the shock, blinded by spears of light.
Then they ended the game, as always,

Bearing me gently back onto the sand.
And host upon host, bleeding away in the foam,
Moistened and cooled me with their floods.

The careful personification, the refined metaphors of blood and waves, and the chiseled rhymes cannot hide the fact that a historical and formed consciousness is at work here. The poem seeks to be simple and balanced, yet only arranges and stylizes elements that are already at hand. One should not forget the historical background to this sort of variation of randomly disposable linguistic clichés. While the Nazis preferred heroic and community-oriented forms, readers could always find in an apolitical neoclassicism an exclusive domain, "with nothing of any resistance ... nothing violent, nothing revolutionary, but only speech which was, so to speak, different within itself" (Heissenbüttel, 13). The various attempts to reach back in time that we have found in Kaschnitz's other work are representative of almost all lyrical attempts at orientation among her generation. One may find for example a Klopstockian elegy, Matthias Claudius's song-form, occasional imitations of Hölderlin's hymns, Rilke's sonnet form, and above all the forms of Stefan George, which Kaschnitz explicitly evoked in her poem *Carpet of Life* (Teppich des Lebens). Just as in George's own *carpet*, reality is here moved into the domain of art and then interpreted; yet precisely this poem betrays something else at work. Marie Luise Kaschnitz could not attain the profundity and aesthetic completion of her model, but instead varied her theme in nine strophes and sought to replace lost quality by quantity. The evident artistic deficits here are connected to the poetic interest itself, which had changed under the dictatorship. Non-Nazi poets wanted to keep language self-consciously pure and yet make it a form of secularized pastoral care of the soul, as we may see in Wolfdietrich Schnurre's poem *The Test* (Die Bewährung): "Not in the call of the glowing earth/nor in need and swamp alone/does the Lord speak the words: Let there be!" (*Eckart* 1943, 125). All poets rejected any mere cult of form for its own sake. Thus Kaschnitz's poem *Carpet of Life* does not end, as did George's, in the domain of the hermetic, but rather—like Schnurre's—offers a populist and cozy Biedermeier form of consolation (Kaschnitz, *Poems* [Gedichte], 104):

And yet I learn more clearly every day:
Mourning must weigh far less than joy,

The sun's rays stream more than the shadows darken,
And in the light a thousand tree-tops rock,
Where morning's gleam and sunshine brightly sparkle
Around that lonely tree the storm must break.

The shoot pushes to light with every drive
And deeper roots than hate's are found in love.

The thematic groups around which Kaschnitz organized her poems in 1947 are also representative of her generation: *Homeland* (Heimat), *Southern*

Landscape (Südliche Landschaft), *In the East* (Im Osten), *The Bountiful Years* (Die reichen Jahre), and *Dark Time* (Dunkle Zeit). In the last thematic group, one may detect a prominence of the sonnet; twenty-three out of forty-six texts are written in this strict form.

Poets as diverse as Andres, Becher, Bergengruen, Brecht, Brenner, Britting, Edschmid, Hagelstange, Haushofer, Hausmann, Holthusen, Kaiser, Kolmar, Krolow, Lange, von Niebelschütz, Nossack, Penzoldt, Peterich, Schneider, Thor, Weinheber, Wolfenstein, and Paul Zech all wrote sonnets. The fashion for sonnets among poets both in exile and in *inner emigration* has long been remarked on. It is instructive that this form reaches its culmination between 1940 and 1950. This evidently proves what Walter Mönch stated about the history of the form: namely, "that in times that follow on great crises, the sonnet begins to run rampant" (Mönch, 257). As Rudolf Hagelstange explained, regarding the origins of his *Venetian Credo* (Venezianisches Credo, 1944): "The theme was the overcoming of temporal chaos through reflection on supra- and extra-temporal forces of man, and the sonnet form offered itself like a stone block with which one could build. In this strict form, it seems to me, there was already an external manifestation of a rejection of formlessness, the will to a new law" (Bender, 38). The conscious distance from chaos would allow no sonnets of any sublime aesthetic attractiveness to be written. The formal consciousness was too programmatic to allow for any stylistic experiments, such as those Rilke had undertaken with the sonnet form. Even the countless poems that referred directly back to Rilke, like Holthusen's moving *Dirge* (Totenklage), were much simpler than Rilke's. Adherence to the sonnet was above all an ethical matter, and the "simple handicraft" of the form was easy to learn.

The ode was not quite so widely practiced as the Mediterranean sonnet, probably because the ode was seen as "Germanified" and thus had a special place in the formal canon of Nazi poetry. The ode is more conscious of its public than is the sonnet. In the eighteenth century, it was praised not only for its lofty heights, but also for its effect on people. Friedrich Georg Jünger tried to revive the ode tradition of Klopstock while keeping it free of *völkisch* impulses. His volume of poems, *Taurus* (1937), was widely regarded and served as a model for Johannes Bobrowski in his Russian odes, several of which were published with the help of Ina Seidel in 1944 in the magazine *Das Innere Reich*. The plans of Count Moltke, a brother of the resistance plotter, to print a volume in Riga in 1944 were however a failure. In contrast to F. G. Jünger, Bobrowski worked in a way that was more open to objects and to the real environment. War destruction and the Russian landscape around the Ilmensee were not timeless themes, but rather an immediate reality confronting the young soldier. The older texts that Eberhard Haufe has printed from Bobrowski's posthumous manuscripts show that the poet managed to succeed in overcoming the pallor of prior attempts in the odes published in *Das Innere Reich*. As he wrote in 1942 to Ina Seidel, "I wanted to make the odes more directly visual, since they had always seemed to me as if spoken through a wall" (Haufe, 56). He did not manage to attain the lively warmth of his postwar poetry, but these odes from 1944 represent a summit of achievement within the poetry of those who stayed in Germany. As it says programmatically in *The Call* (Anruf), "High above the lake, silent Novgorod./Yet well may I sense this, and the heart/Contracts within me,-though still a/Peace is prepared in destruction./But to name it!" (*Das innere Reich* 1944, 353). One must read this poem within the context of Nazi ode poetry in order fully to appreciate its value. While Bobrowski named destruction and asked the old Christian God for reconciliation, Tumler, on the other hand, called up—heroically—the new spirit of the *Volk*: "To thee I sing, new God/who opens his eyes in children/and in the mothers of the *Volk*" (Tumler, 25). Tumler's odes do not exactly belong "to the most chaste and uncorrupted works … that were to be found in contemporary poetry" (Krolow, *Gegenwartslyrik*, 178). Instead they mark, together with Gerd Gaiser's hymn *Rider in the Sky* (Reiter am Himmel, 1941) and the poetry of Franz Fühmann, a successful attempt to legitimize *völkisch* ideology with the help of German classicism.

Along with the classicism that can be found among all groups, there was an extremely broad renovation of Anacreontic poetry and its wish "to make language delicate and light" and refine it "into filigree" (Jünger, 272). One could then observe among many German poets a tendency to "take lightly a playing with language" (Hesse, 671) and a "certain coziness typical of the Biedermeier, which enclosed suffering and pleasure alike in an amicable rhyme" (von Heiseler, 488). This play was however never for its own sake, but was always the expression of a new culture of sociability that had developed under the totalitarian regime. On the one hand, there was a reevaluation of the poetry of drinking, which was mingled with erotic motives—for example, Georg Britting's *Wine's Praise* (Lob des Weines, 1944)—and on the other, titles such as *Little Pastoral* (Kleine Pastorale), *Song of the Seasons* (Jahreszeitenlied), and *Year's Circle* (Reigen des Jahres) point to a renewal of the bucolic tradition. The moralistic collections *The Shepherd* (Der Hirte, 1934), *Homeland Is Good* (Heimat ist gut, 1935), and *The Neighbor* (Der Nachbar, 1940), all by the Swabian minister Albrecht Goes, articulate a sentimental and Christian redefinition of Anacreontic poetry, wherein sentimental moments are mostly integrated into easy and graceful forms (Goes, 4):

Rain and the rain-wind
Sing me awake,
Black is the window-cross,
Quiet my chamber.
Blanket moves softly now,
Spouse breathing pure,
Maiden cries gently,
Falls back asleep.
Tower clock says midnight,

Life-day's at rest.
All is near homeland,
Homeland is best.

If Krolow offered his readers a *Repast under Trees* (Mahlzeit unter Bäumen), it was not meant in a moralizing sense as in Goes's poetry, but on the whole, it was still indebted to the same intimate style of Neo-Biedermeier, even if Krolow gave more weight to erotic moments (Krolow, *Poems* [Gedichte], 10):

And we cut the bread and cheese.
White wine runs upon our chins.
Thus within our flesh we could
Intuit the released spirit of the plum.

Hands wander over the basket.
Resolve of the mouth was vouchsafed.
Soft limbs made now brown
Flow within the moving leaves.

Archaisms in both Goes ("chamber," "spouse," "maiden") and Krolow ("upon our chins," "vouchsafed") try to import into these artificial images something gritty and down-to-earth, and yet only increase an impression of decorative art, of arts and crafts. Right after the war, Elisabeth Langgässer condemned these poems in the strongest terms. In her essay "Writers under the Hitler Dictatorship," she wrote: "It is clear that not everything was tasteless, inartistic, unpoetic; there was no smell of blood around this Anacreontic trifling with flowers on the edge of the mass graves that those flowers covered over—yet it was completely irresponsible, irrelevant, lacking any relation to the world and thus worthy only of repugnance" (Langgässer, 39).

Elisabeth Langgässer nonetheless spared the nature-magical poems of Loerke and Lehmann from this reproach; here her judgement is unfair and must be explained by a lack of knowledge of these texts. Just as in the case of narrative prose and functional prose forms, one may find within poetry a contrary impulse to that of the idyll and secularized soul-saving. Along with Bobrowski, it was the poetry of Hermann Lenz, Lange, Eich, Huchel, and Celan that faced the "terror of the age" (Lehmann, 58). With the exception of Lenz's *Poems* (Gedichte, 1936) and Lange's *Song Behind Fences* (Gesang hinter den Zäunen, 1939), the works of these poets were published diffusely or were only published after 1945. This poetry is characterized by the simultaneity of Anacreontic and Existentialist motifs. In Lenz's case, works such as *The Shepherdess* (Die Hirtin), *The Meadow* (Die Wiese), *The Flute* (Die Flöte) and *For a Gypsy Woman* (An eine Zigeunerin) testify to a graceful bucolic aspect; on the other hand, *The Leaf* (Das Blatt) formulates a programmatic retreat ("I would like to crawl into a rolled-up grape leaf/And listen to its brittle death"), which finally names outright the destruction set off by its withdrawal: "I hummed there and saw also that which was right:/As the spider weaved trembling and distracted,/ And how in the delicate filigree/Of the leaves' veins no blood could run" (Lenz, *Gedichte*, 1). Lange's *Song Behind the Fences* contains a few lullabies and cradle songs, but most of the works reach beyond the limits of the domestic and seasonal cycle. The poem *Dark Waters* (Dunkle Wasser) circles, like Langgässer's cycle *Leaf Man* (Laubmann), around the redemption of the "cold and exiled creature" (Lange, *Gesang*, 23). The harsh images, recalling the Baroque, are ambiguous; there are similes, which must be referred to nature and man's lostness. Eich wrote, with similarly consoling intent, *Early Evening Lullaby* (Schlaflied am frühen Abend), in order to let the abyss of the time open up in other verses. The poem *Path through the Dunes* (Weg durch die Dünen), previously viewed as a postwar work, had already been written in 1934 and published in 1935. Eich sent it in as a contest entry for the competition sponsored by *Die Dame*. The poem shows that the revaluation of natural signs into a negative signature was due not to the experience of war, but rather to an unspecific feeling of anxiety. Within the circles of the beach grass and the traces of birds in the sand, the poem's subject deciphers in fear a "fatal infinitude." It is striking that Huchel's poem *Late Time* (Späte Zeit) represents nothing other than this same crushing feeling of transience. The verses appeared under the title *In Wet Sand* (Im nassen Sand) in *Die Dame* (October 1941, 34):

Quietly the leaves lament on the ground.
The moss and the soil both freeze alone.
Above all the hunters there hunts
high in the wind a strange dog.

Everywhere in the wet sand
lies the powder-burn of the woods,
acorns like hand grenades.

Autumn fired off its shots,
softened shots above a grave.

Hark: the crowns of the dead rustle,
Fog draws on, and with it demons.

The verses are to be read as a poem of autumn, but also one of war and death. Here Huchel's hermetic technique, as we know it from the late poem *Theoprast's Garden* (Der Garten des Theophrast) is already fully worked out. There are not only associations with the gunfire of salutes over a soldier's grave, but also intimations of the causes of death. The lamenting leaves, the strange effect of the constellation of Sirius, and the demons moving along with the fog may be brought into connection with the rule of violence. But Huchel had no intention, any more than did Lange, Kaschnitz, Koeppen, and others, of directly criticizing Nazi dictatorship; the poem was, for him, above all a means to free himself from depression, bent meditatively over a cluster of natural signs. It is not by chance that the poem betrays the influence of Trakl's poetry of solitude.

The melancholy tone was, however, for those times, unusually concrete and multivalent. The poem had to have had a provocative effect, if it was indeed at all grasped in its many levels. Hermann Lenz based his poem *Russian Fall* (Russischer Herbst) directly on his own war experience; it was published by Georg van der Vring in his anthology *The Young Front* (Die junge Front, 1943). Here it is a question of mice that "defend themselves in vain from the snakes," as also of their wet blood and the red burned leaves. The wine of autumn will be "darker and cloudier … from sheer ash/And from the earth of death" (50). The poem recalls Paul Celan, who referred in similar fashion in his 1945 *Death Fugue* (Todesfuge) to metaphors of ashes and serpents. Lenz dedicated his poem *Dressed for Night* (Nächtlich geschürzt) to Celan in 1954. This is not by chance. The models of the Rumanian-German poet were almost identical with those of his generational contemporaries living in the Reich. In Celan's personal library, there was a volume of Rilke, an edition of Trakl and of Hölderlin, along with the *Little Flower Book* (Kleines Blumenbuch) of the Insel publishing house, in which Celan noted the names of the plants depicted in German, Rumanian, Russian, Hebrew, and Greek, among others. The poems Celan wrote in Czernowitz and, from the summer of 1942 onward, in a work camp near Buzäu, which were largely not published, are, like the poems of Bobrowski, Huchel, and Lenz, characterized by an association of nature and war. The poem *Notturno*, written in 1942–43, begins with a call to vigilance very typical of this poetry: "Don't sleep. Be on your guard./The poplars with singing step/march along with the warlike people./The ponds are all of your blood." Other poems that were written at the same time and quickly became known after 1952, such as *Aspen Tree* (Espenbaum), *The Sound of Iron Shoes* (Ein Knirschen von Eisernen Schuhn), and *Death Fugue* (Todesfuge), are also constructed on two levels. In *Aspen Tree* the things of nature and everyday life evoke, strophe after strophe, the fate of Celan's mother killed in the concentration camps: leaves recall her hair, dandelions the Ukraine, the rain cloud tears, the round star a fatal bullet, and so on. As with Huchel, the relatively simple structure, tied to the folksong, is characteristic; only in the postwar years was the aristocratic and hermetic character of Celan's work to be accented. But even in his early work, one should beware of exaggerating the references to contemporary political events. As with his poetic colleagues in Germany, Celan's view of the world was formed by a fundamental experience of fear, and war only radicalized this basic attitude. The menacing element was in fact virtually longed for. As the 1938 poem "Wish" already states: "The roots bend crooked./A mole must live below;/or maybe a dwarf…/or only the earth/and a silver streak of water…/ but blood would be better."

In 1930, Frank Matzke noted: "And typical for our time is not the engineer who has, at home, the images of the New Objectivity on his walls, but rather the engineer who leafs through folios of Rembrandt" (Matzke, 135). Elsewhere he added: "From all sides, nineteenth-century realism urges itself upon us once more" (229). If there is any stylistic aspect common to the works written by the younger generation in the 1930s and 1940s, it is to be found in the literature of the turn of the century and also in the classical and realistic tendencies of premodernist writing. It was already habitual around 1930 to talk about the end of the New Objectivity. Willy Haas coined then, in the *Literarische Welt*, the concept of "the restoration of art" to describe the general tendency of culture, and observed a digging in on the "last assured previous aesthetic position ... that is, circa 1914" (16 May 1930, 2). Fritz Schmalenbach had noted the same phenomenon in painting at the time. After viewing an art exhibition in Essen in 1936, he noted: "New Objectivity has been fairly well pushed to the side." In 1939, he wrote in an essay that extreme tendencies had petered out and been "neutralized and blended down." This newly arisen "middle-of-the-road painting" made an extremely unified and moderate impression; it was in principle "closely kin to Impressionism" (Schmalenbach, 54–55). With those words, Schmalenbach could also have described quite exactly the stylistic evolution of literature at the time. However, only rarely did the authors discussed here attain the nuanced and finely shaded writing style of their impressionistic models. The descriptions seem heavier, more artificial, as if produced through great effort inside a studio. Thus we read in Schirmbeck: "On the trellises, there glowed the yellow flesh of apples, pears and quince, and the leaves rustled like liquid silver. In the distance a dog barked. The sounds of the night came and ebbed like the wind, which went through the branches in odorous waves" (Schirmbeck, 26). As if writers mistrusted any nonsensual impressions, they often complemented their descriptions with commentary. In Lange's *Ulans' Patrol*, we read: "The visible has a particular insistence, as if it wanted never to be forgotten. Music tinkles along behind it for a long time, flowing like a thin riddle in the dark, drowning out here and there ... a soft laugh or a half-whispered male aside" (Lange, *Ulanenpatrouille*, 33). In another passage, the author describes in glowing tones a sultry image recalling less Renoir than Makart: "The mouths were moist, the eyes gleamed, their limbs were loose, pink womanly skin, spread thighs and heavy, full breasts, which molded themselves into the hands of her companion" (173).

A comparison between Lange and Schnitzler, Hofmannsthal, or Bang shows how important the nineteenth century had become again for the younger author. Schmalenbach, again, stressed in the painting of the 1930s and 1940s a certain departure from Impressionism, and observed expressly a "mixture" of Cézanne, Matisse, and Hans von Marées. Objects were often drowned in painterly virtuosity. If one relates this observation to literature, one might say that things are dissolved or drowned in a flood of mere speech. The struggle for nearness to life led frequently to a forced choice of words, to stylized comparisons and an unnatural syntax. But this impression of artifice and preciosity is hardly restricted to inner-German writing alone; it is rather a question of general traits that are typical of most work of exile writers as well. While the emigrants covered over their lack of relationship to their environment with rhetoric, the younger writers at home in

Germany cultivated instead an almost anxiously antirhetorical and nuanced style. They recognized the danger of mere exquisite trifles and sought characteristic adjectives, expressive verbs, and precise nouns. This often compulsive precision had little to do with New Objectivity any longer. One can only speak of objective sharpness in exceptional cases (Friedo Lampe, Felix Hartlaub). Alfred Döblin, who had as recently as 1929, in *Berlin Alexanderplatz*, still worked with the montage of various sorts of texts and with a heightened use of spoken idiom, had to be quickly banned from memory, in light of the muted stylistic principles favored by the younger authors. In his roughly 600-page village novel *Black Willow* (Schwarze Weide), Horst Lange used only some twenty-four vernacular expressions. The literary ideal consisted in a harmonious overall impression. Classicism influenced even those authors who wanted to testify to lived reality. The criteria according to which Walter Boehlich characterized Nossack's *The End* (Der Untergang) make clear a goal shared by all works of the younger generation. Nossack's language, according to Boehlich, was "controlled in the highest degree, and an unflinching calm" emanated from it (Nossack, *Untergang*, 81).

The authors of the younger generation were receptive to an interest in a visual style of description, yet bounds were set from the start to curb any Expressionistic cult of the image. There are, however, sections where the decorative and refined metaphors of the fin de siècle break in. Thus Lange, in his *Flares* (Leuchtkugeln), could observe "frozen blood in coral twigs on the blue skin" (113) and Schirmbeck spoke of a mouth that "looked out of the shimmering alabaster skin like a lotus flower, rocking itself in a dream over a pale silvery mirror" (34). Usually this sort of opulence of figure was muted, however. The ever popular metaphor took the place of sharply observed images or of collage, which was rejected as inorganic. When Koeppen sketched in a street scene in *The Wall Is Swaying* (Die Mauer schwankt), he remained very much in the tradition of New Objectivity with his series of persons and objects, such as "tourist buses, newspaper sellers and policemen, high hedges, carts of various goods, horses, wagonloads, bicycles and cars." Yet in a final popular image that rounded off the whole, he acknowledged the change in taste. The observer perceives, through his half-closed eyes, "only a scurrying of ants ... struggling and dying for a shovel full of earth" (Koeppen, 106). Krämer-Badoni proceeded just as simply when, in *Jacob's Year* (Jacobs Jahr), he compared the salesmen standing outside the shop windows to "startled birds of prey," and the traffic to a "maelstrom" (13). In his travelogue *The Lost Face* (Das verschwundene Gesicht*, 1939), Hocke described the Italian city of Bari using decorative images, yet the deployment of finery is tied up with a clear decline: "The giant hotels seemed like pleasure castles in an Arabian fairy tale world. A silver ray shot out of the beacon, spotlights threw their balls of light into the sky, a magic hand lay a sparkling string of pearls around the Petruzelli theater in a fraction of a second" (217). It may be said in general about the imagery of the 1930s and 1940s that metaphors were used sparingly, usually in agreement with experience in nature or lowered to the level of everyday speech usage. In poetry there was no longer any interest in short imagistic impulses drawn from different domains. The goal was always, despite the typological structure one finds in Huchel or Celan, a unitary level of comparison. Only later on in the 1950s can one find a renewed complication and autonomy of images.

The split worldview suggests that allegory should have experienced a renewed popularity. Yet hardly anyone made use of conceptual allegories such as those from the eighteenth century or the Biedermeier period. Most often, allegories were dissolved in a realistic image. Koeppen's builder von Süde may meet with Duty in person, but only "as an angel on a tombstone from the stone-mason's front garden at the new cemetery" (Koeppen, 367). Nossack's perspective would have seemed made for allegory, and yet one constantly senses an aversion to yielding completely to the allegorical tradition. Instead, Nossack preferred to objectify his allegories. As one may read in *The End*, "I saw an allegory ... before a burned out house. In the rubble in the front garden, there lay like a harp the charred frame of a piano. Through the blackened trash and the sprung wires, a rose grew and blossomed. Earlier, none would have hesitated to put an inscription under this image: Flowering and Transience" (70). Courtly mythology received new attention along with the renewal of Antique material, yet the rejection of the concept of ornamentation led to a moderate use of these means. Since mythology was in contradiction to naturalness and plausibility, many tried to give the gods a sensual and believable form. In Eich's story *Catherine* (Katharina), the children enter an overgrown castle park and discover a stone figure of the goddess Diana on the ground: "a salamander crept out from under Diana's arm, and on the huntress's naked breast, a bug with living antennae was taking a sunbath" (47). It is hardly by chance that the mythological figures in Wilhelm Lehmann's poetry increased during the Third Reich and then gradually diminished after the war. In his *Green God* (Grüner Gott, 1942), he tried to bring distant mythology into some relation to life through a "dose of objectivity" but rejected the cosmic mythologies of Mombert and Däubler as mere tinsel.

These various observations may, one hopes, be sufficient. The literary works discussed in the present study were characterized by a moderate style, one that sought balance. This style was especially well suited to continue its development after World War II, fused with a heightened reception of modern classics from overseas. Bobrowski, Huchel, Eich, Kaschnitz, Koeppen, Nossack, and others, seemingly freed from their withdrawal, adopted no new positions after 1945. The concepts of "zero hour" and "clearing" obviously meant metaphors of an existential conversion. It was only a mystification when Koeppen continued to maintain, in a 1974 speech honoring Hermann Kesten, that after 1945 "the handing down of techniques, that which had been tested, of materials, themes, styles—that is, a handshake from craftsman to craftsman" (*FAZ* 244, 21 October 1974, 21) had not been possible, since everything was lacking. After 1945, the younger generation simply forgot, or diminished the value of, the works written during the Third Reich along with the contradictory experience of that time. We can see that poems of Huchel or Hermann Lenz, Lampe's short novels, Lange's *Black Willow*, Winkler's essays, and the reports of Hartlaub and Nossack (which were only published after the war) are certainly comparable in quality to postwar literature. Scholarly literature has similarly isolated 1950s culture from the Hitler state by concerning itself exclusively with Nazi or religious-confessional writing during the Third Reich. In this way the connection with overseas and various internal German currents are blurred; it was this connection that allowed the younger writers to survive, despite their increasing isolation. After 1950, most of these authors began to make their careers in West Germany, along with the classics of modernism. In this process, which forced the confessional writers and the classicizing traditionalists off the market, the kinship between the desire for "formal fulfillment" that had emerged in 1930 and the reduction of thought to linguistic complexes, which was typical of the Adenauer era, was carefully concealed. When Walter Jens pleaded for an "abstract literature" in 1955, he repeated the values of the new turn taken around 1930, and yet did not acknowledge this point of departure. The ideals he praised were "intellectual precision … coldness and concision," which hardly propagated a return to the 1920s. His appeal ended in a synthesis of "mythical world" and "artistically pure craftsmanship" in an institutionalizing of classical modernity, which is what had been called for at the end of the Weimar Republic in countless manifestos (Jens, "Plädoyer," 514). The political catchword of 1957, "no experiments," can be applied to the literary movements of both the 1930s and the 1950s. Artists agreed to go on living in a "post revolutionary situation" (Holthusen, 347). Now as then, people in the Federal Republic of Germany were afraid of any too immediate experience of their own time and longed for metaphysical unity. It is clear that in such a climate, only a few writers could abandon their distance from the traditions of the Enlightenment and from analytical representational techniques. Ernst Kreuder wrote as early as 2 March 1946 to Horst Lange: "The old emigrants are concerned with a naturalistic working through of the Nazi period. But now we need another frame of mind" (Kreuder, 224). And on 17 January 1947 he wrote: "Any sort of so-called realism is alien to me. That is just another kind of history-writing. Thus all the realistic descriptions of writers who merely observe leave me cold. It is a question rather of spiritual, immaterial truth" (224).

Jens's prophecy that time was working day by day for an abstract literature would not be fulfilled. In the second half of the 1950s, the first dissident voices of a new generation began to make themselves heard. In *Akzente* in 1955, Helmut Krapp and Karl Markus Michel criticized, with their *Notes on Avant-Gardism*, the restorative climate of West German literature. "Our time stands under the sign of being too late: too late is the comeback of Kafka, Proust, Musil, or Karl Kraus; too late was the adaptation of great foreign literature between the wars" (400). Krapp and Michel demanded, instead of an abstract literature, a concrete one that would above all be concentrated on the "medium of speech." On the one hand, so-called experimental poetry continued certain classical artistic traditions through the late 50s and early 60s. On the other, the restriction to linguistic material led to a diminution in existential substance and to a stronger emphasis on rationally checkable experience. In retrospect, this literature appears as a transitional phase and an early sign of the change in climate that would take place in 1965 with the dominance of politically engaged poetry and a new realism. Instead of objective descriptions, transfiguration of form and melancholy, there emerged, in a time of new and unexpected prosperity, new projections such as information surveys and group thinking. People wanted not only an accuracy to life, but the totality of life itself, with its "simultaneous confusion of sounds, colors and spiritual rhythms," and in consequence, there was a return to the experiments of Naturalism and the 1920s. As Jürgen Becker noted in 1965 in the documentary volume he edited with Wolf Vostell, titled *Happenings* and characteristically subtitled *Fluxus – Pop Art – Nouveau Réalisme*: "Arno Holz's motto was that art has a tendency to become again nature itself ... and this was first ratified by Dada and by the art we are discussing here" (Becker, 9). In light of the anti-classical attitudes then becoming popular, along with social Utopias, it has been difficult to gain an accurate image of the poetry that preceded the 1960s and was attacked. But in a period of renewed historical thinking, it seems not inappropriate to look more dispassionately than we have in the past at the non-Nazi literature of the Third Reich and its foundations around 1930.

The question of the aesthetic value of this literature can only be answered in the case of individual works. The fact that many of the postwar writers published during the Hitler dictatorship should no longer be cause for moral disapproval. "We didn't know what would happen," Hans Paeschke recalled. "We lived in darkness." Literature, with its own inner dividedness, participated in the paralyzed consciousness of the epoch led by the Nazis, an epoch that knew only "ideologies or military explosions as a way out" (Heist, 206). It is mostly a question of attempts to save oneself from slavery to the objective world of technology or the subjugation to party dictates through withdrawal. In a few cases, some writers managed to bring the "shaky ground" to speech in their "ownmost retreat." Others calmed their fears with plants and stones, closed themselves off in old forms, or sketched out little embroidered ribbons of consoling wisdom. In so far as the younger writers perceived their loss of viewpoint and the petrification of appearances, they gave testimony—impotent spectators that they were—to the decay of the future.

Translated by Larson Powell

Works Cited

Albertz, Heinrich. "Das Ziel der Geschichte." Review of Rudolf Schneider, *Macht und Gnade: Gestalten, Bilder und Werte in der Geschichte.* In *Eckart* 17 (1941): 159.

Andres, Stefan. *Der Dichter in dieser Zeit: Reden und Aufsätze.* Munich: Piper, 1974.

Barth, Emil. *Gesammelte Werke in zwei Bänden.* Vol. 2. Ed. Franz Norbert Mennemeier. Wiesbaden: Limes, 1960.

———. *Lemuria. Aufzeichnungen und Meditationen.* Hamburg: Claassen & Goverts, 1947.

Bauer, Walter. [Title unknown]. *Die Literatur* 40 (1937/38): 241.

Becker, Jürgen, and Wolf Vostell, eds. *Happenings: Fluxus – Pop Art – Nouveau Réalisme. Eine Documentation.* Reinbek: Rowohlt, 1965.

Bender, Hans, ed. *Mein Gedicht ist mein Messer. Lyriker zu ihren Gedichten.* Heidelberg: Rothe, 1955.

Böhme, Herbert. "Junge deutsche Dichtung." *Der deutsche Student* 2 (1934): 634.

Bussmann, Aline. *Erinnerungen an Wolfgang Borchert. Zur zehnten Wiederkehr seines Todestages am 20. November 1957.* Hamburg: Rowohlt, 1957.

Drews, Richard, and Alfred Kantorowicz, eds. *Verboten und Verbrannt. Deutsche Literatur – 12 Jahre unterdrückt.* Berlin and Munich: Ullstein/Kindler, 1947.

Eckert, Gerd. *Die Literatur* 41 (1938/39): 561.

Eich, Günter. *Katharina.* Leipzig: List, 1936.

Goes, Albrecht. *Heimat ist gut. Zehn Gedichte.* Hamburg: Verlag der Blätter für die Dichtung/ Heinrich Ellermann, 1935.

Grosser, J. F. Gottlieb, ed. *Die Große Kontroverse. Ein Briefwechsel um Deutschland.* Hamburg, Geneva, and Paris: Nagel, 1963.

Hartlaub, Felix. *Das Gesamtwerk.* Frankfurt am Main: Fischer, 1955.

———. *Felix Hartlaub in seinen Briefen.* Ed. Katharina Kraus and Gustav Friedrich Hartlaub. Tübingen: Wunderlich, 1958.

Haufe, Eberhard. "Zur Entwicklung der sarmatischen Lyrik Bobrowskis 1941–1961." *Wissenschaftliche Zeitschrift der Universität Halle* 25, no. 1 (1975): 56.

Heiseler, Bernt von. "Über meine Lyrik." *Hochland* 34, no. 2 (1937): 488.

Heissenbüttel, Helmut. "Zur Lyrik Max Kommerells. Ein Versuch in Hermeneutik." *Max Kommerell, Gedichte, Gespräche, Übertragungen.* Olten und Freiburg im Breisgau: Walter, 1973.

Heist, Walter. *Genet und andere. Exkurse über eine faschistische Literatur von Rang.* Hamburg: Claassen, 1965.

Hennecke, Hans. "Die Sprache der deutschen Lyrik I. Zu den Neuerscheinungen der letzten Jahre." *Europäische Revue* 14, no. 2 (1938): 722.

Hesse, Hermann. "Hermann Hesse über Albrecht Goes." *Neue Rundschau* 46 (1935): 671.

Hocke, Gustav René. *Das verschwundene Gesicht. Ein Abenteuer in Italien.* Leipzig: Rauch, 1939.

———. *Der Französische Geist. Die Meister des Essays von Montaigne bis Giraudoux.* Leipzig: Rauch, 1938.

———. "Rheinisches Europäertum. Zum 10. Todestag von Ernst Robert Curtius." Radio transmission WDR, 24 April 1966.

Hohoff, Curt. "Über Eugene O'Neill." *Hochland* 36, no. 1 (October 1938/March 1939): 46.

Holthusen, Hans Egon, and Friedhelm Kemp, eds. *Ergriffenes Dasein. Deutsche Lyrik 1900–1950.* Ebenhausen: Langewiesche-Brand, 1953.

Ibel, Rudolf. "Von der Würde und Fragwürdigkeit der Ausdruckskunst in der Dichtung." *Die Literatur* 38 (1935/36): 405.

"Jahresbericht 1940 des Hauptlektorats 'schöngeistiges Schrifttum.'" *Lektoren-Brief. Vertrauliche Informationen des Amtes Schrifttumspflege bei dem Beauftragten des Führers für die Überwachung der gesamten geistigen und weltanschaulichen Erziehung der NSDAP* 4, nos. 5/6 (1941): 4.

Jens, Inge, ed. *Max Kommerell: Briefe und Aufzeichnungen, 1919–1944*. Olten und Freiburg im Breisgau: Walter, 1967.

Jens, Walter. "Plädoyer für die abstrakte Kunst." *Texte und Zeichen* 4, no. 1 (1955): 505–515.

Jünger, Friedrich Georg. "Klopstocks Oden." *Die Literatur* 42 (1939/1940): 272.

Kaschnitz, Marie Luise. *Elissa*. Frankfurt am Main: Insel, 1937.

———. *Gedichte*. Hamburg: Claassen & Goverts, 1947.

———. *Orte. Aufzeichnungen*. Frankfurt am Main: Insel, 1973.

Koch, Werner, ed. *Selbstanzeige. Schriftsteller im Gespräch*. Frankfurt am Main: Fischer, 1971.

Koeppen, Wolfgang. *Die Mauer schwankt*. Berlin: Cassirer, 1935.

Korn, Karl. *Lange Lehrzeit: Ein deutsches Leben*. Frankfurt am Main: Societäts-Verlag, 1975.

Krämer-Badoni, Rudolf. *Jacobs Jahr*. Hamburg: Goverts, 1943.

Kreuder, Ernst. "'Man schreibt nicht mehr wie früher.' Briefe an Horst Lange." *Literaturmagazin* 7 (1977): 217.

Krolow, Karl. *Gesammelte Gedichte*. Frankfurt am Main: Suhrkamp, 1965.

———. "Zur Gegenwartslyrik." *Das Innere Reich* 10, no. 2 (1943): 178.

Lampe, Fredo. *Das Gesamtwerk*. Hamburg: Rowohlt, 1955.

———. "Briefe." *Neue deutsche Hefte* 3 (1956/57): 112.

Lange, Horst. "Landschaftliche Dichtung." *Der weisse Rabe* 5/6, no. 2 (1933): 23.

———. *Die Leuchtkugeln. Drei Erzählungen*. Hamburg: Goverts, 1944.

———. *Gesang hinter den Zäunen*. Berlin: Rabenpresse, 1939.

———. *Schwarze Weide*. Hamburg: Goverts, 1937.

———. *Ulanenpatrouille*. Hamburg: Goverts, 1940.

Langgässer, Elisabeth. "Schriftsteller unter der Hitlerdiktatur." *Ost und West* 1, no. 4 (1947): 39.

Lehmann, Wilhelm. *Der grüne Gott. Ein Versbuch*. Berlin: Müller, 1942.

Lenz, Hermann. *Gedichte*. Hamburg: Verlag der Blätter für die Dichtung. Heinrich Ellermann, 1936.

Marcuse, Ludwig, ed. *War ich ein Nazi? Politik – Anfechtung des Gewissens*. Munich: Rütten & Loening, 1968.

Matzke, Frank. *Jugend bekennt: so sind wir!* Leipzig: Reclam, 1930.

Mönch, Walter. *Das Sonett. Gestalt und Geschichte*. Heidelberg: Kerle, 1955.

Nebel, Gerhard. *Bei den nördlichen Hesperiden. Tagebuch aus dem Jahr 1942*. Wuppertal: Marées, 1948.

Nossack, Hans Erich. *Der Untergang. Ein Bericht*. Frankfurt am Main: Suhrkamp, 1967.

———. *Pseudoautographische Glossen*. Frankfurt am Main: Suhrkamp, 1971.

Rauch, Karl. "'Täglich ein Gedicht lesen …'" *Die Dame* 3 (1935): 38.

Schaefer, Oda. *Auch wenn Du träumst, gehen die Uhren. Lebenserinnerungen*. Munich: Piper, 1970.

Schirmbeck, Heinrich. *Die Fechtbrüder*. Berlin: Suhrkamp, 1942.

Schmalenbach, Fritz. *Die Malerei der Neuen Sachlichkeit*. Berlin: Mann, 1973.

Schnurre, Wolfdietrich. "Die Bewährung" [The Test]. *Eckart* 19 (1943): 125.

Schonauer, Franz. *Deutsche Literatur im Dritten Reich: Versuch einer Darstellung in polemischdidaktischer Absicht*. Olten und Freiburg im Breisgau: Walter, 1961.

Splett, Oskar. "Die lebenden Generationen." *Prisma* 3, nos. 19/20 (1948): 42.

Tgahrt, Reinhard, ed. "Hermann Kasack 1896–1966." *Marbacher Magazin* 2 (1976): 28.

Tumler, Franz. *Anruf. Gedichte*. Munich: Langen, 1941.

Ullrich, Kurt. "Zur Situation der amerikanischen Literatur." *Neu Amerika. Zwanzig Erzähler der Gegenwart*, 12. Berlin: Fischer, 1937.

von der Vring, Georg, ed. *Die junge Front. Gedichte junger Soldaten*. Munich: Piper, 1943.

Winkler, Eugen Gottlob. *Briefe 1932–1936*. Ed. Walter Warnach. Bad Salzig: Rauch, 1949.

Wulf, Joseph. *Musik im Dritten Reich*. Gütersloh: Mohn, 1963.

Zeller, Bernhard, ed. "Als der Krieg zu Ende war." *Literarisch-politische Publizistik 1945–1950*. Stuttgart: Klett, 1973.

Chapter 4

CULTURE AS SIMULATION
The Third Reich and Postmodernity

Hans Dieter Schäfer

In February and March 1945, as the Red Army amassed along the Oder River in preparation for the upcoming battle for Berlin, Hitler spent an "endlessly long" time in the bunker of the Reichskanzlei before a wooden model of the planned redesign of Linz. "At such moments [he] forgot the war," his secretary remembered. "He no longer felt any exhaustion and explained to us ... all the details of the changes which he planned for his hometown" (Zoller, 57). The mirage inside the bunker made the wasteland outside the concrete walls, for which Hitler was responsible, vanish. From 1933 onwards, set pieces from theater and film architecture (see Bartetzko) had created scenarios that allowed the state leadership and populace alike to collectively deceive themselves about the death throes of reason and reality. Hitler himself derived a part of his legitimation from the cult-of-the-artist that the bourgeoisie had established. As Goebbels explained about the Führer in 1937: "His entire work testifies to an artistic spirit: his state is a construction of truly classical proportions. The artistic formation of his politics places him, as befits his character and his nature, at the head" of culture (Dröge and Müller, 56).[1] The Third Reich replaced bourgeois values, all of which had been emptied of meaning by modernization, with imitations resembling traditional values such as personal identity shaped by experience, German history, the sublime, building for eternity. Countless imitations gave form to private everyday life and appeared to lend a collective meaning to the madness occurring everywhere. Those writers, painters, and composers supported by National Socialism largely abandoned complexity and, unlike the Bohemians, no longer had the goal "of attaining self-consciousness" through the image "of their own destruction" (210).

Spatial Productions in the Third Reich

In this mixture of disparate traditions, art revealed itself to be extraordinarily aggressive and was adaptable to prevailing ideology as a model for late-capitalistic consumer culture. Even then, the quality of the individual work of art was of less importance than its integration into the media network. When Werner Peiner exhibited his pictures at the Prussian Academy in 1938, he received several state commissions and was personally asked by Hitler to do a special exhibition (Hesse, 119). In his decorative tapestries for the Auswärtige Amt or the Reichskanzlei, Peiner combined the style of Indian and Asian miniatures with the formal arsenal of European murals to "facilitate" National Socialism's "integration into German history" (331). In the face of allegorical representations of the continents, the forced stylization reduces the whole to a beauty equivalent to that emanated by the coarse star-portraits of film placards (Hesse, 404–11). If the Goblin promised taste through materials and expenditure, then the natural stone surfacing of National Socialist buildings suggested the eternal. In 1938, Hitler had maintained: "[W]e do not build for our current time, we build for the future! Therefore, we must build *big, solidly* and *permanently*" (Mittig, 20).

The monuments were to replace the "trash architecture" of the Weimar Republic but were nonetheless subjected to quicker and cheaper construction materials along with reinforced concrete and steel, so that today damages to Berlin's Olympic Stadium or to the grounds of the Reichsparteitag in Nuremberg are incurring substantial renovation costs (Mittig, 21).[2] While National Socialism compelled "hundreds of thousands ... on forced marches" with "clipped" songs throughout the country (Ekelöf, 48), it inveigled with a Reich built on masonry blocks lasting for a thousand years. The incessant mobilization in the *Kolonne* (marching brigade) and the stage effects simulating eternity merged together, negating time in a way that appealed to the emotions of many "because industrialism had come into a deep crisis and now endangered their existence" (Damus, 302). Thirty river basin and road maps, which Werner Peiner illustrated in 1933–34 for Shell AG for advertising purposes, extol: "Germany is beautiful!" The pictures reference the landscapes at hand but also describe "historical monuments and architectural styles, national traditions and scenes from working life" (Hesse, 33). Kasimir Edschmid, who wrote the texts for the Rhine River map, declared the river "to be Germany itself, the mirror of its becoming, the witness of its eternal, wonderful resurrection." Even though a plane can be seen circling a Shell gas station, rural scenes and historical edifices dominate on the map; only two automobiles hover on the map surface, taking up less space than deer and wild boars, thus giving the impression of a homogeneous landscape from which the cathedral of Cologne rises "majestically into the sky, like a marvel with thousands of stones and peaks, figures and portals." The map persuaded the "worthless" automobile tourist of his participation in German greatness in order to reverently refocus his gaze from below upwards.[3] Because he wished to save the reader from his emotional isolation, Reinhold Schneider's *Fahrt ins Reich* also transformed the present into an imaginary space and demanded new order and control by conjuring up old truths. For as he writes about the *Marienburg* (Schneider, 111–12), whose flying buttresses divide "like jets of water ... that then are then recombined to create a vault of light" (110), nothing is "hated more by the peoples of the plain [below] ... than form and the consciousness of the overlordship contained within it." Because many people felt themselves to be objects of inscrutable powers, the Third Reich made an effort to present unity as form and to declare foreigners to be the antagonistic embodiment of chaos. Many of the staged spaces altered time beyond recognition in order to conceal the movement that defined the nature of National Socialism.

Joseph Weinheber's *Gemäldegedicht* "Albrecht Dürer"

Not infrequently, the technical ability of less successful artists served as a basis for a career in the production of delusions, with whose flickering gleam Hitler set in motion the destruction of national history, including historical monuments. Josef Weinheber regarded himself, "after Rilke and beside George," as the "greatest lyric poet of the German language" (Berger, 277). This exceedingly inflated claim stood in contrast to the conservative and ahistorical formal style, which recombined fragments from the past into billboards. Weinheber had written monthly, class-based, and zodiac aphorisms for the annual calendars of the Phönix Insurance Company in Vienna, which he then collected and expanded with pictorial poems in 1937 to form a twelve-part cycle entitled *O Mensch, gib acht!* The following poem (Weinheber, 348–49) is for the month of April:

Albrecht Dürer
Selbstbildnis in der Alten Pinakothek in München

Von meiner Stirne geht das deutsche Licht.
Die Schläfenfurche Traum und Grübeln spricht.
Durchsichtig fast, der Braue ferner Schwung
nennt heilig unsre Überlieferung.
Das treue Aug erfaßt die reiche Welt,
nichts ist so klein, es werde wohlbestellt.
Von meinen Locken geht ein Leuchten still,
sie sind des Christus, wo er deutsch sein will.
Die Nase, südlich schmal und streng geführt,
gibt Maß und läßt der Form, was ihr gebührt.
Im Schnurrbart lebt das Volk nach seiner Art:
Es ist ein heller, dünner Frankenbart,
wie jener, dunkler um das Kinn herum
von harter Kraft sagt, Stand und Herrentum.
Der Mund, keusch, fest und voller Innigkeit,

hat in den Winkeln schon den Schwank bereit,
indes die Wange, trauerschön genug,
aufzeigt den ewigen deutschen Leidenszug.
Es ruht die Hand, Einfalt und Stolz zugleich,
dem Mantel auf, als hielte sie das Reich.
In diesen Fingern, weg- und hergebracht,
hab ich gedeutet, was den Künstler macht.
In ihnen webt der bildsam hohe Geist,
der euch das Rätsel und die Lösung weist.
Wahrhaftig steckt die Kunst in der Natur:
Reißt sie heraus, ihr habt sie, klar und pur.
Als meines Volkes gültige Gestalt,
für alle da, so hab ich mich gemalt.
Euch völlig zugewandt ist mein Gesicht.
Wend't ihr euch ab von ihm, so seid ihr nicht.

Albrecht Dürer
Self-Portrait in the Alten Pinakothek Museum in Munich

From my brow a German light is shining.
The temple's crease speaks of dream and brooding.
Almost invisibly, the eyebrows' arching lineage
Names our sacred heritage.
The steadfast eye encompasses the world so rich,
Nothing is so small to escape its reach.
My curls give forth a soft illumination,
They are of Christ, who would want to be German.
The nose, southernly narrow and strictly defined
Shows proportion and form most refined.
The Volk resides in its way in the mustache:
It is a light, thin Franconian panache,
Like that darker one on the chin all around
Bespeaks rugged strength, class and mastery that abound.
The mouth, chaste, firm and full of intensity,
Holds in its corners a lively propensity,
The cheek reveals, with sorrowful beauty enough,
The eternal German inclination to suffer.
The hand holds, at once in simplicity and pride,
Open the coat as if it held the Reich.
In these fingers, plying back and forth,
I have shown what makes an artist's worth.
In them is woven the high formative power
That supplies the riddle and its answer.
Truly Art resides within nature:
Grasp it, you'll have it clear and pure.
As the definitive figure of my people,
For all to see, thus I have painted me.
My face turns toward all of you to see,
If you turn away, you'll cease to be.

(trans. Neil H. Donahue)

Weinheber composed the *Selbstbildnis* (Self-Portrait) from the forehead, the temple-furrows, the brow, the eyes, curls, the nose, and the mustache over the mouth and cheeks all the way down to the hand, in order to allow Dürer to interpret the nature of his art at the end of the poem. The open "answer" to the "riddle" quotes a half-sentence from *Bücher von menschlicher Proportion* (Books of Human Proportion): "Dann wahrhaftig steckt die Kunst in der Natur, wer sie heraus kann reißen, der hat sie" (Then truly, art is in nature, and whoever can tear it out, will have it, Dürer, 198).[4] To lend the poem the appearance of prophecy, Weinheber bound the iambic pentameter with the old-fashioned rhyming couplets of the *Meistersang*. As in the edifices of National Socialist architecture, the "will to achieve a form, which is self-contained and resting in itself" results "in an expression of inaccessibility and absoluteness of authority" (Damus, 308); unlike in postmodernity, the poem does not play with its sources as if they were masks but rather hallucinates a false radiance into empty eye sockets. Weinheber swore the reader to the national ideology, which prevails over the "German light" mentioned in the first line by way of expressions such as "heilig unsre Überlieferung" (our sacred heritage), "ewige[r] deutsche[r] Leidenszug" (eternal German inclination to suffer), "das Reich," and "meines Volkes gültige Gestalt" (definitive figure of my people). In the process, he could refer to the cult of Dürer, which had since the early nineteenth century enthusiastically anointed the painter as the "embodiment of the artist" (Hinz, 11). Reproductions of *Die Betenden Hände* (Praying Hands) and *Der Hase* (The Hare) were not the only works circulated in large numbers; *Selbstbildnis* was used as title page adornment for the *Kunstgewerbeblätter* and as a model for a postage stamp (Hinz, 66, 75).

Like Hitler, Weinheber felt himself to be a misunderstood genius. Insulated from the empirical world, he worshiped the priestly "heroes in art, piousness, wisdom," which—to him—included Dürer, Michelangelo, and, above all, Hölderlin and his "own nobility" (Berger, 280). A "characteristic feature" of our century's history is "that it has swept away person and personality" (Kertész, 3). The poem seems intent on opposing this process, yet "Albrecht Dürer" provided Hitler's split personality with a blinding mask, behind which he could pursue the liquidation of independent lives and livelihoods. Since the Führer's name was omitted, a particularly strong vacuum emerged that seemed to hunger for a form: "Euch völlig zugewandt ist mein Gesicht./Wend't ihr euch ab von ihm so seid ihr nicht" (My face is completely turned toward you./If you turn away, you'll cease to be). The end contorts the historical truth into its opposite, for only a renunciation of the illusion would have been able to protect the German Reich and its people from catastrophe.

Gottfried Benn's *Künstlergedicht* "Chopin"

In response to the monumental rubbish of such stage decor, Gottfried Benn wrote a poem in October 1944 that thematized a non-German artist and the perfection of his "small hand" (*Sämtliche Werke I*, 180–81).

Chopin

Nicht sehr ergiebig im Gespräch,
Ansichten waren nicht seine Stärke,
Ansichten reden drum herum,
wenn Delacroix Theorien entwickelte,
wurde er unruhig, er seinerseits konnte
die Notturnos nicht begründen.

Schwacher Liebhaber;
Schatten in Nohant,
wo George Sands Kinder
keine erzieherischen Ratschläge
von ihm annahmen.

Brustkrank in jener Form
mit Blutungen und Narbenbildung,
die sich lange hinzieht;
stiller Tod
im Gegensatz zu einem
mit Schmerzparoxysmen
oder durch Gewehrsalven:
man rückte den Flügel (Erard) an die Tür
und Delphine Potocka
sang ihm in der letzten Stunde
ein Veilchenlied.

Nach England reiste er mit drei Flügeln:
Pleyel, Erard, Broadwood,
spielte für 20 Guineen abends
eine Viertelstunde
bei Rothschilds, Wellingtons, im Strafford House
und vor zahllosen Hosenbändern;
verdunkelt von Müdigkeit und Todesnähe
kehrte er heim
auf den Square d'Orléans.

Dann verbrennt er seine Skizzen
und Manuskripte,
nur keine Restbestände, Fragmente, Notizen,
diese verräterischen Einblicke-,
sagte zum Schluß:
"meine Versuche sind nach Maßgabe dessen vollendet,
was mir zu erreichen möglich war."

Spielen sollte jeder Finger
mit der seinem Bau entsprechenden Kraft,
der vierte ist der schwächste

(nur siamesisch zum Mittelfinger).
Wenn er begann, lagen sie
auf e, fis, gis, h, c.

Wer je bestimmte Präludien
von ihm hörte,
sei es in Landhäusern oder
in einem Höhengelände
oder aus offenen Terrassentüren
beispielsweise aus einem Sanatorium,
wird es schwer vergessen.
Nie eine Oper komponiert,
keine Symphonie,
nur diese tragischen Progressionen
aus artistischer Überzeugung
und mit einer kleinen Hand.

Chopin

Not much given to conversation
Opinions were not his strength,
opinions were always beside the point,
whenever Delacroix developed his theories,
he became unsettled, for his part he could not
even explain his Notturnos.

A diffident lover;
Shadow in Nohant,
where George Sand's kids
did not listen to his advice
on their upbringing.

Consumptive of that kind
With bleeding and scar tissue buildup,
that drags on and on;
quiet death
contrary to one
with paroxysms of pain
or before a firing-squad:

His grand piano (Erard) was put against the door
And Delphine Potocka
Sang to him in his last hour
A sentimental song.

He traveled to England with three pianos:
Pleyel, Erard, Broadwood,
played for 20 Guineas evenings
a quarter-hour
at the Rothschild's, Wellington's, in the Strafford House
and before countless of the Garters;
gloomy from exhaustion and mortality
he returned home
to the Square d'Orléans

Then he burns his drafts
And manuscripts,
just no remnants, fragments, notations,
these revealing glimpses—
he says at the end:
"My efforts are complete to the extent of what
was possible for me to achieve."

Each finger should play
With the force corresponding to its structure
The fourth is the weakest
(Only a Siamese twin to the middle finger)
When he began, they lay
On E, F-sharp, G-sharp, H, C.

Whoever heard him play
certain Preludes,
in a country home or
on a mountain retreat,
or through the open terrace doors,
for example, of a sanatorium,
will hardly forget it

Never composed an opera,
no symphony,
only these tragic progressions
of artistic conviction
and with a delicate hand.

(trans. Neil H. Donahue)

The reader is directly confronted with disparate fragments, which, at
first sight, elude a unified "view"; unrhymed and free verse groups afford
the poem an open character. Presumably, what fascinated Benn about
Chopin was "the manifold playfulness that does not go in depth."[5] Benn
characterized Chopin as a "diffident lover" and as a "shadow in Nohant,"
whose "advice on their upbringing" would have been ignored by George
Sand's children. Following the topic of failure in everyday life, the third
verse thematizes illness and death, in order to deal with his artistic performance in the next verse. Benn clarifies that the preludes are not meant
"for everybody" by referencing the semipublic play in England to which
Chopin had been invited by Jews and the nobility. Because he wished to
leave only complete works behind, Chopin is said to have burned his
"drafts and manuscripts" before his death.

Benn justified his form of writing to Oelze (18 January 1945) by referring back to the montages of Dos Passos, in order to "bring new topics,
new realities into the insipid German lyricism and move away from
moods and sentiments to objects ..." (*Briefe*, 377–78). When Wilhelm
Lehmann asked the poet about the poetic substance of the poem, he mentioned the Chopin biography by Guy de Pourtalès, *Der blaue Klang* (The
Blue Sound).[6] The poem disregards the intimate; the reader learns nothing

about the break that George Sand brought about in order to pass "judgement" on "physical and intellectual vitality" (290). In contrast, Benn opened his mind to Chopin's artistic credo; like Weinheber, he lets his "hero" speak for himself: "My efforts are complete to the extent of what it was possible for me to achieve" (307). Already in the original version, the words have the character of a last will; they are spoken after the dying man had "in no small measure regained the use of language." Obviously, "the thought of imperfection and incompleteness [struck him] as intolerable" (297) directly before death, for Chopin not only wanted to make sure that all his manuscripts had been burned, but also expressed a desire that all his "roughly sketched" compositions should be "given unto the fire" (307). "No remnants, fragments, notations,/these revealing insights," Benn added. The penultimate verse focuses on Chopin's technical advice for the piano, which Pourtalès had summarized after the failed dialogue with Delacroix. The composer, he wrote, was to be like Liszt, ever conscious of "the activity" of "each individual finger." Each one was to play "with the inherent force of its structure," whereas "the fourth is the weakest of them all" (199). Pourtalès called the fourth finger the "Siamese twin-brother of the middle finger" and stipulated that all of them should rest "on the *E, F sharp, G sharp, B flat* and *B* keys," so that right from the start, the hand would be placed "in an advantageous position" (200).

The end of the poem thematizes the reception of Chopin after his death; Benn shifted his music away from the massive cultural industry and associated it with a "country home" and "high countryside," interwoven with morbidity. The poet then modified three sentence fragments from *Der blaue Klang* for inclusion in the final five lines. First, Benn integrated the fact that Chopin had "never felt a strong desire to compose an opera" (202). Second, Benn converted Heine's "harmonic" (206) into "tragic progressions" in order to recall the "delicate hand" with his last words. As it is written in the original: "wenn man seine kleine Hand ergriff, überraschte deren feste Knochenbildung,... es sei eine knöcherne Soldatenhand mit Frauen-muskeln gewesen" (when one took his small hand, one was surprised at its solid bone structure,... as if it were a bony soldier's hand with women's muscles, 200). With the poem, Benn created a reflection of himself: he sympathized with Chopin's "profound brotherly modesty" ("Totenrede für Klabund," 198), and shared in his rejection of great works, without however wanting to sacrifice "enduring structures" ("IV. Block II, Zimmer 66," 137). His own nature corresponded to Pourtalès's assessment that Chopin had striven for "something more perfect and exquisite than the loud clapping of the masses" (Pourtalès, 202). Though excluded from publication by the National Socialists from 1938 onwards, Benn's written correspondence with a member of Bremen's upper class, F. W. Oelze,[7] enabled his Bohemian art to survive periods of "endless depression" and "petrification" (*Briefe*, 159: 6 December 1936). Even though "Chopin was not played" ("Teils-teils," 317) in his parents' home, Benn objected to trashing such music in his "Nachtcafé" (1912) (*Sämtliche Werke I*, 19):

H moll: die 35. Sonate.
Zwei Augen brüllen auf:
Spritzt nicht dies Blut von Chopin in den Saal,
damit das Pack drauf rumlatscht!
Schluß! He, Gigi!

B-minor: the Sonata Op. 35.
Two eyes raise a roar:
Don't spray the blood of Chopin around the room,
Just so these louts can wallow in it!
Stop! Hey, Gigi!

(trans. Neil H. Donahue)

Because Chopin's "aristocratic celebrity" (Pourtalès, 214) limited itself to "technical training" (199), Benn felt drawn to his piano music. Benn opposed Weinheber's bold and mendacious projection of meaning "out of artistic conviction" with another image of the artist, which, even though it professes to a playful "as if," is not grounded in postmodernism. "Artistry," as Benn later explained in "Probleme der Lyrik" (Problems of Lyric Poetry), is "an enormously serious and a central concept. Artistry is the art's attempt to experience itself as content at a time of the general decline of content and to form a new style from this experience" ("Probleme der Lyrik," 14). By defending unique expression, Benn successfully attempted to rescue both the bourgeois "I" as well as the "elegiac secret" of modernity.[8] The Chopin poem ruptures the chronological but does not offer synchronicity; especially because so much attention is devoted to dying, it couples the past with a possible future. However, Benn was able to preserve modernity during the Third Reich only because he had struggled to reach the truth after his error of 1933–34. A few months before he wrote the poem, Benn delivered in "Block II, Zimmer 66" a harsh report on the state of affairs of the fifth year of the war in all its "details" (128): "There are no more artificial limbs for the wounded, for there is no material left," he wrote, speaking as a doctor. "There are no more shoelaces and no dentures, no gauze bandages and specimen glasses.... But the Führer awards stripes and determines the width of the wreath ribbons for military burials" (132). In the midst of shabbiness, he continued, propaganda continued "auf hohen Touren" (at full speed). Benn distinguished between a "coarse" and a "mild" method of political propaganda, among which he counted the misuses of Rilke and Hölderlin. "Dir ist, Liebes, keiner zuviel gefallen" was the most often used quotation of the latter (131). While "the decay ... oozes out of all pores," he would assemble pictures from an illustrated magazine into his report: "Nera and Sehra, the 'Heinzelmännchen of Mostar,' are so happy to finally be allowed to work in the large organization of Todt: Goebbels smiles with his white teeth for the wounded; Göring comes as a Santa Claus—the fairy-tale spins a web around us" (132). In a military base in Landsberg an der Warthe, "high up, with a splendid view over the city and the river basin" (letter to Oelze, 30 August 1943; *Briefe*, 342: cf. Heintel), Benn found the necessary detachment to shed light on National Socialism's strategy to obscure blunt materialism and to let reality move behind a great wall of smoke and mirrors: irresponsible "gamblers" had assumed the reign, "who had come to Monte [Carlo] with a nebulous system in order to break the bank" (126); reason had been surrendered to the illusion through the "vacuum" (129) created by prohibitions and through the "state-bred decline in education" (130); conversations at the base were those "of nice, harmless people, from whom no one could surmise what threatened him and the Fatherland" (125); they "essentially think only of how they might bring back mushrooms for their wives on their next leave" (126).

The End of Public Responsibility

Unlike Benn, most of the artists in the Third Reich were deprived of direction and only rarely found themselves in a position to create distance. Goebbels had abolished literary criticism; everything not disqualified by his bureaucracy and allowed to be printed was deemed to be good. For a large part of the younger generation, a willingness existed right from the start—in spite of their opposition to the ideology—not to question the political conditions of the Hitler-state. One rarely denied oneself material enticements, while at the same time one hoped to be able to keep the core of one's soul pure. Only gradually did it become evident that this started a process of divisiveness, which appeared to permit a relative autonomy in the cultural sector—beyond the invented *Stunde Null*—particularly since the subconscious had been exposed to a form of colonization through the immense expansion of the media. If the interest in ideological criticism that characterized the generation of 1968 had led to a critical examination of the edifying literature of the "inner emigrants" and of the national literature of the state itself, then subsequent research since the mid 1970s had returned the hitherto ignored portions of its history to postwar literature. While Fritz J. Raddatz morally executed authors who had published in the Third Reich in a sensational report for *Die Zeit* entitled "Wir werden weiterdichten, wenn alles in Scherben fällt ..." (We will continue writing, when everything breaks into fragments),[9] the author of this essay maintained in various publications (see bibliography) that they had partially preserved the vitality of modernity in obscurity. As much as the observations about the disparate politics of literature and its niches turned out to be accurate (Barbian, 844), and though some older and younger writers who attained recognition only after 1945 continued with postexpressionist motifs and writing styles, the approach was flawed on two accounts: it stipulated a "young generation," which had not existed in that form, and it worked with the concepts of epoch and style of a bourgeois culture, the foundations of which, in reality, had crumbled away. Also not sufficiently considered was that most works of any importance were written by authors such as Eugen Gottlob Winkler, Felix Hartlaub, and Friedo Lampe, who had not survived the Third Reich, while others such as Horst Lange hardly found their way back to their old form. After all, those literary excavations resulted in a new evaluation of individual authors and of the diffuse culture of the Third Reich (see, among others, Scheffel, Arntzen, Kirchner, Schütz, Caemmerer and Delabar, Wolz, Graf, Czucka). Previously unpublished texts of the *Stunde Null* authors, by now made accessible, for the most, document their origins and occasionally shed light on their entanglements. My research has shown the journal *Die Kolonne* (founded in 1929 and suspended in 1932) as the paradigm of a modern tradition that could also survive in the Third Reich. Uncovered documents exposed divergent interests that would soon tear apart the literary circle to which Günter Eich, Peter Huchel, Horst Lange, and Martin Raschke belonged. Lange's letters to Ernst Kreuder repeatedly reference a "vacuum" (27 February 1939) and a "paralyzing feeling of isolation" (26 April 1939); the individual artist had "to rely upon himself and had nothing within close proximity that could serve as a point of orientation" (27 February 1939). Lange lamented the flight of friends "with whom 7 or 8 years ago one had formed a small front of young talents" into "lucrative and less demanding occupations" such as radio broadcasting (27 February 1939), and he regretted the expulsion of "ideologically engaged" authors such as Anna Seghers and Heinrich Mann, writing that "we now lack a literature, which can fan the flames in the fireplace" (11 January 1940). In contrast, most contemporary books appeared to him to be "reminiscent of the time before 1890. Everything that followed is being denied and erased," but "we need a literature that is alive" (6 May 1939).

While Martin Raschke submitted completely to the delusional ideas of National Socialism to glorify the war (see Schäfer, "Der Mythos der jungen Kolonne"), Eich was disgusted by the senseless destruction, yet nonetheless put his talents at the disposal of anti-British propaganda directly before the start of the Western Campaign with his recently rediscovered (1993) play for radio *Rebellion in der Goldstadt* (Rebellion in Gold City). Personal self-interest prompted him to trade military service for a four-week work detail in Berlin. In a letter to Arthur A. Kuhnert, Eich spoke of "wretched work" but, "honoraris causa," he hoped for "a prompt broadcast date with a hook-up to all the stations in the captured and occupied regions."[10] Here the veiled materialism of the leadership intermingled with the honest materialism of the young writer. Eich had openly declared as early as 1930: "Responsibility toward the time? Not in the least. Only to myself" (*Gesammelte Werke*, Vol. 4, 457). Horst Lange lamented in 1934 that he and Eich "had gone into different directions" and noted that while he had been pleased by Eich's "successes," he had read, "not without sadness his bad poems in the *Bücherwurm* some time ago." With "Späte Zeit,"[11] Peter Huchel wrote a poem that encrypted the truth, but the piece is the only jewel of its kind. Whether or not he had written an anti-British radio program with "Die Greuel von Denshawai" is in dispute (see Parker); however, there is much evidence suggesting that he had suspended his work on it (see Nijssen). Key terms of National Socialist ideology permeate the language of his radio play about Rubens (1940), in which he calls upon the painter to "represent the human body as being more powerful, as it had been in the past: heroic and beautiful." Next to Roman fencers and rowers, Huchel counted Africans in the category of human beings that had not yet become "so degenerate and weak." In doing so, he did not craft a veiled critique of National Socialist racial policies;[12] Hitler had purchased Werner Peiner's triptych *Das schwarze Paradies* (The Black Paradise) for the Reichskanzlei to publicly state the German claim to the colonies (Hesse, 121–27; fig. 397).

Sham Existences and Opportunism

In the last two decades, research and journalism have succeeded in restoring résumés not only to postwar authors but also to industrialists, lawyers, legal clerks and judges, architects, scientists, journalists, and others; now and then one discovers completely falsified biographies such as these of Peter Grubbe or Hans Schwerte, who made their own past disappear with new names in order to successfully launch new careers. When Werner Höfer's propaganda article on the execution of the pianist Kreiten was pointed out by Fred K. Prieberg in the *12 Uhr Blatt* to the Executive Board of the WDR, he received a reply that the accused person had appeared "as a representative of liberal journalism in the past decades" and that he had "shown himself to be a credible figure" (Wieser, 166). Only after *Der Spiegel* published other intimate musings by Höfer and revealed them to be enveloped in horror did supporters withdraw from the journalist without considering the fact that he had been similarly employed as a *"Weichzeichner"* (a person who sees the world through rose-tinted glasses) after the war in order to avoid any basic criticism in his programs. Since the 1950s, the sales-promoting strategy of the news magazine has been to disclose the National Socialist past of politicians and companies of the *"Wirtschaftswunder"* (economic miracle). By Aryanizing the underwear manufacturer Carl Joel in 1938, Neckermann had laid the foundation for his mail order business; he had "guaranteed"[13] the supply of winter uniforms for the Eastern Front from 1942–43 onwards; Grundig's capital stemmed from the production of transformers for communications equipment manufactured by Eastern European female forced laborers and prisoners.[14] The DGB (Deutsche Gewerkschaftsbund) employed nearly the same personnel and similar plans to continue the construction business of the Deutsche Arbeitsfront and even co-opted the term *Neue Heimat*, which Ley had coined in 1939.[15] Only recently has it become known that this brand of investigative journalism was partially run by former *SS-Hauptsturmführer*; their articles contained "insider-knowledge that could only have come from those directly involved" (see Hachmeister). The "past" of his department head Georg Wolff, whose main responsibility in the *Sicherheitsdienst* in Norway from 1940 to 1945 had been to provide situational reports to Berlin, had "not [been] a factor," Augstein explained in an interview (16),[16] forgetting that he himself had published a sentimental story about a farmer's woman in her traditional costume in the *Völkischer Beobachter*. ("Her blue-black hair, parted in the middle, fell down along her half-bronze cheek and entwined itself in the back into a knot").[17] When Hans Werner Richter was confronted with five prose works he had written during the Third Reich, he could not "remember anything" about it. As the founder of the Group 47 explained: "I wanted to live, and I think everybody was writing somewhere, because otherwise it wouldn't have been possible for them to emerge quite of a sudden—no one falls from the sky" (Wehdeking, 179–80). Wolfgang Weyrauch is one of the few younger authors to have admitted to his past after the "collapse." In an "Offenen Brief" (Open Letter) to Johannes R. Becher, he confessed that he had identified Hitler with Germany and further did not want to leave the public sphere exclusively to the party hacks ("Letter," 588).

An impressive example for the *"sanfte Tour"* (mild tour) of war propaganda is rendered in the article *"Verse für dich"* (Verses for you), in which the author, writing from the front, asks his "sweetheart" to join him in taking the very same "small green book" in hand that he has, because "we want to hold on to everything which is great and beautiful now that it appears that the earth is shaking." Weyrauch quoted a verse from Hölderlin's "Tod für's Vaterland" (Death for the Fatherland): "Du kömmst, o Schlacht, schon wogen die Jünglinge hinab von ihren Hügeln, hinab ins Tal, wo keck herauf die Würger drängen" (You come, o battle, already the youths flow downward from their hilltops into the valley, where the stranglers surge upward, NHD) to find a noble purpose for the slaughter with these "prophetic lines, written for us, for 1945" (*Das Reich*, 1 April 1945). Having returned home from captivity to his girlfriend, who in the meantime "had borne a child" ("Letter," 588), he addressed the *"Würger"* (stranglers) from the past familiarly in the poem "The Red Army Man" (Der Rotarmist) (*Gedichte*, 32):

Du denkst an Marfa, ich denk an Marie,
wir beide lieben unsre Fraun und die,
die mit uns über Tal und Hügel rollen,
doch einmal Arzt und Lehrer werden wollen.
Komm, lieber Bruder, gib mir deine Hand,
wir alle haben nur ein Vaterland.

You think of Marfa, I think of Marie,
we both love our wives and those who
with us over hill and vale do come,
and someday want to become doctors and teachers.
Come, dear brother, give me your hand,
we all have only one fatherland.

(trans. Neil H. Donahue)

In the open letter, Weyrauch admitted to having acted "without any conscience" during the Third Reich, and to feeling ashamed of it, yet at the same time concealed the new censorship practice. After his liberation by the Red Army, he had "been allowed to work as he wished, and no one told me what to do" ("Letter," 589). For both Hitler and Stalin, he feigned the existence of an artistic autonomy that had been destroyed long ago, only to dedicate himself shortly thereafter to the popularization of the avant-garde and modernism. In the 1959 afterword to his anthology *Expeditionen* (Expeditions), Weyrauch exhorted his readers at the start of mass motorization "Do you really want to ride in stagecoaches?... Please, then, abstain from it in lyricism as well" (*Expeditionen*, 161).

"Controlled Schizophrenia"

Behind such opportunism lay a lack of orientation that also confused young people who opposed National Socialism. For example, though Irmgard Keun left her exile in Holland on 13 May 1938 to visit her friend Arnold Strauss in the United States (Kreis, 210), she returned to Amsterdam in July only to inform him shortly thereafter of her impending deportation: "The people in Europe are all completely mad.... I literally did not know anymore, where, where, where [to go]" (Kreis and Strauss, 251).

Wolfgang Koeppen, who lived in the Netherlands supported by the Jewish family Michaelis, was also affected by deportation, so that he returned to Germany in the autumn of 1938. UFA (Universale Filmanstalt) took the place of private patronage at this time, engaging him for four film projects as a scriptwriter (Döring, 115–18). Unlike Irmgard Keun, Koeppen had written in Holland not only for readers in exile but also for readers in the Reich. The novel *Die Mauer schwankt* (The Wall Is Swaying), which had been published by the Jewish publishing house Bruno Cassirer in 1935, thematizes his fundamental experience: "Did you know something? You knew nothing. Each step was a step into the darkness. You could fall at any moment, and if you wanted to do good, you were in greater danger of doing wrong" (Koeppen, 247). Occasionally, this disorientation resulted in an overpowering materiality. "Up to now, I have only seen Nakel [Naklo] from the conquered region, houses in ruins, dirty women and arrested *Franctireurs* [a derogatory term for French saboteurs and resistance fighters]. But the bread rolls were good and the apples cheap," Eich wrote in a letter dated 20 September 1939 (Vieregg, *Sünden*, vi–vii). The expected execution of the resistance fighters triggered no compassion; fear had fundamentally extinguished the relationship to other human beings, transforming everything else into objects. Such a way of thinking permitted no access to experiential reality.

Expressions such as "resistance" and "camouflage," used recently to try to rescue a large portion of inner German literature as "regime-critical," presuppose a distance, not a separation, from contemporary events (see Denk). Even a concept such as "mimicry" (Heukenkamp, 24) is a poor choice, as it suggests that the artist had only ostensibly adapted himself in order to protect his personality, which of course was the primary casualty of the schism. Many of the negative pictures encountered in literature should be read less as masked criticism than as an expression of an ambivalent attitude toward life. "Reality" was perceived "no longer as the total sum of hard, unavoidable facts," Hannah Arendt remarked about the destruction of consciousness by the National Socialists, "but as a conglomerate of constantly changing events and slogans, where something could be true today, which will already be false tomorrow" (Arendt, 30–31).

In a conversation in 1977, Wolfdietrich Schnurre referred to life during the Third Reich as a "controlled schizophrenia" (Sandmeyer, 195). According to research by Bateson and his students, schizophrenia is triggered by contradictory messages (Bateson, 25); in the Third Reich as in other mass cultures, the shift between "warm and tender" care and "cold" rejection can be observed even in everyday life. Caught between function and soul, man cannot develop a stable identity. "What counts, is melding with the moment";[18] a temporal connection with the past and the future is nearly impossible to attain. Joseph Gabel described the career of a schizophrenic as that of a "failure," who "wants to restart his life, put it on hold and later make the time run backwards." The afflicted person enters a state of "delusional inhibition of his temporal organization with all its consequences" (Gabel, 121) that leads him to "start over 'at the *Stunde Null'*" (Gabel, 123) again and again. Though Schnurre supplied a convincing diagnosis of the phenomenon, the conversation documents the fact that he himself was helpless against this schizophrenia. He had written "only for himself," because "if I had had to think of others while writing, consideration would have been required. Instead I could be inconsiderate and postpone my literary debut until 1946. But then I immediately thought of the others while writing" (Sandmeyer, 194). Presumably, Schnurre emphasized his willingness to assume responsibility in this way because an inner barrier kept him from talking about film reviews, stories, and poems he had published during the Third Reich (Blencke, 138). In 1939, he had, along with his graduating high school classmates, volunteered for war duty "due to a desire for adventure ... and a vague ... feeling of camaraderie" (Sandmeyer, 192), but was later sentenced to several weeks' arrest. In 1944, Schnurre conjured up the "spiritual world" as an "untouchable landscape"[19] in his *Front und Heimat* (Frontline and Homeland); however, he had lost the ability to separate the inside from the outside world. He described the "human heart" as an "internal battlefield" and advised authors to direct their gaze to the "fight between our soul with the powers of chaos and destruction";[20] in such images, the self surrendered to the mutilating impulses.

Wolfgang Borchert

Even Wolfgang Borchert, who had been placed into custody from 1942 to 1944 on suspicion of undermining the military, had difficulties maintaining his independence under "controlled schizophrenia." Appearing on 13 July 1943 in the *Hamburger Anzeiger*, the prose piece "Requiem für einen Freund" (Requiem for a Friend) first makes concrete the blinding dynamics of marches; despite his use of crassly realistic elements and despite the lamentation so typical of the author—"Where is God—the grenades scream! Where is God—the stars scream! Where is God—we pray!"—the experience of time in the end is reduced to a biological concept of survival (Borchert, *Allein*, 262):

> Da gelobe ich dir, daß ich aushalten will—für dich. Denn in mir bist du—du warst mein Bruder und hattest den heiligen Glauben an das ewige Leben. Du mußtest darum sterben—wir wollen, wenn es uns vergönnt ist, dafür kämpfen und leben!
> Und als es in der Frühe tagt, sitzt auf dem Helm, den wir dir auf das Birkenkreuz taten, ein kleiner grauer Vogel und singt—
> Und ganz weit im Osten geht groß die Morgensonne auf.

> I swear to you that I will hold on—for you. Since you are in me—you were my brother and had the sacred belief in eternal life. Therefore you had to die—for that, we want, if such is granted to us, to fight and live!
> And as the day begins, a small grey bird perches on your helmet that we had put on the birch cross, and sings—
> And far away in the East the morning sun rises.

> (trans. Neil H. Donahue)

This is very different from his short stories written after the "collapse." With the "miserable night" in which "fear and desperation stretched their fingers out toward me," Borchert himself unconsciously supplied the reason for the outpouring of delusional thinking that blends in with the final passages with National Socialist ideology. A few months later, Borchert succeeded in expressing the truth with an uncommon consciousness of language (*GW*, 292):

Brief aus Rußland

Man wird tierisch.
Das macht die eisenhaltige
Luft. Aber das faltige
Herz fühlt manchmal noch lyrisch.
Ein Stahlhelm im Morgensonnenschimmer.
Ein Buchfink singt und der Helm rostet.
Was wohl zu Hause ein Zimmer
mit Bett und warm Wasser kostet?
Wenn man nicht so müde wär!

Aber die Beine sind schwer.
Hast du noch ein Stück Brot?
Morgen nehmen wir den Wald.
Aber das Leben ist hier so tot.
Selbst die Sterne sind fremd und kalt.
Und die Häuser sind
so zufällig gebaut.
Nur manchmal siehst du ein Kind,
das hat wunderbare Haut.

Letter from Russia

One becomes an animal.
The iron-filled air does
that. But the wrinkled
heart sometimes still feels lyrical.
A steel helmet in the glow of the morning sun.
A chaffinch sings and the helmet rusts.
But back home what is the cost of
a bed and warm water?
If only one weren't so tired.

But my legs are heavy.
Do you have a piece of bread?
Tomorrow we'll take the woods.
But life here is so dead.
Even the stars are distant and cold.
And the houses are
so haphazardly built.
Only sometimes you see a child
that has wonderful skin.

(trans. Neil H. Donahue)

Presumably, Borchert had recited the poem in September 1943 in the Hamburg Bronzekeller, together with songs and cabaret pieces; the tone of the genre lends the "Letter" flip expressions such as "eisenhaltige Luft" (iron-filled air) and "faltiges Herz" (wrinkled heart), and rhymes such as "tierisch/lyrisch" (animal/lyrical) or "rostet/kostet" (rusts/costs). By asking for the price of a hotel room at home, Borchert denied the steel helmet the transfigurative meaning it possessed in the "Requiem"; he no longer spoke of the "eternal," but of everyday life, which he identified with being "so dead," and in this way sabotaged the simulated inwardness of contemporary lyric poetry. On 20 February 1943, Borchert wrote to Hugo Sicker from Minsk: "meanwhile, I have experienced a lot, both terrible and wonderful." The letter mentions "patrols" through "horrible forests" and a stay in a quarantine hospital, "where each night the dead were carried out," finally ending with a fairy-tale-like story of "a few unreal, magical days with a tender Russian girl—Fina—in Smolensk" (Borchert, *Allein*, 99).

Horst Lange's Story "Das nie betretene Haus" (The House Never Entered)

A similar desire for truth characterizes Lange's "The House Never Entered," which was published in the *Frankfurter Zeitung* on 26 May 1943. The narrative describes a train trip taken by a man ("His uniform was threadbare and faded") together with a girl. The views through the window—"a roughcast brick house, a garden, a fence, a few fruit trees"—appear as "a slight allegory of peace, which time did not want to grant them." The visible objects seem to interchange with one another and do not create any spatial experience ("everything seemed to flow"). The slanted position in a curve makes apparent the unrest that threatens the couple because of the separation: "The horizon rose, the trees leaned to the side and stood crooked for a moment, as if they had also been grasped by centrifugal force." Out of this "*Schauder*" (shudder), the soldier and the girl invent a house with pigeons, many rooms, and poplars for themselves ("When the wind comes, it sounds like water"). However, when the conversation touches upon the potential architect, contact with life's reality is reestablished by memory ("… if he had not been killed. In Russia"). At this point, Lange converts the dialog into a soliloquy of the protagonist and creates awareness of time: "He didn't answer himself, he watched the clock and calculated, how many hours would still pass, until they would reach the destination. 'The only question is,' he said so loudly that he startled himself, 'whether we'll ever get there, where we belong?'"

The periodicals in which Lange's stories appeared on 23 May 1943 show how difficult it was not to suffer a loss of time in the fragmented experience of reality. The *Frankfurter Zeitung* was then still being published in two daily editions; not until the end of August did the bureaucracy order a suspension of the publication within the framework of a "media consolidation necessitated by the war effort." Both editions of 23 May 1943 contain fourteen pages. Nonpolitical news and commentary had the largest share with 3.75 pages, followed by 3.35 pages of classifieds and advertisements, 3.1 pages of culture, and 2 pages of business news; political news and commentaries appeared on only 1.8 pages. Page one of the first edition, which begins with a travel essay by editor-in-chief Rudolf Kircher on the "Burg von Tomar" (Castle of Tomar) in Portugal, demonstrates how problematic it was to distinguish between nonpolitical and political texts, especially during the Third Reich. Clearly separated by a line on the right-hand side, one can read the "Reports from the Führer's Headquarters" and a commentary on the German-Italian Friendship Pact. The lower third is reserved for Lange's long narrative. This seemingly objective layout tempts the reader to assume a linkage between the allegedly independent articles. The news that the "Local offensives of the Soviets in the area north of Lissitschansk … had failed … in hand-to-hand combat and [the Soviets] suffered great bloody losses" is glorified by references to the "truly occidental idealism" with which the Christian knights mentioned in the travel essay had "hurled themselves at [the approaching] Islamic [forces]" and by references to the depiction of the "most distinctive" church, "gleaming in gold and pale colors." Only the readers' consciousness could decide whether Lange's story participated in this process or whether it could unfold its potential of revoking heroism. In both editions of 23 May, "The House Never Entered" does not exist in isolation. It positions itself next to and thus creates a connection to other texts, for example, to Christian Grunert's study of flowers on the Kaiserkrone. Lange's experience of time, however, is echoed in only one contribution to this issue, and that is Friedrich Sieburg's sketch "A Parisian Summer," a passage from his *Robespierre* (1935), which presents a picture of a feverish desire at the end of the revolution: the rich, though under threat of arrest and death, are still openly eating ice cream, apple pastries, and sturgeon in white wine in front of cafés; fashion exposes "carnal beauty" during this summer, while there is neither bread nor fat for most of the people; "no soap, no shoes," yet "Paris tries to live, as if everything was just like it was before."

This immersion into the private sphere mirrors—in connection with the 23 May 1943 issue of the *Frankfurter Zeitung*—the consciousness of the Germans. Twenty-six movie theaters were advertised in the entertainment section for Frankfurt, hotels promoted themselves and their swimming pools with cafés that were "fully operational," as did German theaters in The Hague, Cracow, Oslo, Strasbourg, and Paris. Although weekly meat rations had to be reduced by another 100 grams, there was still "an abundant selection of skin creams, lipsticks." The *Handelsblatt* reported that "Lindes Eismaschinen distribute another 5% profit" and reprinted New York's "stock market news." The state cynically feigned being a caretaker when the barbaric destruction reached its apex: "Goethe's summerhouse in Weimar has fallen into great disrepair over the last years due to ground water levels. The northern side wall will now be renewed in order to protect the house in which Goethe had lived six years from further damage." The Öffentliche Bausparkasse (Public Savings Bank) promised a "house of one's own," a "blissful island in the river of life"; the Badenia GmbH announced "an information session on 'financing and building after the war'" for 27 May 1943 that included a "display of modern homes." The doubt expressed in Lange's "The House Never Entered"—"whether we'll ever get there, where we belong"—was quickly assuaged in such a context. The wishful thinking that was destroying every realistic experience of the times was also being supplemented by the distorted images of the official ideology. Thus, Alfred Rosenberg presented stereotypical projections of madness in a speech published on the front page of the second edition of 23 May 1943 designed to remove the chaotic presence from the perception of reality; he consigned the "madness" to the past of the Republic, "when Germany tore itself apart in civil war and interior conflict," or to Bolshevism, which was making a last attempt "to dissolve and crush Europe."

The "Model Case" of Alfred Andersch

When Hitler's order regarding the final solution was put into action, Alfred Andersch applied for a divorce from his half-Jewish wife. His brother remembered this decision—"his own development" was "more important" to him (Reinhardt, 82)—since Andersch could only become a member of the Reichsschrifttumskammer only after the separation, which took effect on 6 March 1943. Unlike the prose of Horst Lange, the language of his stories, which he submitted to the Suhrkamp Verlag for publication (see *Erinnerte Gestalten*), is replete with key terms of the official propaganda. In 1943, Andersch applied for a transfer to a propaganda unit, yet apparently his plan failed because of his political past. As a "green soldier," he was disappointed in life on the military base and complained in December 1943 that he found himself in a "mixed-up heap, in which no camaraderie exists and in which the many sick persons etc. create a nauseating atmosphere of slacking and shirking" (*Tagebuch*, 20). The war itself seemed to Andersch a travel adventure. "I sit in Kufstein and drink a red wine, and far below the Inn flows by," he wrote home on 27 May 1944 (39). With the U.S. Army advancing, Andersch changed sides. In his report *Die Kirschen der Freiheit* (The Cherries of Freedom, 1952), he glorified his communist past by almost exclusively and provocatively presenting his incarceration in a concentration camp in 1933 and his desertion in 1944. "My book seems to have hit the bull's eye," Andersch wrote in a letter. "I believe that now I have really become a famous man; the PEN-Club has already contacted me" (78).

As we know from the biography by Stephan Reinhardt, Andersch is actually a "model case" for the compulsion to legitimize that postwar society had imposed upon itself, so that fabrications and a successful reconstruction blur together. Only by ignoring his life in the Third Reich, beyond acknowledging the most important dates, could Andersch sell himself as a "moral authority" (Heidelberger-Leonhard, 51). Completely devoid of irony, *Kirschen* takes up the empty pathos of his early stories, except that it no longer propagates an integration into but rather a departure from the *Kolonne*. This retreat has all the characteristics of an attack, as if the direction of the movement no longer mattered: "And the full-mooned, acacia-scented troop movement raced down the street, with moon and dust along the Aurelia, in the thunderous roar of the columns, in the wild, furious grating of the tanks' caterpillar tracks, in the flying hair of the men who stood in the hatch of the tanks" (Und der vollmondige, akazienduftende Feldzug raste die Straße entlang, mit Mond und Staub die Aurelia entlang, im donnernden Gedröhn der Kolonnen, im wilden, aufreizenden Knirschen der Raupenketten, im fliegenden Haar der Männer, die in den Luke der Panzer standen). Negative expressions such as "dusty muffled cries of commando-calls" or the "moon-pale triumph of wafting billows [Fahnen-flags] of dust," sprinkled into the text later, merely create a dark backdrop for the heroic style (51). Detached from factual reality, Andersch succumbed in *Kirschen* to the fascination emanating from speed and its inherent violence; transit itself, not the message delivered by the troops, was of importance. The desertion to the Americans did not begin a new time for Andersch but merely opened up a new space, in which it was necessary to make connections as quickly as possible. It is not the fact that the author exploited his stay in a concentration camp and his desertion at the expense of the entire truth that is remarkable, but rather his memories, which are adversely affected and devoured by the experience of space. With his prose story "Erste Ausfahrt" (First Exit), published in 1944 in the *Kölnische Zeitung*, Andersch had already thematized the space into which the narrator plunges with knapsack and camping stove on a bicycle tour; in the place of fear and alienation, giddy euphoria flares up: "Then there was space, space, space!" However, the "bright glowing consciousness" and the "future" lose all temporalization; they harden into stereotypes (*Erinnerte Gestalten*, 169). The inability to comprehend the present situation as a moment of history does not allow for experience of temporal dimensions; being overwhelmed by space is an expression of the very same fragmentation with which the Third Reich operated its "Territorial Expansion Economy" (*Raumwirtschaft*), "Expansion Research" (*Raumforschung*), and "Politics of Greater Expansion" (*Großraumpolitik*), in order to argue, in a delusional way, for a "new territorial division of the earth."[21] National Socialist architecture had a preference for undeveloped surfaces. One tore down mature structures or separated the new buildings from adjoining old buildings by dividing walls (Bartetzko, 55–56); a space created in such a way was construction and picture at the same time. The Third Reich presented itself as a swift series of transitional landscapes, which one had to traverse block by block so that the gruesome reality of the "collapse" was perceived ahistorically. *Kahlschlag* ("clear-cutting" of overblown literary style), *Stunde Null* (Zero Hour), *Tabula-Rasa-Situation* (clean-slate situation) were the slogans, with which the self continued to value space over time in order to establish itself comfortably in the soon-to-be-cleared expanses of rubble.

Postwar Culture and Postmodernism

Hannah Arendt was surprised after a visit in 1950 by how little the "nightmare of destruction and terror" had penetrated into consciousness. "In the midst of piles of rubble," the Germans would write "postcards with pictures … of churches and market places … that no longer existed" (Arendt, 24). The absence of mourning, she noted, had been covered up by "feverish activity," while little of the "old virtue to achieve as splendid a final product as possible independent of work conditions" remained. Everywhere, "mediocre production" (35) prevailed along with the "exaggerated hope … that the country would become Europe's most modern" (28–29). In the arts, the "German flight from reality" (21) and the related compulsion to demolish and modernize corresponded with the attempt "to liberate themselves from a lack of connectedness with the outside world" (Krolow, 13) and to quickly participate again in the "world language of poetry" (Bender, 10). Although the postwar writers did not tire of confessing the guilt of the Third Reich, the ease with which they had, almost without exception, ignored their own history is surprising; thus, "they served more the institutional forgetting rather than a cathartic remembrance, just as the mechanically ... repeated ceremonies of official mourning did" (Kertész, 18). Art then operated on the same plane as politics—a plane antagonistic to reality. Everything functioned, often in the most spectacular way, to give the impression of reconstructing a pre-National Socialist world. Most important now became the most modern design—a façade behind which actual dependencies of the Third Reich could hide, along with their personal histories. As director of radio programming and editor of the journal *Texte und Zeichen*, Andersch assumed a key role in spreading the avant-garde. "Andersch is a *very* influential man, who can be not only very useful but also, if one makes him an enemy, very damaging," Arno Schmidt noted (Rauschenbach, 209: letter to Josef Bläschke on 4 July 1959).

The fact that government agencies and institutions and private economic entities gradually began to acknowledge violations of taboos exposes the historical break between the new culture and the bourgeois Boheme. While exuberant rejection of all limits characterized the arts after World War I, the Group 47 soon found itself on the verge of becoming a commercial trust in order to integrate its members into the cultural entertainment establishment. "Even a whole set of managers, editors, broadcasters, and journalists was present, and their presence gave the meeting something of the character of a literary stock exchange," it had already been noted in a 1951 symposium report (see Rohnert, 147). We almost all forgot that several painters and writers who had been defamed in the Third Reich registered this development apprehensively. Thus, during the awards ceremony of the *Deutscher Kunstpreis* in 1950, Karl Hofer deplored "indifference" and spoke of a "new kind of artistic craftsmanship with beautifully colored ... surfaces, organized with subtle refinement" (Hofer, *Katalog*, 645). In the debate with Will Grohmann that took place in 1955 shortly before his death, Hofer's goal was not to denounce abstract art, of which he had been wrongly accused, but rather to deplore the quick self-satisfaction with mediocre products that had been observed by Hannah Arendt.

He clairvoyantly revealed cultural industry's technique of compensating for diminishing emotions by continually creating new slogans and replacing the idols of the avant garde as soon as the public mood changed. Thus Hofer predicted a "naturalism that had already passed through a stage of abstraction" as a countermovement, without expecting a renewal of art, because "anything too conscious and intentional bears the stigma of the transient" (Hofer, "Zur Situation der Bildenden Kunst," 428). Gottfried Benn expressed himself even more critically than Hofer in his letters to Oelze. On 19 July 1946, he failed to see personal "standards, guidelines, [and] laws" in "several leading personalities of the press and in Berlin literature [who were supplied] with huge cars again." According to Benn, everything bowed "without any shame or thought to the key terms the public demanded and espoused" (*Briefe*, 38–39). Two years later, he diagnosed in his young visitors "harmless smooth brains that did not think of anything independently," and he asked Oelze "whether we had been as empty, when we were 20 years old" (*Briefe*, 146: 22 July 1948). Adorno reached a similar conclusion after returning from his American exile. In his first essay published in the German Federal Republic (1950), he discovered the contradiction of a "desperate will to culture" (*verzweifelten Kulturwillens*) with a fearful search for protection in the "conventional and what had been" (*Herkömmlichem und Gewesenem*) and argued that, compared with Expressionism, „an eerie traditionalism prevailed without any binding tradition." Because the new artists nourished themselves from the stocks of the avant-garde of old "they destroy what they themselves profess" (Adorno, 473).[22]

The criticism that had been silenced as stabilization of the Federal Republic progressed had oriented itself anachronistically to the standards of the Bohemian culture of the *Kaiserreich* and of the Weimar Republic. Therefore, it recognized the fundamental nature of social change. Not until the Adenauer era did the reductionist argument take root that the violent nature of the Third Reich was exclusively responsible for cultural and civilizational losses. This argument did not take into account the epochal changes that occurred, with certain delays, in all industrial societies. For a long time this transformation was difficult to comprehend because the majority still rejected the formal arsenal of the avant-garde as a means of provocation; this fact masked all too well the paralysis that afflicted most of the works succeeding it. Since National Socialism had already denounced modernity as a bluff, each inquiry into its rank (or position) could be misunderstood as reactionary. In addition, traces of Bohemian art kept on occurring in the works of individual authors writing as late as the 1970s. Rolf Dieter Brinkmann with *Rome, Views* (Rom, Blicke, 1979), and Bernward Vespers with *The Trip* (Die Reise, 1977) turned to the most inconspicuous details of their "universe of fear and death" in order to confront the reader directly with the truth of everyday barbarism; in retrospect it appears too optimistic to consider this fact an indication of the renewal of the bourgeois avant-garde. If postmodernist theoreticians now openly admit their imitations of modernist patterns and propagate a kind of computer game (Ortheil, 59), then they have only drawn the obvious conclusion from a practice that has been in place for a long time, which cannot be simply reversed. Already Hofer had recognized that "the art of our time ... definitely corresponds to our time and from this fact derives its legitimacy" (Hofer, *Katalog*, 647).

In opposition to postmodernism, many postwar authors hid behind values of the Bohemian culture, which included, among others, independent personality, a claim of truthfulness, distance and detachment and thinking in categories of time, as well as a sense of responsibility and an authentic voice. The support and popularization both of authors of the *Stunde Null* and of artifacts and genuine products of modernity legitimized the German Federal Republic as the successor state to the Weimar Republic and distanced it from both the Third Reich and the GDR. With the silent collapse of the eastern block, "the last remnants of a bourgeois ideology had left the stage of history" (Kondylis, 292). The resulting vacuum no longer required opposition and diminished even further the importance of the older forms of thought and life. National Socialism dramatically accelerated the dissolution of regional *Sonderkulturen* (special cultures) and the sense of being rooted in a social class; the mechanisms of the welfare society perforated the sense of responsibility toward strangers and weakened the ability to perceive unbearable living conditions. One must also consider the sphere of the arts a part of this process, with its unparalleled upward mobility and its nearly perfected system of benefits.

The bourgeois Bohème and its independence were replaced by a large number of producers and a network of privileges and obligations, which entrapped artists of almost all branches who became art bureaucrats and entrepreneurs. The brutal regime of the government and the institutionalized "antimodernism" have long misled scholars, keeping them from considering the period from 1933 to 1945 under this aspect. Yet while National Socialist boycotts of excellence (i.e., excellent art) led to a decline of public life, the party also increased its expenditures on prizes, stipends, and purchases to tie the majority of artists and artisans to itself. In both of his speeches on culture in 1937, Hitler expressly defended "well-meaning, decent average performance" (7 September 1937: Domarus, 718) and promised "an unheard of blossoming of German art," since "never before" had "the allocation of the necessary funds [been] more generous ... than in National Socialist Germany" (19 June 1937: Domarus, 708). After the "collapse," political dictatorship no longer affected the cultural sector of the West; the popularization of "degenerate art," however, merely created an illusion of a new high culture. Even though bourgeois-democratic values were being propagated and the connection to the obliterated Bohème had been formally acknowledged, paralysis held sway due to social and spiritual impoverishments, such as the dominance of economics in public places and the tendency born of insecurity to sacrifice the truth on the altar of immediate success. "Art for everyone," the whittling down of complex language into simple images, mass production by the media conglomerate, and the waning of critical distance connect the culture before and after 1945 to a postmodernism that no longer tries to use projections of meaning to conceal fragmentation. Imre Kertész does not consider "violence and destructivism" a "unique misstep" but regards them as "the primary characteristic" (Kertész, 10) of our age, which could break out any time under a new guise. The "dichotomy of the human being" between his private sphere and the functional conditions of its maintenance drives "the individual as well as society into a situation which is becoming more and more schizophrenic" (10); "categories of space ... still determine" thought (Jameson, 61); our production of imagery, like that of the National Socialists, is "obsessed with pseudo events and spectacular happenings" (ibid., 63), so that the illusion euphorically asserts itself in the place of reality. It is contrary to history to demand a return to the norms of high culture, because with this return, "modernism itself would be pressed into service of an anti-modern resentment" (Huyssen, 30). It may not be important to unmask postmodern art as rubbish, but it is important to unmask the illusion behind which a humankind that is exposed to ever increasing pressure threatens to disappear.

Translated by Damon O. Rarick

Notes

1. See Dröge and Müller, *Die Macht der Schönheit. Avantgarde und Faschismus oder die Geburt der Massenkultur* (1995). The following thoughts are beholden to this important book.
2. I owe thanks to Hans-Ernst Mittig for the reference to Eckart Dietzfelbinger, *Der Umgang der Stadt Nürnberg mit dem früheren Parteitagsgelände* (21–22), in which he writes about the dilapidation of the Zeppelin-grandstand "due to decades-long frost damage and water permeation" and the costs "pertaining to historical preservation laws." Cf. also Hans-Ernst Mittig, "Dauerhaftigkeit, einst Denkmalargument" (11–34).
3. Prof. Werner Peiner (design) and Kasimir Edschmid (text), *Der Rhein von Köln bis Bingen*, Shell-Rheinkarte.
4. Reinhard Tgahrt pointed out the quote to me.
5. Compare Benn's letter to Oelze on 11 April 1942 about Alexander Lernet-Holenia, where it is written: "... sondern ins Elegante und Gesellschaftliche. Also etwas Undeutsches" (*Briefe*, 312).
6. At the meeting 1952 in Knokke. Conversation of the author with Wilhelm Lehmann on 14 May 1965. Compare also the letter to Oelze dated 29 March 1936 (*Briefe*, 124): "Pourtalès ist ein netter Schriftsteller. Ich las sein Buch über *Chopin* 'Der blaue Klang' (oder ähnlich). Gefiel mir gut" (Pourtalès is a nice writer. I read his book about *Chopin* "The Blue Sound" [or something similar]. I liked it).
7. See H. D. Schäfer, *Herr Oelze aus Bremen* (2001).
8. Compare to the relationship of bourgeois identity as a "monad-like container" and "unique style" in Jameson, 60.
9. Raddatz, 33–36. Cf. Reich-Ranicki. For a summary of the responses in this debate, see also the German original of this article.
10. According to the recording of the radio play *Rebellion in der Goldstadt* (1997). See H.D. Schäfer, "Eichs Fall" (2002).
11. Dated 1933 in *Gedichte* (Berlin 1948, 77), with the title "Im nassen Sand" in *Die Dame* 22 (October 1941): 34; cf. Schäfer, this volume, "The Young Generation's Non-National Socialist Literature," 73.
12. Nijssen, 628. The radio play is not publicly accessible and is archived at Monica Huchel's estate in Staufen.
13. "Neckermann. Katalog gegen Kartelle," *Der Spiegel* 44 (10 October 1955): 24–25.
14. "Grundig. Die neuen Größen," *Der Spiegel* 3 (15 January 1958): 20.

15. "Wohnungsbau. Neue Heimat," *Der Spiegel* 10 (4 March 1959): 27–28.
16. "'Ich hake diesen Fall auch ab.' Frau Christiansen fragt, Herr Augstein antwortet," *die tageszeitung*, Ausgabe West (4–5 January 1997): 16.
17. "Rudolf Augstein: In eigener Sache," *Der Spiegel* 52 (21 December 1992): 75–76 with a copy of the "Frau aus der Fremde," the story that the author claimed had been submitted to the *Völkischer Beobachter* without his knowledge by an agency; this discovery was made by Christian Michelides in *Forum* 468 (1992): 11–12.
18. "Die Tyrannei des Kindlichen," *Der Spiegel* 9 (24 February 1997): 223.
19. Wolfdietrich Schnurre, "Vom inneren Reifen. Trost und Verheißung im Alltag des Krieges. Vom Obergefreiten Wolfdietrich Schnurre," *Front und Heimat* (December 1944): 7.
20. Wolfdietrich Schnurre, "Das Schlachtfeld des Herzens. Wenn der Soldat zur Feder greift. Die Frage nach Stil und Gehalt, beantwortet von Wolfdietrich Schnurre," *Front und Heimat* (December 1944). Both essays follow Engler, 409. The index of books lists more than a dozen *Truppenbetreuungsblätter* with the same title: "die Angaben verdanke ich den (unvollständigen) Notizen des Autors auf den Artikeln,… ich hatte noch die Möglichkeit, ein paar Stunden das Schnurre-Archiv einzusehen, bevor es an die Akademie der Künste ging" (Jürgen Engler, letter to author dated 18 March 1997).
21. Hans Havemann, "Im Bann des Raumes," *Das Reich* 13 (26 March 1944). Literatur/ Kunst/Wissenschaft mit Hinweisen auf die inflationäre Verwendung des Begriffs; als Beweggrund des Raumdenkens nannte Havemann neue Medien wie Kino sowie die Revolution im Transportwesen: "Es geht so schnell durchs Bunte und Wechselnde, daß wir ständig wendebereit und raumorientiert sein müssen."
22. See H. D. Schäfer on postwar culture, *Avantgarde* (2001).

Works Cited

Adorno, Theodor. "Auferstehung der Kultur in Deutschland?" *Frankfurter Hefte* 5 (1950).
Andersch, Alfred. *Die Kirschen der Freiheit: Ein Bericht*. Frankfurt am Main: Frankfurter Verlags-Anstalt, 1952.
———. "… *Einmal wirklich leben": ein Tagebuch in Briefen an Hedwig Andersch, 1943 bis 1975*. Ed. Winfried Stephan. Zürich: Diogenes, 1986.
———. *Erinnerte Gestalten: Frühe Erzählungen*. Zürich: Diogenes, 1986.
Arendt, Hannah. *Besuch in Deutschland*. Berlin: Rotbuch, 1993.
Arntzen, Helmut. "Nebeneinander. Film, Literatur, Denken und Sprache der Dreißiger Jahre." In *Ursprung der Gegenwart: Zur bewusstseinsgeschichte der Dreißiger Jahre in Deutschland*, ed. Helmut Arntzen, 1–168. Weinheim: Beltz Athenäum, 1995.
Augstein, Rudolf. "'Ich hake diesen Fall auch ab.' Frau Christiansen fragt, Herr Augstein antwortet." *die tageszeitung* (4–5 January 1997): 16.
———. "Rudolf Augstein: In eigener Sache." *Der Spiegel* 52 (21 December 1992): 75–76.
Barbian, Jan-Pieter. *Literaturpolitik im Dritten Reich: Institutionen, Kompetenzen, Betätigungsfelder*. Munich: Deutscher Taschenbuchverlag, 1995.
Bartetzko, Dieter. *Illusionen in Stein. Stimmungsarchitektur im deutschen Faschismus: ihre Vorgeschichte in Theater- und Film-Bauten*. Reinbek bei Hamburg: Rowohlt, 1985.
Bateson, Gregory. *Schizophrenie und Familie: Beiträge zu einer neuen Theorie*. Theorie. Vol. 2. Frankfurt am Main: Suhrkamp, 1969.
Bender, Hans. *Vorwort zu Widerspiel. Deutsche Lyrik seit 1945*. Munich: Hanser, 1962.
Benn, Gottfried. *Briefe an F. W. Oelze 1932–1945*. Foreword by F. W. Oelze. Ed. Harald Steinhagen and Jürgen Schröder. Wiesbaden: Limes, 1977.
———. "Chopin." In *Sämtliche Werke*. Vol. 1: *Gedichte I*, ed. Gerhard Schuster, 180–81. Stuttgart: Klett-Cotta, 1986.

———. "IV. Block II, Zimmer 66." In *Sämtliche Werke*. Vol. 5: *Prosa III*, ed. Gerhard Schuster, 122–39. Stuttgart: Klett-Cotta, 1991.

———. "Nachtcafé." In *Sämtliche Werke*. Vol. 1: *Gedichte I*, ed. Gerhard Schuster, 19. Stuttgart: Klett-Cotta, 1986.

———. "Probleme der Lyrik." In *Sämtliche Werke*. Vol. 6: *Prosa IV*, ed. Holger Hof. Stuttgart: Klett-Cotta, 2001.

———. "Teils-teils." In *Sämtliche Werke*. Vol. 1: *Gedichte I*, ed. Gerhard Schuster, 317–18. Stuttgart: Klett-Cotta, 1986.

———. "Totenrede für Klabund." In *Sämtliche Werke*. Vol. 3: *Prosa I*, ed. Gerhard Schuster, 196–200. Stuttgart: Klett-Cotta, 1987.

Berger, Albert. "Götter, Dämonen und Irdisches. Josef Weinhebers dichterische Metaphysik." In *Österreichische Literatur der dreißiger Jahre: Ideologische Verhältnisse, institutionelle Voraussetzungen*, ed. Klaus Amann and Albert Berger. Vienna: Bohlau Verlag, 1985.

Blencke, Katharina. *Wolfdietrich Schnurres Nachlass: Katalogisierung, Systematisierung und Darstellung der Werkgeschichte, mit einer Bibliographie der Primär- und Sekundärliteratur*. Literatur- und Medienwissenschaft. Vol. 19. Paderborn: Igel, 1993.

Borchert, Wolfgang. *Allein mit meinem Schatten und dem Mond: Briefe, Gedichte und Dokumente*. Ed. Gordon J. A. Burgess and Michael Töteberg. Reinbek bei Hamburg: Rohwolt, 1996.

———. *Das Gesamtwerk* [GW in text]. Hamburg: Rowohlt, 1949.

Caemmerer, Christiane, and Walter Delabar, eds. *Dichtung im Dritten Reich? Zur Literatur in Deutschland 1933–45*. Opladen: Westdeutscher Verlag, 1996.

Cuomo, Glenn R. *Career at the Cost of Compromise: Günter Eich's Life and Work in the Years 1933–1945*. Amsterdamer Publikationen zur Sprache und Literatur (APSL). Vol. 82. Amsterdam: Rodopi, 1989.

Czucka, Eckehard. "Tatsachen-Bilder. Literatur zwischen 1930 und 1940. Zum Beispiel Friedo Lampe und Wilhelm Lehmann." In *Ursprung der Gegenwart: Zur Bewusstseinsgeschichte der Dreißiger Jahre in Deutschland*, ed. Helmut Arntzen, 419–86. Weinheim: Beltz Athenäum, 1995.

Damus, Martin. "Postmoderne und regionalistische Architektur." In *Inszenierung der Macht: ästhetische Faszination im Faschismus*, ed. Klaus Behnken and Frank Wagner. Berlin: NGBK (Neue Gesellschaft für Bildende Kunst), 1987.

Denk, Friedrich. *Die Zensur der Nachgeborenen: zur regimekritischen Literatur im Dritten Reich*. Weilheim in Oberbayern: Denk-Verlag, 1995.

Dietzfelbinger, Eckart. *Der Umgang der Stadt Nürnberg mit dem früheren Reichsparteitagsgelände*. Beiträge zur politischen Bildung. Vol. 26. Nuremberg: Pädagagogisches Institut, 1990.

Domarus, Max, ed. *Hitler Reden und Proklamationen, 1932–1945*. Vol. 1. Munich: Süddeutscher Verlag, 1965.

Döring, Jörg. "Eulenspiegel schreibt Gespenstergeschichten. Wolfgang Koeppen im Dritten Reich." In *Dichtung im Dritten Reich? Zur Literatur in Deutschland 1933–45*, ed. Christiane Caemmerer and Walter Delabar, 115–18. Opladen: Westdeutscher Verlag, 1996.

Dröge, Franz and Michael Müller. *Die Macht der Schönheit: Avantgarde und Faschismus oder die Geburt der Massenkultur*. Europäische Bibliothek. Vol. 21. Hamburg: Europäische Verlagsanstalt, 1995.

Dürer, Albrecht. *Schriften und Briefe*. Reclam-Bibliothek. Ed. Ernst Ullmann. 6th ed. Vol. 26. Leipzig: Reclam Verlag, 1993.

Eich, Günter. *Gesammelte Werke in vier Bänden*. Ed. Axel Vieregg. Vol. 4. Vermischte Schriften. Frankfurt am Main: Suhrkamp, 1991.

———. *Rebellion in der Goldstadt. Tonkassette, Text und Materialien*. Ed. Karl Karst. Frankfurt am Main: Suhrkamp, 1997.

Ekelöf, Gunnar. "Ein Schicksal der dreißiger Jahre." In *Der Weg eines Aussenseiters: Erzählungen und Essays*. Vol. 1015. Reclams Universal-Bibliothek. Leipzig: Reclam, 1983.

Engler, Jürgen. "Die 'Schizophrenie' des Anfangs. Wolfdietrich Schnurre—ein Autor der 'Trümmerliteratur.'" In *Unterm Notdach: Nachkriegsliteratur in Berlin 1945–1949*, ed. Ursula Heukenkamp. Berlin: Schmidt, 1996.

Gabel, Joseph. *Ideologie und Schizophrenie: Formen der Entfremdung*. Frankfurt am Main: S. Fischer Verlag, 1967.

Graf, Johannes. *Friedo Lampes Erzählung 'Am Rande der Nacht.' Konservative Philosophie und avantgardistische Form*. Master's thesis. Freie Universität Berlin, 1989–90.

Grubbe, Peter. "'Ich bin mit mir im Reinen.' Der linksliberale Autor Peter Grubbe über seine nationalsozialistische Vergangenheit als Kreishauptmann in Kolomea." *Der Spiegel* (9 October 1995): 250–52.

Hachmeister, Lutz. "Mein Führer, es ist ein Wunder!" *die tageszeitung* (27 December 1996): 12; *Der Spiegel. Sonderausgabe 1947–1997*: 14–15.

———. "Der Amnesie-Klub. Auch zum 50sten Jubiläum ist beim *Spiegel* eine Analyse der eigenen Geschichte unerwünscht." *die tageszeitung* (18–19 January 1997): 30.

Heidelberger-Leonhard, Irene. "Erschriebener Widerstand. Fragen an Alfred Anderschs Werk und Leben." In *Alfred Andersch: Perspektiven zu Leben und Werk*, ed. Volker Wehdking. Opladen: Westdeutscher Verlag, 1994.

Heintel, Helmut, ed. *Block II, Zimmer 66: Gottfried Benn in Landsberg, 1943–1945. Eine bildliche Dokumentation*. Stuttgart: Urachhaus, 1988.

Hesse, Anja. *Malerei des Nationalsozialismus. Der Maler Werner Peiner (1897–1984)*. Studien zur Kunstgeschichte. Vol. 94. Hildesheim: Georg Olms Verlag, 1995.

Heukenkamp, Ursula, ed. *Unterm Notdach: Nachkriegsliteratur in Berlin 1945–1949*. Berlin: Schmidt, 1996.

Hinz, Berthold. *Dürers Gloria: Kunst, Kult, Konsum* (Ausstellung der Kunstbibliothek Staatliche Museen Preussischer Kulturbesitz Berlin, 24. September bis 28. November 1971). Berlin: Mann, 1971.

Hofer, Karl. *Katalog Staatliche Kunsthalle*. Berlin: Staatliche Kunsthalle Berlin 1978.

———. "Zur Situation der Bildenden Kunst." *Der Monat* 8 (1955): 428.

Huyssen, Andreas. "Postmoderne—eine amerikanische Internationale?" In *Postmoderne: Zeichen eines kulturellen Wandels*, ed. Andreas Huyssen and Klaus R. Scherpe. Reinbek bei Hamburg: Rowohlt, 1986.

Jameson, Frederic. "Zur Logik der Kultur im Spätkapitalismus." In *Postmoderne: Zeichen eines kulturellen Wandels*, ed. Aendreas Huyssen and Klaus R. Scherpe. Reinbek bei Hamburg: Rowohlt Taschenbuch Verlag, 1986.

Kertész, Imre. *Meine Rede über das Jahrhundert. Angesichts unseres Jahrhunderts*. Vol. 5. Hamburg: Hamburger Edition, 1995.

Kirchner, Doris. *Doppelbödige Wirklichkeit: Magischer Realismus und nicht-faschistische Literatur*. Stauffenburg Colloquium. Vol. 27. Tübingen: Stauffenburg, 1993.

Koeppen, Wolfgang. *Die Mauer schwankt*. Berlin: B. Cassirer, 1935.

Kondylis, Panajotis. *Der Niedergang der bürgerlichen Denk- und Lebensformen. Die liberale Moderne und die massendemokratische Postmoderne*. Weinheim: VCH, 1991.

Kreis, Gabriele. *"Was man glaubt, gibt es." Das Leben der Irmgard Keun*. Zürich: Arche, 1991.

Kreis, Gabriele, and Marjory S. Strauss, eds. *Ich lebe in einem wilden Wirbel. Briefe an Arnold Strauss 1933–1947*. Düsseldorf: Claassen, 1988.

Krolow, Karl. *Aspekte zeitgenössischer Lyrik*. Munich: List, 1963.

Lange, Horst. "Das nie betretene Haus." In Horst Lange, *Windsbraut: Erzählungen*, 36–44. Hamburg: Claasen and Goverts, 1947.

Mittig, Hans-Ernst. "Dauerhaftigkeit, einst Denkmalargument." In *Mo(nu)mente: Formen und Funktionen ephemerer Denkmäler*, ed. Michael Diers and Andreas Beyer. Vol. 5. Artefact. Berlin: Akademie Verlag, 1993.

———. "NS-Architektur in uns." *Beiträge zur politischen Bildung* 10 (1991): 20

Nijssen, Hub. "Peter Huchel als Propagandist? Über die Autorschaft des Hörspiels 'Die Greuel von Denshawai.'" *Neophilologus* 77, no. 4 (1993): 625–57.

Ortheil, Hanns-Josef. "Das Lesen—ein Spiel. Postmoderne Literatur? Die Literatur der Zukunft." *Die Zeit* (17 April 1987): 59.

Parker, Stephen. "Peter Huchel als Propandist? Huchels 1940 enstandene Adaption von Georg Bernard Shaws 'Die Greuel von Denshawai.'" *Rundfunk und Fernsehen* 39, no. 3 (1991): 343–52.

Pourtalès, Guy de. *Der blaue Klang: Friedrich Chopins Leben.* Freiburg: Urban, 1928.

Raddatz, Fritz J. "Wir werden weiterdichten, wenn alles in Scherben fällt." *Die Zeit* 42 (12 October 1979): 33–36.

Rauschenbach, Bernd, ed. *Arno Schmidt, der Briefwechsel mit Alfred Andersch: mit einigen Briefen von und an Gisela Andersch, Hans Magnus Enzenzberger, Helmut Heissenbüttel und Alice Schmidt.* Vol. 1. Zürich: Arno Schmidt Stiftung im Haffmans Verlag, 1985.

Reich-Ranicki, Marcel. "Verleumdung statt Aufklärung. Deutsche Schriftsteller im Dritten Reich. Zu einem *Zeit*-Dossier von Fritz J. Raddatz." *Frankfurter Allgemeine Zeitung* 243 (18 October 1979): 25.

Reinhardt, Stephan. *Alfred Andersch: eine Biographie.* Zürich: Diogenes, 1990.

Rohnert, Ernst Theodor. "Symposion junger Schriftsteller." *Das literarische Deutschland* (20 May 1951). In *Die Gruppe 47: Ein kritischer Grundriß,* ed. Hans Ludwig Arnold. Munich: edition text + kritik, 1980.

Sandmeyer, Peter. "Schreiben nach 1945. Ein Interview mit Wolfdietrich Schnurre." In *Literaturmagazin 7,* ed. Nicolas Born, Jürgen Manthey, and Delf Schmidt. Reinbek bei Hamburg: Rowohlt, 1977.

Schäfer, Hans Dieter. "Avantgarde als Werbung und Geste der Langen Fünfziger Jahren oder Hölderlin im Turm." In *Aufbruch ins 20. Jahrhundert: Über Avantgarden,* ed. Heinz Ludwig Arnold. Munich: edition text + kritik, 2001.

———. *Das Gespaltene Bewußtsein: Über deutsche Kultur und Lebenswirklichkeit 1933–1945.* Munich: Hanser, 1981.

———. "Der Mythos der jungen Kolonne." In *Martin Raschke 1905–1943: Studien und Quellen,* ed. Wilhelm Haefs, 29–40. Dresden: w.e.b. Universitätsverlag, 2002.

———. "Die nichtfaschistische Literatur der 'jungen Generation' im nationalsozialistischen Deutschland." In *Die deutsche Literatur im Dritten Reich: Themen, Traditionen, Wirkungen,* ed. Horst Denkler and Karl Prümm, 459–503. Stuttgart: Reclam, 1976. [Revised for inclusion in *Das Gespaltene Bewußtsein*]

———. "Eichs Fall." In *Martin Raschke 1905–1943: Studien und Quellen,* ed. Wilhelm Haefs, 115–33. Dresden: w.e.b. Universitätsverlag, 2002.

———. *Herr Oelze aus Bremen: Gottfried Benn und Friedrich Wilhelm Oelze.* Göttingen: Wallstein, 2001.

———. "Zur Periodisierung der deutschen Literatur seit 1930." *Literaturmagazin* 7 (1977): 95–115. [Included in revised form in *Das Gespaltene Bewußtsein*]

Scheffel, Michael. *Magischer Realismus: die Geschichte eines Begriffes und ein Versuch seiner Bestimmung.* Stauffenburg Colloquium. Vol. 16. Tübingen: Stauffenburg, 1990.

Schneider, Reinhold. *Auf Wegen deutscher Geschichte: Eine Fahrt ins Reich.* Leipzig: Insel Verlag, 1934.

Schütz, Erhard. "Zwischen 'Kolonne' und 'Ethos des bescheidenen Standhaltens.' Zu den Romanen Horst Langes und August Scholtis während des Dritten Reichs." In *Dichtung im Dritten Reich? Zur Literatur in Deutschland 1933–45,* ed. Christiane Caemmerer and Walter Delabar, 77–95. Opladen: Westdeutscher Verlag, 1996.

Schwerte, Hans. "'Ich bin doch immun.' Spiegel-Reporter Walter Meyer über das zweite Leben des SS-Mannes Schneider." *Der Spiegel* (8 May 1995): 94–97.

Sieburg, Friedrich. "Ein Pariser Sommer." In Friedrich Sieburg, *Robespierre,* 199–208. Frankfurt am Main, 1935.

Steinhagen, Harald, Jürgen Schröder, and F. W. Oelze, eds. *Gottfried Benn: Briefe an F.W. Oelze, 1932–1945.* Vol. 1. Briefe. Wiesbaden: Limes, 1977.

Vieregg, Axel. *Der eigenen Fehlbarkeit begegnet: Günter Eichs Realitäten, 1933–1945.* Eggingen: Edition Isele, 1993.

———, ed. *Unsere Sünden sind Maulwürfe: die Günter-Eich-Debatte.* Vol. 36. Amsterdam: Rodopi, 1996.

Wehdeking, Volker. *Anfänge westdeutscher Nachkriegsliteratur. Aufsätze, Interviews, Materialien.* Aachen: Alano Rader, 1989.

Weinheber, Josef. "Albrecht Dürer. *Selbstbildnis in der Alten Pinakothek in München.*" In *Sämtliche Werke,* ed. Josef Nadler and Hedwig Weinheber. Vol. 2: *Die Hauptwerke,* ed. Friedrich Jenaczek, 348–49. Salzburg, 1954.

Weyrauch, Wolfgang. *Expeditionen: Deutsche Lyrik seit 1945.* Munich: Paul List, 1959.

———. "Letter from Wolfgang Weyrauch to Johannes R. Becher." *Aufbau* 7 (1948): 588.

———. *Von des Glücks Barmherzigkeit: Gedichte.* Berlin: Aufbau-Verlag, 1947.

Wieser, Harald. "Tod eines Pianisten. Spiegel-Autor Harald Wieser über das Naziopfer Karlrobert Kreiten und den Schreibtischtäter Werner Höfer." *Der Spiegel* (14 December 1987): 166.

Zoller, Albert. *Hitler privat. Ein Erlebnisbericht seiner Geheimsekretärin.* Düsseldorf: Droste, 1949.

Chapter 5

TARGETING THE READER, ENTERING HISTORY

A New Epitaph for the *Inner Emigration*

Frank Trommler

The View from Switzerland

In 1944, one of the most respected Swiss journals, *Neue Schweizer Rund-schau*, published an unusual article about the intellectual undercurrents in Germany. Under the pseudonym Angrivarius, the author tried to profile German intellectual elites in their rather faint attempts to counter the Nazi regime with essayistic, literary, and journalistic expressions of disapproval, even condemnation. The author refrained, with one exception, from mentioning names of the most outspoken critics in order not to endanger their lives. While careful not to exaggerate their influence, he made clear that they represented an important force for the period after Hitler's defeat—*if*, as he stressed, they truly disentangled themselves from the Prussian legacy of nationalism and militarism, the "Fridericus-Bismarck-Realpolitik-Komplex" (376).

The article was unusual in its dual perspective—Swiss observers might have called it neutral—combining insider information with a critical look from a non-German point of view. It is worth some attention as it provides a distancing, though sensitive approach to the ambivalent stance of cultural and political circles between preserving intellectual continuity with German history and resisting the "totalitarian" state. The author enumerated four areas around which oppositional thinking and literature crystallized: (1) the rejection of totalitarianism with its defining characteristics (the absence of freedom and rights, the empowerment of the masses, collectivism, imperialism, and mendacity), (2) the fear of the inevitable catastrophe, (3) the vague hope for an anticollectivistic social order, and (4) a disgust for political gigantism and a longing for privacy and the simple life. He highlighted these areas with some examples, which pointedly emphasize their traditional middle-class (*bürgerlich*) orientation, and found them best represented in Rudolf Pechel's journal *Deutsche Rundschau* and its circle of contributors and readers. The article projected neither the notion of resistance (Widerstand) as a political movement nor the concept of *inner emigration* (innere Emigration) as a form of intellectual existence. Its rather unassuming assessment seems almost an antidote to the fiery, often vicious battles that ensued over these concepts and their applicability after Germany's defeat, and helps frame the question of how the cultural elites, though labeled apolitical, were able to sustain the notion that they would be instrumental in determining Germany's future shape.

This question illuminates the role of literary writers both during the course of the Third Reich and in the political and cultural transformations after its catastrophic demise. If there was a legacy of writers such as Ernst Wiechert, Ricarda Huch, Werner Bergengruen, Reinhold Schneider, Albrecht Haushofer, and Friedrich Reck-Malleczewen, it lay in their often courageous stand on those core issues mentioned in the article: the suppression of freedom, the fight against tyranny, the longing for privacy and the simple life. Their careers and public reputation had been shaped by their literary articulation of these and related topics; they relied on special segments of the middle-classes as their reading public; they were closely observed by the authorities. Ernst Wiechert was put in a concentration camp, as were writers of the Left. Adam Kuckhoff was executed in Plötzensee. Reck-Malleczewen died in Dachau shortly before the end of the war. Albrecht Haushofer was put in prison and killed by the SS.

Yet, was this legacy also the core of the contributions with which inner emigrants participated in postwar literary life? In what way was it part of the effort to move Germany out of the self-inflicted moral misery of postwar academics, journalists, and other professionals, though tightly monitored by the occupation forces? Indeed, numerous networks around churches and political, religious, and academic groups traced their origins back to activities before 1945. While Berlin drew immediate attention thanks to the Russian interest in co-opting the German intelligentsia, cultural activities of similar stature sprang up in Heidelberg, Frankfurt, Hamburg, Munich, and Darmstadt, mostly supported by journals such as *Die Wandlung, Die Gegenwart,* and *Frankfurter Hefte.* Freer from the control of the occupying powers than the newspapers, they established an intellectual public sphere that furthered the transition to a new democracy even if contributors were rather unclear in their conception of what democracy entailed. Karl Jaspers, author of the widely discussed treatise *Die Schuldfrage* (1946), expressed it in the words: "We are allowed to talk publicly with one another. Let's see what we have to say to one another. Since we can again freely talk to one another, the first task is to really talk to one another. This is by no means easy" (Waldmüller, 54). Jaspers coedited what is arguably the most prominent of these journals, *Die Wandlung,* together with Alfred Weber, Werner Krauss and Dolf Sternberger, who defined as the journal's mission the discussion of guilt and resistance under National Socialism as the basis of a new political commitment (see Sternberger, "Die Herrschaft der Freiheit"). The title *Die Wandlung* was to indicate participation, maybe even leadership, in what the Swiss observer called "the largest and most important psychotherapeutic cure that the world has seen so far" (Angrivarius, 376).

Compared with this postwar work toward a profound *Wandlung* in all areas of cultural and political life, the prominent authors who had provided moral reflection during the reign of Hitler rarely took initiatives, as did, for instance, Ernst Wiechert with his "Rede an die deutsche Jugend" in November 1945 in Munich, or Erich Kästner, who helped establish the political cabaret "Schaubude" and, besides editing the cultural section of *Die Neue Zeitung*, published the critical youth magazine *Pinguin* from 1946 to 1949. Kästner successfully capitalized on his fame as an author of children's books and reached out to the young generation. While he used satire as part of political enlightenment, Wiechert, in his speech to the young generation, conjured the biblical image of Nazi Germany as Sodom and Gomorrah, where a few righteous people preserved humanity, though not without the guilt of the bystander. Wiechert belonged to those who were disenchanted with the unwillingness of their countrymen to address the past, even though his new novels, *Die Jeromin-Kinder* and *Missa sine nomine*, were extremely successful in Germany, while his earlier novels were reissued and reached a dedicated readership. In 1948 he moved to Switzerland.

The public profile of *inner emigration* as a unified phenomenon—which it never was[1]—drew its arguments mainly from the assumption that these writers, in their veiled opposition to the Hitler regime, represented a considerable portion of the German population, thus helping postwar Germany to regain moral credibility (Berglund, 219). That this was done at the expense of exile writers, as in the vitriolic letter exchange between Walter von Molo and Frank Thieß, on the one side, and Thomas Mann on the other, poisoned the air for many years, though it reflected the thinking of many Germans (see Grosser). This schism was not offset by the attempts at the first German writers' congress in Berlin in 1947, whose opening speakers Elisabeth Langgässer and Alfred Kantorowicz called for the building of a community between exile writers and those who had stayed in Germany. The onset of the Cold War, dramatically interrupting the congress,[2] destroyed what was left of the openness to addressing the disastrous entanglement of German culture with Nazism and instilled a new obsession with the division of Germany as part of the hostilities of the occupying powers. The language of common responsibility that undergirded the notion of *Wandlung* lost most of its weight.

The Academy of Inner Emigrants

It is hardly surprising that the most official step in assembling writers who had survived the Third Reich without undue moral compromise was taken explicitly without a program of action. Founded in the Frankfurt Paulskirche in 1949, the Deutsche Akademie für Sprache und Dichtung, whose seat was to be in Darmstadt, borrowed as its rationale the maxim of the French academy, proclaiming its desire to become "the highest body in the sanctioning of the current usage of language" (Assmann and Heckmann, 16). The list of its founding members, here given in toto, reads like a proclamation that the *inner emigration* was the basis for this kind of official recognition:

> Stefan Andres, Emil Barth, Werner Bergengruen, Heinrich Berl, Richard Gerlach, Albrecht Goes, Adolf Grimme, Wilhelm Hausenstein, Bernt von Heiseler, Gustav René Hocke, Walther von Hollander, Oskar Jancke, Christian Jenssen, Erich Kästner, Marie Luise von Kaschnitz, Jakob Kneip, Gottfried Kölwel, Horst Lange, Elisabeth Langgässer, Wilhelm Lehmann, Gustav Lindemann, Theodor Litt, Friedrich Märker, Karl August Meissinger, Werner Milch, Günther Müller, Rudolf Pechel, Josef Pieper, Hans Reisiger, Harry Reuss-Löwenstein, Luise Rinser, Otto Rombach, Oda Schaefer, Friedrich Schnack, Reinhold Schneider, Franz Joseph Schöningh, Rudolf Alexander Schröder, Werner von der Schulenburg, Bruno Snell, Hermann Stahl, Max Stefl, Gerhard Storz, W. E. Süskind, Otto Frhr. von Taube, Frank Thiess, Fritz Usinger, Leo Weismantel, Joseph Winckler, Leopold Ziegler. (Assmann and Heckmann, 22)

The academy's first decisions gave due recognition to writers of the *inner emigration*: it chose Rudolf Pechel as its first president in 1950 and Gottfried Benn as the first winner of the Büchner Prize in 1951. As an institution of aging writers with a particular legacy, it represented more or less itself, with a vague commitment to keeping out writers who had been tainted by National Socialism. It declined membership to Friedrich Sieburg, who became the most influential literary critic of the 1950s but who had been close to the German occupation forces in France. Increasingly committed to celebratory acts of representation in the new republic (also founded in 1949), the academy did not fulfill the mission of cleansing the German language; this task was more effectively accomplished by critics who, like Dolf Sternberger, were working in political science, journalism, or politics.[3]

The relative obscurity of this academy in the intellectual and scholarly debates about the course of West German literature since 1945 stands in contrast to the initial hopes for its role in the life of the Federal Republic. It maintained the legitimacy of those who had opposed Hitler and received full support from the highest official of the new republic, Theodor Heuss, who himself was a member; it offered a prestigious forum for writers who tried to revitalize literary life by calling on literary traditions that harkened back to the 1920s and before. As a matter of fact, despite the unwillingness to invite émigré writers—the "Emigrantenkomplex" (Assmann and Heckmann, 6)—the academy hearkened back most sympathetically, even longingly, to the colorful literary life of the Weimar Republic.

The hope to institute a measure of normalcy in matters of literature and culture after the devastations of the Nazi period was born by the rather extensive (and expensive) project of a literary journal in the tradition of the famed *Literarische Welt,* edited by Willy Haas in the 1920s. In the years 1950–52 under the title *Das literarische Deutschland,* edited by Gertrud von le Fort, Rudolf Alexander Schröder, Bruno Snell, and Gerhard Storz, and in 1952–53 under the title *Neue literarische Welt,* edited by Frank Thiess, the journal assembled an impressive array of contributors whose essays, poems, and reviews were to project what most members of the academy felt was missing in the contemporary scene: literary quality. The traditional German concept of *Dichtung* received a modernized reading. Longer articles about writers tended to bestow the term *Dichter* on them. A few months before the demise of the *Neue literarische Welt,* Heinz-Winfried Sabais, one of the most efficient cultural mediators on the conference scene and organizer of some of the intellectually most stimulating public discussions of the early 1950s, the "Darmstädter Gespräche," summarized the belief in the transforming power of *Dichtung* that shaped the journal's agenda. Under the headline, "Verändern die Dichter die Welt?" (Do Writers Transform the World?), Sabais asserted the power of literature in history:

> *Dichtung* is the uninterrupted catharsis and renaissance which takes place in the subject of mankind. Its dynamic toward meaning is superior to the dynamic of the external upheavals which are directed toward limited goals. Revolutions only result in a new state constitution or social structure; *Dichtung* writes the constitution of mankind on which all other constitutions depend. Therefore the fight over a poem often penetrates deeper into the core of an epoch than the fight over a section of the law. (Sabais, 2)

Reflecting this kind of literary self-empowerment, Sabais pointed to the fact that Claus von Stauffenberg, the leader of the conspiracy against Hitler on 20 July 1944, had belonged to the circle of devotees around Stefan George, and that many a soldier in the war, degraded to "human material," was able to remain a human being because he carried with him a volume of Rilke's poems.

The fact that the academy and the journal provided only a forum, not an engine, for new literary life has been attributed to provincialism or traditionalism, but the journal reintroduced such authors of modernism as Kafka, Hofmannsthal, Joyce, and Gide, and promoted a lively exchange with contemporary foreign authors, especially French ones, including the existentialists. This ambiguity or ambivalence about the journal's mission reflects a dilemma that is closely related to the legacy of the *inner emigration*: Can one really create a new post-Hitler moral and intellectual legitimacy by merely asseverating and reiterating one's integrity under Hitler? How can one create a post-Hitler literature by trying to remake normality without thematizing the terrible moral break with cherished traditions that the Nazis caused (and not diminishing this break by pointing to a general catastrophic downturn in modern history)? Promoting the integrity of writers under Nazism to representational status in postwar Germany was not necessarily successful as a basis for new literary sparks and identities. In other words, by insisting on their lived integrity, inner emigrants, unless they volunteered to embrace the moral break as part of their existence, reached a broad audience but hardly initiated a new literature. No wonder that other writers who conjured the break, even if it was often to cover up earlier involvement in the Nazi apparatus, found a way of writing themselves more conspicuously into the founding narrative of the Federal Republic. They knew how to use the notion of *Stunde Null* (point zero or Zero Hour) 1945.

Even in East Germany, which built its cultural legitimacy on the uninterrupted tradition of the literature of the Left, the mere adherence to this tradition—the so-called exile bonus—wore out soon. In his September 1948 address "Der Künstler im Zweijahrplan" (The Artist in the Two-Year Plan), Walter Ulbricht complained that writers still kept thematizing their exile experiences instead of committing their writing to the construction of the new socialist society.

Tracing Literary Opposition

The study of the fortunes of inner emigrants after 1945, as sketchy as it is, yields insights into a both neglected chapter of West German cultural life and the precarious public commitment of writers who had established their rapport with readers in a rather ambiguous relationship with politics. The separation of the scholarship on *inner emigration* from that of postwar literature, which, in pursuit of the founding myth of the Federal Republic, usually became a narrative of the ascent of Group 47, has hindered a differentiated assessment of the underlying poetics. As a consequence the success of these writers with German audiences between the 1930s and 1950s has seldom been acknowledged, let alone thoroughly analyzed as a constitutive part of twentieth-century literary history.

Scholars have usually concentrated on the question of whether inner emigrants' claims that they took great risks in opposing the Hitler regime in their writings were justified.[4] Their research destroyed certain legends and found many similarities with conformist writers in the Third Reich. This provided more insights into the resurgence of the conservative current of German literature and thought after 1930, which was not just a reaction to the prominence of the progressive literary life in the Weimar Republic but also a fight for redistributing literary markets. Writers of the *inner emigration* profited from this development. Yet, as scholars maintained the methodological and thematic separation of their archeology of Nazi and anti-Nazi positions from the narrative of a new West German literature, the contours of the conservative current remained blurred, often hard to distinguish from the *völkisch* or explicitly National Socialist tendencies that continued to resonate with some of the reading public in West Germany and Austria. After interest in the founding narrative of the (old)

Federal Republic waned with the (re-)unification of 1990, the narrow focus on Group 47 seems to have become itself historical.

Now it is possible to trace literary opposition within the resurgence of a traditional, at times antimodernist, current in literature since the early 1930s, with a focus on two aspects that received new momentum from this current of traditionalism, but that also contained modern elements in the various stages of producing, marketing, and reading literature in mid-century. They are: (a) the active concern with reading and the reader in both the conceptualization and reception of the work; and (b) the promotion of the author and his or her heritage, constituting part of the literary structure as well as a tool for a particularly devoted, at times therapeutic reception.

It is one thing to establish a close relationship with readers that carries over through a terrifying historical period; it is another thing to establish a forward-looking literary life in a war-torn country without a capital. As writers such as Bergengruen, Wiechert, Carossa, Schröder, Gertrud von le Fort, and Reinhold Schneider saw many editions of their works through the decades capturing a sizable portion of the West German market for novels and textbooks (*Lesebücher*),[5] the weight of their message made itself felt more through the individual reading experience than through participation in a fledgling literary life. Was the extent to which the reading experience determined the appeal of these authors before 1945 so different? Responding to the lack of a "normal" literary life under National Socialism, their intensive work toward a particular kind of sensitive reading appears to have been an important part of their oppositional message. While committed to different ideological, political, and social issues, these writers shared concerns about a particular form of reading that distinguished them from the celebrated propagators of *völkisch* thought and heroic lifestyles, though there was, as scholars have shown, a broad area of overlap (see Schnell, also Caemmerer and Delabar). Still, the writers' often idiosyncratic maneuvers to instill an element of imperviousness (*Widerständigkeit*; however, *Widerstand* is also political resistance) in the reading process were indispensable for the "right" political or moral understanding, which is difficult for later generations to reconstruct.

The extinction of a "normal" literary life under National Socialism did not necessarily mean that there was no literary public sphere. It existed, though more as a project than a reality, constantly monitored by several official institutions between Goebbels, Göring, and Rosenberg. For a large proportion of publications, what was prescribed and accepted was less crucial than what was restricted. In many cases it served only as a backdrop against which writers built their individual "public" sphere, i.e., a sphere of communication in which careful reading distinguished between participation and exclusion. Establishing invisible reading communities was of itself nothing new; rather, it continued trends from earlier decades that had shaped the publication industry and given publishing houses profiles and devoted audiences. Churches and certain organizations were able to maintain their reading audiences, yet national socialist literary policy was intent on restricting or monitoring these forms of communication. To complicate the reading process was not necessarily suspicious by itself; the sense of participation resulted more from testing the readers' presence of mind while drawing them into the reading community than from their successful deciphering of specific symbols, which usually remained ambiguous. Although the individual figures in Ernst Jünger's *On the Marble Cliffs* point to representatives of the Nazi regime (the Oberförster as Hitler, etc.), the narrator guides the reader like a novice in a covert community through the book's overall atmosphere of a mythical *Widerständigkeit*.

In view of the crucial place of the reading experience as constitutive for the phenomenon of *inner emigration*, one would have expected discussion to more actively involve theories of reading and reception that have contributed greatly to recent literary criticism. While Stanley Fish's notion of interpretive communities—as applied, for instance, to Gertrud von Le Fort's writings of spiritual salvation (see M. K. Devinney; also S. Fish)—can help define the vague term "reading communities," Wolfgang Iser's marking of textual gaps and interstices (*Leerstellen*) as indispensable for the active involvement of the reader can further the analysis of texts that have become difficult to decipher (see Iser). Yet, the focus on the production of political and ideological messages in these texts has hindered a more forthright study both of the implied and the actual reading.

Whether in the case of Elisabeth Langgässer or that of Horst Lange, of Werner Bergengruen or Ernst Wiechert, the works of these writers demonstrate how the aesthetic invention of an *inner emigration* usually shapes the political message, not vice versa, as it unfolds a particular tension between fiction and the political unconscious, as Fredric Jameson has called literature's larger frame of reference. Jameson's assertion (in his 1981 work *The Political Unconscious: Narrative as a Socially Symbolic Act*) that all literature must be read as a symbolic meditation on the destiny of community illuminates the extent to which this literature can be called political. When the Nazis tried to endow the symbolic meditation on the destiny of community with their brand of a mythical *Schicksalsgemeinschaft* (destined community) in the hand of the inspired leader, they picked up on currents that were by no means restricted to the Right. In fact, one cannot easily separate their appropriation of antihistorical histories and individualist formulations of anti-individual ideologies from the techniques used in counter-discourses. In the depression years after 1930, many disillusioned middle-class writers, from Joseph Roth and Ödön von Horvath, who emigrated, to the writers around the periodical *Die Kolonne*, who did not emigrate, turned to a mythic conception of reality in their literary works. The search for fictional or poetic zones of timeless nature or humanity with which writers such as Oskar Loerke and Wilhelm Lehmann, Friedo Lampe and Ernst Wiechert, Eugen Gottlob Winkler and Hermann Kasack tried to establish distance from the rhetoric and the ready-made phrases of official language, cannot always be distinguished from the mythification of timeless moments in *völkisch* narratives.

Still, one can determine that, under this system, fiction and the political unconscious create a momentum in which the reader is moved toward a critical attitude, an impulse toward probing existing views on reality. It is no less an attitude or disposition (*Haltung*) than the mindset propagated in the proclamations for a National Socialist literature that Ralf Schnell has convincingly analyzed on the basis of a 1937 article by Gerhard Schumann (103–19). Where Schnell points to a *Haltung* instead of an ideology or specific topic as the core of National Socialist literature, one can argue that oppositional writing is also to a large extent defined by a specific *Haltung*, which the author instills in the reader.[6] Reading is projected and practiced as an individualizing activity; speaking of a reading community points to the participation in an internalized communality, not a collective practice.

The Nazi Policies of Reading

The focus on reading and reception, helpful in determining what constituted literary opposition, warrants even more attention with the realization that in the areas of culture, literature, education, and libraries the Nazi leadership made the issue of reception a crucial target in its policies. Uwe-Karsten Ketelsen, Jan-Pieter Barbian, and others have shown that the programmatic phase of Nazi arts policy took place in the first four years of the regime, as a follow-up to the book burnings of 1933. It seems necessary to emphasize what historians have often overlooked in their studies of the Third Reich as a twelve-year dictatorship: that there is a distinct difference between the first years of prewar National Socialism, in which "revolutionary" innovations were imposed on German society, and the second phase, whose dynamics resulted from the organization of resources for the war effort with a different type of systemic radicalization. Schnell's helpful analysis of a National Socialist literature and performance culture based on a specific *Haltung* remains a project—indeed, often only a project—of the first phase. Already around 1938 its organizing efforts were seen more or less as a failure, masked by the internal battles between Goebbels and Rosenberg and their bureaucracies. Although the propaganda apparatus expanded its range in the late 1930s, at this time the creation of a new *völkisch* literature by advancing the careers of new National Socialist poets and playwrights was considered a flop, notwithstanding the fact that, thanks to official promotion, authors such as Eberhard Wolfgang Moeller, Josef Weinheber, and Gerhard Schumann rose to national prominence. The assessment of the failure of a particular *völkisch* literature has remained valid as much as it concerned the attempt to formulate art and literature policy as a device for new artistic production.

However, this is only one part of the story, and it has been overemphasized at the expense of the other. The other is a broader and more comprehensive attempt at transforming the *reception* of art and literature in Germany into a new kind of *völkisch* undertaking (for which certain necessary structures existed only in music, thanks to the tradition of public organization of *Musikpflege* in Germany and Austria). Volker Dahm has given an account of the tremendous effort invested in building numerous regional and local structures for adult education, public libraries, literary prizes, and reading and lecture organizations, including the "Reichswerk Buch und Volk." The network of public libraries received increased attention. While the Weimar Republic built the *Volksbüchereiwesen*, the system of public libraries, mostly as a private or nongovernmental structure, with strong input from the Social Democratic program for *Volksbildung*, the real innovation of the 1930s was the decision to provide public funding for several layers of local libraries and reading-related activities involving schools and youth organizations. The so-called transformation of the literary culture of the Weimar Republic meant, in connection with the book burnings in 1933, the installation of rigorous censorship and replacement of personnel with questionable (i.e., democratic) credentials. But it also meant a tax-supported building program of large proportions, projecting a public library in every village of five hundred or more, supplying funds for filling their shelves, and encouraging reading and library use among broad segments of the population, especially the younger generations.

If reading received so much attention, which kind of reading was meant? Wasn't there a discrepancy between the individualizing momentum and the official propagation of a life of adventurous heroism, of action and collective participation? In his path-breaking studies of reading under National Socialism, Norbert Hopster has summarized the answer: "The leadership was aware of the fact, if literature was to be made useful in the service of the regime, it was possible only on the basis of a new reading paradigm, meaning that it could be substantiated only through a new form of literary reception which was enclosed in the comprehensive model of political education" (Hopster, 101). The latter phrase refers, of course, to the propaganda of National Socialist totalitarianism and ideological coordination, or *Gleichschaltung*.

The first step in this agenda was elevating reading to a socially significant activity. In his article "Observations about the Book" (Betrachtungen über das Buch, 272), Hans Frank remarked that after a long period of overestimating the book, an acute danger loomed of underestimating the book. The fact that the regime put in such effort to energize libraries and reading constituted not just part of its ideological outreach but also an endeavor to fill a void in the offerings to the population as consumers of goods. Though less accentuated than later in East Germany, book production and propagation of reading was a way of compensating for the lack of consumerism. The former increased as the latter, in the form of consumer goods and recreational activities, decreased. Its precedent was the enormous increase in the production of reading material during World War I, which had become the "biggest reading event in the 20th century" (Natter). Similarly, the National Socialist regime gave publishers like Bertelsmann the opportunity for enormous growth by marketing reading material for the armed forces (*Wehrmachtsausgaben*) during World War II (see Sarkowicz and Mentzer, 49f.). Continuities with the period after the war are hard to overlook, not only with regard to the strategies of compensating for the lack of a functioning book market but also in maintaining a particular kind of compensatory use of the conservative cultural tradition, a kind of *Volksausgabe* (popular edition) for rough times.

The second step, the specific National Socialist step, was to apply a particular *Haltung* to reading by concentrating on its communal and ritualistic potential. In the words of Hans Frank:

> As beneficial as public help [in enhancing the book] is, the decisive step can only be made by the individual who takes the book home, experiences it and makes its experience available to those with whom it has, in some ways, a communal bond; and by trying to make sure that word does not remain word, but again finds back the path where all important books come from: to an exemplary, deeply rooted, *volkhaft* life. (Frank, 273)

In other words, reading is not supposed to remain a solitary activity but should become the basis for a collective experience. The reader should become part of a reading community, a *lesende Volksgemeinschaft*. Youth organizations, and of course the Hitler youth, were the preferred targets of this policy. Caring for books in school and youth camp libraries and communal reading in classrooms and meetings became part of everyday duties. Reading often was a euphemism for listening to and practicing speech-making for purposes of political indoctrination.

As indicated by Schnell's analysis, reading as collective participation was the formula for the first "revolutionary" phase of Nazi art policy. Its ideas concerning the *Volksgemeinschaft* were not intended to be revolutionary; however, the organizational fusion of production and reception in Nazism corresponds to strategies of the collective practice of art that were articulated elsewhere around 1930, most effectively in Soviet Russia by Sergej Tretjakov. National Socialist practice stands on one side of the scale of collectivization of the art experience, whose other side—Tretjakov's project of a collective newspaper—impressed Walter Benjamin so much that he integrated it in his address at the Institute for the Study of Fascism in Paris in 1934, "The Author as Producer."

In the second, war-oriented phase of the Third Reich, this transformation of reading was promoted with considerably diminished energy (and resources). The Nazis did not find a way to transform reading from the uncontrollable private act to a social or collective affair with certainty. They constantly warned against "reading rage" (*Lesewut*) as an antisocial activity. A look at official policies and practices helps outline the area where oppositional writers were able to draw readers toward their own *Haltung*. While deeply entangled in the thematic and linguistic ambiguities of the 1930s and 1940s, they rarely produced new plots or stories or aesthetic innovations. What they intended and often were able to do was activate readers, so that they reconnected with the political unconscious in a critical way. A crucial part of their literary strategy was to subvert the official pressure on reading as a communal activity: hence, the isolating nature of much of their writing. When criticizing them as individualists in a self-styled cocoon, one should not forget to what they responded: not just a threatening reality full of political fervor but also an onslaught on the reader's independence and integrity. They might not have been able to save themselves as great writers in the annals of literary history, but they might have saved reading as a critical activity, through the period of Nazi rule in the 1930s and early 1940s, in order to build a bridge of continuity between Weimar Germany in the 1920s and the Federal Republic in the 1950s.

Resurrecting the Role of the *Dichter*

The link between the fortunes of the literary opposition and the resurgence of the conservative current that prevailed for more than a decade after 1945 can also be traced in the ways that the image of the author was given central importance. Resuming the traditional veneration of *Dichtung*—in opposition to the notion of the use-value of literature that liberal and leftist writers of the 1920s had propagated—inner emigrants such as Wiechert, Carossa, Bergengruen, and von Le Fort had little problem using the *Dichterverehrung* (which was part of the *völkisch* legacy) to conceptualize and market their works as part of a higher mission. The perception of *Dichtung* as a natural, and therefore higher expression of human endeavors than *Literatur*, which tended toward ideology and mere entertainment, directly reinforced their moral authority (see Conrady). What middle-class readers considered lacking in the novels of Heinrich Mann, Lion Feuchtwanger, or Arnold Zweig, they attributed to these authors: that they presented their audiences with a template for the internalization of war, alienation, and moral redemption.

It might have to do with the somewhat therapeutic understanding of the role of the *Dichter*—in contrast to the politically committed intellectual in the 1920s—that a substantial number of *Dichterinnen* (women writers) rose to high prominence in this period, from the officially celebrated Agnes Miegel and Ina Seidel to the officially shunned Ricarda Huch, who left the Prussian Academy in protest over the exclusion of left-liberal authors in 1933 but who remained in Germany, and Gertrud von Le Fort, who continued to emulate the image of the saintly woman in historical narratives. Representatives of a younger generation rose to similar prominence after 1945, among them Elisabeth Langgässer, Ilse Langner, Luise Rinser, and Marie-Luise Kaschnitz, who began to disassociate their works from the traditional motherly image of female identity.

The most effective display of the role of the *Dichter* followed the well-established pattern of the *Goethe-Kult*, which helped Gerhard Hauptmann and Stefan George gain superior status in the public eye. Continued by Carossa and Wiechert in careful self-projections as solitary masters of the wisdom of life (see Thoenelt), it helped shape the resonance of male writers who addressed present social and cultural conditions without direct confrontations. This display took central stage between the Goethe anniversary years 1932 and 1949, roughly the period of the most intensive recasting of art and aesthetics at a distance from the sphere of production and—though hardly practiced by writers in their individual careers—the market. Omitting public references to the dependency on the market was not difficult during the Third Reich (although it had in no way become less important), and while it was even less of an issue right after the war until the currency reform in 1948, when consumer goods became accessible again and the value of reading material, at least in the Western zones, dropped.

This strategy of distancing the creation of the literary work from the modern production process did not come to an end in 1945 after the war (see Pfeiffer). On the contrary, a look at the *Frankfurter Hefte* and their left-leaning editors, Walter Dirks and Eugen Kogon, as well as at other publications and media, shows a strong tendency to refer to the special intuition with which writers (in the highest sense: *Dichter*) address the trials and tribulations of this period of catastrophe and guilt. Aesthetic criteria are woven into the analysis of the plight of the Germans. The role of the *Dichter*, a construct in which the literary opposition anchored its moral authority, became a catalyst for writers and critics in their own plight to project authority, at least until 1950 (Kretschmer, 219).

That this staging of literary creation (*Inszenierung von Autorschaft*) entails both retrograde and progressive elements, has not escaped notice (Hass, 168). It represents on the one hand a continuation of the topos of the *poeta vates* that elevated George and invigorated the Expressionists; on the other, a crucial ingredient of literature in an age in which the authority of the literary text is dwindling and increasingly needs the author as a "visible partner," as the literary critic Karl August Horst has called it. Under the ominous title "Epitaph auf eine Epoche," Horst delineated the conclusion of a period in which the literary form and the writer's truth were made identical. He looked beyond the immediate appeal of autobiographical prose about war and postwar experiences, and exposed the characteristics of a representational structure in which the literary work, in order to overcome the leveling effect of its narrative, needs the "real" author as part of its literary appearance. "Didn't one notice," Horst asked, "that with increasing objectivity the writer and the artist in general step forward from their anonymity, because they become indispensable as partners of their model?" (Horst, 1168; see also Trommler, "What Should Remain?" 162). Answering this question in the affirmative leads back to the Expressionists and the *Inszenierung von Autorschaft* in the Weimar Republic, yet it is equally revealing for the more remote, seemingly "natural" and "untainted" reprise of *Dichtertum* on the part of inner emigrants.

However, one should not overlook the political justification for the interest in staging a particular *Dichtertum* descending from Goethe's image, the *Dichtertum* of an older man who is firmly anchored in a profession and writes from inspiration and accumulated wisdom. In the revealingly affirmative essay, "The Profession of the Poet and Bourgeois Existence" (Dichterberuf und bürgerliche Existenz, 1953), the conservative Germanist Paul Kluckhohn raved about the fact that most of the worthwhile *Dichter* of the period, including Hans Grimm, Kurt Kluge, Hermann Stehr, Wilhelm Schäfer, Hermann Claudius, Ernst Wiechert, Rudolf Alexander Schröder, and Hans Carossa held a professional position and were not totally dependent on their literary production. Kluckhohn's point was that writers with a nonliterary profession are less vulnerable to political and economic blackmail, unlike for example, Josef Weinheber, who became dependent "on the powers of the day which pulled him down into the abyss" (Kluckhohn, 69). Indeed, by reliving an older ideal of the *Feierabenddichter* (Sunday poet), who in his spare time weaves the poetic fabric that provides comfort and, at times, excitement for his contemporaries, Kluckhohn marks the conditions under which writers tried to avoid financial dependency on the marketing of literature. He provides some insight into the reasons why the creation of the oppositional *Haltung* more often than not presupposes a rather secure middle-class existence—which, at the same time, makes it vulnerable to certain political pressures.

Gottfried Benn, for example, took himself completely out of the literary circuit when he entered the military in 1935. A physician, he did not feel comfortable assuming the role of a medical Goethe as did his medical colleague Hans Carossa. As a matter of fact, Benn's literary work—produced in the leisure hours after his daily duties during the war—became the pursuit of an absolute *Haltung* of rejection to the extent that his earlier entanglement with Fascism almost disappeared from sight when he reentered the literary scene with *Statische Gedichte* in 1948. This stylization was so radical and unforgiving in its posture of the aesthetic *Phänotyp* that in subsequent years the author Benn indeed became, to use Horst's words, a prominent partner of his model of static poetry. By pushing the role of the disentangled aesthetic observer to the extreme, he—and likewise Ernst Jünger—was able to pull away from any association with the traditional aesthetics of inner emigrants. He became a new role model for younger male writers in the Federal Republic who, like Hans Magnus Enzensberger, tried to assemble a position of aesthetic distance from the oncoming new normality.

Two Ways of Entering History

Can one create a post-Hitler literature without focusing on the break with cherished tradition that the Nazis perpetrated? The question has been answered. Calling the efforts of inner emigrants rather unsuccessful does not mean that the described activities, including public exchanges such as the "Darmstädter Colloquia" (*Gespräche*), were not at times impressive attempts to regenerate West Germany's intellectual elites, the first efforts in a country without a capital to provide more literary and intellectual substance to public life than could just the first ten years of Group 47. Yet this group, by capitalizing on the mostly unspoken projection of a new beginning after war and Nazism, was able to write itself conspicuously into the founding myth of the Federal Republic.

Many factors contributed to this success, among them: (1) the well-honed myth of youth (although several of the leading figures were close to forty years old), relating back to the early 1930s when most of the early representatives of the Group had started out (see my "Mission ohne Ziel" esp. 45–46); (2) the successful collaboration with radio stations in the mid 1950s that became both a financial sponsor and public relations engine; (3) the growing production of literary works that helped attract a new and younger audience; and 4) the ways in which writers of Group 47, most impressively Heinrich Böll, inserted themselves as authors into public discussion (literary and otherwise), remaining visible, in Karl August Horst's terminology, as partners of their models (Trommler, "What Should Remain?" fn. 29, 162–64). In the public mind their projection of the writer as the disillusioned young German soldier who came out of the war as a victim rather than a perpetrator, as exemplified by Wolfgang Borchert, signaled a decisive departure from the role of the writer as *Dichter* or *Dichterin*, steeped in tradition and concerned with keeping the literary mission intact against the evil forces of the time. The new writer-figure assured a younger audience that it could recognize its own experience in and after the war, although it was an almost obsessively male projection. Johanna Moosdorf's bitter comment—"It was just impossible to depict a woman who takes action, a woman protagonist. One had to take a male person" (Venske, 201)—is an apt reflection of the situation and shows the problems women authors had in gaining access to the new self-styled paradigm of postwar German literature.

Calling the ascent of these writers successful does not mean that they were free from entanglement with National Socialism. On the contrary, recent inquiries into the lives of Alfred Andersch, Hans Werner Richter, Peter Huchel, Erich Kuby, Luise Rinser, and other representative literary figures, which followed upon Glenn Cuomo's research into Günter Eich's substantial production for radio stations in the Third Reich, have demonstrated that their claim of a new beginning was based more on hope and intention than on fact (see Denk). Such important research, taken in total, as summarized in this volume, completes this survey of *inner emigration* and its contribution to Germany's moral survival and regeneration. It helps locate the impulses for a new literature and literary life by determining that the delayed resistance (*Die nachgeholte Résistance,* Trommler) of those who claimed to have come from a "point zero" corresponds at times with a degree of psychological and professional collaboration within the Nazi system.

While these writers rose after 1950 with the bonus of a new beginning, those who had taken many risks to publish oppositional literature increasingly fell under the suspicion of complicity or were plainly discarded as out of date. Their ways of elevating and complicating reading within the reflections of a terrifying system and the lack of political conscience of a larger community became antiquarian, the last remnant of an outdated German tradition before modernism returned. Now that the literature of exiled writers has been reintegrated (also) into the West German book market and scholarly discourse in recent decades, the dissociation from the contribution of inner emigrants seems unwarranted, indeed a questionable remnant of the now outdated founding narrative of the Federal Republic for postwar German literature.

Notes

1. See Elisabeth Langgässer's critical views in Ursula El-Akramy, *Wotans Rabe*.
2. About Melvin Lasky's intervention at the congress, see *Erster Deutscher Schrift-stellerkongreß 4.–8. Oktober 1947: Protokoll und Dokumente*, eds. Ursula Reinhold, Dieter Schlenstedt and Horst Tanneberger (Berlin: Aufbau, 1997), 48–51, 294–302.
3. Cf. Dolf Sternberger, Gerhard Storz, W. E. Süskind, eds. *Aus dem Wörterbuch des Unmenschen* (1957). This work is based on the columns under the same title in the first three volumes of *Die Wandlung*, 1945–48.
4. See Michael Philipp, "Distanz und Anpassung" (1994). For a new and promising methodological approach, see Heidrun Ehrke-Rotermund and Erwin Rotermund, *Zwischenreiche und Gegenwelten* (1999).
5. See Hans Sarkowicz and Alf Mentzer, *Literatur in Nazi-Deutschland* (2000). About book market, literature in education, and concepts of traditionalism, see *Literatur in der Bundesrepublik Deutschland bis 1967*, ed. Ludwig Fischer.
6. The term *Haltung* is hard to translate as it encompasses more of a cultural directive than *Habitus* and the word *attitude*. It is more localized in the process of literary reception than Reinhold Grimm's term *Lebensform* in his article, "Innere Emigration als Lebensform."

Works Cited

Angrivarius. "Geistige Unterströmungen in Deutschland." *Neue Schweizer Rundschau* N.F. 12 (November 1944): 371–89.
Assmann, Michael, and Herbert Heckmann, eds. *Zwischen Kritik und Zuversicht: 50 Jahre Deutsche Akademie für Sprache und Dichtung*. Göttingen: Wallstein, 1999.
Berglund, Gisela. *Der Kampf um den Leser im Dritten Reich: Die Literaturpolitik der "Neuen Literatur" (Will Vesper) und der "Nationalsozialistischen Monatshefte."* Worms: Heintz, 1980.
Caemmerer, Christine, and Walter Delabar, eds. *Dichtung im Dritten Reich? Zur Literatur in Deutschland 1933–1945*. Opladen: Westdeutscher Verlag, 1996.
Conrady, Karl Otto. "Gegen die Mystifikation von Dichtung und Literatur." In *Literatur und Dichtung: Versuch einer Begriffsbestimmung*, ed. Horst Rüdiger, 64–78. Stuttgart: Kohlhammer, 1973.
Cuomo, Glenn R. *Career at the Cost of Compromise: Günter Eich's Life and Work in the Years 1933–1945*. Amsterdam and Atlanta: Rodopi, 1989.

Denk, Friedrich. *Die Zensur der Nachgeborenen: Zur regimekritischen Literatur im Dritten Reich.* Weilheim: Denk-Verlag, 1996.
Devinney, Margaret Klopfle. *The Legends of Gertrud von Le Fort: Text and Audience.* New York: Lang, 1989.
Ehrke-Rotermund, Heidrun, and Erwin Rotermund. *Zwischenreiche und Gegenwelten: Texte und Vorstudien zur 'Verdeckten Schreibweise' im "Dritten Reich."* Munich: Fink, 1999.
El-Akramy, Ursula. *Wotans Rabe: Elisabeth Langgässer, ihre Tochter Cordelia und die Feuer von Auschwitz.* Frankfurt: Verlag Neue Kritik, 1997.
Fischer, Ludwig, ed. *Literatur in der Bundesrepublik Deutschland bis 1967.* Vol. 10 of *Hansers Sozialgeschichte der deutschen Literatur vom 16. Jahrhundert bis zur Gegenwart,* ed. Rolf Grimminger. Munich: Hanser, 1986.
Fish, Stanley E. *Surprised by Sin: The Reader in "Paradise Lost."* Berkeley and Los Angeles: University of California Press, 1971.
Frank, Hans. "Betrachtungen über das Buch." *Schule der Freiheit* 9, nos. 13/14 (1942): 272–74.
Grimm, Reinhold. "Innere Emigration als Lebensform." In *Exil und innere Emigration: Third Wisconsin Workshop,* ed. Reinhold Grimm and Jost Hermand, 31–74. Frankfurt: Athenäum, 1972.
Grosser, J. F. G., ed. *Die große Kontroverse. Ein Briefwechsel um Deutschland.* Hamburg, Genf, and Paris: Nagel, 1963.
Hass, Ulrike. *Militante Pastorale: Zur Literatur der antimodernen Bewegungen im frühen 20. Jahrhundert.* Munich: Fink, 1993.
Hopster, Norbert. "Literatur und 'Leben' in der Ästhetik des Nationalsozialismus." *Wirkendes Wort* 43 (1993): 99–115.
Hopster, Norbert, and Ulrich Nassen. *Literatur und Erziehung im Nationalsozialismus: Deutschunterricht als Körperkultur.* Paderborn: Schöningh, 1983.
Horst, Karl August. "Epitaph auf eine Epoche." *Merkur* 16 (1962): 1162–69.
Iser, Wolfgang. *The Act of Reading: A Theory of Aesthetic Response.* Baltimore: Johns Hopkins University Press, 1978.
———. *The Implied Reader: Patterns of Communication in Prose Fiction from Bunyan to Beckett.* Baltimore: Johns Hopkins University Press, 1974.
Jameson, Fredric. *The Political Unconscious: Narrative as a Socially Symbolic Act.* Ithaca: Cornell University Press, 1981.
Ketelsen, Uwe-Karsten. *Literatur und Drittes Reich.* Schernfeld: SH-Verlag, 1992.
Kluckhohn, Paul. *Dichterberuf und bürgerliche Existenz.* Tübingen and Stuttgart: Rainer Wunderlich, 1953.
Kretschmer, Michael. "Die Dichterrolle als Reflexionsmedium literarischer Praxis in Deutschland 1945–1950." *Poetica* 11 (1979): 207–32.
Natter, Wolfgang G. *Literature at War, 1914–1940: Representing the "Time of Greatness" in Germany.* New Haven and London: Yale University Press, 1999.
Pfeiffer, Johannes. *Die dichterische Wirklichkeit: Versuche über Wesen und Wahrheit der Dichtung.* Hamburg: Richard Meiner, 1962.
Philipp, Michael. "Distanz und Anpassung: Sozialgeschichtliche Aspekte der *Inneren Emigration.*" *Exilforschung: Ein internationales Jahrbuch* 12 (1994): 11–30.
Reinhardt, Stephan. *Alfred Andersch: Eine Biographie.* Zurich: Diogenes, 1990.
Reinhold, Ursula, Dieter Schlenstedt, and Horst Tanneberger, eds. *Erster Deutscher Schriftstellerkongreß 4.–8. Oktober 1947: Protokoll und Dokumente.* Berlin: Aufbau, 1997.
Sabais, Heinz-Winfried. "Verändern die Dichter die Welt?" *Neue literarische Welt* 4, no. 15 (1953): 1–2.
Sarkowicz, Hans, and Alf Mentzer. *Literatur in Nazi-Deutschland: Ein biografisches Lexikon.* Hamburg and Vienna: Europa, 2000.
Schnell, Ralf. *Dichtung in finsteren Zeiten: Deutsche Literatur und Faschismus.* Reinbek bei Hamburg: Rowohlt, 1998.
Sternberger, Dolf. "Die Herrschaft der Freiheit." *Die Wandlung* 1 (12 July 1946): 556–71.
Sternberger, Dolf, Gerhard Storz, and W. E. Süskind, eds., *Aus dem Wörterbuch des Unmenschen.* Hamburg: Claassen, 1957.

Thoenelt, Klaus. "Innere Emigration: Fiktion oder Wirklichkeit? Literarische Tradition und Nationalismus in den Werken Ernst Wiecherts, Hans Carossas und Hans Falladas (1933–1945)." In *Leid der Worte: Panorama des literarischen Nationalsozialismus*, ed. Jörg Thunecke, 300–20. Bonn: Bouvier, 1987.

Trommler, Frank. "What Should Remain? Exploring the Literary Contributions to Postwar German History." In *Beyond 1989: Re-reading German Literature since 1945*, ed. Keith Bullivant, 153–76. Providence, R.I., and Oxford: Berghahn, 1997.

———. "Die nachgeholte Résistance: Politik und Gruppenethos im historischen Zusammenhang." In *Die Gruppe 47 in der Geschichte der Bundesrepublik*, ed. Justus Fetscher, Eberhard Lämmert, Jürgen Schutte, 9–22. Würzburg: Königshausen & Neumann, 1991.

———. "Mission ohne Ziel: Über den Kult der Jugend im modernen Deutschland." In *"Mit uns zieht die neue Zeit": Der Mythos Jugend*, ed. Thomas Koebner, Rolf-Peter Janz, and Frank Trommler, 24–49. Frankfurt: Suhrkamp 1985.

Venske, Regula. "Schriftstellerinnen gegen das Vergessen: Johanna Moosdorf." In *Frauenliteratur ohne Tradition? Neun Autorinnenporträts*, ed. Inge Stephan, Regula Venske, and Sigrid Weigel. Frankfurt: Fischer, 1987.

Waldmüller, Monika. *Die Wandlung: Eine Monatsschrift – Herausgegeben von Dolf Sternberger unter Mitwirkung von Karl Jaspers, Werner Krauss und Alfred Weber 1945–1949*. Marbach: Deutsche Schillergesellschaft, 1988.

Chapter 6

ABSENCES OF TIME AND HISTORY

Poetry of *Inner Emigration*

Leonard Olschner

> dein aber ist das Schreiten,
> dein die Grenze, die Zeit,
> *glaube* den Ewigkeiten,
> *fordre sie nicht zu weit,*
>
> yours though is the striding,
> yours the border, and time;
> believe the eternities,
> demand not too much of them,
>
> —Gottfried Benn, "Mediterranean"
> (Mittelmeerisch; *SW*, 1:212)

Much of the poetry written within Germany between 1933 and 1945—or, to be more precise, since the phenomenon is not restricted to the years the Nazis were in power, between the latter 1920s and early 1950s—is characterized, first, by a stubborn though ultimately comprehensible sense of stasis, and second, by a remarkably depersonalized mode of voice, to the extent that authors' names frequently appear to be arbitrary, interchangeable, and thus irrelevant.[1] Both of these characteristics appear to be symptomatic of deeper-lying cultural exigencies beyond the sphere of individual psychology and closer to unreflected and anxious conformism. Admittedly this may in part result from the unoriginal, imitative nature of the texts. While still in exile Adorno wrote in 1944 of the "separate and apocryphal existence" of art and thought, years before the Nazis came to power, of the "hiding places" of this existence: "Whoever did not conform had to retreat into an inner emigration years before the outbreak of the Third Reich ..." (*GS*, 4:64). Hermann Korte speaks of *inner emigration* as the "program" of *Naturlyriker* around 1930: "They sought their position outside cities and [cultural] centers and made themselves at home, as it were, in remote and esoteric regions. They did this in order to pit a new type of perception against a temporal perspective dedicated to 'grand,' topical temporary problems: a view of the insignificant, unnoticed detail" (Korte, 632). It is precisely the opposition to and consequences of this "temporal perspective" that demand our attention.

Many of the recognized and legally publishing poets of the nazi years seriously saw themselves as part of both a great tradition and a time of renewal. Photographs of writers meeting reveal, apart from ideological purpose, a new elite's air of significant self-importance and possibly satisfaction at a newly established consensus after dissenters had departed or been coerced to depart.[2] Gottfried Benn for his part held the literary journals of these people to be little more than "collective dilettantism" (*Gemeinschaftsdilettantismus*) (*Briefe*, 76: letter to Oelze, 7 October 1935). Having in mind Hans Friedrich Blunck, recipient of the Goethe-Medaille in 1938, he noted: "Do we not have among us talents with the resonance of a watering can and the pathos of a person who has drowned?" (*SW*, 4:282). The lack of originality reminds one of Schiller's distich "Dilettante": "Just because a verse comes to you in a cultured language/that writes and thinks for you, you believe you are a poet" (302). This bon mot points toward formative cultural forces at work outside the poets' minds, forces from which the less original writers escaped only with difficulty.

Between Rilke and Celan shifts occurred with regard to sensing time as a historical dimension, one into timelessness and again one out of it. We might choose as textual markers Rilke's "Transience" (Vergänglichkeit, 1924) and Celan's "Corona" (1948), both of which affirm time and transition even with the subtextual wish to transcend them.

VERGÄNGLICHKEIT

Flugsand der Stunden. Leise fortwährende Schwindung
auch noch des glücklich gesegneten Baus.
Leben weht immer. Schon ragen ohne Verbindung
die nicht mehr tragenden Säulen heraus.

Aber Verfall: ist er trauriger, als der Fontäne
Rückkehr zum Spiegel, den sie mit Schimmer bestaubt?
Halten wir uns dem Wandel zwischen die Zähne,
daß er uns völlig begreift in sein schauendes Haupt. (Rilke, 159)

TRANSIENCE

Wind-borne sand of the hours. Quietly persevering shrinking
of even the happily blessed edifice.
Life breathes always. The no longer supporting columns
protrude already without connection.

But decay: is this sadder than the fountain's
return to the mirror that it dusts with shimmer?

We should place ourselves between the teeth of change,
so that it grasps us fully into its seeing countenance. (author's translation)

CORONA

Aus der Hand frißt der Herbst mir sein Blatt: wir sind Freunde.
Wir schälen die Zeit aus den Nüssen und lehren sie gehn:
die Zeit kehrt zurück in die Schale.

Im Spiegel ist Sonntag,
im Traum wird geschlafen,
der Mund redet wahr.

Mein Aug steigt hinab zum Geschlecht der Geliebten:
wir sehen uns an,
wir sagen uns Dunkles,
wir lieben einander wie Mohn und Gedächtnis,
wir schlafen wie Wein in den Muscheln,
wie das Meer im Blutstrahl des Mondes.

Wir stehen umschlungen im Fenster, sie sehen uns zu von der Straße:
es ist Zeit, daß man weiß!
Es ist Zeit, daß der Stein sich zu blühen bequemt,
daß der Unrast ein Herz schlägt.
Es ist Zeit, daß es Zeit wird.

Es ist Zeit. (Celan, 37)

CORONA

Autumn eats its leaf out of my hand: we are friends.
From the nuts we shell time and we teach it to walk:
then time returns to the shell.

In the mirror it's Sunday,
in dream there is room for sleeping,
our mouths speak the truth.

My eye moves down to the sex of my loved one:
we look at each other,
we exchange dark words,
we love each other like poppy and recollection,
we sleep like wine in the conches,
like the sea in the moon's blood ray.

We stand by the window embracing, and people look up from the street:
it is time they knew!
It is time the stone made an effort to flower,
time unrest had a beating heart.
It is time it were time.

It is time.

(trans. Michael Hamburger, *Poems of Paul Celan* [London: Anvil Press, 1995], 61)

Even without a detailed explication, both poems demonstrate the centrality of time as a dominating historical presence (in Rilke "Wind-borne sand of the hours" in connection with "decline" [*Verfall*]; in Celan "It is time it were time"). In the period between these texts "time" becomes both the problem of the texts and the key to their understanding. If we follow Aristotle, time implies movement and change in nature (the basis being the movement of heavenly bodies). Stasis rather than dynamis characterizes his understanding of nature, with form and place taking precedence over time.[3] I do not wish to look at Augustine's critique of Aristotle in his examination of how the mind senses time—Augustine's meditations on time, in book XI of the *Confessions*, are instructive in this context (see Whitrow, 64)—but rather to emphasize the oppositions involved in time versus timelessness and change versus stasis. In the rush to flee from the contradictions—both inward and outward—poets, ostensibly choosing the timeless and hence something "pure," chose stasis.

Stasis lies at the heart of a substantial amount of the poetry during this period and becomes both a retarding and blocking element with regard to new impulses, that is, to poetic renewal even of the most modest and rudimentary kind, not to mention traces of the avant-garde. Christoph Meckel speaks of how his father Eberhard Meckel (1907–69), a fairly respected poet in his day as well as friend and contemporary of Günter Eich and Peter Huchel, wrote poems

> in which time is not perceptible. He was not alone with this attitude. All kinds of writers of his generation—an entire phalanx of the youngest intellectuals—continued to live in an astonishing atemporality. They withdrew into nature poetry, hid themselves in the seasons—in what seemed eternal, perennially valid, supertemporal—and in the beauty of nature and beauty of art, in a notion of consolation and a belief in the passing of time-bound misery. (Christoph Meckel, 22)

Much of Eberhard Meckel's poetry does indeed thrive on the negation of time, of concrete place and of genuine movement, such as his poems in the *Anthology of New Poetry* (*Anthologie jüngster Lyrik*, Fehse and Mann, 1929). One of these illustrates the point at hand:

SOMMER

Wochenmüde sich fallen lassen in tiefes Gras.
Hänge umher, Wiesen, und nichts als Sonne!
Weiter und nähere Landschaft unter einem Riesigen,
Das blau umgrenzt den Liegenden, den Schauenden.

Körper ohne Zeit, summender Sonntag geworden,
Das bin nicht ich, das ist alles und muß immer sein.
Das bist du, Blume, Wald, Berg und Wind,
das bist du, Acker, alter, wachsender. (119)

SUMMER

Weeks of tiredness, letting oneself fall in deep grass.
Hills everywhere, meadows, and nothing but sun!
Farther, in a nearer landscape under a giant [sky]
that outlines in blue the one lying and looking.

Body without time, having become a humming Sunday;
that is not I, that is everything and must always be.
You are this: flower, forest, mountain and wind,
you are this: field, old and growing. (author's translation)

A poem on the becoming of a poem, entitled "Invocation of a Poem" (Anrufung um ein Gedicht) and published in *Das Innere Reich* in 1936–37, contains the ambiguous line "Am I singing the song originating in time?"

Sing ich das Lied, das der Zeit entsprang?
Ach, es erfüllt zu sehr die Brust.
Hol ich für Deutschland den ernsten Gesang
tief hervor aus Jubel und Lust?

Am I singing the song originating in time?
O it fills too fully my heart.
Do I obtain for Germany from deep below
the serious song of jubilation and desire? (author's translation)

The quoted verses (ll. 5–8) give the text a sense of uncertain identity and origin, and the reader, today at least, must wonder if Meckel was considering whether his poem articulated a period of apparent cultural rejuvenation or indeed wished to transcend such attachment. Were it not for the bitter memoir of his son, Eberhard Meckel might have disappeared from literary history altogether; his name, generally absent in biographical dictionaries, and his texts are remembered perhaps chiefly in the Freiburg im Breisgau region, from which he came and to which he returned.

Such conspicuous lack of time, place, and movement explains in part the flood of nature poetry good, bad, and indifferent in its thematizing of the timeless cycle of seasons and its recycling of images, cadences and gestures from the Romantic canon (see Emmerich, esp. 83–91). Adorno calls nature poetry "anachronistic" not just because of its themes, but even more because the truthfulness of its context has evaporated; he writes, "Nature poetry is anachronistic not only with regard to its subject: its truth content has shrunk" (author's translation; *Ästhetische Theorie*, 325). Time becomes a paradigm for the forces at work on the production of the texts as well as for the texts themselves, and this mirrors the conscious or subconscious expectations among readers when anticipating this poetry. Time is taken not as a theme but as an inadvertent focus; the poetry shows how time as a concept is "treated," confronted, developed, avoided, transformed. An implicit poetics of time—and perhaps a poetics of history *ex negativo* as well—emerges. Hans Carossa demands, sometime before 1940:

O verlerne die Zeit,
Daß nicht dein Antlitz verkümmre
Und mit dem Antlitz das Herz!
Leg ab deine Namen! (Carossa, 61)

O forget what time is,
that your countenance not waste away
and with the countenance your heart!
Cast off your names! (author's translation)

Such an explicit desire to negate time, or rather a consciousness of or for time ("O forget what time is") may be infrequent, but certainly not rare. The underlying attitude remains widespread.

Adorno's essay "On Poetry and Society" was delivered on radio in Berlin in the early 1950s. For all of its subtlety and differentiation, the essay's major thesis—namely, that poetry always stands in some definable relation to and emanates from the society in which it is written—has today nearly the quality of a truism. But the audience Adorno addressed in the West Germany of the early 1950s continued or inherited a still predominant cultural force of engaged tradition, to which Adorno himself to some degree subscribed (Hohendahl, 114), as well as interiority (*Innerlichkeit*), timelessness (*Zeitenthobenheit*), and an antagonistic attitude toward history (*Geschichtsfeindlichkeit*). With much justification the designation "restoration" became part of public debate, at the latest by 1950 in an essay by Walter Dirks, which appeared in *Frankfurter Hefte*. Concurrently the desire for a literature of consolation, apparently best accomplished through poetry, provided a climate of expectation. It is by no means an exaggeration to speak of a tendency toward, if not a predominance of, paraphrases of Goethe's lyrical *Lebensweisheit* and a renaissance of Biedermeier sensibility as revealed in much of Mörike's verse.

Part of Adorno's radio essay is particularly germane for the present context, for in an implicit rhetorical move its author anticipates objections that, being something pure unto itself, poetry had nothing to do with society. To the contrary, Adorno retorts, this poetry has the strongest of links to society. The central statement is this:

> However, this demand on poetry—namely, that of virgin language—is in and of itself social. It implies the protest against a social condition which each individual experiences as hostile, alien, cold and depressing, and this condition impresses itself negatively onto the text: the heavier this condition weighs, then the more stubbornly the text opposes it by refusing to yield to anything heterogenous and by constituting itself according to its own laws. Its distance to pure existence becomes the measure of what is false and wrong in it. In protesting against it, poetry articulates the dream of a world in which things are different. (author's translation; Adorno, "Rede über Lyrik," *GS*, 11:52)

The last two sentences address the problem with particular acuity. At this point in his argument Adorno seems to have in mind Rilke, whose "cult of objects" (*Dingkult*) he cites directly after this passage, along with George and Mörike; and in doing so he nods almost benevolently toward utopian readings of the canonized poets. But his insight remains valid even for completely different writers.

Indeed, a poem by Eberhard Meckel, "Youth and Maiden in the Countryside" (Jüngling und Mädchen in Landschaft)—a title more suggestive of a painting—actually contains the lines: "All existence outside the countryside demands/a grand forgetting."

JÜNGLING UND MÄDCHEN IN LANDSCHAFT

Siehe dir an alle die Dinge umher,
das ist Landschaft für uns, das ist der Berge
klare Gestalt, der Hügel bewaldeter Schwung,
Ebene hier, Bauern, bestellte Felder.

Alles Dasein außer der Landschaft erfordert
ein großes Vergessen. Oh, wären wir immer Erde,
so tief und einfach verwurzelt in Wiese und Acker
wie Bäume, im Regen, im Wind, besonnt und bestirnt. (Fehse and Mann, 120)

YOUTH AND MAIDEN IN COUNTRYSIDE

Look at all things around you:
that is countryside for us, that is the clear
shape of the mountains, the forested sweep of the hills,
plain here, farmers, cultivated fields.

All existence outside the countryside demands
a grand forgetting. O, if only we were always earth,
so deeply and simply rooted in meadow and field
like trees, shone upon by sun and by stars, in rain, in wind. (author's translation)

This slight text would appear to resume a position one would have thought overcome in Lessing's Laokoon essay, namely of literature attempting to emulate the representational stasis of a painting. In his *Aesthetic Theory* Adorno observes that what becomes apparent in works of art is their temporal core (*Zeitkern*); to analyze these works becomes tantamount to gaining an awareness of the history immanently stored in them:

> By means of its determination as a phenomenon, art experiences its own negation teleologically; the violent opening up of the phenomenon denies aesthetic appearance. But the appearance and its explosion at the site of the work of art are essentially historical. The work of art is not—as historicism would have it—existence removed from becoming, but rather a becoming as existence. What appears in it is its inner time, and the explosion of the appearance interrupts its continuity. Its monadological kernel mediates actual history. History may be understood as the content of works of art. Analyzing works of art is equivalent to becoming aware of the history inherent in them. (author's translation: Adorno, *Ästhetische Theorie*, 132)

One might extrapolate: history is locked up in works of art, in poems—repressed, denied—because it was so threatening. The poets spoke unabashedly of *Time* and *History* as though they were speaking of time and history and not of eternity and destiny. Titles of poetry volumes just for 1948 betrayed their uninterrupted preoccupation: Georg Maurer, *Songs of the Time* (Gesänge der Zeit); Rudolf Hagelstange, *The Current of Time* (Strom der Zeit); Reinhold Schneider, *The Star of the Time* (Stern der Zeit). A year later Hans Egon Holthusen went a transcendental step farther: Here in Time (*Hier in der Zeit*). That this poetry was still as antimodernist as that of certain strains in the late 1920s, indicates the continuity and consistency of poetic writing in Germany. The young Günter Eich stated uncompromisingly in 1930: "Responsibility to my time? Not at all. Only to myself" ("Innere Dialoge," 457)—a position Eich would rescind in the immediate postwar period.

Few texts articulate an attitude both of withdrawal and opposition with the decisive clarity of Hermann Kasack's "Gang ins Innere," written, according to its author, in 1934 and published in the volume *Eternal Being* (Das ewige Dasein, 1943):

GANG INS INNERE

Galleria del Pace am Lago Averno

Die meine Tage teilen, folgen nicht,
Sie sind in ihnen schon verglitten.
Vor meinen Augen glänzt das innere Licht:
So bin ich in die Unterwelt geschritten.

Dort geben tote Freunde das Geleit.
Sie warten meiner, stille Wächter,
Den Weg zu weisen ohne Zeit,
Darunter rieselt Sandgelächter.

Die Stollen, bleiern, füllt ein Schein,
Drin leuchten die erfrornen Seelen.
Die Herzen werden glatt, Gestein,
Dem blühend alle Moose fehlen.

Ich taste traumhaft mich einher,
Vom eignen Labyrinth gefangen.
Gestorbnen gleich weiß ich nicht mehr,
Bin ich oder die Welt vergangen.

Wohl pocht es mahnend an das Tor,
Mich wieder in den Tag zu schrecken.
Doch was sich in sich selbst verlor,
Kann keine Sehnsucht mehr erwecken.

Wie Perlen nie zu Tränen schmelzen,
Laß ich mich nicht zurückbesinnen.
Gebt auf, die Steine von mir abzuwälzen:
Die Ströme münden nur nach innen. (Kasack, 190)

STEPS WITHIN

Those who share my days do not follow,
they have already slipped away in them.
Before my eyes an inner light shines:
thus I strode into the underworld.

Dead friends there provide an escort.
They, quiet watchmen, wait for me
to show the way without time,
beneath which the sand-laughter trickles.

A glow fills, leadenly, the gallery
where the frozen should shine.
Our hearts become smooth, rocks,
which, blossoming, lack all moss.

I grope dreamlike therein,
captured by my own labyrinth.
Just like the dead I no longer know:
am I or is the world gone?

True, I hear a knocking, warning, at the gate,
shocking me back into the day.
But no longing can again awaken
what has lost itself in itself.

Just as pearls never melt into tears,
let me not think back.
Give up trying to push the stones from me:
the currents flow only towards my innermost being. (author's translation)

The voice of this poem speaks in paradoxical images of without/within (ll. 3–4). In this underworld, friends accompany the speaker, "to show the way without time" (l. 7). This may be an allegorical space, but it is significantly "without time." Interiority dominates the scene, so it is hardly surprising that a dream or dreamlike state originates within (ll. 13–14). In many texts that in some way problematize temporality, the speakers turn to dreams, perhaps as a convention of escape from the corner into which they have backed themselves (cf. Adorno's "dream of a world in which things are different"; cf. also Reinhold Schneider, "Terrible home between time and dream," 282). By ending his poem with the lines "Give up trying to push the stones from me:/the currents flow only toward my innermost being," (ll. 23–24) Kasack admits of no solution for removing the stones of acutely felt political oppression in this historical situation, while at the same time the self retreats into itself without hesitation. The title of the volume, *Eternal Being*, proves to be uncannily appropriate. In its theme of a retreat into interiority, the poem evokes Benn's "Never Lonelier" (Einsamer nie, written no later than September 1936), from his last sanctioned publication during the Nazi period. In it the lines "but where are victory and proof thereof/from the realm which you represent?" (ll. 7–8) and "you serve the counter-bliss, the mind" (l. 12: *SW*, 1:135) demarcate a position of aesthetic alterity against the brutal "aesthetics" and intoxication of the Nazis and their followers. Benn corroborates this reading of the poet's world as a counterworld in a recording of the poem, made sometime between 1950 and 1956, in which he lingers slightly on and stresses the word "dir" (see Koch).

But one might also recall a lesser known poem, Oskar Loerke's "Fuge" (written on 2 July 1933), which is not without clumsy obscurity but which clearly demonstrates a comparable movement toward interiority ("You, star of the penitents,/whip your spirit inwards" [ll. 13–14] and "My realm [*Reich*], my way" [l. 21] *Gedichte*, 407–8). Another of Oskar Loerke's poems, "Timeless Awakening" (Zeitloses Erwachen), written in February 1932 and first published in *Carline Thistle Woods* (Silberdistelwald, 1934), exhibits even before Hitler's ascent to power the symptoms of inner conflict and a sense of its speaker being out of step with the times. Loerke posits a double and oppositional temporality—one historical, the other personal:

ZEITLOSES ERWACHEN

Im Garten wuchs bei Nacht der Norden,
Ich bin von keiner Zeit noch schwer.
So bin ich ausgenommen worden,
Zu altern wie die Welt umher?

Auf Beeten schmilzt die weiße Flocke
Im Ginster-Immergrün und Buchs,
In welkem Farn hängt Haargelocke
Von einem Wolfshund oder Fuchs.

In Vasen wuchs die Zeit und Tassen,
Sie nahmen die Erfüllung hin
Mit horchendem Geschehenlassen—
Nur meine Zeit ist nicht darin.

Vielleicht hat sie der Traum betreten,
Der nicht nach meinen Träumen fragt,
Und ihre Schleppe ziehn Kometen
Durch eine Nacht, die mir nicht tagt.

Armaden ruhn von Schlacht und Böe
Dort aus, das Erz im dichten Stahl,
Das Ammonshorn ruht auf der Höhe
Des Berges aus vom Meer im Tag.

Für Völkerzüge der Vandalen
Ist Raum darin, für Zelt und Vieh—
In Vasen wuchs die Zeit und Schalen
Und wächst, doch über fließt sie nie.

Ein Tropfen mag es einmal wagen,
Er neigt sich über, hängt am Rand,
Vom Altern ausgenommen und verschlagen
Wie außer Leib und außer Land. (*Die Gedichte*, 395–96)

TIMELESS AWAKENING

In the garden the north grew by night,
and still I am not heavy with time.
So have I been exempted
from aging like the world surrounding me?

On garden beds the white flake melts
in the evergreen broom and beech,
in wilted fern the hair hangs
from a wolfhound or fox.

In vases time grew and in cups,
they accepted fulfillment
passively, and listening—
only, my time is not within.

Perhaps a dream entered it,
not inquiring about my dreams,
and comets drag their tails
through a night which won't give way to day for me.

There armadas rest from battle and wind gusts,
the ore in the thick steel,
the ammonite rests from the sea in day
on the height of the mountain.

For the migration of the Vandals
space is there, for tent and beasts—
In vases time grew and in bowls
and grows, but never does it overflow.

A drop might dare it once,
it leans over, hangs on the rim,
exempted from aging and displaced
as if outside body, outside land. (author's translation)

Zeit (time) occupies the center of the poem's innermost inception, but also structures its argument by clarifying the position from which the voice speaks. The opposition of duration and transitoriness assumes the form of the "evergreen" in the garden and the suggestion of cut flowers in vases— only, since this cannot be a literal reading, the "evergreen" takes the meaning of the lasting while that which no longer lives ("In vases") appears to be growing. The *Beete* (garden beds) may be cultivated and receptive to organic growth, although the *Ginster* (broom) is, tautologically, a wild evergreen anyway; but the "vases" as vessels are artifacts and constructs for retaining time by delimiting and hence measuring it. The ephemerality ("In vases time grew") grew and grows ("wuchs"; "wächst") in inverse relation to the withering of flowers, if these were in fact flowers and not the image in a poem. This opposition is without doubt complex, harboring the contrast of historical time and the speaker's time ("only, my time is not within"). The question of non-aging as a premise for refusing to go with the times ("So have I been exempted/from aging like the world surrounding me?" ll. 3–4) develops into a more certain hypothesis of non-aging ("A drop … /exempted from aging and displaced/as if outside body, outside land"). One is reminded of Kasack's "I no longer know:/am I or is the world gone?" This *Tropfen*, not bound by region or nation or narrow qualities, becomes the shy "drop" and minute bit of time that has dared to escape the confinement of definable parameters in order to participate in something like eternal truths or values. The speaker posits a moment of truth outside the collective historical and ideological movement. The oppositional perception of self and political-historical reality, of interiority and exteriority cannot enter a dialectic process of cognition or action, unless in the form of the poem as the site of working through the dilemma. No resolution and hence no closure is possible under current conditions. In August of 1932 Loerke committed an entry to his diary, as foreshadowed in "Timeless Awakening": "Perhaps desperation over the dire political circumstances. Life has lost its meaning" (Diaries; *Tagebücher*, 265). Weighed down by history, though understanding himself as being nonpolitical, Loerke could not realize a nature poetry in which nature was isolated and free from history (Schulz, 383). Time caught up with the poet and entered into poetic speech.

Eight years later, after Germany's attack on Poland but before Stalingrad, Georg Britting published in *Das Innere Reich* 7 (1940–41) a little poem entitled "Violets," which in its preoccupation with simple-minded harmlessness creates the illusion of some sort of normalcy and consolation under duress. Without referring specifically to Britting's poem, Schäfer revives the designation *Anakreontik* for verse such as this (56–58).

VEILCHEN

Wo die Veilchen stehn
Im ersten Gras—
Im Vorübergehn
Siehst du das:

Eine alte Frau,
Die sich zu ihnen bückt,
Und sich eines pflückt,
An die Brust sich steckt
Das junge Blau.

Und die Frau erschrickt,
Als hätte sie getan,
Was sich nicht für sie schickt,
Als gäbs für Blumenraub
Nur eben eine Zeit:

Die Zeit im Mädchenkleid,
Da Brust an Brust sich drückt—
(Nun wird sie rot)—

Als sei für Veilchen das,
Und ihnen vorbestimmt,
Der schönste Tod. (74)

VIOLETS

Where the violets stand
in the first grass—
this you can see
when walking past:

An old woman
who bends down to them
and picks one
to place it on her bosom,
that young blue.

And the woman starts,
as though having done
what was not quite fitting,
as though for robbing flowers
there were only one time:

the time of the little girl's dress,
when breast presses against breast—
(now she is turning red)—

as though for violets this were,
and predestined for them,
the most beautiful death. (author's translation)

Such dalliance at a time of war and the mechanization of death, which Britting himself had intensely experienced during World War I, follows an agenda differing markedly from that of the poems by Kasack and Loerke, although "Violets" attempts in feigned naïveté to negate time. Its disingenuousness lies in its gesture of wanting to emulate Goethean simplicity, perhaps as a conscious echo of his poem "Found" (Gefunden) an allusion his readers would have immediately understood, but also in a male fantasy about what female sentiment might or indeed should be. Furthermore, to speak of death in such a poetic context, and especially in the form of teleological fulfillment ("predestined"), when so much dying was occurring elsewhere, takes on conspicuous significance. One wonders whether the closing stanza, whether consciously intended or inadvertently uttered by the author, supports preparedness for death and suggests a desirability of death as the supreme sacrifice to the fatherland in time of war.

In view of such benign or possibly not entirely so benign reflection on transience and the presence of the past, one might compare the poem with Günter Eich's "On a Very Old Photograph" (Zu einer sehr alten Photographie), first published in *Der Bücherwurm* under the much different circumstances of 1934.

ZU EINER SEHR ALTEN PHOTOGRAPHIE

Aus vergilbtem Bilde
über dem Bücherbrett
atmet ein Lächeln milde
hin zu Wand und Bett.

Aus dem schwarzen Rahmen
und aus toter Zeit
blickst du, ohne Namen,
du, Vergangenheit.

Aber die Sekunde,
die dich festgebannt,
wurde Zeit und Stunde,
hielt dich unverwandt.

Und das Lächeln schwebte
immer noch im Raum,
unverändert lebte
im Aug' derselbe Traum,

als schon die bittre Lauge
der Zeit geätzt das Haar
und als das müde Auge
schon längst geschlossen war. (*GW*, 1:194)

ON A VERY OLD PHOTOGRAPH

From yellowed image
over the bookshelf
a smile breathes gently
over towards wall and bed.

From the black frame
and from dead time
you glance, nameless,
you, the past.

But the second
that captured you
became time and hour,
held you steadfastly.

And the smile floated
still in the room,
unchanged the same dream
lived in your eye,

as the bitter solution
etched your hair
and as the tired eye
was already long closed. (author's translation)

The actual "theme" of the poem is not the ancient photograph itself but at once "the past" (*Vergangenheit*) in terms of seconds and hours and the timelessness of the past ("in toter Zeit"). The photograph becomes pretext for the allegorical vehicle with which Eich attempts to concretize a vaporized instant—just as this poem itself became such a "photograph" for later readers looking back to a text looking back to a visual image. The eye (l. 16), apparently fixed on the viewer of the photograph, provides a privileged yet illusory and, one might add, escapist link between the past of the photograph and the present of the poem. From this photograph, and hence from the past and transitoriness, emanates an aura which, according to Walter Benjamin, is inexorably bound to the "here and now" of the individual so portrayed in the photograph. "In the fleeting expression of a person's face," Benjamin writes, "the aura appears from old photographs for the last time. This is what constitutes their melancholy and incomparable beauty" (author's translation, 489). The six years separating the texts by Britting and Eich also unavoidably separate historical consciousness; they also account for a shift of reader expectation placed on such texts, since Britting, writing around 1940, was anticipating the actual catastrophe of war, while Eich averted his gaze from the early preparations for this catastrophe.

The war's end of course did not preclude a continuation of unpolitical mainstream writing, which in turn came under no immediate challenge from returning exile writers. Obviously all writers after May 1945 had at some level to face the reality of mass destruction of life, the reality of responsibility and guilt, though few felt duty-bound to thematize this so quickly. In 1946 Karl Krolow wrote on poetry in his time: "Poetry in our time must follow its urge in that it simultaneously raises time." (author's translation; 7). Just how was poetry supposed to elevate time —however this concept might be understood—onto a higher plane? In April 1947 Wilhelm Lehmann wrote his "German Time 1947" (Deutsche Zeit 1947), a title suggesting a direct reckoning with the times as evoked in the initial lines:[4]

Blechdose rostet, Baumstumpf schreit.
Der Wind greint. Jammert ihn die Zeit?
Spitz das Gesicht, der Magen leer,
Den Krähen selbst kein Abfall mehr.

Verlangt nach Lust der dürre Leib,
Für Brot verkauft sich Mann und Weib.
Ich lache nicht, ich weine nicht,
Zu Ende geht das Weltgedicht.

Da seine Strophe sich verlor,
Die letzte, dem ertaubten Ohr,
Hat sich die Erde aufgemacht,
Aus Winterohnmacht spät erwacht.

Zwar schlug das Beil die Hügel kahl,
Versuch, versuch es noch einmal.
Sie mischt und siebt mit weiser Hand:
In Wangenglut entbrennt der Hang,
Zu Anemone wird der Sand.

Sie eilen, grämlichen Gesichts.
Es blüht vorbei. Es ist ein Nichts.
Mißglückter Zauber? Er gelang.
Ich bin genährt. Ich hör Gesang. (173)

Tin-can rusts, tree-stump screams,
the wind complains. Is it lamenting the times?
The face drawn, the stomach empty,
not even rubbish for the crows.

The emaciated body demands lust,
man and woman sell themselves for bread.
I laugh not, I cry not,
the poem of the world is at an end.

Since the stanza, the last,
lost itself to the deafened ear,
the earth has opened,
awakened late from winterly impotence.

The ax may have struck the hills bald,
try, try it yet again.
It [the stanza] mixes and sifts with a sage hand:
the slope begins to burn as a glow of cheek,
the sand becomes anemone.

They hurry with sullen face.
It blossoms past. It is nothing.
Did the magic fail? It worked.
I am nourished. I can hear song. (author's translation)

The poem's opening gambit anticipates Böll's designation of *Trümmer-literatur* for the writing about observable reality in the immediate postwar period. The poem, reminiscent of Meckel's "Invocation of a Poem" (see above), may recall, but only superficially, the disillusioned laconism of Eich's poem "Inventory" (Inventur), first published in 1948 in *Distant Farmsteads* (Abgelegene Gehöfte), but Holthusen's "Tabula rasa" (written, according to its author, as early as 1943 and first published in 1945 in *Die Wandlung*) proves a closer relation. Lehmann's initial gesture seems to suggest a new vocabulary, not to mention new attitudes, motifs, and imagery, for poetry emerging from the chasm. Since universal poetry is at an end ("the poem of the world is at an end"), the poet's first and ultimately only responsibility would here seem to be a recuperation of poetic speech, and in this vein the poem closes: "Did the magic fail? It worked./ I am nourished. I can hear song." The implicit conclusion indicates that timeless, poetic values can transcend even the most irritating and threatening of circumstances and that the poet can and indeed should resume his vocation.

For his poem "Taking a Breath" (Atemholen), written in August of the same year, Lehmann had considered two other titles, "Day in August without Time" (Augusttag ohne Zeit) and "Timelessness in the Garden" (Zeit-losigkeit im Garten), both of which reveal the unerring proclivities of the text. The poet assumes a continuity of time on a grand scale, and so in the larger context of the origins of poetry recent history finds itself relegated to secondary importance: "The war of the world is now history become still."

Toward the end the text articulates a central concern: "Time is standing
still" (ll. 5–6, 17).

ATEMHOLEN

Der Duft des zweiten Heus schwebt auf dem Wege,
Es ist August. Kein Wolkenzug.
Kein grober Wind ist auf den Gängen rege,
Nur Distelsame wiegt ihm leicht genug.

Der Krieg der Welt ist hier verklungene Geschichte,
Ein Spiel der Schmetterlinge, weilt die Zeit.
Mozart hat komponiert, und Shakespeare schrieb Gedichte,
So sei zu hören sie bereit.

Ein Apfel fällt. Die Kühe rupfen.
Im Heckenausschnitt blaut das Meer.
Die Zither hör ich Don Giovanni zupfen,
Bassanio rudert Portia von Belmont her.

Auch die Empörten lassen sich erbitten,
Auch Timon von Athen und König Lear.
Vor dem Vergessen schützt sie, was sie litten.
Sie sprechen schon. Sie setzen sich zu dir.

Die Zeit steht still. Die Zirkelschnecke bändert
Ihr Haus. Kordelias leises Lachen hallt
Durch die Jahrhunderte. Es hat sich nicht geändert.
Jung bin mit ihr ich, mit dem König alt. (180)

TAKING A BREATH

The smell of the second hay harvest floats on the path,
it is August. No clouds.
No rough wind moves along the ways,
only thistle seed sways slightly enough for it.

The war of the world is now history become still;
a play of butterflies, time is lingering.
Mozart composed, Shakespeare wrote poems,
thus it is ready to hear.

An apple falls. Cows tear at grass.
Through a gap in the hedge the sea shines blue.
I hear Don Giovanni plucking the zither,
Bassanio rows Portia over from Belmont.

Those who are incensed also want to be invited,
Timothy of Athens and King Lear as well.
What they suffered protects them from forgetting.
They are already speaking. They sit down with you.

Time is standing still. The snail spirals
its house. Cordelia's quiet laughing echoes
through the centuries. It has not changed.
With her I am young and old with the king. (author's translation)

One wonders what, if anything, has really changed in the intervening years for the poet or for the voice in his poetry. We should make a clear distinction between Lehmann's strategies of writing, which include, significantly, avoidance, withdrawal, and compensation, and, for example, Loerke's work in the 1930s. For Loerke poetry seems by contrast driven by a strong if submerged modernist impetus and by a more confrontational mode of speech, despite his inherently conservative and traditionalist stance, in which the raw presence of history was not welcome. It is as if time and history had guided Loerke's pen against his will, whereas Lehmann dealt more cunningly with comparable temporal and historical pressures on his writing.

All of the poems mentioned, and many others as well by poets such as Günter Eich, Josef Weinheber, Hermann Claudius, Bodo Schütt, Reinhold Schneider, and Hans Egon Holthusen, evince historical time and voice, regardless of how convoluted, deeply buried, or willfully negated the former, how constructed the latter. It would be necessary to ascertain to what degree poets consciously reflected on these thoughts or even incorporated them into their explicit poetics, although the poets tend to argue on different (aesthetic) levels and not on how their poetry might have originated in sublimated, repressed, or compensated poetic concepts. Here too we might find suggestiveness, a sense of drift, unintended snatches of betrayed truthfulness. Only a few contemporary essays appear to claim much relevance to this specific topic, although these few do span the period from 1927 to 1952. For example, Rudolf Paulsen's brief essay, "The Poet and the Times" (Der Dichter und die Zeit, 1930), argues for the timelessness of great art as part of the intense debate in the late 1920s on the death of lyric poetry when threatened by urban industrial society, new media and new genres. In this essay he rehearses an all too familiar standpoint: "The poet is guided, not by conditions of external existence in time, but by what is absolute. Thus he is always dealing with primeval phenomena." In a similarly structured traditionalist argument, delivered to Munich students with considerable personal risk in 1935 as a public lecture, Ernst Wiechert's "The Poet and the Times" (Der Dichter und die Zeit) claims that poetry belongs to a realm of timelessness and expresses skepticism about the role of contemporary poets. He rejects the notion of any present—including, his argument implies, that of 1935—mistaking its values for eternal values and doing so in poetry (12). He states what is most on his mind: "But the poet beyond time: that is what the hungry are waiting for. For there are many, many hungry people in our time who do not wish to stand at the periphery, since the fate of their people is in a burning way their own fate" (author's translation, 15).

In the immediate postwar period, Fritz Usinger's 1946 essay "Coming Home to Time" (Heimkehr in die Zeit) proves remarkable in its articulation, one fears, of a consensus:

Germans have a profound relationship with time.... In their very being, Germans are not people of the present.... But Germans are threatened by the infinitude of time, just as they are by the infinitude of space. That is, they are susceptible to feelings of forlornness to which the insight into time's infiniteness can lead. (author's translation, 161)

What Usinger has to say lies not in the communication but in the position from which he speaks: his point of departure is an attitude and mentality with roots in pseudomystical, pseudometaphysical abstraction. One might call it merely simplistic and naïve if Usinger had written it in isolation from historical events and genuine reflection on their meaning.

In this period of *inner emigration* under the Nazis, the absence of historical time functions as a prerequisite and justification for the very existence of poetry. While an implied poetics of extratemporality would seem to preclude time, the evocative power of language is not questioned and the ineffable is present at best in the form of a coquettish "trope of the unutterable" (*Unsagbarkeitstopos*). Silence, a modernist dilemma, is nowhere seriously threatening, except perhaps in the vein of Benn's observation, made in late 1943 or early 1944: "One calls those writers visionary, whose verbal gifts are not adequate to their view of the world" (Schriftsteller, die ihrem Weltbild sprachlich nicht gewachsen sind, nennt man in Deutschland Seher, *SW*, 4:356). In the end the question becomes what the text accomplishes as a poetic text, and this includes its responsibility toward its own time. A new mode of poetic speech is conceivable within subversive oppositional writing, but it is doubtful whether strictly speaking it would belong to *inner emigration* at all or merely to the fringes thereof, becoming a poetic exercise of writing along historical fault lines.

Notes

1. On questions of period threshold and synchronicity of poetic consciousness, see Olschner, "Die Gleichzeitigkeit des Ungleichzeitigen."
2. See the photographs of Hans Grimm and others in *"Das Innere Reich, 1934–1944."* Werner Volke, ed., *Marbacher Magazin* 26 (1983): 29, 42.
3. "Not only do we measure the movement by the time, but also the time by the movement, because they define each other" (*Physica*, iv. 220 b). See Whitrow, 42. Aristotle's definition of time entails the "'numbering' of motion and change in relation to before and after" (Whitrow, 61). Cf. the related notions, in English and German, of "count"/ "recount" and "zählen"/"erzählen."
4. Walter Dirks rejected the poem in 1947 for *Frankfurter Hefte* and Lehmann published it in a collection in 1950; he in turn considered and rejected other titles: "Poem of the World" (Das Weltgedicht), "Sustenance" (Nahrung), "End and Beginning" (Ende und Anfang), "Sustenance of the Poet" (Nahrung des Dichters).

Works Cited

Adorno, Theodor W. *Gesammelte Schriften* [GS in text]. Ed. Rolf Tiedemann in collaboration with Gretel Adorno, Susan Buck-Morss, and Klaus Schultz. Frankfurt am Main: Suhrkamp, 1997.

——. "Minima Moralia. Reflexionen aus dem beschädigten Leben." *Gesammelte Schriften*. Ed. Rolf Tiedemann in collaboration with Gretel Adorno, Susan Buck-Morss, and Klaus Schultz. Vol. 4. Frankfurt am Main: Suhrkamp, 1997.

——. "Noten zur Literatur." *Gesammelte Schriften*. Ed. Rolf Tiedemann in collaboration with Gretel Adorno, Susan Buck-Morss, and Klaus Schultz. Vol. 11. Frankfurt am Main: Suhrkamp, 1997.

Benjamin, Walter. "Das Kunstwerk im Zeitalter seiner technischen Reproduzierbarkeit." (2. Fassung). In *Gesammelte Schriften*, ed. Rolf Tiedemann und Hermann Schweppenhäuser. Vol. 1. Frankfurt am Main: Suhrkamp, 1974.

Benn, Gottfried. *Sämtliche Werke* [SW in text]. Ed. Gerhard Schuster in collaboration with Ilse Benn. Stuttgart: Klett-Cotta, 1986–.

——. *Briefe an F. W. Oelze 1932–1945*. Foreword by F. W. Oelze. Ed. Harald Steinhagen and Jürgen Schröder. Frankfurt am Main: Fischer, 1979.

Celan, Paul. *Gesammelte Werke in fünf Bänden, 1: Gedichte 1*. Ed. Beda Allemann and Stefan Reichert with Rudolf Bücher. Frankfurt am Main: Suhrkamp, 1983.

Carossa, Hans. *Sämtliche Werke*. Vol. 1. Frankfurt am Main: Insel, 1978.

Dirks, Walter. "Die restaurative Charakter der Epoche." *Frankfurter Hefte* 5 (1950): 942–54.

Eich, Günter. *Gesammelte Werke* [GW in text]. Ed. Axel Vieregg. Frankfurt am Main: Suhrkamp, 1991.

——. "Innere Dialoge." *Gesammelte Werke*. Vol. 4: *Vermischte Schriften*. Ed. Axel Vieregg. Frankfurt am Main: Suhrkamp, 1991.

Emmerich, Wolfgang. "Kein Gespräch über Bäume. Naturlyrik unterm Faschismus und im Exil." In *Natur und Natürlichkeit. Stationen des Grünen in der deutschen Literatur*, ed. Reinhold Grimm and Jost Hermand, 77–117. Königstein/Ts.: Athenäum, 1981.

Fehse, Willi and Klaus Mann, eds. *Anthologie jüngster Lyrik*. Preface by Rudolf G. Binding. Hamburg: Enoch, 1929.

Hohendahl, Peter Uwe. "The Displaced Intellectual? Adorno's American Years Revisited." In *Die Resonanz des Exils. Gelungene und mißlungene Rezeption deutschsprachiger Exilautoren*, ed. Dieter Sevin, 110–20. Amsterdam and Atlanta: Rodopi, 1992.

Holthusen, Hans Egon, and Friedhelm Kemp, eds. *Ergriffenes Dasein*. Ebenhausen: Langewiesche-Brandt, 1953.

Kasack, Hermann. *Das ewige Dasein*. Berlin: Suhrkamp, 1943.

Koch, Thilo, ed. *Gottfried Benn liest: Der Ptolemäer, Soll die Dichtung das Leben bessern? Urgesicht, Gedichte*. Deutsche Grammophon 2757 001, n.d.

Korte, Hermann. "Lyrik am Ende der Weimarer Republik." In *Literatur der Weimarer Republik 1918–1933 (Hansers Sozialgeschichte der deutschen Literatur vom 16. Jahrhundert bis zur Gegenwart, 8)*, ed. Bernhard Weyergraf. Munich: dtv, 1995.

Krolow, Karl. "Das Gedicht in unserer Zeit." In *Das Gedicht in unserer Zeit*, ed. Friedrich Rasche. Das Forum. Eine Schriftenreihe zu Fragen der Zeit. Hanover: Adolf Spoonholtz, 1946.

Lehmann, Wilhelm. *Sämtliche Gedichte: Gesammelte Werke in acht Bänden* [SG in text]. Vol. 1. Ed. Hans Dieter Schäfer. Stuttgart: Klett-Cotta, 1982.

Loerke, Oskar. *Die Gedichte*. Ed. Peter Suhrkamp. Rev. Reinhard Tgahrt. Frankfurt am Main: Suhrkamp, 1984.

——. *Tagebücher 1903–1939*. Ed. Hermann Kasack. Frankfurt am Main: Suhrkamp, 1986.

Meckel, Christoph. *Suchbild. Über meinen Vater*. Frankfurt am Main: Fischer, 1983.

Olschner, Leonard. "Die Gleichzeitigkeit des Ungleichzeitigen. Lyrische Tendenzen zwischen *Ewiger Vorrat deutscher Poesie* (1926) and *Transit* (1956)." In *Schwellen. Germanistische Erkundungen einer Metapher*, ed. Nicholas Saul, Daniel Steuer, Frank Möbus, and Birgit Illner, 185–195. Würzburg: Königshausen & Neumann, 1999.

Paulsen, Rudolf. "Der Dichter und die Zeit." *Der Schriftsteller* 18, no. 9 (1930): 40–41.

Rilke, Rainer Maria. *Sämtliche Werke, 2: Gedichte. Zweiter Teil.* Ed. Rilke-Archiv, in collaboration with Ruth Sieber-Rilke and Ernst Zinn. Wiesbaden: Insel, 1963.

Schäfer, Hans Dieter. *Das gespaltene Bewußtsein. Über deutsche Kultur und Lebenswirklichkeit 1933–1945.* Frankfurt am Main, Berlin, and Vienna: Ullstein, 1981.

Friedrich Schiller, *Werke, 1: Gedichte in der Reihenfolge ihres Erscheinens 1776–1799.* Ed. Julius Petersen and Friedrich Beißner. Weimar: Böhlau, 1943.

Schneider, Reinhold. "Blauschwarzer Himmel, Wolken." *Lyrik.* Sel. and afterword by Christoph Perels. Frankfurt am Main: Insel, 1981.

Schulz, Gerhard. "Zeitgedicht und innere Emigration. Zu Oskar Loerkes Gedichtbuch 'Der Silberdistelwald' (1934)." In *Zeit der Moderne. Zur deutschen Literatur von der Jahrhundertwende bis zur Gegenwart,* ed. Hans-Henrik Krummacher, Fritz Martini, and Walter Müller-Seidel. Stuttgart: Kröner, 1984.

Usinger, Fritz. "Heimkehr in die Zeit." *Welt und Wort* 1 (1946).

Volke, Werner, ed. *Das Innere Reich, 1934–1944. Eine Zeitschrift für Dichtung, Kunst und deutsches Leben.* Exhibit catalogue. *Marbacher Magazin* 26 (1983).

Whitrow, G. J. *Time in History: Views of Time from Prehistory to the Present Day.* Oxford and New York: Oxford University Press, 1989.

Wiechert, Ernst. *Der Dichter und die Zeit. Rede, gehalten am 16. April 1935 im Auditorium Maximum der Universität München.* Ed. and foreword by Friedrich Witz. Zurich: Artemis, 1945.

Chapter 7

DEPICTIONS OF THE STATE IN WORKS OF THE *INNER EMIGRATION*

Colin Riordan

The ability of non-Nazi writers inside Nazi Germany to express dissidence, or even to practice resistance through their work remains a matter of debate. In J. M. Ritchie's view, "writing idylls, historical novels, or 'pure' poetry could be forms of protest against Nazi brutality" (Ritchie, 113). Similarly, Wolfgang Brekle argues that much nonfascist literature composed or published in Germany may be seen as offering resistance in the form of "the literature of passive resistance" (this and all other translations by the author). His definition of literary *inner emigration* thus includes both "the literature of the intellectual opposition, which consciously offers humanistic alternatives [*Gegenbilder*]" (8) and *samizdat* attacks on the regime. Ralf Schnell, in the best and most comprehensive work on the topic, prefers to highlight (11–12) the distinction between the clear oppositional stance of illegal underground resistance literature on the one hand, and on the other, the published work of bourgeois Christian writers, in which any oppositional stance must at most emerge through implication. Reinhold Grimm acknowledges the difficulty of defining the term, but concludes: "Only a visibly oppositional attitude deserves the name *inner emigration*" (411). What none dispute is that a group of conservative Christian writers, some initially sympathetic to the regime, harbored increasing doubts that they attempted to express in work published in Germany after 1933.[1] Werner Bergengruen, Ernst Wiechert, and Reinhold Schneider all belong to this group.

Initially, it was the writers themselves who raised the question of instrumentality, or, as Ralf Schnell puts it, "the question of the function of literary inner emigration in the Third Reich and its possible effects" (13). The riskiest means of using legally published literature for oppositional purposes was encoding. There are relatively few examples for obvious reasons; if the allegory was too clear, then the writer concerned risked non-publication at best, imprisonment or death at worst. For example, although Ernst Wiechert's novella *The White Buffalo* (Der weiße Büffel, written in 1937) was not published until after the collapse of the regime, the writer's imprisonment in Buchenwald in 1938 was in part due to his having read excerpts publicly.[2] Safer but more obscure metaphorical representations, on the other hand, might not be recognized by readers. Perhaps aware of the effective limitations of such encoding, Werner Bergengruen argued in his memoirs *Memories at My Desk* (Schreibtischerinnerungen, 1961) for an additional form of instrumentality, contending that the most that could be hoped for was to encourage the like-minded, to stiffen the collective backbone of a readership that might range from irresolute Party members through the indifferent to those afraid to voice their opposition. Bergengruen claims that his readers confirmed this effect: "Innumerable people have assured me that the books helped them to stave off despair and bring them to the decision that those years demanded of everyone, to find courage within" (208). While reader reaction is relatively difficult to gauge, there existed a third form of instrumentality that can be judged more reliably. Both Werner Bergengruen and Ernst Wiechert subsequently claimed that their literary activity during the twelve years of Nazism, which by force of circumstance could never be overtly oppositional, at least attempted to establish a *Gegenbild*, an opposing image, an alternative system of values to those which prevailed (See Bergengruen, 176; Wiechert, 689).[3] Using literature to represent a *Gegenbild* to Nazism was both less risky and easier for the audience to assimilate. While it would be reductive to imagine that these three are the only possible categories of instrumentality, and simplistic to suppose that any one work might be unable to combine various shades in various combinations, the notion of *Gegenbild* represents the focus, the ideal outcome of any form of resistance, and so is worthy of special attention.

To put it another way, these writers' reservations about National Socialism raise the question of what they favored in its place. While individual views naturally varied, all political values had to be defined in relation to the National Socialist state. The omnipresent state was the overwhelming problem that they all faced, and so the conception of the state implied by their works, that is, of an alternative constitution or form of government, is of primary importance. The conservative, nationalistic views of all the prominent inner emigrants, and the frequent recourse to history as a background for muted dissidence, justify an enquiry into whether there was a particular historical model for the kind of state that was implied by their works. The question has been posed before: Ralf Schnell considers the constitutional historian Carl Schmitt to have provided the model for Werner Bergengruen and Reinhold Schneider, while Bill Niven sees Prussianism as the model for Ernst Wiechert (see Schnell, 132–34; Niven, 1–20). But neither explores in detail the historiographical implications of such models, nor do they locate depictions of the state in the context of German constitutional tradition and historical evolution. As the starting point for my examination, Werner Bergengruen's *The Grand Tyrant and the Court* (Der Großtyrann und das Gericht; hereafter *GG*) offers fertile material for teasing out at least the principles of an implied constitutional framework.

Published in 1935, *The Grand Tyrant and the Court* is, in effect, a detective novel with a highly complex plot, yet a simple premise. The ruler of Cassano, a city-state in renaissance Italy, resolves to test the loyalty of his subjects and closest advisers by demanding that the murderer of a monk, Fra Agostino, be brought to justice within three days. On the pattern of *Oedipus Tyrannus*, it eventually transpires that the tyrant himself had committed the murder as part of his test, the twist being that he ultimately admits the sin of "wanting to resemble God" ('*Gottähnlichseinwollen*'). Not only his subjects, but he himself has learned a bitter lesson. What is of interest for my purposes, however, is not merely the character of the tyrant himself, but the way in which the dictatorship, or tyranny, is depicted in the novel.

The early part of the novel may easily be read as a coded representation of aspects of the dictatorial state in which it was written. Surrounding himself with an aura of fear maintained by his "security forces" (*Sicherheitsbehörde*; *GG*, 11), the tyrant has left a toothless senate intact as a sop to the citizens' previous autonomy (*GG*, 17). The head of the security authority, Nespoli, has managed to create the general illusion of total power: "it was almost omnipotence, almost omniscience, that was exaggeratedly ascribed to him" (*GG*, 21). There is even a reference to the tyrant's "chancellory" (*Kanzleiraum*; *GG*, 36), which can hardly have failed to arouse echoes of the Reich chancellor himself. The impression of a state that in a number of key aspects resembles Nazi Germany peaks with a description no contemporary reader could fail to recognize: "So mighty was the shadow which the grand tyrant threw over all aspects of life in Cassano that even the most trusted friends speaking privately hardly dared to utter a derogatory or even critical word about him. Everyone had the sense of his possible presence" (*GG*, 60). It seems clear, then, that the tyrant does arouse echoes of Hitler, and the city-state Cassano of Germany. The crucial question is whether the reader is invited to approve or disapprove. The answer is both, for from about chapter 15 of the first book onwards, a more positive picture of the tyrant and of his chief of secret police begins to emerge. Moreover, a sophisticated analysis of the nature of an absolutist state takes place, to a point that invites agreement with the advantages offered by such a constitution.

The change in the way both the state and its chief leaders are presented is transmitted in at least three portrayals: those of Nespoli, of the tyrant, and of the constitution of the state itself. Arousing the reader's sympathy for Nespoli is a relatively straightforward matter, for the first book is narrated from his point of view, revealing his fear of the threat hanging over him. Moreover, he is involved in a love story, which provides a further human dimension to the character. The tyrant, too, is gradually presented in a positive light. Again, the change comes about from about chapter 15 of the first book onwards. The tyrant is popular: "he was loved by the simple people, just as is almost any tyrant" (*GG*, 77). In this transitory phase, the positive commentary is two-edged, but stands in stark contrast to the image of unrelenting oppression which has previously been presented. At the end of chapter 17 it appears, contrary to the previous impression, that the tyrant's treatment of Nespoli is not sadistic, but educative: "'Whether you are doing *the right thing* or not—act. It matters less whether a person is doing the right thing, than whether his actions drive him to acquiring new strengths that he didn't have before'" (*GG*, 78). While the sentiment certainly has fascistic overtones, the impression of a merely brutal oppressor is further eroded. As the novel progresses, we are invited to sympathize with the tyrant, who reveals a more human side to his nature by pardoning Diomede for hasty behavior (for which the young man might have expected imprisonment at the very least), and even commends him for supporting his father (see *GG*, 143). The tyrant begins to appear less capriciously dangerous than beneficently strict. His discussion with Diomede in chapter 12 of book 3 makes him seem intelligent, reasonable, and open-minded. In book 3, chapter 23, he is willing to think the best of Diomede even though the reader is aware of the thorough deception that the young man is practicing. Finally, at the end of the novel the tyrant learns his lesson and repents.

So far as the notion of any *Gegenbild* is concerned, the acid test is the way in which the *system* is portrayed; that is, in this case, the authoritarian ruling structure. Strikingly, the novel offers no challenge to hierarchical authoritarianism itself. For all his conversion, the tyrant remains the dictator of an absolute state. What is of interest, then, is the *nature* of the tyranny that Bergengruen depicts. There are many indicators that allow us to construct a picture of the kind of constitution that obtains in Cassano. Nearly all are contained in book 3, the pivotal of the five books, in which the transformation in the tyrant, or in our view of him, takes place. Chapters 12, 21, and 22 are of particular interest in this respect. All three consist of conversations with Diomede where the wiser, more experienced tyrant gradually makes clear to the young, intelligent but inexperienced Diomede what the advantages of absolutist rule are.

In the first of these episodes, Diomede appears furiously before the tyrant, complaining about the accusations against his father Confini (see *GG*, 139). The tyrant promises that the guarantee not only of justice, but also of fairness, resides in his person alone: "I promise you … that I will embark on this task in all fairness. But you need to recognize that I have to protect not only the line of Confini, but also justice in Cassano" (*GG*, 140). Yet the tyrant does believe in the proper administration of justice and in the rule of law: "we all serve justice" (*GG*, 141), he comments, and in response to Diomede's claim that rumor has it that his father will not receive a Christian burial and his property will be confiscated if he is found guilty, the tyrant replies tersely: "In accordance with the law" (*GG*, 141).[4] This impels Diomede to point out that he is in favour of absolutist rule, and, indeed, is antidemocratic, being in favor of "a state constitution with a strong man at the top. This gives every last one of its people a strength they cannot have if furriers and wool merchants are squabbling over political office" (GG, 142). The positive portrayal of both the tyrant and Diomede in these scenes suggests that Bergengruen endorses this view. In the state of Cassano, the tyrant is the ultimate instance; he is both the source and the guarantor of justice in the state. While Diomede accepts this unquestioningly, he draws attention to the potentially conflicting demands of justice and political expediency that are, to one extent or another, always the problem of any state: " under certain circumstances a state can be better served with an unjust verdict than with a just one" (GG, 190). The tyrant suggests in response that the interests of "the safe standing of a community" (GG, 190) and those of "divine justice" (GG, 190) are identical: "would you not wish to grant me the latitude to administer justice in the way that best serves as its highest goal the continuation of the mighty and prospering community of Cassano, even if thereby perhaps the lesser claim to justice of some market woman is lost?" (GG, 190). At this stage it is axiomatic for the tyrant that the demands of justice and those of the state are identical.

The final discussion strives to make clear the advantages of absolute rule over democracy, oligarchy, or other systems where power is distributed. The tyrant explains that the reason the building works had never been completed before was that "the dominant alliances among the parties of the ruling families and guilds changed so frequently that nobody trusted themselves to drive such projects through" (GG, 226). Again, not only is there no challenge to the "strong man" theory of government, but the views of both the tyrant and Diomede on this point are not ironic. The tyrant then amplifies his view when Diomede refers to him in passing as "the will of the people" (GG, 231). Though reluctant to accept this at face value, he does admit to being "the hidden will of the people" (GG, 231). Diomede objects that a ruler might be mistaken in his belief that he can separate the open will of the people from their hidden will, and that only a god could do this. The tyrant brushes the objection aside and asserts that in practical terms, he, as the ruler of Cassano, has to take action to cut through the indecision of "the rule of parties" (GG, 235). Although the tyrant has appeared patient, thoughtful, and reasonable throughout these discussions, as the chapter ends he arrogantly reiterates his claim to be able to administer justice in a divine manner. His only sin is hubris, it seems. In all other respects the absolutist system of government is presented as positive.

It would be perverse to ignore the striking similarities to the Hitler state that appear in these depictions of the constitution of Cassano. The parties that previously ruled have been brushed aside; the absolute ruler wields absolute power while claiming to provide peace and order. Since this state of affairs appears in a positive light, the text could easily be read as an endorsement of the Nazi state with the single caveat that the leader refuses to have recourse to religion to lend his position legitimacy. The argument then seems to be that dictatorship is an acceptable system so long as the dictator acknowledges the supremacy of divine justice. The Nazi state would thus be recommended with that one change. And indeed this would be a possible, if superficial reading of the text: it explains why the *Völkischer Beobachter* declared it to be "*the* dictator novel [*Führerroman*] of the Renaissance period." But this would only be part of the story: there is also a case for suggesting that the novel *does* present a *Gegenbild* to National Socialism. For it would be equally perverse to ignore the differences between the form of state in *The Grand Tyrant and the Court*, as apparently endorsed in the narrative stance, and the National Socialist state.

The discussions between the Grand Tyrant and Diomede depict the ruler as intelligent, thoughtful, reasonable, and genuinely concerned for the well-being of all his subjects. He is concerned to improve their lot, while the use of fear as an instrument of power is shown to have been a mistake. Even after the murder of Fra Agostino, nobody in the novel is physically harmed by the tyrant or his men. Even the intimidation he practices has an educative function. Far from being a brutal barbarian, this ruler is able to recognize faults and change his ways. The impression we are left with is of an absolutist ruler who has a rational and compassionate approach to ruling the state, but who has no intention of relinquishing power. While unquestionably a despot, he is, arguably, an enlightened despot. Indeed, for all the tyrant's Machiavellian deviousness, much in evidence earlier in the novel, by the end, with Bergengruen's sanction, he has begun to look very much more like an enlightened absolutist than either a renaissance prince or a Hitler.

Indeed, it is my contention that enlightened absolutism does constitute the historical model that figures as the *Gegenbild* in the novel. My argument rests on two pillars: firstly, the historiographical topicality of enlightened absolutism both in 1930s Germany and elsewhere, and secondly, thematic resemblances between its doctrines of government and those to be found in the novel. I shall deal with these issues in turn.

First used in the second half of the eighteenth century, the phrase "enlightened despotism" is still seen today, even though its internal contradictions were pointed out as early as 1786. The term "enlightened absolutism" is preferred by modern historians, although this too has a long history. The primary source of the theory of enlightened absolutism, and the origin of the term itself, is to be found in the writings of German historians in the nineteenth and early twentieth centuries.[5] The phrase was coined in 1847 by the German historian Wilhelm Roscher. His ideas were developed by nationalist historians such as Reinhold Koser and Heinrich von Treitschke, who were "confident about the beneficent role of the state and saw enlightened absolutism primarily in terms of the growth of its power" (Scott, 6). The influence of Roscher and his successors on German historiography can hardly be underestimated: it seems reasonable to suppose that the nationalist, highly conservative writers of *inner emigration*, choosing as they so often did historical themes, would have at least been aware of their ideas, and more probably, were familiar with them. This supposition is lent further weight when one considers that internationally, the theory of enlightened absolutism was developed most intensively during the late 1920s and the early 1930s. In 1928 the International Committee of Historical Sciences (ICHS) launched an enquiry into enlightened despotism, "one of a series which aimed to identify common developments and shared experiences in the past, and thereby to increase mutual understanding in the present" (Scott, 8). The final report was made in 1937, although the debate was documented in the ICHS bulletin from 1926 onwards, with articles in 1930, 1931, 1933, and 1936. The topic was therefore on the international historical agenda throughout the period under discussion, and one might reasonably expect that a cultivated, conservative writer of historical novels would have been aware of the debate.

In essence, enlightened absolutism was an attempt to create a method of government that retained all power in the hands of the monarch, yet directed that power in domestic policy toward improvements in educational, social, and economic conditions. The preeminent example of the type was, of course, Frederick II of Prussia, although Joseph II of Austria and Catherine the Great are commonly cited, while a host of minor rulers have also been included in the category. Germany's contribution to the new philosophy of kingship was thus considerable. Studies of enlightened absolutism identify cameralism as an essential factor. This was "a distinctive body of economic ideas which emphasised the primacy of a state's wealth and the prosperity of its subjects.... Its advocates believed that the best foundation for a wealthy and strong state was a happy and prosperous population, and this led rulers to regulate the lives of their subjects in considerable detail" (Scott, 18). German theories of natural law were similarly influential. These ideas "fostered the idea of a social contract by which the people pledged obedience and loyalty in return for a ruler's protection and his efforts to advance their interests" (Scott, 19). Enlightened absolutism, then, amounted to a transformation in the principles of government in authoritarian states: "Proprietary, divine right monarchy gave way to the new sense of the duties and responsibilities of kingship, epitomised by Frederick the Great's famous aphorism that 'the king was the first servant of his people'" (Scott, 19).

At the same time, it is important to be aware of the limitations of enlightened absolutism. In particular, the Enlightenment provided only the broad framework within which the ideas of enlightened absolutism flourished. Few historians have been successful in showing that a particular measure derived from a particular enlightenment doctrine. Attempts to do so were somewhat discredited when a series of quotations which, it had long been supposed, purported to show the enlightenment origins of Joseph II's reforms, turned out to be forgeries. And enlightened absolutists were still absolutists: none of them succeeded in abolishing serfdom, for example. Similarly, it was considered progressive that Frederick II reduced the number of executions to a mere fourteen or fifteen a year, and reserved the use of torture for only the most pressing cases. Nonetheless, this was unquestionably progress by comparison with his father's reign.

This very combination of ruling by force with an enlightened approach in broadest sense appears in *The Grand Tyrant and the Court*. That the tyrant rules by force and demands total obedience needs no further proof. But by the same token, all the main elements of enlightened absolutism are present in the novel: education, readiness to reform, and an interest in the welfare of the common people as the guarantee of a strong state. As shown above, the attitude of the *Großtyrann* toward Nespoli and Diomede is educative, rather than even merely didactic. The tyrant's willingness to enter into debate with Diomede on the principles of government, and his final acceptance of the young man's ideas (he promises to employ him as an adviser) speak of a willingness to reform. Just as important is the tyrant's attitude to the country and his subjects: "'A beautiful country, Massimo!' he said. 'And a useful people! I hope to be able to do a great deal more for both before I die'" (GG, 71). This benevolent attitude is certainly more reminiscent of an enlightened absolutist than of an unreconstructed dictator. He has the interests of his community at heart: "I have … a particular interest in building. But I try to direct this interest so that what comes into being is appropriate and useful to the community" (GG, 227). Moreover, the very structure of the plot points in this direction. The whole impetus is toward understanding, improvement of everybody's lot, and indeed, enlightenment. The parallel with enlightened absolutism here is striking. For enlightened absolutists believed in the possibility of change for the better without radical restructuring of society or anything approaching social equality. And certainly this is the upshot of Bergengruen's novel: while reform is not only possible, but desirable, crucially, it need not involve any radical changes to the way in which hierarchic authoritarianism is used to rule the state. The clearest possible historical model for this is enlightened absolutism, typified by Frederick the Great of Prussia.

There are objections that could be made to this analysis. The major one concerns religion. In particular, it might seem perverse to connect enlightened absolutism with the *Großtyrann*, who, after all, is depicted as regaining the very sense of divine right to rule that the enlightened absolutists sought to supersede with the idea of the social contract. Frederick the Great, it might be argued, was at his most scathing when dismissing Christianity as a farrago of myth. But Frederick also made religious toleration a main plank of his policy, as Kant noted with approval (39) in the seminal essay "Answer to the Question: What is Enlightenment?" (Beantwortung der Frage: Was ist Aufklärung?) Furthermore, while he was the most influential, Frederick II was certainly not the only enlightened absolutist ruler in Europe, nor the only one amongst the German states. To quote Charles Ingrao on the smaller German states:

Germany was a Christian society with deeply held religious beliefs. Enlightenment ideas could survive in Germany only when they could exist with Christian thinking and values. The great Enlightenment figure Christian Wolff had, in fact, effected a marvellous synthesis of the two by placing the forces of nature and natural law under God's protection, and by making human reason an instrument for rationally studying the world He had created. (Scott, 226)

Thus it was possible for enlightened rulers to retain Christian belief, but to recognize that they no longer ruled by divine right for their own benefit, and that their paramount responsibility was to serve the welfare of the state (Scott, 228). Furthermore, examples of progressive ruling can be found among the seventy-odd prince-bishops and other ecclesiastical rulers who held sway over about a third of the German population.

A similar objection might be made to the concept of justice in the novel. How can it be enlightened for an absolute ruler to assume all the judicial offices in his own person? Frederick II, for example, regarded independent processes of law, and the principle of equality before the law, as crucial to his reforms. But the tyrant, too, upholds that principle, as his treatment of Diomede shows: he is determined to adhere to the processes of law, consults "jurists" (*Rechtsgelehrte*) and makes it clear throughout that justice as a principle is paramount. Furthermore, Frederick II was not always consistent in adhering to his own theories; at times he interfered in the process of law and took command, as it were, of a particular case. Be that as it may, how can a rational, enlightened view of a state's legal system consider the will of God to be the ultimate arbiter? In fact, precisely that view prevailed in Frederick's Prussia, despite the king's own beliefs. As T. C. W. Blanning illustrates, the legal reforms that were the mainstay of the transformation in the Prussian state were in fact initiated in the reign of Frederick William I by Samuel Freiherr von Cocceji and continued under Frederick II. Cocceji, too, believed that "all law had its origin in the will of God" (Scott, 266). The conversion of Bergengruen's tyrant to this point of view does not, then, conflict with the historical model of enlightened absolutism.

One final objection may be to the notion that the tyrant embodies in his person the will of the people. This assumption is made initially by Diomede, and is ultimately accepted by the tyrant (though with reservations). If the image presented of the tyrant is to be taken as a positive one, then we must assume that Bergengruen, too, endorses this view. While it would seem at first sight to be contrary to any rational approach, there is an important precedent. In the above-mentioned essay "What is Enlightenment?" of 1784, Kant specifically refers to Frederick the Great, although in a manner that clearly indicates the limitations to absolutist power: "those matters that even a people may not decide for itself can be decided even less by a monarch for the people, since his legislative authority resides in the fact that he unites the will of the people in his own" (Kant, 39–40). This, in effect, is the lesson that the tyrant has to learn in the novel.

The constitutional model for Cassano, then, is to be found neither in renaissance Italy nor in Hitler's Germany, but in the enlightened absolutist states of the eighteenth century. Before considering the implications of this analysis, however, I wish to take another example: that of Ernst Wiechert, in whose novel *The Simple Life* (*Das einfache Leben;* hereafter *EL*) Frederick the Great lurks as a ghostly presence. Wiechert's novel is much less overtly concerned with constitutional questions and the role of the state than is Bergengruen's, but suggests more clearly a *Gegenbild.* The alternative presented is summarized by the title, the novel advocating, in an unambiguous, if long-winded, manner, a retreat from the hurly-burly of urban life, living in harmony with nature and the seasons, and attaining a lofty disinterest in base politics through spiritual contemplation. Thomas von Orla is the central protagonist, a naval officer haunted by memories of the Kiel mutiny. He is repulsed by life in the Weimar Republic, all the vices of which are represented by his wife, whom he leaves to live a simple life as a fisherman and writer. His retreat is in the heart of Prussia, and it becomes clear that Prussian values are of primary importance in the novel. The question of what might be meant by "Prussian values" is not, however, as straightforward as it might appear.

Bill Niven argues that such values were wholly pernicious, and that Wiechert was a secret or subliminal Nazi sympathizer: "one might be forgiven for seeing in *The Simple Life* an intended panegyric of the spiritual forefathers of National Socialism and thereby, implicitly, of National Socialism itself" (13). In Niven's view, the Prussianism in the novel "suggests that the best social unit is a hierarchy based on military and war-time structures" (13). Curiously, however, one aspect that emerges strongly from the novel is its antimilitarism, which is remarkable given the circumstances of its writing. It seems to me that to see the Prussianism of the novel as merely a precursor of National Socialism, and therefore to conclude that Wiechert harbors a "secret admiration" for those he claims to hate, is something of a simplification (Niven, 12; he includes Bergengruen and Jünger in this assessment). Moreover, the notion of the writer of *The Simple Life* as a Nazi sympathizer sits uneasily with his dissident speeches to students, public protest over the treatment of Niemöller, his subsequent arrest, multiple interrogations by the Gestapo, and two months' imprisonment in Buchenwald. In the light of this disparity, the portrayal of social structures and the implied theory of the state underlying *The Simple Life* would repay closer investigation.

The most obvious distinction between *The Simple Life* and *The Grand Tyrant and the Court* is that Wiechert eschews a historical setting, choosing instead to date the events of the novel from the Weimar Republic, little more than ten years before the time of writing. Bill Niven is right to point out that "Wiechert's novel is not purely a cipher novel" (14), and that the novel is written at least as much against the post–World War I period as against Hitler's Germany. But this does not mean that earlier historical models must necessarily be absent. For the Weimar Republic is mostly present only as a threatening shadow, mainly represented by the behavior of Orla's wife, who neglects him and their son as she spends her time partying, spending money, and taking lovers and drugs in great quantity.

Orla soon leaves Berlin for the countryside, where the sordid realities of Weimar Germany (as Wiechert perceived them) rarely penetrate. In fact, the novel is set overwhelmingly in a world redolent of preindustrial Germany. Orla inhabits a mythic landscape, a rural idyll that can never have existed. And, as Niven himself notes, there are a number of thematic references to the Prussia of Frederick the Great.

The most obvious of these is the General's manservant, who is of a stature and dress reminiscent of Frederick the Great's personal bodyguard. The element of contrivance that characterizes the introduction of this more than faintly ridiculous figure is at least partly offset by the mildly ironic stance of the latter part of the description. But the very contrivance draws attention to the implication: the General, an old warrior, as a Frederick II figure. Other references make this notion more than mere idle speculation. The hall in the General's residence is decorated with "swords from Frederickean battles" (129), for example. Orla's role is that of a vassal to the General, who tells him he is: "An officer and nobleman, who would have been a source of joy to the great king" (*EL*, 253). The impression is created of a microcosmic model of eighteenth-century Prussia. Yet surprisingly, given the conjunction of a retired general and a retired naval captain, the aggressive militarism that was the enduring characteristic of Frederick the Great's Prussia is by no means the most prominent here. Indeed, the novel is pervaded by a sense of disillusionment with militarism, or at least with the abuse of military virtues as they are perceived.

In a clear parallel with Wiechert himself, Orla writes two books on the navy and the philosophy of warfare, which incur the displeasure of the right. From the very beginning a strong sense that war is no longer a useful means of achieving one's ends characterizes the text. The tone of deep disillusionment with war, or at least its consequences, is all too apparent when Orla contemplates his fellow passengers in a Berlin train: "Cripples, many cripples, the bloody witnesses of a great sacrifice, who looked numbly or full of hatred at the healthy; who had been told that they were heroes, and who now believed that others looked on them as poor fools, an unwelcome army that now had to be dragged along on the way to a new destination" (*EL*, 17). It cannot easily be argued that this is merely disillusion with the betrayal of Versailles, for the novel by no means advocates renewed feats of the military glory that characterized Prussia in its heyday. Orla certainly eschews any such ambition: "No experiences, no heroic roles, no aura around the head" (*EL*, 75). Warfare, at least in its modern manifestation, finds little place.

Probably the most revealing episode in this respect takes place later in the book. Bildermann asks Orla if he would take part in some local war games. Orla considers the request before finally agreeing. His obvious reservations about becoming involved in this effort to circumvent in an amateur way the provisions of Versailles do not sit easily with an analysis of the novel that sees a romantic notion of militarism as a hallmark of the kind of Prussianism advocated, especially since he chooses to take on the job of umpiring rather than being directly involved himself. This is not to say that Orla is against what are in the novel perceived as military virtues: he certainly is not. But his views do differ from those of the colonel in charge of the exercise, who notes that in his book, Orla had expressed "odd views," but that "all men loyal to the king had to stand together against these rogues" (*EL*, 275). Orla's reply is instructive:

> Which rogues did the Herr Oberst mean? That was another thing they didn't usually do on the island, calling a whole class of people rogues, even if they did something wrong or evil, or even intended to do so. And the salvation of the fatherland, which they all desired, seemed to him only possible if the people as a whole stood together, but not if a fatal abyss were to remain open between the caste of gentlemen and the caste of rogues. (275)

Orla's brand of Prussianism is clearly not the vainglorious, militaristic kind promoted under National Socialism, an ideology that made the condemnation of whole supposed categories of people a central murderous element of its policy. In fact, he derives his values less from Frederick II's external military exploits than from his domestic reform and philosophy of government. The interpretation of enlightened absolutism disseminated by the nineteenth century German historian and biographer of Frederick the Great, Reinhold Koser, remained prevalent in Germany until well past the middle of the twentieth century. Koser saw a "crucial and novel element in enlightened absolutism to be the acceptance by the monarch of a social contract, imposing obligations in return for the obedience and support derived from the population at large" (Scott, 7). In effect, the people would pledge obedience and loyalty in return for protection and welfare. For this to work, social cohesion was essential. In *The Simple Life* it is these elements of Prussianism that are celebrated, rather than exclusively those highlighted by Niven.

Indeed, the novel reveals much evidence of contractual obligations in ways that recall, in microcosm, the social contract. The first and most detailed of these is the contract that Orla signs on entering the General's employment. Significantly, the General reminds Orla of one of the Prussian kings in the conversation they have before the contract is presented. This contract sets out the duties and rights of both parties, and exchanges loyalty for welfare and protection:

> Thomas read what he would possess in rights and duties, in salary and "produce," discovered … that he would have to "be a faithful servant to his lordship always," just as the latter swore to "keep him well in all needs of body and soul." It seemed to him, once he had read this slowly, that the contract might well have come from the time of that laconic king. (EL, 69–70)

Not even Wiechert means this entirely seriously, of course, but a serious point lies behind it. Orla and the General are entering into more than an employment contract; this is a social contract that depends on a hierarchy in which each party agrees to their place and is content to accept it for the benefits that accrue to both sides. This is the whole basis of enlightened absolutism. The substance of the contract is, moreover, reinforced both by the archaic formulations and the references to "that laconic king" as well as the "Frederickean giant" (71) who conducts Orla to and from the interview. Significantly, however, it is the domestic, reformatory aspect of Prussianism that is stressed here, rather than the aggressive militarism.

Nor is this an isolated example. In a sentimental scene, the General's granddaughter, Marianne, seals a contract of understanding with Bildermann, much older than she but her social inferior:

> "Yes, now we're here," she repeated, "and now we'll stay here, isn't that right, Bildermann?"
> "*For ever*, little lady!" he said.
> She puts her small hand in his, and they know that they are sealing a contract. (*EL*, 151)

That this is not merely a coincidence, but is meant to reprise the previous contract, seems clear from a similar occasion near the end of the novel when Marianne seals a contract with Thomas Orla that explicitly refers to the one between him and the General:

> "We have sealed a contract, the two of us, haven't we Thomas?" He nodded.
> "To be a faithful servant to his lordship always; isn't that right, Thomas?"
> "Indeed. And to keep him well in all needs of body and soul."
> "And the contract is irrevocable, grandfather, do you hear? A lifelong contract!" (*EL*, 362)

This emphasis on contracts implies a relationship between social classes in an unchallenged hierarchical system, but it is a relationship that works by agreement, not terror. While this *Gegenbild* might be criticized for being idealistic and nostalgic, its allusion to enlightened absolutism does show that the notion of the state implied by the novel need not be interpreted as the threshold to fascism. The challenge to Nazism in the novel refers to the source of power and the exercise of it. And there is a possibility that this approach may well have been more effective in winning over potential but conservative opponents of Nazism than any amount of fiery condemnation (which could not have been written or published anyway), or, indeed, than coded direct criticism. As in the case of Bergengruen, the *Gegenbild* is thus much more coherent than has hitherto been supposed, and what is more, is locatable to a specific historical model.

Finally, Reinhold Schneider's *Las Casas before Charles V* (1938; Las Casas vor Karl V, hereafter as *LC*) differs from both *The Grand Tyrant and the Court* and *The Simple Life* in that it is not only more strongly Christian, but a genuine historical novel, set in the time of the conquistadors. Like *The Grand Tyrant and the Court*, its centerpiece is a constitutional debate, but one conducted on a more sophisticated level and around which the whole of the plot revolves. The historical figure at the center of Schneider's novel is Bartolomé de Las Casas, the Dominican friar who devoted his life to improving the lot of the native inhabitants of the South American countries colonized by Spain in the sixteenth century. In 1550 the Holy Roman Emperor Charles V called an assembly at Vallalodid to resolve the question of whether wars for conquest might justly be waged against the Indians. The resolution was to be achieved by means of a disputation between Las Casas and Gines de Sepulveda, his principal opponent and a constitutional lawyer. Sepulveda represented the view that, given the sinful and barbaric nature of the natives, it was lawful to make war on them in order to achieve their conversion to Christianity, and that this result could only be achieved by subjection. Las Casas argued that the Christian faith could not countenance the brutal treatment meted out to the Indians, that their human dignity should be respected, and that the result of this policy would benefit both sides. Although Sepulveda won the disputation formally, the moral victory may be considered to have been with Las Casas (see MacNutt, 288).

Schneider keeps closely to the main outline of the historical characters and events. The core of the disputation, as in the historical record, is a conflict between religion and the state. Schneider glosses Sepulveda's error as a readiness to sacrifice the interests of justice (in the abstract sense) to those of the state when he has Las Casas refer to "men of the ilk of Sepulveda, who for the sake of the state shattered the one clear and majestic law into a thousand splinters, which could be exploited arbitrarily" (*LC*, 64). The subordination of the demands of natural justice to the expediency of the state was, in 1938, naturally a matter as important to dissidents as was the persecution of whole peoples. And Sepulveda's arguments must have had a seductive logic in the context of 1930s Germany: "For how can faith be helped, if not by an orderly state?" (*LC*, 92). Christianity depended on the security of a Christian state, and therefore all means were acceptable to enforce the security and well-being of the state. The welfare of its subjects would automatically flow from that.

Las Casas's argument begins with the subjects: if the Emperor protected the interests of his subjects, not only would they more readily convert to Christianity, but their loyalty and affection would result in a more secure state that would be cheaper to maintain. At no time does Las Casas dispute the right of Spain to colonize South America and convert the inhabitants. He mounts no challenge to fundamental structures. Both sides agree on those and on the aims of the state: the dispute concerns methods. As in the case of the renaissance city-state Cassano, the values that emerge are not those most typical of the politics and society of the historical period. Rather, Schneider focuses on the politics of reform, even if the reform derives its inspiration from religion. The supremacy of the state is not called into question; that the state may capriciously breach any moral, ethical, or legal boundaries, is. The role of the state and the opportunities and limitations offered by statecraft are at the forefront.

The possibilities of reform emerge through Las Casas's success in converting the Emperor to his point of view, and thus, in the end, converting a technical loss into an overwhelming victory in the disputation. The portrait of Charles V that emerges is of a humane ruler who has the best interests of all his subjects at heart. Las Casas believes that the Emperor called the disputation "out of true sympathy for the fate of his Indian peoples" (LC, 79). The Emperor's willingness to introduce reform, which Schneider saves as the dramatic and sudden dénouement, is uncompromising: "'These' said the Kaiser … 'are the New Laws. Read and consider them: it is nothing trivial. I want to free the Indians'" (LC, 136). Schneider has adapted the historical circumstances to his own purposes; although in 1542 Las Casas had persuaded the Emperor to issue legislation to improve conditions for native peoples, it was not and could not have been the kind of sweeping liberation that Schneider, for dramatic and political purposes, postulates in his novel. The enlightened absolutist principle, however, is clear throughout: the rights and dignity of human beings must be respected by the state, for the sake of both the state and its citizens.

In each of these novels, then, a *Gegenbild* emerges that derives its inspiration not from the specific historical settings of the novels, but from a period in European history characterized by reform and the improvement of the citizens' lot. Admittedly, such an approach might be construed as hopelessly nostalgic and thus an empty attempt at aesthetic dissidence. Yet it would be wrong to equate the authoritarian structures of enlightened absolutism morally with Nazism, or to view them merely as the original patterns that ultimately gave rise to Nazism. For those eighteenth-century states were reformist: the values that are derived are on the whole positive ones, the notion of the state one that is beneficial to the individual by comparison with what had gone before. And there is more to it than this. The leading enlightened absolutist was Frederick II of Prussia. His military exploits and status as one of the founders of modern Germany led to his being glorified in an almost hysterical manner in Nazi Germany. Drawing attention to his domestic virtues rather than external aggression was surely a necessary counterbalance. This was, of course, also done in a more direct way by writers such as Reck-Malleczewen, or, even more appositely, Jochen Klepper in his novel of Frederick Wilhelm I and his son, *The Father* (Der Vater). Yet in the novels under discussion here the emphasis is less on the specifics of the rise of Prussia than on the values, approach, and tendency toward improvement that characterized enlightened absolutism and that were in many ways the direct opposite of those that characterized contemporary Germany. However great one's reservations concerning the political views of these writers, their *Gegenbild* offered a more attractive, if ultimately inadequate, position for conservatives reluctant to support National Socialism.

Notes

1. A study devoted to this group may be found in H. R. Klieneberger, *The Christian Writers of the Inner Emigration* (1968). Other useful studies include Reinhold Grimm, Jost Hermand, eds., *Exil und innere Emigration* (1972); Ernst Loewy, *Literatur unterm Hakenkreuz. Das dritte Reich und seine Dichtung. Eine Dokumentation* (1990); Sigrid Bock and Manfred Hahn, eds., *Erfahrung Nazideutschland. Romane in Deutschland 1933–45* (1987); and Lothar Bluhm, *Das Tagebuch zum Dritten Reich: Zeugnisse der Inneren Emigration von Jochen Klepper bis Ernst Jünger* (1991).
2. Surprisingly, the apparently more direct coded criticism of Ernst Jünger's *Auf den Marmorklippen* was published with no personal consequences for the author, perhaps because of his earlier closeness to the National Socialist cause.
3. See the investigation of this question in Eric Dickins's "'Gegenbild' and 'Schlüsselschrift.'"
4. Later, Vittoria comments: "His lordship is known as a lover of justice" (*GG*, 172). In the context, this seems more than mere flattery.
5. The following account draws substantially from H. M. Scott, ed., *Enlightened Absolutism. Reform and Reformers in Later Eighteenth-Century Europe* (1990).

Works Cited

Bergengruen, Werner. *Der Großtyrann und das Gericht*. Munich: dtv, 1987.
———. *Schreibtischerinnerungen*. Zurich: Verlag der Arche, 1961.
Brekle, Wolfgang. *Schriftsteller im antifaschistischen Widerstand 1933–45 in Deutschland*. Berlin and Weimar: Aufbau-Verlag, 1985.
Dickins, Eric. "'Gegenbild' and 'Schlüsselschrift': Wiechert's *Das einfache Leben* and Bergengruen's *Der Grosstyrann und das Gericht* reconsidered." *German Life and Letters* 38 (1985): 97–109.
Grimm, Reinhold. "Im Dickicht der inneren Emigration." In *Die deutsche Literatur im Dritten Reich: Themen, Traditionen, Wirkungen*, ed. Horst Denkler and Wolfgang Wippermann, 406–26. Stuttgart: Reclam, 1976.
Kant, Immanuel. *Werke*. Vol. 8. Berlin and Leipzig: de Gruyter, 1923.
Klieneberger, H. R. *The Christian Writers of the Inner Emigration*. Mouton: The Hague, 1968.
MacNutt, Francis Augustus. *Bartholomew de Las Casas. His Life, His Apostolate, and His Writings*. New York and London: The Knickerbocker Press, 1909.
Niven, Bill. "Ernst Wiechert and his role between 1933 and 1945." *New German Studies* 16 (1990–91): 1–20.
Ritchie, J. M. *German Literature under National Socialism*. London and Canberra: Croom Helm, 1983.
Schneider, Reinhold. *Las Casas vor Karl V*. Frankfurt am Main: Suhrkamp, 1990.
Schnell, Ralf. *Literarische Innere Emigration 1933–45*. Stuttgart: Metzler, 1976.
Scott, H. M., ed. *Enlightened Absolutism: Reform and Reformers in Later Eighteenth-Century Europe*. London: Macmillan, 1990.
Wiechert, Ernst. *Das einfache Leben*. Frankfurt am Main: Ullstein, 1995.
———. *Sämtliche Werke*. Vol. 9. Vienna: Desch, 1957.

Chapter 8

THE LIMITS ON LITERARY LIFE
IN THE THIRD REICH

Volker Dahm

No matter how controversial many questions about the period of National Socialism have been and still are, the verdict on National Socialist cultural policy appears unambiguous: culture was consistently and systematically misused by those in power in order to propagate their ideology and carry out their political goals. However, since 1983, when Hans Dieter Schäfer pointed out the existence during the Third Reich of a non-National Socialist literature by younger authors that was nevertheless tolerated by supervisory offices, more recent historical and empirical research into particular areas of National Socialist cultural policy has made it clear that the cultural reality of the Third Reich cannot adequately be grasped by such a generalizing approach (see Steinweis; Barbian).[1] Indeed, in order to understand this reality it is necessary to analyze the systemic formation of National Socialist cultural policy and the cultural maneuvering space that resulted from that formation.

On 7 February 1934, at a conference of the presiding officers of the Reich Chamber of Culture (Reichskulturkammer, or RKK) and of its subsidiary chambers, Propaganda Minister Joseph Goebbels made a statement on the subject of artistic freedom in the National Socialist state. Among other things, he declared:

> Fundamentally even in the National Socialist state the point of view must be maintained that art is free.... In itself, art can thrive only if it is given the greatest possible freedom of development. And those who believe that they can constrict or abbreviate art, or even all of culture, are thereby committing a sin against art and against culture. When I say that art is free, however, I would, on the other hand, like to protest against the point of view that such a statement would mean giving free rein to an absolutely anarchical cast of mind in art. This cannot be the case, and if it is the case, then the problems that we have had to

register again and again ... in the last fourteen years will appear. As free as art must be and can be in its own developmental laws, it must feel itself equally bound to the laws of the national life of a people. Art and culture arise in the maternal soil of a people; hence they will always be bound to the ethical, social, national, and moral foundational laws of the state. But within the framework and the limits of national laws of life, art must be given freedom to develop ... for art is never produced by organizations but always by single human beings, by individuals.[2]

This statement by Goebbels reveals *in nuce* the fundamental structural problem of National Socialist cultural policy, which resulted in a specific kind of totalitarian cultural management. To be sure, as a totalitarian mass movement National Socialism rejected the elitist conception of art held by both the liberal bourgeoisie and nationalist and *völkisch*-bourgeois groups; however, in principle it held fast to a bourgeois conception of culture, according to which artistic works and cultural values could come into existence only through individual creative accomplishments. At the same time, National Socialist cultural criticism was governed stereotypically by the belief that the supposed decline of art and culture in the era of the parliamentary system (the commercialized cultural sphere of Weimar, the hegemony of so-called civilization and asphalt art; in a word, "cultural bolshevism") was the result of unrestrained individualism, unleashed primarily by elements alien to the race and the people, which threatened to destroy the life foundations of people and nation. For this reason the freedom of art was supposed to develop only within the framework of "national laws of life." The unfettered artistic individual wrought by liberalism, the individual who recognized only his own personal interests, who was responsible only to himself, and who could be controlled and limited only by bourgeois penal law, was to be replaced by the artist as a servant and member of his people and nation. The relationship of National Socialism to art and culture was thus characterized, on the one hand, by a bourgeois-individualist conception of art, and on the other hand, by a monolithic social and racial self-understanding.

The magic means for transcending this contradiction, for reconciling the individual and society, was the idea of a Germanic "racial community" (*Volksgemeinschaft*). The "racial community" was, in the imagination of Hitler, a revolutionary social model that would eventually overcome the historic disunity of the German people: its splitting into clans and tribes in the Germanic period, into dynasties in feudal society, and into religious groupings, political parties, and class organizations in more recent times and up to the present.[3] At one point Hitler formulated the essence of the racial community thus: "Above and beyond classes and social positions, professions, religious denominations, and all other confusions of life rises the social unity of the German people, irrespective of social position and background, founded in blood, brought together through a thousand-year life, and bound together by fate to thrive or to perish."[4] Conflicting individual and group interests, it was believed, ought to be settled not in social battles and by social contracts, as in the defunct pluralist-parliamentary system, but through actions by everyone oriented toward the collective good of people and nation. In November of 1933 Goebbels wrote in the official newsletter of his ministry: "National Socialism does not want ... a coercive state; it wants members of the people who, through free, creative work, achieve the best for the common good."[5] But this common good was determined not by the people's community itself but by the ideological elite of the new society as incorporated in the National Socialist leadership.

In practice the political realization of the ideology of the racial community (*Volksgemeinschaft*) occurred via the elimination of political parties, trade unions, and similar interest groups, as well as of employers' organizations, on the one hand, and via the creation of new National Socialist community organizations on the other. These new mass organizations were supposed to be dominated by a unified will, which would regulate the actions of the individual and correspond to the interests of the entire people.

In the area of culture the RKK law of 22 September 1933 forced everyone active in the arts, culture, or cultural scholarship into "professional collectives" (*Berufsgemeinschaften*). Writers, booksellers, publishers, and librarians went into the Reich Chamber of Literature (Reichschrifttumskammer, RSK); painters, sculptors, gallery operators, art publishers and art dealers into the Reich Chamber of Visual Arts (Reichskammer der bildenden Künste); composers, conductors, musicians, music publishers, and sellers of music into the Chamber of Music, etc. The RKK law not only did away with freedom to organize, it also eliminated freedom of commerce. Anyone in a cultural profession had, in essence, to be licensed, and the various cultural organizations, now gathered together and ideologically coordinated (*gleichgeschaltet*), became agents of the state (see Dahm).

The principle of admission into an organized profession was based on a combination of required organizational membership and the possibility of rejection or removal from the relevant organization. According to paragraph four of the first regulation on the implementation of the RKK law, anyone involved "in the production, in the reproduction, in the intellectual or technical processing, in the dissemination, in the preservation, in the merchandizing, or in negotiations leading to the merchandizing of cultural value" had to be a member of the special chamber responsible for that activity; and, according to paragraph ten of the same regulation, "membership in a particular chamber [could] ... be denied or a member expelled" if "facts" showed "that the person in question does not possess the reliability and aptitude requisite for the carrying out of his activity."[6] The question of when "reliability" and "aptitude" were to be affirmed or negated was intentionally left to the unregulated decision-making power of the respective chamber presidents. In practice, however (and one cannot imagine it otherwise), procedures leading to rejection or expulsion could be carried out only if internal criteria for judgement were available.

At first improvised and then fully developed by about 1936, these criteria were developed by the chambers with the controlling assistance of the various cultural-political special departments and of the legal department of the Propaganda Ministry.

Until now the implementation of rejection and expulsion procedures has been explained only on the basis of examples, primarily by Jan-Pieter Barbian in his overview of National Socialist literary policy, considered a standard work on the topic. Within the framework of my study of the Reich Chamber of Literature (in progress), I have carried out a systematic examination of these procedures. One of the important results of these investigations is that aesthetic criteria played a relatively minor role; i.e., as a rule they were used not at all or in only an auxiliary way. The primary reason for this lies in the fact that most of the representatives of artistic and literary ideas rejected by the National Socialists either emigrated in 1933, or withdrew from public view, or brought themselves into political and aesthetic conformity. To be sure, expulsion procedures were instigated again and again as a result of literary productions that, in the view of one or another Party or state office, conflicted with the political or cultural political goals of National Socialism, but personal features always stood at the center of such procedures. The overwhelming majority of cases dealt with bourgeois notions of morality and value that were now radicalized and brought together with specific National Socialist criteria into a catalogue of personal characteristics. Those affected by the procedures were not just former political opponents of the left or right, Jews, "Jewish mixed-bloods" and their spouses, as well as the members of other "racial" minorities, but also criminals, homosexuals, people with psychological illnesses, and spiritual and religious sects, a spectrum only slightly at variance from the whole spectrum of those persecuted by the National Socialist police. However, there were only two "sets of circumstances" that made expulsion compulsory: active opposition to the regime, as proven by a court judgement or by incarceration in a concentration camp, and the "characteristic of being non-Aryan." For racists, nothing in the world could extenuate the latter blemish.

The ban from a profession (*Berufsverbot*) was a modern, highly efficient instrument of totalitarian cultural policy because it had not simply an executive but also—and above all—a preventive function. By threatening to punish offenses against cultural-political norms—which were codified nowhere, but which, given any sensitivity at all to the spirit of the times, were easily recognizable—with the destruction of the offender's economic existence, such control induced the desired intellectual orientation of an entire professional group. Further measures contributed: first, the creation of a new leadership elite in public cultural institutions, i.e., the removal immediately after the "seizure of power" of all cultural leaders seen as protagonists or beneficiaries of Weimar cultural activity, and their replacement by politically "reliable" and aesthetically conformist leaders in cultural administrations, in state and city theaters, museums and libraries,

172 | *Volker Dahm*

and in state-owned factories, publishing houses, and film production companies; second, the institution of massive cultural propaganda and subsidies, in all areas of culture and aimed at all social classes, which measures, since productive and not repressive, have received generally less attention by scholars. Taken together, these measures were intended not just to reward and pave the way for artists and authors who conformed to political-aesthetic norms, but also to break the educational privileges and the literary monopoly of the bourgeoisie. In particular, books were supposed to have the broadest reception.

These instruments and measures—the purging of personnel and the intellectual disciplining of professional groups via the RKK, the cultural-political changing of the elites, and cultural propaganda and subsidies—combined to create a broad-based system of cultural-political control that would reduce administrative interference in cultural production and distribution to a minimum and thus maintain the principle of an artistic and entrepreneurial freedom of creation limited only by basic national interests.

Hence censorship, the classic instrument of totalitarian control of public opinion, played a smaller role in principle and in reality than is generally assumed. Of course, the situation varied during particular phases of the regime and in particular areas of culture. Whereas the banning of art, music, and literature was carried out intensively in the first years of the regime in order to "cleanse" the market as well as the collections of museums, libraries, and book stores, such banning later functioned only as the final line of defense—to use military terminology—against any violations of rules and norms that still managed to slip through the system in individual cases. The area of literature was the most difficult to survey because of mass production. The regime was able to do without systematic censorship of new publications before or after printing because it could rely on denunciations of undesirable literature if such literature did make it to the market. Official and private denunciations were a part of everyday life in the Third Reich. Another means of interfering in cultural production and distribution via hidden administrative measures was the issuance of informal instructions given individually to particular persons—publishers, writers, etc.—which, in more important cases, were made generally applicable by publication in the confidential newsletters of the special professional groups in the separate chambers. In the area of literature such generalized instructions tended to occur in the case of bans on dealing with particular issues, on advertising or merchandizing specific books, or on engaging in forbidden business relationships, especially with Jewish companies abroad.

Above and beyond the actual tasks of cultural policy, the state and Party interfered massively in the area of cultural events that had previously been dominated by city governments and commercial sponsors. The chief protagonist here was the National Socialist organization "Strength through Joy" (*Kraft durch Freude*, KdF) with its bureaus "After the End of the Workday" (*Feierabend*) and "German Program for Adult Education"

(*Deutsches Volksbildungswerk*). The goal of both bureaus was to promote meaningful and—at the very least—politically "unproblematic" leisure activities for the broad masses. While the national adult education program (into which all city-sponsored adult education programs, among others, had been absorbed) offered lectures and classes in virtually all areas of life, the "End of the Workday" bureau made it possible for ordinary people, who might previously have been prevented from entering bourgeois artistic institutions by lack of money or by fears of social discomfort, to visit the theater, the opera, the operetta, and concerts. The mass effectiveness achieved by KdF is shown by the following figures: in 1938 alone the "End of the Workday" and adult education bureaus carried out 252,000 events with about 61 million participants.

All in all, the cultural constitution of the National Socialist state offers a rather peculiar model of totalitarian culture. Just as in the economy the private method of production was combined with state and plan elements, so too in the realm of culture, individual freedom of creation was mixed with state direction and intervention. The limitations on individual freedom of creation, on the one hand, stood in relation to, on the other hand, the limits of state effectiveness. The discrepancy between the two, the gap in this twofold limitation, constituted in effect a space of freedom for art and culture, a space that resisted all norms and arose pragmatically through the structural correlation of cultural production and cultural administration.

The analysis of a great number of membership and prohibition files of the RSK, and of the lists of banned books and the advertisements for new publications in the booksellers' magazine, has shown that the bureaucracy overseeing literature tolerated anything that was politically indifferent and that betrayed no noticeable aesthetic connection to condemned modernist artistic and stylistic movements. In practice, the Chamber of Literature and the Propaganda Ministry limited themselves to combating anything viewed as anti-National Socialist or as critical of the regime on racial, political, moral, or formal grounds. National Socialist fiction and poetry were desired and promoted, but were not demanded, let alone coerced. In spite of the exclusion of so-called decadent literature and of all kinds of "Marxist" writing, permissible literature hence still included a relatively broad spectrum: from genuine Party literature and writing in sympathy with National Socialism—which, in comparison to the Weimar period, had moved clearly to the right on the scale of political opinion—through works of nonfiction and entertainment, to non-National Socialist literature.

Very similar observations were made years ago about the public libraries, which were supervised professionally and ideologically by the Reich Ministry of Education. Although these libraries were subjected to a systematic political purging between 1933 and 1936, and although the rebuilding of collections in mid-sized and smaller libraries was centrally coordinated, with few exceptions the public libraries did not develop into militantly National Socialist libraries. Such a development was forestalled by the notorious dearth of new conformist belletristic fiction—a dearth caused by the intellectual and formal barrenness of the National Socialist *Weltan-schauung*—and by the personal preferences of readers, as well as, above all, by the unavoidable informational needs of a modern industrial society characterized by the division of labor. To be sure, a core of National Socialist and related literature, estimated to be about 20 percent of the total, was available everywhere, but this core was surrounded by a persistently broad spectrum of literature "oriented … to the diverse nature of groups of users and not limited to a propaganda function" (Boese, 344). Things were no different in the theater. Although the positions of director were occupied by individuals considered politically and artistically reliable, and in spite of the supervisory activities of the *Reich Dramaturge*, one can speak of Nazi infected, but not of National Socialist theatrical programs. From 1934 to 1944 productions were divided in the following way: 19.5 percent, classics; 16 percent, right-wing theater (i.e., Nazi and Nazi-related plays); and 52.5 percent, entertainment theater (see Dussel).

To sum up, the Third Reich was characterized by widespread aesthetic trivialization and a dramatic shift of intellectual standards toward the ideological right wing, but not by a complete or even extensive saturation of cultural production and of cultural life by National Socialist ideology. Inherent in the structure of the system itself, not due to a failure (of enforcement) by the regime, there existed a zone with unclear borders between what was clearly and unambiguously desirable and what was clearly and unambiguously not allowed. This zone offered artists the possibility of withdrawing from the totalitarian claims of the regime by means of aesthetic conventionality or political neutrality, but it also gave those with the necessary willingness to take risks the opportunity to explore the limits of individual freedom of creation. Anyone who wanted to write and publish was certainly subject to many restrictions on content and form—but no one was forced to become a National Socialist writer or poet. Those who became National Socialist literary figures either did so out of conviction or succumbed to the temptation of seeking success and fame through a change of their own opinions.

Translated by Stephen Brockmann

Notes

1. For some time the author of this essay has been working on an examination of the Reich Chamber of Literature. The primary source materials for this study are the membership files of the Chamber in the Berlin Document Center (BDC) of the Bundesarchiv, Berlin (BA).
2. BA R 43 II (*Neue Reichskanzlei*)/1241, fol. 18: Reich Minister Dr. Goebbels on the corporate structure of the cultural professions, in *Deutsches Nachrichtenbüro*, no. 288, 8 February 1934.
3. On Hitler's view of history, see his secret speech to young German officers on 30 May 1942, in H. Picker, 493–504.
4. Speech by Hitler on Heroes' Memorial Day (*Heldengedenktag*, 10 March) 1940 at the Berlin Zeughaus (armory), in M. Domarus, 1479.
5. *Nachrichtenblatt des Reichsministeriums für Volksaufklärung und Propaganda* 21, no. 1 (November 1933): 132.
6. The first regulation for the implementation of the Reich Chamber of Culture law of 1 November 1933, in *Reichsgesetzblatt* 1 (1933): 797–800.

Works Cited

Barbian, Jan-Pieter. *Literaturpolitik im "Dritten Reich". Institutionen, Kompetenzen, Betätigungsfelder*. Frankfurt am Main: Buchhändler-Vereinigung, 1993.

Boese, Engelbrecht. *Das öffentliche Bibliothekswesen im Dritten Reich*. Bad Honnef: Bock + Herchen, 1987.

Dussel, K. "Provinztheater in der NS-Zeit." *Vierteljahrshefte für Zeitgeschichte* 38, no. 1 (1990): 75–111.

Dahm, Volker. "Anfänge und Ideologie der Reichskulturkammer. Die 'Berufsgemeinschaft' als Instrument kulturpolitischer Steuerung und sozialer Reglementierung." *Vierteljahreshefte für Zeitgeschichte* 34, no. 1 (1986): 53–84.

Domarus, M. *Hitler. Reden und Proklamationen. 1932–1945*. Part II. Vol. 3. 4th ed. Leonberg: Pamminger, 1988.

Picker, Henry. *Hitlers Tischgespräche im Führerhauptquartier 1941–1942*. Stuttgart: Seewald, 1963.

Schäfer, Hans Dieter. *Das gespaltene Bewußtsein. Über deutsche Kultur und Lebenswirklichkeit 1933–1945*. Munich: Hanser, 1981.

Steinweis, Alan. *Art, Ideology and Economics in Nazi Germany: The Reich Chambers of Music, Theater, and the Visual Arts*. Chapel Hill: University of North Carolina Press, 1993.

Chapter 9

OPPOSITION OR OPPORTUNISM?

Günter Eich's Status as *Inner Emigrant*

Glenn R. Cuomo

When I first approached the topic of Günter Eich's life and work two decades ago, my intention was to reconcile the "anarchistic noncon-formist" image Eich had cultivated in the last decades of his life with the circumstances of his professional activity under National Socialism. After all, this was the author who had received a devotional letter from Gudrun Ensslin in 1963 (Herbst, A 330), and whose last wish had been to have his ashes deposited in Switzerland next to those of the anarchist Mikhail Bakunin.[1] Would we find evidence of the Eich of *Dreams* (Träume) and *Moles* (Maulwürfe) in the pernicious atmosphere of Hitler's Reich, where the critical stances toward the established powers advocated in these works would have cost a person's freedom, if not life? How did the author of the dictum "Be sand, not the oil in the gears of the world!" (Seid Sand, nicht das Öl im Getriebe der Welt!), which became the motto of the APO (Ausserparlamentarische Opposition) and die Grünen, avoid friction with Himmler's Gestapo? In particular, I was interested in judg-ing Eich's own writings under Nazism according to the standards for authors he presented in his Büchner-Prize speech in 1959: "If our work cannot be understood as criticism, as opposition and resistance … then we are positive and decorate the slaughterhouse with geraniums" (Eich, *Vermischte Schriften*, 627). Was Eich just as controversial a writer twenty-five years earlier, or did he produce "geraniums" as an accommodation to National Socialism?

Any scrutiny of Eich's work in the years from 1933 to 1945, however, was seriously challenged by the relative vacuum that this period repre-sented in Eich's biography. In the first place, the bulk of his writing under Nazism consisted of radio broadcasts that appeared to be almost all nonex-tant and of little significance, according to Eich's postwar assessment: "In those times my radio plays were hardly noticed" (From a letter Eich wrote to Horst-Günther Funke, cited in Funke, 108). In the second place, a great deal has been made out of the apparent focus of Eich's writing during the Nazi period on broadcast texts, to the detriment of his work in other genres, especially poetry. Thus we were confronted with a Nazi-era oeuvre consisting of a "corpus" of works that were largely missing or in obscurity, on the one hand, or unwritten, on the other.

The lack of any substantial "corpus delicti" of texts left postwar critics considerable space for speculation and little grounds on which to question Eich's own claims about his minor role as an author under Nazism. Most telling was the curious form of ex-negativo argumentation, whereby several critics directed more attention to the texts Eich supposedly had not written than to the ones that he had. Drawing upon Brecht's "Schlechte Zeit für Lyrik" (Bad Time for Poetry), they represented Eich's alleged hiatus from poetry as a deliberate act of renunciation, "the poet's supreme sacrifice of self-imposed silence," which protested the political conditions under Hitler (Krispyn, 40–41; see also Müller-Hanpft, 30–31; Schafroth, 26; and Richardson, 18 and 47–48). This "oppositional gesture" of withdrawal into silence, together with criticism of the Nazi regime Eich had allegedly written between the lines of some broadcast texts,[2] allowed him to approach the status of an *inner emigrant*, as problematical as the designation itself is (Brekle, 67–68). In his early overview of Nazi literary policy, Dietrich Strothmann went so far as to denote Eich an "undesirable author" in the eyes of the censors (Tabelle 7a: Buchproduktion 1933–1944: unerwünschte Autoren).

Now, here we have to note in all fairness that in the immediate postwar period Eich had admitted quite candidly that he had not performed any active resistance and should not be considered part of "the secret Germany" associated with the "Inner Emigration" (letter of 1 November 1947 to Willi Fehse, cited in Karst, 88; see also Müller-Hanpft, 31). At the same time, however, in the twenty-seven years he lived after the war Eich volunteered few details about the true extent of his writing career after 1933. Instead he allowed such noninformative reductions to stand as: "He was a soldier from the first to last day of the war" (Groll, 98), which cast him as a "victim of fascism."

Only in the last two decades did we arrive at a series of revelations about Eich's professional activity in the Nazi period as a result of renewed scrutiny of sources from the Third Reich period, especially of new materials that surfaced from the former East Bloc. Among other things, the claims about any conscious renunciation after 1933 of poetry or other literary genres evaporated in the face of an additional story ("The Shadow Battle" [Die Schattenschlacht], 1936) and thirty-five poems Eich had published between 1933 and 1938, in addition to at least thirty poems we know he used in his broadcasts. Moreover, the discovery of some 160 radio broadcasts for which Eich was either the sole author or co-author and the multiple accolades his radio plays received in the Nazi press between 1933 and 1940 place him among the most prolific and respected authors who worked for Goebbels's broadcasting system. Finally, the discovery of several letters that Eich wrote to fellow writers during the Hitler regime provide useful insights into his perception of his career in both the prewar and war years.

In the following pages, I want to explore some of these new findings and touch on the controversy they have sparked. We have one camp of researchers, such as myself, who have been labeled "Denunzianten" (denouncers) for besmirching Eich's character (Storck). On the other side are critics who are stubbornly trying to downplay the evidence of the political compromises that marked his Nazi-era career and construct some form of oppositional stance.

The most difficult piece of evidence to refute is Eich's card in the Nazi Party Master File, indicating that he had applied for NSDAP membership on 1 May 1933 and that in November of that same year the membership process had been stopped on the basis of a letter. This letter has not been preserved in Nazi Party Correspondence files, so we cannot determine whether Eich himself had withdrawn his application or he had failed the Party's background check. However, the latter possibility is highly unlikely in the light of Eich's subsequent professional accomplishments. If the Nazi Party had actually deemed Eich to be "politically unreliable," he would have found it difficult to join the compulsory writers' organization, the Reichsschrifttumskammer (Reich Chamber of Literature), as he did in December 1933 and maintain his membership until the very end, since the chamber followed a strict political and racial screening process. Most importantly, as an "undesirable author" Eich could never have spent the next seven years writing for Goebbels's broadcasting system, the most strictly controlled of all the media, from which authors were barred for the slightest reason, even if their works could still appear in print.

Axel Vieregg recently speculated that Eich had entered and exited the Nazi Party on a "bet" with friends (15). If true, this would bespeak a strikingly cavalier attitude toward the political circumstances, since the membership form required affirmations of one's "Aryan background" and support for the Nazi Party's platform. To be sure, Eich signed on to (and from?) the Nazi Party at a point when the Hitler regime had barely started its criminal acts. In this respect we would have more grounds to condemn Eich's fellow poet Wilhelm Lehmann, who as a professor "felt compelled" to join the party on 1 January 1940,[3] fourteen months after the Kristallnacht and three months after the outbreak of Hitler's aggressive war. But in early 1933, Eich could have had no doubts about the regime's vicious antisemitic and racist agenda, which had constituted the foundation for the Party's program since Hitler announced the NSDAP's twenty-five points in February 1920 (Buckreis, 436–39).

Notably, Eich's flirtation with the Nazi Party was a solo action. None of his immediate colleagues—Martin Raschke, Walter Bauer, Jürgen Eggebrecht, Horst Lange, Peter Huchel, or A. Artur Kuhnert—went this route.[4]

Nor did the prominent poet Gottfried Benn ever join the party, although this mentor figure from whom Eich and Raschke sought guidance and support in 1933 did compromise himself with his early proclamations in support of the new regime and against such émigrés as Klaus Mann.[5] Even the conservative-nationalistic author Hans Friedrich Blunck, the first president of the Reichsschrifttumskammer, did not enter the Nazi Party until the membership rolls were reopened in 1937. Far from qualifying him as an *inner emigrant*, the 1 May entry placed Eich squarely in the company of Martin Heidegger, Herbert von Karajan, and other "March Fatalities" (*Märzgefallene*), who had rushed to accommodate the new regime.[6] And as a "temporary Nazi" for just a few months, Eich was too "tainted" to have lived up to words with which Joachim Kaiser eulogized him in 1973: "Through the Nazi Period he saved himself, somehow and unblemished [*makellos*]" (83, emphasis added).

The mainstay of Eich's lucrative career with the National Socialist broadcasting system was the highly successful *Königswusterhäuser Rural Postman* (Königswusterhäuser Landbote) series, which he wrote in collaboration with his friend Martin Raschke. Their monthly episodes consisting of scenes from contemporary life in the provinces, poems, and songs ran from October 1933 until May 1940. It therefore was a major find when Raschke's copies of the broadcast texts turned up in his papers in Dresden, together with some of Eich's correspondence. The texts themselves did not differ significantly from the excerpts that had been published in 1936 in a commemorative book (Eich and Raschke, *Das festliche Jahr*). But the ones from the later 1930s did indicate that the "heile Welt" (intact world) of the German province that Eich and Raschke depicted was at times also a "Heil Hitler! Welt" (world saluting Hitler) in which the contemporary political situation and even the war could intrude. The most blatant example of this is not a broadcast text, but one of Eich's letters to Raschke, in which he outlines the points for an episode where their *Landbote* character encounters a "Strength-through-Joy" (*Kraft-durch-Freude*)-sponsored group hike in the country. Among the points Eich wants the broadcast to emphasize are: "disciplined hiking in contrast to the 'Wandervogel hordes' and the community-building power of the Strength-through-Joy hiking movement."[7]

Interestingly, Eich closes this same letter with an observation that warrants scrutiny, since it has been taken as evidence that he had tried to maintain some "distance" from the political manipulation of his broadcasts:

> By the way, I heard, not in the radio, but from confidential sources, that bad things are being said about the *Landbote* in Darré's staff. It is rejected in the strongest terms as romantic and liberalistic. (Vieregg, 68)

This passage's significance lies not so much in its indication that Eich and Raschke's rural representations might have been at odds with people associated with Hitler's Reich Peasant Leader (*Reichsbauernführer*) R. Walter Darré, which would be no surprise, but in Eich's perception of his broadcasts as contentious in the eyes of the authorities. The fact was that the broadcasting sector under Goebbels's control pursued a far more liberal cultural policy than did the Nazi Party's extremist faction represented by Alfred Rosenberg, Darré, and others, whom Goebbels ridiculed as "our nationalistic idiots" in his confidential diary entries (Cuomo, "Diaries," 211). Goebbels frequently quashed efforts to sabotage the radio's popular appeal through an infusion of the "Nordic kitsch" favored by some of his rivals in the Party leadership. Therefore the suggestion Eich made at his letter's close that he and Raschke should wind up the *Landbote* series in the coming fall before it was cut from the program was an unnecessary precaution, which Raschke did not heed in any case. Their series survived the first wave of program changes in late 1939 and lasted until Goebbels's wartime propaganda measures eliminated radio play broadcasts from the program in favor of entertaining music in the spring of 1940.

Eich's perception of his works' unacceptable nature to the Nazis also plays a role in the most sensational discovery that has been made in his pre-1945 oeuvre, namely the intact recording on wax plates of his final broadcast text for the Nazi airwaves: *Rebellion in the City of Gold* (Rebellion in der Goldstadt; hereafter *Rebellion*). Eich's broadcast opens in London, where stockholders of the South African gold mines plot to boost the value of their stocks by mandating that higher-paid white workers be replaced by lower-paid blacks. It then shifts to the fates of two married Johannesburg miners, Mike, an Irishman, and Pieter, a Boer, whose livelihoods are threatened by the wage cuts. When an overwhelming military force puts down the ensuing mineworkers' strike, Mike is killed in the bombing attack on the workers' stronghold. Before his wife's eyes, Pieter is subsequently dragged from his apartment and summarily executed as a conspirator.

Now there is no question that Eich had written this work as a contribution to an anti-English radio play campaign starting in January 1940, for which Goebbels and Reichsschrifttumskammer President Hanns Johst had solicited topic proposals from experienced authors (Cuomo, *Career* 62–63). Among the authors who participated were Hans Rehberg, Rudolf Stache, and two of Eich's colleagues from the *Kolonne* days of the Weimar Republic. A. Artur Kuhnert, with whom Eich collaborated on eleven broadcasts between 1933 and 1939, proved to be quite prolific in this campaign and produced two anti-English pieces. Broadcast on 14 February 1940, Kuhnert's "Erika, a Big Deal!" (Erika, ganz groß!) presented a caricature of British diplomats, troops, and gold speculators in Persia. His "Dr. Mackenzie's Mission" (Die Mission des Dr. MacKenzie), broadcast on 2 April 1940, alleged that a British physician had helped hasten the death of the cancer-stricken Kaiser Friedrich III. Peter Huchel, the former *Kolonne* writer who later served as the first editor of the GDR's literary journal *Sinn und Form*, also contributed to Goebbels's propaganda campaign. Huchel's broadcast on 23 January 1940, "The Denshawai Horror" (Die Greuel von Denshawai), has generated just as much controversy among scholars as Eich's *Rebellion in der Goldstadt* ever since I revealed evidence of its existence over a decade ago. Initial claims that Huchel had no part in the anti-British radio campaign have been refuted by Stephen Parker's discovery in Huchel's library of the Propaganda Ministry's special edition of George Bernard Shaw's critique of British colonial policy, in which "The Denshawai Horror" appeared (Cuomo, *Career*, 63 and 153; Parker, "Peter Huchel als Propagandist" and "On Peter Huchel's Adaptation"; also Nijssen).

In Eich's case, Goebbels's propaganda campaign offered not only one last chance to earn a broadcast honorarium, but also the opportunity to secure a work furlough (*Arbeitsurlaub*) from his tedious, but totally safe military duties on the home front. Assigned to the Luftwaffe ground personnel, he was chauffeuring around low-ranking officers in his car and operating a telephone switchboard, hardly the desperate situation that justified further compromise.[8] When we consider Gottfried Benn's famous designation of the army in late 1934 as being "the aristocratic form of emigration" (Benn, 39), we find a striking irony in Eich's action. For unlike Benn, Ernst Jünger, and eventually even Gustaf Gründgens,[9] who all used military service as a way of escaping the clutches of Goebbels's propaganda machinery, Eich was using that very same machinery to escape the military, at least on a temporary basis. He would do it again in October 1940, when he exploited the opportunity to participate in a training course for film writers in occupied France (Vieregg, 57–58).[10] Here we have to consider the timing of all of this, just as we have done with Wilhelm Lehmann's decision to join the Nazis in 1940. Eich was now proffering his services to a regime whose criminal nature was increasing exponentially with every month Hitler's war continued.

With the newly discovered recording of *Rebellion*, considerable effort has been made to demonstrate how this "bloody glove" from Eich's Nazi-era career did not really fit the author. The lack of an actual broadcast text in Eich's handwriting has left room for all sorts of conjecture, some of which evokes the theories from the 1970s, when the title was treated in isolation from the context of the anti-British propaganda campaign. One critic writing in 1978 believed that Eich's text had an apparently "anti-English and anti-capitalist tendency," which lent itself to exploitation by Nazi propagandists but had never been intended for such a purpose (Würffel, 150). The 1997 edition of the radio play text, recording, and related materials follows a similar line of argumentation. It claims Eich had accommodated the anti-British campaign halfheartedly and submitted a broadcast text on an "inappropriate topic" with a "leftist tendency," which propagandists reworked before it reached the airwaves. Much was made out of the fact that the wax plate with the broadcast's longest recorded scene and three other opening scenes were not numbered in sequence with the other plates, which suggests they were later insertions by a third party and not part of Eich's missing "original" (*Urtext*) (Karst, 68–69).

Here the notion that Eich's material had been manipulated by the Propaganda Ministry for use in its anti-English campaign recalls the defensive strategy the film director Veit Harlan employed when discussing his films *Jud Süß* and *Kolberg*. Harlan claimed to have made high quality feature films that Goebbels first banned and then completely reworked into the infamous works of propaganda we now know (Harlan, passim).

The other tactic of associating the pronounced "anti-capitalist tendency" of Eich's *Rebellion* with some form of antifascism ignores both the context in which it was produced and Nazi propaganda's long-standing vilification of the speculative capitalism of war profiteers and *Börsenmakler* (stockbrokers) in the Western "plutocracies." A good example is Adolf Weber's July 1939 broadcast "Gold für Wallstreet," which represented Wall Street as "… the infamous scene of international plutocracy in New York, that den of the dangerous American finance hyenas" (*Die Sendung* 16, 28 [1939]). As I have demonstrated elsewhere, Nazi propagandists were especially fond of George Bernard Shaw's turn-of-the-century caricatures of Great Britain's decadent and unprincipled upper class and continued to stage his plays after 1939 (Cuomo, "Saint Joan"). Eich's two characters Lord Pembroke and his fickle daughter Lilian conform to Shaw's types, especially when Lilian spontaneously switches her passion from the cause of the oppressed working class to ballroom dancing.

As with the *Kraft durch Freude* episode in the *Landbote* series, we have a letter in which Eich revealed a conflicted attitude toward his *Rebellion* as he reported to A. Artur Kuhnert the results of his weeklong furlough:

> Despite the radio people's help I needed a week before a story came about, which above all did not raise any objections with all instances. Well, it is the gold miners' strike in 1922 in Johannesburg, a subject which I would reject with hands wrung in dismay, if I were the Propaganda Ministry. I assume that it will never be broadcast, which would be a shame on account of my lack of funds. (letter of 13 March 1940, cited in Karst, 60–61)

There is curious contradiction between the first two sentences, since it is hard to understand how a subject that "raises no objections with all instances" would be so repulsive to the Propaganda Ministry. Here we have to keep in mind that the operative term is Eich's *Thema* (subject) and not *Hörspielmanuskript* (radio play manuscript).

It is true that Eich's historical source, the 1922 Witwatersrand mine strike, had some problematical features. The most prominent victims of the military crackdown were communist labor organizers who were fighting to maintain the job color bar, a law that excluded black workers from better paying jobs. But the average listener would not know these details,[11] and Eich emphasized the military, not the socialist solidarity among the *Kameraden* on strike. As with his radio adaptation in 1937 of Rudolf Brunngraber's novel *Radium*, a broadcast that shows thematic and stylistic parallels to *Rebellion*, Eich simplified the conflict and created stark contrasts between classes. He personalized the plight of the South African workers by focusing on the families of the Irish and Boer workers, past and present victims of British imperialism. In short, he wrote an effective propaganda radio play and should not have been surprised that it was broadcast in the anti-British campaign during the Western offensive.

Rebellion marked not only the end of Eich's radio career, but also of his compensated professional activity under National Socialism, since the film course did not result in any profitable engagement as a screenplay author equivalent to Eich's seven years in radio. As of yet nobody has conjectured that this was due to a conscious decision on his part to refrain from further collaboration. But we can discern from his letters of the late 1930s and early 1940s a consistently self-deprecatory attitude toward his work for the Nazi broadcasting industry. Almost three years before *Rebellion* such self-critique resulted in the "poet" Chabanais, a character Eich added to his adaptation of *Radium* and whose name in French was associated with prostitution.[12] Unable to earn a livelihood with his trite lyrics and desperate to pay for his wife's medical care, Chabanais becomes the propagandist for the unscrupulous radium producer Cynac and sings the praise of his employer's products in his verse. [13] Only after seventeen young girls die of radium poisoning in Cynac's luminous watch dial factory does Chabanais gain insight into his wrongdoing and flee into the jungle.

With Eich it is telling that the opportunity to sell his works to the Nazi radio disappeared before we could find any evidence that he had emulated his character's flight from complicity. At the same time, however, the radical transformation of his position on an author's accountability to the times from the late Weimar years to the early postwar period indicates that the experience under National Socialism had left its mark. In early 1930 he had championed the poet's right to aloofness: "And accountability to the times? Not in the slightest way. Only to myself," *Die Kolonne* 1, no. 2 [Feb. 1930]: 7; rpt. in Eich, *Vermischte Schriften*, 457), and in 1932, the last year of Weimar democracy, he continued to advocate "disengaged poetry" in defiance of the trend toward "socially relevant" literature:

What is the essential characteristic of an age? Certainly not its outward appearances, airplane and dynamo, but rather the transformation that the person experiences through them.... The transformations of the self are the problem of the lyric poet. That will have the formal consequence that in general he avoids vocabulary that encompasses a time-bound, i.e., a problem that doesn't directly interest him. Yes, I believe the lyric poet *must* use 'old' vocabulary, which, having become free of problems itself, first acquires its new meaning through the 'I'. So many temporally determined associations adhere to terms such as 'dynamo' or 'telephone cable' that they usually distort the 'I'-problematic of the poem through their own problematical nature. ("Antwort an Bernard Diebold," *Die Kolonne* 3, no. 1 [1932]: 3; rpt. in Eich, *Vermischte Schriften*: 458–59)

For the years 1933 to 1945 we have no record of any similar poetological statements, save for Eich's representation of the alcoholic poet Patt in his adaptation of Karl May themes in the radio play *Tracks in the Prairie* (Fährten in der Prärie) in 1936 or his aforementioned poet turned "propagandist" Chabanais in Radium from 1937. Yet there can be no doubt that Eich had come to question fundamentally the tenability of the apolitical position he had advocated during the Weimar Republic. Indeed, the remarks Eich made in an interview with *Der Spiegel* in 1950 refute virtually verbatim his earlier insistence on poetry's "timeless vocabulary":

> Is the poet allowed to be moved by the moonshine in the woods, not however by the rubble of our cities? Whoever believes the poem has to exclude the phenomena of the time as coincidences and only speak of the 'eternal things' is from experience confusing eternity with the past.
>
> An aesthetic that considers reality or parts of it as not poetic is soulless and hostile to authentic poetry. And therefore I believe that the poet's avoidance of the vocabulary of civilization and technology must finally be done away with. (*Der Spiegel* 27 [6 July 1950]: 39)

It is not fortuitous that the eighteen years that separate Eich's diametrically opposed poetological stances represent the most traumatic generational transition in modern German history. Perhaps it took the compromising experiences of his flirtation with Nazi Party membership and his accommodation of propagandistic aims in his radio broadcasts to dislodge Eich from his neo-romantic aloofness. The insights he had gained from seven years of compromise as an author for Goebbels's broadcasting system might have served as the catalyst for his transformation into a postwar activist. In this regard the 150 broadcast texts he wrote between 1933 and 1940 could be seen as the stations on the path to Eich's antiestablishment engagement in the 1950s and 1960s. Without such works as *Rebellion* Eich might never have written the controversial radio play *Dreams* and his *Moles*, the highly provocative experimental prose that marked his final phase.

Notes

1. This is according to a biographical sketch about Eich's second wife, the author Ilse Aichinger, which includes an account of his final illness and last request that his urn be placed next to Bakunin's in Berne. This request was denied (Serke, 119).

2. Krispyn, for example, finds "hidden barbs" against the Hitler regime in one of the episodes Eich had written for the long-running *Königswusterhäuser Landbote* series (37).

3. See the NSDAP Membership Form (Anlage zum Antrag auf Aufnahme in die NSDAP), signed and dated 1 January 1940—Berlin Document Center: *Partei-Korrespondenz/Wilhelm Lehmann*.

4. Axel Vieregg's claim that Kuhnert joined the NSDAP after the membership rolls were reopened in 1937 lacks substantiation (18). The NSDAP Master File has no membership card for him or any other evidence of an application, and as late as 19 December 1941 documents regarding Kuhnert from the NSDAP Gauleitung München-Oberbayern indicate no affiliation with the Party (Berlin Document Center: Reichskulturkammer/Personnel File: A. Artur Kuhnert).

5. In his discussion of Benn's influence over Eich and his colleagues, Peter Horst Neumann claims that Eich must have dissociated himself from Benn after the latter's notorious broadcast on 24 April 1933 in support of the Hitler regime, "Der neue Staat und die Intellektuellen" (38). However, Neumann's assertion that Benn and Eich had parted ways in early 1933 does not jibe with the fact that in July 1933 both Eich and Raschke utilized Benn as a reference on their membership applications for the *Reichsverband Deutscher Schriftsteller*, which transformed soon into the Reichsschrifttumskammer. Moreover, Martin Raschke subsequently wrote an enthusiastic overview of Benn's oeuvre, including his latest essay volume *Der neue Staat und die Intellektuellen*, which contained both the aforementioned speech and Benn's "Antwort an die literarische Emigration"— "Gespräche um Gottfried Benn," *Die Literatur* 36 (Oct. 1933): 8–11).

6. Originally used to commemorate the hundreds of civilians who died in the barricade battles in German and Austrian cities during the failed Revolution of March 1848, the term *Märzgefallene* was later applied facetiously to the thousands of opportunistic Germans who joined the NSDAP in the weeks after Hitler's appointment as Reich Chancellor on 30 January 1933. The conductor Herbert von Karajan actually joined the NSDAP twice. He first joined the Austrian branch of the Party in April 1933 and was then inducted into the German NSDAP as of 1 May 1933 with the membership number 3 340 914 (Rathkolb, 203–12). The fact that Martin Heidegger was assigned the membership number 3 125 894 and Eich 2 634 901 suggests that Eich had applied for Party membership earlier than either Martin Heidegger or Herbert von Karajan (Berlin Document Center: NSDAP Master Files for Günter Eich and Martin Heidegger).

7. Eich's letter to Raschke, 17 April 1939: *Nachlass Martin Raschke/Sächsische Landesbibliothek*, Dresden.

8. In this respect, Eich's military duties were reminiscent of the situation he represented in the early postwar story "Das schöne Kommando." In order to prolong their pleasant assignment in the peaceful Bavarian Alpine meadows, two Wehrmacht soldiers eventually murder the renegade Russian POW they have been sent to capture.

9. Eight days after Goebbels's "Total War" declaration on 18 February 1943, Gründgens sought Göring's permission to leave the Preussische Staatstheater and enlist in the Wehrmacht (Riess, 229–31).

10. It is noteworthy that we have a relevant report of 5 October 1940 from the Sicherheitsdienst of the SS, which noted that the programming cutback in radio plays had caused "talented writers" to seek opportunities in film. Both Eich and Kuhnert are mentioned as examples of such "talent" (Bundesarchiv: R 58/1089, Bl. 173–74; cited in Hörburger, 418–19).

11. At best, some listeners might have recalled that the gold miners' strike in 1922 had played a peripheral role toward the conclusion of Hans Grimm's nationalistic bestseller

Volk ohne Raum. Several commentaries on Eich's upcoming broadcast had made this connection to Grimm's work.

12. See Cuomo, *Career*, 110–14; Vieregg cites a letter in which Eich confirms my earlier association of Chabanais with prostitution (47).

13. Here Eich's designation of his poet's occupation is noteworthy. Although in German "propaganda" can also refer to commercial advertising as well as political agitation, at the time Eich wrote *Radium*, Goebbels's Propaganda Ministry issued a directive to limit the use of the term to the political realm. Businesses were supposed to use the term *Werbung* to designate advertising (*Börsenblatt für den deutschen Buchhandel* 126 [5 June 1937]: 492).

Works Cited

Benn, Gottfried. *Briefe an F.W. Oelze 1932–1945*. Vol. 1. Wiesbaden: Limes, 1972.

Brekle, Wolfgang. "Die antifaschistische Literatur in Deutschland (1933–1945): Probleme der inneren Emigration am Beispiel deutscher Erzähler." *Weimarer Beiträge* 15, no. 6 (1970): 67–128.

Buckreis, Adam. *Politik des 20. Jahrhunderts: Weltgeschichte 1901–1936*. 3rd ed. Nuremberg: Panorama-Verlag, n.d. [1936].

Eich, Günter. *Vermischte Schriften*. Ed. Axel Vieregg. Vol. 4 of *Gesammelte Werke in vier Bänden*. Ed. Karl Karst et al. Frankfurt am Main: Suhrkamp, 1991.

Eich, Günter, and Martin Raschke. *Das festliche Jahr*. Oldenburg: Gerhard Stalling, 1936.

Cuomo, Glenn R. "The Diaries of Joseph Goebbels as a Source for the Understanding of National Socialist Cultural Politics." In *National Socialist Cultural Policy*, ed. G. R. Cuomo, 197–245. New York: St. Martin's Press, 1995.

———. "'Saint Joan before the Cannibals': George Bernard Shaw in the Third Reich." *German Studies Review* 16, no. 3 (1993): 435–61.

———. *Career at the Cost of Compromise: Günter Eich's Life and Work in the Years 1933–1945*. Amsterdam and Atlanta: Rodopi, 1989.

Funke, Horst-Günther. *Die literarische Form des deutschen Hörspiels in historischer Entwicklung*. Diss. Erlangen-Nuremberg 1963. Erlangen: privately printed, 1963.

Groll, Gunter, ed. *De Profundis: Deutsche Lyrik in dieser Zeit. Eine Anthologie aus zwölf Jahren*. Munich: Kurt Desch, 1946.

Harlan, Veit. *Im Schatten meiner Filme: Selbstbiographie*. Gütersloh: Sigbert Mohn, 1966.

Herbst, Helmut. "Günter Eich: Ein Rückblick." *Börsenblatt für den Deutschen Buchhandel* 69 (30 August 1988): A 327–30.

Hörburger, Christian. *Das Hörspiel der Weimarer Republik: Versuch einer kritischen Analyse*. Stuttgart: Akademischer Verlag Hans-Dieter Heinz, 1975.

Kaiser, Joachim. "Günter Eich, der Poet, ist gestorben." In *Günter Eich zum Gedächtnis*, ed. Siegfried Unseld, 82–86. Frankfurt am Main: Suhrkamp, 1973.

Karst, Karl, ed. *Günter Eich, 'Rebellion in der Goldstadt': Texttranskript und Materialien*. Frankfurt am Main: Suhrkamp, 1997.

Krispyn, Egbert. *Günter Eich*. New York: Twayne, 1971.

Müller-Hanpft, Suzanne. *Lyrik und Rezeption: Das Beispiel Günter Eich*. Munich: Hanser, 1972.

Neumann, Peter Horst. *Die Rettung der Poesie im Unsinn: Der Anarchist Günter Eich*. Stuttgart: Klett-Cotta, 1981.

Nijssen, Hub. "Peter Huchel als Propagandist? Über die Autorschaft des Hörspiels 'Die Greuel von Denshawai.'" *Neophilologus* 77, no. 4 (1993): 625–35.

Parker, Stephen. "Peter Huchel als Propagandist. Huchels 1940 entstandene Adaption von George Bernhard Shaws 'Die Greuel von Denshawai.'" *Rundfunk und Fernsehen* 39, no. 3 (1991): 343–53.

————. "On Peter Huchel's Adaptation of Shaw's 'Denshawai Horror' and Related Matters." *Neophilogus* 79, no. 2 (1995): 295–306.

Rathkolb, Oliver. *Führertreu und Gottbegnadet: Künstlereliten im Dritten Reich.* Vienna: Österreichischer Bundesverlag, 1991.

Richardson, Larry Leroy. *Committed Aestheticism: The Poetic Theory and Practice of Günter Eich.* New York: Peter Lang, 1983.

Riess, Curt. *Gustaf Gründgens: Eine Biografie.* Hamburg: Hoffmann und Campe, 1965.

Schafroth, Heinz F. *Günter Eich.* Munich: Beck, 1976.

Serke, Jürgen. *Frauen Schreiben: Ein neues Kapitel deutschsprachiger Literatur.* Frankfurt am Main: Fischer, 1982.

Storck, Joachim W. "Anatomie einer Denunziation: Der 'Fall' Günter Eich." In *Widerspruche im Widersprechen: Historische und aktuelle Ansichten der Verneinung,* ed. Peter Rau, 156–81. Frankfurt am Main: Peter Lang, 1996.

Strothmann, Dietrich. *Nationalsozialistische Literaturpolitik: Ein Beitrag zur Publizistik im Dritten Reich.* Bonn: Bouvier, 1960.

Vieregg, Axel. *Der eigenen Fehlbarkeit begegnet: Günter Eichs Realitäten 1933–1945.* Eggingen: Edition Isele, 1993.

Würffel, Stefan Bodo. "'… denn heute hört uns Deutschland'—Anmerkungen zum Hörspiel im Dritten Reich." In *Kunst und Kultur im deutschen Faschismus,* ed. Ralf Schnell, 129–55. Stuttgart: Metzler, 1978.

Chapter 10

CONSERVATIVE OPPOSITION

Friedrich Reck-Malleczewen's Antifascist Novel
Bockelson: A History of Mass Hysteria

Karl-Heinz Schoeps

For authors of the *inner emigration* it was not possible to comment with impunity on the contemporary political situation within the Third Reich using contemporary subjects. Therefore, authors were forced to find modes of indirect critique that would, first, avoid censorship and reprisal, and second, deliver critical commentary staking out positions at odds with state ideology, or at least allowing for an openness of interpretation, even if it at times amounted to inscrutability. One way to accomplish this sort of indirect critique was through "historical camouflage,"[1] that is, by using the past to illuminate the present. One of the best examples of this technique is Reinhold Schneider's *Las Casas before Charles V* (Las Casas vor Karl V., 1938). Another method of critical indirection (and here, dislocation) was to use exotic lands as the setting, as did Werner Bergengruen in his novel *The Supreme Dictator and the Court* (Der Großtyrann und das Gericht, 1935), Ernst Jünger in his novel *On the Marble Cliffs* (Auf den Marmorklippen, 1939), or Ernst Wiechert in his short novel *The White Buffalo* (Der Weiße Büffel, 1937, first published in 1946). Though less well known than all of these other authors of the *inner emigration*, the Protestant East Prussian turned Catholic Bavarian monarchist Friedrich Percyval Reck-Malleczewen (1884–1945) used the historic Anabaptist rule of 1534–35 in the city of Münster to present the most trenchant criticism of National Socialist rule to appear in print in those years within Germany.

In 1533, four hundred years before the Nazis came to power in Germany and in the wake of Martin Luther's reformation, the Westphalian city of Münster experienced increasing inner turmoil that threatened to erupt in civil war. Lutheranism had reached Münster in the early 1530s as it had all other German lands, but neither Catholicism nor Lutheranism was firmly in control in the city. Under the leadership of Bernhard Rothmann, who had the support of the guilds, the Reformation was officially recognized in the Treaty of Dülmen in February of 1533 (after an attack on the episcopal court in Telgte in 1532). Soon the Lutherans who dominated the city council set out to secure the reformation. But this was only the beginning of the bloody struggle that was to rage in Münster for the next two years. For Rothmann, the city reformer, Luther's reform did not go far enough; he wanted to introduce what he perceived as true Christianity in Münster. At issue were communion (Rothmann favored Zwingli's "that means the body of Christ" vs. Luther's "that is the body of Christ") and baptism (Rothmann opposed the baptism of children, thereby turning against the prevailing law of the land ["geltendes Reichsrecht"]). Rothmann left Lutheranism behind and became an Anabaptist. He and his followers challenged the city council and, after fierce clashes, gained a majority in the council elections of 23 February 1534. To quote Hans-Jürgen Goertz, an authority on the age of reformation: "The Anabaptists therefore gained power legally by successfully exploiting an unstable situation where Lutheran and Zwinglian tendencies were competing against each other over the Reformation, and the guilds were struggling for control of the council" (Goertz, 30). The Anabaptist movements were by no means restricted to Münster but found adherents and prophets in all German lands. Some were more radical than others, some were more militant than others. All of them, however, thought they were the chosen few and all of them were more or less brutally persecuted.

However, it was only in the city of Münster that they gained power for a short while—16 months, to be exact, from 23 February 1534 to 25 June 1535, when Münster was recaptured by imperial troops. One of the better known Anabaptist prophets, Melchior Hoffmann, believed in the power of the sword to weed out the infidels (Catholics and Lutherans) and had selected the city of Strasbourg as the new Jerusalem. Instrumental in gaining power in Münster were prophets from abroad and their followers, notably Jan Matthijs (or Matthys), a baker from Leiden and one of Hoffmann's disciples, who had arrived in Münster in February 1534 and, in particular, Jan van Leiden, also called Bockelson (after his father Bockel), an actor, playwright, and tailor who had quit his professions to open a bar. Their teachings appealed particularly to women (Ranke, 541), who played an important part in Mathiys's and Bockelson's ascension to power. But Münster was not enough for their ambition. According to Johan Dusentschuer, one of the new prophets and Bockelson's official spokesman or, in modern terms, "propaganda minister," the Anabaptist revolution should spread throughout the world: "As Johan Dusentschuer proclaimed, the renewal of the world should issue from Münster" (Klötzer, 165). Münster figured as the center of salvation for the whole world (the "salvational center of the imminent renewal of the world," Klötzer, 160). Missionaries were sent into surrounding cities to proselytize their citizens.

When Jan Matthijs died on Easter in 1534 in a fight with imperial troops who beleaguered the city, Jan van Leiden succeeded him as leader. Proclaimed king of the city by Dusentschuer, he erected a theocratic dictatorship, ruthlessly persecuting all enemies. Bockelson abolished the city council and replaced it with a council of twelve elders. Catholic icons in churches were destroyed and pictures, books, documents, and even musical instruments were burned in the marketplace; only the Bible was spared and became the sole ideological guide for the community. Dissidents were either killed or forced to leave town; their belongings were confiscated and became communal property. New laws were introduced that abolished private property and sanctioned polygamy. All valuable metals were confiscated. However, not all of these measures were introduced for purely ideological reasons as Hermann von Kerssenbrock, one of the first and contemporary chroniclers of Anabaptist rule in Münster, claimed (Laubach, 194). According to Ernst Laubach, there was also a military necessity for this measure as the city came under increasing pressure from Bishop Count Franz von Waldeck's forces (Laubach, 184). Metals were needed for defensive purposes, social tensions had to be reduced by abolishing private property, and since women outnumbered men by a vast margin, polygamy seemed to make some sense; it was not done for the personal pleasure of the chief prophet Bockelson, at least not primarily (as Kerssenbrock maintained). The leveling of church spires was not wanton destruction but was carried out to create effective platforms for defensive weaponry and observation posts.

A new city ordinance made the respected citizen and merchant Knipperdolling, who was Bockelson's right-hand man, the official "bearer of the sword," in other words police chief of Münster (not executioner, as Kerssenbrock would have it). Bockelson was a gifted orator and had the support of the majority of the citizens. His claim to be a divinely selected leader was bolstered by his military victories against the sieging forces and by the failure of an ill-prepared coup against him. Bockelson saw himself as a "King on David's throne" whose mission was to prepare the millennium rule of Christ. When the military situation deteriorated after the Bishop's forces had effectively blockaded the city and gained the upper hand, Bockelson emphasized the need for sporting events and games to divert people from the grim realities of hunger, destruction, and the daily chores of keeping up the defenses, a task to which every citizen, whether male or female, young or old, had to contribute. Draconian punishments were meted out for traitors and defeatists. Up to the very end Bockelson and his followers hoped that new weapons and a reserve army of Anabaptists from the Netherlands would change the desperate military situation and lead to final victory. But that was not to be; Bockelson's theocratic dictatorship finally failed. The Bishop's forces finally captured the city at great cost to attackers and defenders alike. Rothmann died in the final battle (or possibly escaped, according to Dülmen, 354), Bockelson and Knipperdolling were captured, interrogated, tortured, executed, and their bodies displayed in iron cages suspended from the tower of the Lamberti church. Münster was again saved for Catholicism (and has remained Catholic to this day).

This then is the historical background for Friedrich Percyval Reck-Malleczewen's chronicle of Anabaptist rule in Münster, *Bockelson: A History of Mass Hysteria,* which was published inside Nazi Germany in 1937. Reck-Malleczewen followed the historical events very closely and used a number of sources including Kerssenbrock and Gresbeck, both eyewitnesses of the events in Münster (albeit with a bias against the Anabaptists), as well as the eminent nineteenth-century historian Leopold Ranke. To lend an air of historical authenticity to his work Reck-Malleczewen quotes liberally from his sources in Latin and low German. He uses footnotes and a bibliography citing his sources. Ranke had postulated that history be studied objectively and "sine ira et studio," that is, without anger and passion. Reck-Malleczewen, in his chronicle, followed the opposite path (i.e., "cum ira et studio"). But Reck-Malleczewen's intention was not to achieve historical objectivity. On the contrary, he openly criticizes Ranke for his misplaced objectivity and asserts: "The times of wanting to understand at any price are gone until further notice. In writing history as well" (136). In searching for a convenient vehicle to publish his criticism of the Nazis within Nazi Germany, Reck-Malleczewen chanced upon the Anabaptist rule in Münster.[2] In this context objectivity and understanding were the last things he needed; both were replaced by attack and polemics. The subject matter Reck-Malleczewen selected for his attack on National Socialism was cleverly chosen because the Anabaptist rule in Münster in the sixteenth century provided, indeed, a number of striking parallels to Nazi rule in Germany in the twentieth century, particularly when seen through the eyes of some of Reck-Malleczewen's sources: Kerssenbrock wrote from a Catholic stance, and Heinrich Gresbeck was a traitor who had deserted to the Bishop's side and helped to bring about the fall of Münster. Even Reck-Malleczewen noted in his book that neither of them had reason to present Bockelson and his rule in a positive light and may have overshot their goal (66), but by and large the conservative Reck-Malleczewen agreed with them and followed their lead. In reading sixteenth-century sources Reck-Malleczewen was struck by the parallels between Bockelson's rule in Münster and Hitler's rule in Germany, as he noted in his diary (published posthumously in 1947 as *Tagebuch eines Verzweifelten,* translated into English in 1970 as *Diary of a Man in Despair*) on 11 August 1936, and I quote this reference to Nazi Germany almost in its entirety:

I have been working on my book about the Münster city-state set up by the Anabaptist heretics in the sixteenth century. I read accounts of this 'kingdom of Zion' by contemporaries, and I am shaken. In every respect down to the most ridiculous details, that was a forerunner of what we are now enduring. Like the Germany of today, the Münster city-state for years separated itself from the civilized world; like Nazi Germany, it was hugely successful over a long period of time, and appeared invincible. And then, suddenly, against all expectation and over a comparable trifle it collapsed....

As in our case, a misbegotten failure conceived, so to speak, in the gutter, became the great prophet, and the opposition simply disintegrated, while the rest of the world looked on in astonishment and incomprehension. As with us ..., hysterical females, schoolmasters, renegade priests, the dregs and outsiders from everywhere formed the main supports of the regime. I have to delete some of the parallels in order not to jeopardize myself any more than I already have. A thin sauce of ideology covered lewdness, greed, sadism, and fathomless lust for power, in Münster, too, and whoever would not completely accept the new teaching was turned over to the executioner. The same role of official murderer played by Hitler in the Röhm Putsch was acted by Bockelson in Münster. As with us, Spartan laws were promulgated to control the *misera plebs*, but these did not apply to him or his followers. Bockelson also surrounded himself with bodyguards, and was beyond the reach of any would-be assassin. As with us, there were street meetings and "voluntary contributions," refusal of which meant proscription. As with us, the masses were drugged: folk festivals, useless construction, anything and everything, to keep the man in the street from a moment's pause to reflect.

Exactly as Nazi Germany has done, Münster sent its fifth columns and prophets forth to undermine neighboring states. The fact that the Münster propaganda chief, Dusentschnur [*sic*], limped like Goebbels is a joke which history spent four hundred years preparing: a fact which I, familiar as I am with the vindictiveness of our Minister of Lies, have most advisedly omitted in my book [he didn't, actually—KHS]. Constructed on a foundation of lies there existed for a short time between the Middle Ages and modern times a bandits' regime. It threatened all the established world—Kaiser, nobility, and all the old relationships. And it was all designed to still the hunger for mastery of a couple of power-mad thugs. A few things have yet to happen to complete the parallel. In the besieged Münster of 1534, the people were driven to swallow their own excrement, to eat their own children. This could happen to us, too, just as Hitler and his sycophants face the same inevitable end as Bockelson and Knipperdolling. (trans. Rubens, 19–20)

In Reck-Malleczewen's interpretation, Bockelson is a precursor of the Nazi dictator with whom he shares many negative attributes. He bears, Reck-Malleczewen writes, "the degenerate traits of a bastard born in the gutter ... who dabbled in literature ... who probably was a great artist in the eyes of his followers" (11).[3] Both Bockelson and Hitler were would-be artists: Hitler was a painter (of sorts) and Bockelson an actor and a playwright (of sorts).[4] For Reck-Malleczewen, Bockelson is nothing but a charlatan and an idle prattler, "basically a miserable and unimportant creature" who could only emerge briefly in times of turmoil. History occasionally allows itself the cruel joke ... to make a nonentity into the center of great events ... but only for a short time" (12). Reck-Malleczewen's chronicle, then, is more than the story of this prophet; it is "the story of a demonic German intoxication during which all those devils and evil spirits escaped into the open from the hidden recesses of the soul, devils and spirits which up to then had only been depicted on Gothic canvases" (12).

Hysterical mobs roamed through the streets of Münster proclaiming the end of the world. "Münster," Reck-Malleczewen comments, "has gone mad overnight" (17). Reck-Malleczewen's description of Anabaptist rule in Münster follows history but with his own slant, emphasizing parallels to National Socialist rule in Germany four hundred years later, omitting events that did not fit his theory, and showing the Anabaptists entirely as victimizers and not as the victims they certainly also were. Occasionally, Reck-Malleczewen's language even mimics Nazi language. After the council elections of February 1534, Reck-Malleczewen constructs an analogy to the appeasement policies toward the Nazis of the 1930s, in which the old council tries to negotiate and appease the Anabaptist rebels instead of opposing their terror with a firm hand. In Reck-Malleczewen's view, determined opposition at this time would have saved thousands of lives later. Thus, the old order collapses without any resistance; its insignia are destroyed and streets are renamed to erase all memory of earlier times—exactly as in Nazi Germany. Some people emigrate, but most citizens fall for this madness. Citing threats from abroad the authorities strengthen their totalitarian rule and ruthlessly persecute traitors. In Reck-Malleczewen's words, "it is the old game of all revolutionary states and cities to divert the attention of the masses from their real plans" (17). The outlook for Münster looks bleak indeed and the Anabaptist Reich is in danger, but Reck-Malleczewen, with clear reference to the situation within Nazi Germany, addresses the city of Münster with words of comfort: "Do not give up and do not bury your head in the sand" (33–34). Adherents of the old beliefs, now called "godless," are forced out of town, even killed, their possessions confiscated.

With the intolerant Nazi policies in mind Reck-Malleczewen describes how Anabaptists destroyed and plundered churches and cathedrals, burned books—except the Bible—and encouraged residents to identify traitors (imagined and real). Knipperdolling is stylized into a Freisler whose sword threatens all who resist, complain or criticize those in power. The influential prophet Dusentschnuer assumes traits of Goebbels: "The word of this limping prophet counts a great deal in Münster. One day in September ... he runs to the market square shouting that Johann Bockelson, God's holy man, will rule as king not only over Münster but over the whole world and all nobility of the Reich" (83). Just like Goebbels, the Anabaptists made effective use of propaganda, the goal being, as Reck-Malleczewen terms it in obvious analogy to the language of the Third Reich (or *lingua tertii imperii [LTI]*, as Victor Klemperer called it), the "propagandistic disintegration of the enemy" (propagandistische Zersetzung des Gegners, 57). Rothmann's propaganda leaflets, spread through missionaries and shot into the Bishop's camps around Münster, have the desired effect; some of the Bishop's soldiers join the Anabaptists and new Anabaptist communities emerge in the country. Reck-Malleczewen's venom is directed especially at Rothmann, the intellectual instigator (*intellektueller Drahtzieher*, 115) behind all the evils of Anabaptist rule. He sarcastically calls him "dear Rothmann" throughout his book and holds him responsible for all the misery and crime committed in the name of the new millennium, the Thousand Year Reich, envisioned by the prophets of Münster.

In describing the end of Anabaptist rule Reck-Malleczewen even anticipates the end of Nazi rule. The new rulers of Münster do not have time to savor their victories; the opposing forces have regrouped and tightened the ring around the city. Shortages of food lead to rationing and hunger. Even games and other entertainment can no longer distract the populace from the misery of their situation and the lavishness of the king's court. The situation seems hopeless, but the king prepares for final victory. He promotes some of his vassals to dukes and promises them lands he has yet to conquer. He responds to criticism with increased terror and forces every remaining citizen to contribute to the defense of the city. The final struggle (*Endkampf*) is a struggle for life and death, which can only end in the destruction of one side or the other. Bockelson wants to defend the city at any cost and appeals to his followers to persevere (*durchhalten*). But in the end the forces of the Bishop capture the city in a bloody battle; the expected relief armies from the Netherlands and the new weaponry in which Bockelson (and the Nazis) believe to the end never materialize. Bockelson and Knipperdolling are caught, tried, and executed; Rothmann is never seen again and probably dies in the fighting. Before his judges Bockelson recants and promises collaboration against other Anabaptists. In Reck-Malleczewen's view, the great king of Zion turns out to be "a reckless psychopath whom history allowed to play for a time at the controls of its vast machinery causing a great deal of damage" (176).

In Reck-Malleczewen's conservative view of history the tragedy of Münster was caused not so much by one individual but by the emerging power of the masses. For him the National Socialist mass hysteria had its origins in the mass hysteria of the Anabaptist state of the sixteenth century. The Anabaptist rebellion had already displayed the evils contained in all subsequent mass movements, be they the French revolution of 1789, the German revolutions of 1848 and 1918/19, or the Bolshevist revolution of 1917. Münster was "the embryo of a modern council republic [*Räterepublik*] on a puritan basis" (45). The Anabaptist war was "the first example of a 'total war'" (40). Reck-Malleczewen sees only the destructive aspect of revolutions and invariably sides with the old order; in Münster's case with the Catholic Bishop Franz von Waldeck. Revolutions are seen not as reactions to oppression and social evils but as "safety valves for the discharge of pent-up mass resentments" (91). In Reck-Malleczewen's analysis "it came to these products of mass hysteria only because of the total breakdown of the social order. It was the unhappy fate of this city that a great political gangster stirred up the fire under this witches' cauldron and it had to pay dearly enough for this" (187).

To even a casual reader with no knowledge of the events that took place in Münster in the sixteenth century, Reck-Malleczewen's chronicle appears subjective and polemical. Nevertheless, some astounding parallels emerge between Nazi rule in Germany in the twentieth century and Anabaptist rule in Münster in the sixteenth century. Both Bockelson and Hitler came to power legally and with the support of the middle and lower middle classes in times of social and economic turmoil (Münster suffered an economic crisis in the wake of a declining Hanse and increasing religious strife; Weimar Germany suffered the results of the Wall Street crash of 1929 and political strife between right and left). Both consolidated their power through terrorism and ruthless persecution of opponents in order to create a dictatorship. Both shared in the idea of a thousand-year Reich, albeit not on the same ideological basis: the Anabaptists saw themselves in religious terms as precursors of Christ's thousand-year rule, whereas the Nazis envisioned one thousand years of their own secular rule and did not see themselves as precursors of some other ruler. Both their leaders, Hitler and Bockelson, came from humble origins. Both had artistic ambitions, both were gifted orators and demagogues, and both came from a foreign country to take over the reigns of government. Yet to describe the Anabaptist rule in Münster solely in terms of Nazi rule or in terms of any other mass movement does injustice to history, as experts have pointed out. According to Richard van Dülmen, the rule of Jan Matthijs and Jan van Leiden cannot be defined in terms of modern mass movements:

> The charismatic leadership established under Jan Matthys and the institutionalized kingdom of Zion under Jan van Leiden are inadequately defined when seen as an outbreak of mass hysteria and rule of arbitrary terror in anticipation of modern totalitarian systems. Though it cannot be denied that those elements existed, social life in the Anabaptist state under conditions of siege was far more rational than generally accepted.... Nor was the Anabaptist rule the result of a "plebeian revolution" or the final act of an early bourgeois revolution. (van Dülmen, 364–65, my translation)

Van Dülmen also points out that the Anabaptists came to power quite legally and with the support of the established wealthy citizens, not just the rabble, and that all segments of the populace participated in their rule, although craftsmen constituted the largest single group (van Dülmen, 365). The beginnings of Anabaptist rule were peaceful; it changed its character to a more militant society only under the onslaught of the Bishop's forces. Jan Bockelson was a charismatic leader but he was neither a "Christian communist idealist," as Ernst Bloch or Georg Lukacs would see him, nor a modern demagogue and leader of the people, as Reck-Malleczewen would have it, at least in van Dülmen's view (316). Perhaps Friedrich Dürrenmatt got it right when he warned in the foreword to his play *Es steht geschrieben* (It is Written, 1947), which also deals with the Anabaptist rule in Münster: "To what extent our times are reflected in it is another question. It would, however, be closer to the author's intention to be very cautious in drawing parallels which are, at best, tentative" (my translation).

But the problem is more general. How legitimate is it to use historical events and figures to transport other ideas? Some critics have pointed out that a number of representatives of the so-called *inner emigration*, not just Reck-Malleczewen, have resorted to that device as mentioned before. But writers and filmmakers closer to the Nazis also used history as a vehicle for their ideas. There were numerous plays and films about Friedrich II of Prussia. One of the more blatant examples is the film *Jud Süß* (Jew Süß), in which the screenwriters Ludwig Metzger, Veit Harlan, and the noted playwright Eberhard Wolfgang Möller used real events that occurred in Württemberg and Stuttgart in the eighteenth century to advance the antisemitic policies of the Nazis in the 1940s. In his seminal work *Literarische Innere Emigration 1933–1945* (1976) Ralf Schnell devotes a chapter to the problems arising from fictionalizing history; one of the authors he singles out is Reck-Malleczewen. One of the main problems in selecting historical parallels is that events that are seemingly similar are chosen and highlighted at the expense of those events that do not fit the theory of historical parallelism. Schnell faults particularly Reck-Malleczewen's *Bockelson* in this respect, but one suspects that Schnell is biased against Reck-Malleczewen for his conservative stance, as he makes amply clear in his discussion of Reck-Malleczewen's *Diary of a Man in Despair* (42–46). In Schnell's view Reck-Malleczewen's conservative stance prevented him from arriving at a genuine analysis of fascism (42). However, it seems to me that Schnell could be faulted for his leftist ideological blindness just as much as he faults Reck-Malleczewen's limitations resulting from his conservatism. In the end it does not really matter whether *Bockelson* is historically accurate (it is not); what does matter is that the book could be published in Nazi Germany in 1937 despite its obvious criticism of Nazi rule. It is, as Günter Scholdt pointed out in a 1982 lecture held at the Deutscher Germanistentag in Aachen, indeed "one of the most astonishing belletristic works to appear in the Third Reich" (Scholdt, 350).

The question arises as to why this book could appear at all. Ralf Schnell suggests as a reason that it is close to Nazi ideology (Schnell, 154; Scholdt, 355). I agree with Scholdt that Schnell is too eager to throw all conservatives into one pot—tempting as that may be. To be sure, Reck-Malleczewen was against all mass movements and revolutions, whether they come from the right or from the left. Reck-Malleczewen's writing was also tainted by racism when he talked about the "*Verniggerung*" (niggerization) of Germany in his *Diary*. But his *Diary of a Man in Despair* (published in 1947) makes amply clear that he was a staunch anti-Nazi, albeit a problematical German conservative. It is more likely that *Bockelson* escaped censorship and was published simply by accident, or more likely, because it found a publisher willing to take the risk of publishing it and because no one denounced it. Reck-Malleczewen's book may also have benefited from the numerous rivals and conflicting opportunists in the cultural bureaucracy of the Third Reich who allowed a number of works to slip through. Jan-Pieter Barbians confirms the possibility of such scenarios in his recent study *Literaturpolitik im 'Dritten Reich'* (1995). Perhaps a censor chose to assume that it was all directed against Bolshevism, which indeed it was to a certain extent, but in Reck-Malleczewen's mind Bolshevism was equated to Nazism. In any case, it was a courageous act to write and to publish such a work. Reck-Malleczewen eventually paid dearly for his antifascist stance. He was denounced to the Gestapo, arrested, and taken to the Dachau concentration camp, where he died in February of 1945. His book *Bockelson: A History of Mass Hysteria*, despite all its shortcomings, is more than another document of *inner emigration*; it is a document, in the guise of historical fiction, of active resistance against an inhumane regime.

Notes

1. Term borrowed from Ralf Schnell, 113.
2. Reck-Malleczewen's *Bockelson* is not the only treatment of the subject matter. Other works dealing with the Anabaptist rule of Münster include Robert Hammerling's epic *Der König von Sion* (1859), Lulu von Strauß und Torney's novel *Der jüngste Tag* (1922), Friedrich Dürrenmatt's drama *Es steht geschrieben* (1947; revised as *Die Wiedertäufer*, 1966) and Franz Theodor Csokor's novel *Der Schlüssel zum Abgrund* (1955).
3. My translation. Page numbers in the text refer to this 1946 edition of the original; all translations are mine.
4. Friedrich Dürrenmatt in his comedy *Die Wiedertäufer* (The Anabaptists), the second version of his play about the Anabaptists, written in 1966, made ample use of the fact that Bockelson was a playwright. The first version dates from 1946 and is entitled *Es steht geschrieben* (It Is Written).

Works Cited

Barbian, Jan-Pieter. *Literaturpolitik im "Dritten Reich": Institutionen, Kompetenzen, Betätigungsfelder.* Munich: dtv, 1995.

Dülmen, Richard van. *Reformation als Revolution. Soziale Bewegung und religiöser Radikalismus in der deutschen Reformation.* Munich: dtv, 1977.

Dürrenmatt, Friedrich. *Werkausgabe in dreißig Bänden.* Edited in collaboration with the author. Vol. 1, *Es steht geschrieben. Der Blinde.* Zurich: Diogenes, 1980.

Goertz, Hans-Jürgen. *The Anabaptists.* Translated by Trevor Johnson. London, New York: Routledge, 1996. [Orig. *Die Täufer. Geschichte und Deutung.* Munich: Beck, 1980, 1988.]

Klötzer, Ralf. "Hoffnung auf eine andere Wirklichkeit. Die Erwartungshorizonte in der Täuferstadt Münster 1534/35." In *Aussenseiter zwischen Mittelalter und Neuzeit. Festschrift für Hans-Jürgen Goertz zum 60. Geburtstag,* ed. Norbert Fischer and Marion Kobelt-Groch. Leiden, New York, and Cologne: Brill, 1997.

Klemperer, Victor. *LTI. Notizbuch eines Philologen.* Leipzig: Reclam, 1946; 5th ed. 1978.

Laubach, Ernst. "Reformation und Täuferherrschaft." In *Geschichte der Stadt Münster,* ed. Franz-Josef Jakobi. Vol. 1. Münster: Aschendorff, 1993.

Ranke, Leopold. *Deutsche Geschichte im Zeitalter der Reformation.* Vol. 3. 2nd ed. Berlin: Dunker and Humblot, 1843.

Reck-Malleczewen, Friedrich Percyval. *Bockelson. Geschichte eines Massenwahns.* Wiesentheid: Droemersche Verlagsanstalt, 1946.

————. *Diary of a Man in Despair.* Translated by Paul Rubens. London: Macmillan, 1970.

————. *Tagebuch eines Verzweifelten.* Lorch and Württemberg-Stuttgart: Bürger-Verlag, 1947.

Schnell, Ralf. *Literarische Innere Emigration 1933–1945.* Stuttgart: Metzler, 1976.

Scholdt, Günter. "Wiedertäufer und Drittes Reich. Zu einer Verschlüsselung im literarischen Widerstand." In *Literatur und Sprache im historischen Prozeß. Vorträge des Deutschen Germanistentages in Aachen 1982,* ed. Thomas Cramer. Vol. 1. Tübingen: Niemeyer, 1983.

Chapter 11

LUISE RINSER'S ESCAPE INTO *INNER EMIGRATION*

Diana Orendi

> What terrible times do we live in, when a conversation about
> trees almost constitutes a crime, because it equals a silence
> about so many atrocities?

> —Bertolt Brecht, 1938 ("An die Nachgeborenen")[1]

These words by Brecht, uttered sometime during the first months of exile
from the fascist regime in Germany, seemed like so many of his sharply
coined phrases, harsh and unforgiving to those who heard and read
them and turned them over in their minds as I have for years. But if we
take them as they were meant, they condemned then, in 1938, any attempt
by anyone to avoid what Brecht considered the right choice. They denied
all Germans, whether they remained in the country or fled the Nazis, the
right to circumvent the moral obligation of being political. To remain
apolitical, Brecht's words implied, is to risk being called a criminal, perhaps not so much by your contemporaries, but irrefutably by later generations. After all, Brecht's phrase was directed at those yet to be born
(*die Nachgeborenen*).

Brecht's maxim sharply limits the realm of what constitutes *inner emigration*. More fundamentally, his words question whether those who
claimed to have migrated into an interior sphere were in fact collaborators
of the fascist regime. Brecht was not the only one to deny German authors
the right to such a refuge. Famously, Thomas Mann issued a verdict on
this matter in his correspondence with Frank Thiess in 1946 (see Grosser,
24). Mann's words about the odor of "Blood and Shame" (*Blut und Schande*)
(Grosser, 31) that he claimed to smell on all the books produced during the
Third Reich within Germany have attained the status of *ultima ratio* on this
matter. Yet at the time, his words were taken, like Brecht's, as the bitter

words of yet another exiled author; Mann's view was dismissed as the jaundiced perspective of someone who begrudged those who had remained in the Reich the security and comfort they were enjoying while he had to endure exile. What his contemporaries did not want to concede at the time was the fact that, in his wholesale rejection, Mann had condemned the inner emigrants as a cowardly lot. In the same breath, he had refused to accord them the right to have their works judged on literary merit.

Fifty-eight years ago, however, when the dust had settled over Germany's bombed-out cities, public opinion was vastly different. Intellectuals as well as society at large sided with those artists in Germany for whom veteran writer Ernst Jünger had become a spokesperson as the author of *On the Marble Cliffs* (1939), the work considered archetypal for *inner emigration*. Jünger coined the motto that "Survival in itself was the major achievement of the day" (*Tagebücher*, 75). Voicing similar support for those who had stayed the course, Frank Thiess asserted that "those who patiently persisted within Germany had collected in the process a treasure of insight and experience which rendered them richer in knowledge and life's wisdom than the ones who had left" (Grosser). To justify his decision to wait it out, Thiess reiterated that "It was much more difficult to maintain one's integrity while within Germany than [it was] sending messages from the outside." Thus, both Jünger and Thiess claimed the moral high ground for writers like themselves who had decided to remain in war-torn Germany. Unashamed of his position, Jünger maintained, then and for the next sixty years of his long life, that it had been the correct decision to withdraw into an inner sanctum from 1933 to 1945. He claimed to have the right to appropriate this space as a refuge where his writings would not be read as political statements. He wanted his literary works to stand not as pronouncements of resistance against the dictator, but rather on their literary merits alone. With this posture, Jünger may have been the most prominent, but certainly not the only representative of *inner emigration* to enter the arena of postwar German literature unscathed by a Nazi past. The case of Jünger's controversial status in postwar literature, where he performed a role very close to that of a cult figure for the reactionary forces, has never received the critical attention it warrants.[2] Suffice it to say here that his was the most visible case that proved it possible to execute a seamless transition from Third Reich popularity to postwar celebrity status.

In fact, many of the authors who began their writing career during the Hitler period, such as Günter Eich, Peter Huchel, Marie-Luise Kaschnitz, Gerd Gaiser, Karl Krolow, and Luise Rinser, became the stars of Adenauer-era literature and beyond. The popularity of authors who, coming out of *inner emigration*, continued to publish in the predominantly conservative forms and genres they had refined during their years in seclusion, enforces Jünger's and Thiess's position for the postwar era.[3] Not only must the postwar reading audience have ignored what Brecht and Mann considered exhibitions of cowardly collaboration; readers must have welcomed and embraced representatives of the *inner emigration*, in whose works they found their own experiences reflected in ways they could easily identify with. While the literary output of exiled authors such as Mann, Brecht, Feuchtwanger, Sachs, and others was met with indifference for the most part, readers eagerly turned to the authors who had remained.

Luise Rinser, one of the most widely read and best-loved German writers of the Adenauer period and beyond, provides an actual test case for examining the dynamics of literary production and audience approval in the immediate postwar era. Closer scrutiny of Rinser, author of a large number of novels, short stories, diaries, and collections of letters, will give some insight into the literary taste of postwar German society. Such an exercise, moreover, could be used as well to answer some of the profoundly troubled questions that historians have raised about postwar German society's sense of collective culpability. It could, for one, throw partial light on the much puzzled-over manner in which Germans dealt (or refused to deal) with the painful burden of working through their collective guilt feelings about complicity in the atrocities of the Nazi regime.

The secret of Luise Rinser's popularity with a postwar audience lies in the fact that her personal history as much as her stories mirrored an ideal that the average German at the time aspired to. Indeed, the typical Rinser reader has always been the average German: usually not members of the intelligentsia, not university educated, Rinser readers are mainstream, often from the same Catholic or secular humanistic background as she. In the years after the war, they would find the often-grim reality of their own lives reflected in Rinser's books. More importantly, the author offered—in easily accessible narratives—visions of an exemplary existence in the face of unbelievable hardships. This was material the readers could readily absorb and take to heart. No doubt, their reading pleasure was driven by the desire to have possessed—*post facto*, so to speak—the same courage that the author herself had, at least in fiction, demonstrated. Moreover, they detected the identical trait of "civil courage" in many of the author's heroines and they found in Rinser's plot scenarios plausible and believable characters who face real-life decisions they could identify with; consequently, readers immersed themselves in the fantasy of having led similarly fearless and uncompromising lives during the disquieting times of the Nazi regime.

This pattern was set into motion with the 1946 publication of Rinser's, *A Woman's Prison Journal*, written after five months of detention in a Traunstein women's prison. In 1944, having discussed the imminent loss of the war with a friend of hers, Rinser had been charged with defeatist remarks. Awaiting trial for treason, she was set free after a highly placed connection intervened on her behalf. Her *Prison Journal* documents the dehumanizing effect of imprisonment as well as the author's indomitable will and life force. The book of fiction, which propelled the forty-year-old in 1950 into the fast-paced life of a best-selling author was *Nina* (*Mitte des Lebens*). The female protagonist of this *Bildungsroman* is an avid resistance fighter from the beginnings of the Third Reich, a fiercely independent woman who risks her life for political and racial victims of the regime. Jailed for treason late in the war, this heroic character has the largesse, upon miraculously being spared the death sentence, to save the life of an SS man who is dying of blood poisoning. In this, her first postwar book of fiction, Rinser immediately begins to sow the seeds of the myth surrounding her past by letting both readers and critics assume that Nina is a portrait of the artist as a young woman. It was a very conscious and highly successful construct in fiction by an author who needed a past commensurate with the autobiographical image she presented to her emerging audience. A history was called for that would fit the activist persona into which she was metamorphosing during the 1950s. As a highly public figure of the past fifty years, Rinser has been connected with numerous social causes. Before she ran—unsuccessfully—for the West German presidency as the candidate of the Green Party in 1984, she had already championed such causes as the antinuclear, the feminist, and the environmental movements, the advancement of the rights of prison inmates, and the fight for the redress (*Wiedergutmachung*) of Nazi and postwar discrimination against the Romany. No one would want to diminish the value of Rinser's social engagement or deny her due esteem for her often passionate commitment to worthy causes. Yet the truth, however little known, is that some chapters in Rinser's history are not as stellar as the author maintained during her long life. Having lived in Italy from 1955 on, Luise Rinser died at age ninety in 2002.

The story of her life presents itself as fairly typical of her time and place, the tale of an only child of a staunchly Catholic Bavarian couple, of a girl who grew up feeling unwanted and unloved by her stern parents. Rinser's autobiography of 1981, *Embrace the Wolf* (Den Wolf umarmen), gives ample evidence of the father's rigidity, the mother's insensitivity, and the daughter's equally unrelenting sense of rebellion. Trying to escape her parents' grasp and the cold atmosphere of her home, the child's desperate search for companions leads her to friendships with society's outcasts. Still inexperienced and unsure of her goals, other than wanting to excel in order to prove her worth to her demanding parents, young Luise is easy prey for the propaganda of the rising National Socialist movement. Small wonder, then, that the 22-year-old teacher trainee from upper Bavaria should march straight from the university lecture halls into the arms of the Nazi Party, or rather the arms of a young SA man. Like so many of her generation, Rinser fell victim to the seductions of fascist ideology and consequently published several blood-and-soil pieces in 1934 in the Nazi journal *Herdfeuer* (a magazine placed on the index of forbidden publications after 1945 by the Allied forces). The most embarrassingly adulatory of these publications is a hymn to the Führer, entitled "Young Generation." The student-teacher, who had led a ski camp for the BDM (the Nazi association for girls) during the previous winter, evinces enthusiastic yet naïve support with the lines "Unsheltered, we keep an icy watch on towers and summits during sharp morning storms,… cool, hard, and knowing is this conscious generation," in whose name the author swears to be loyal until death, "A sworn guardian of the sacred soil/the great Führer's silent ambassadors," who will "wake, die, or win/because we are faithful."

There are, of course, anthologies full of similarly banal devotional pieces to Hitler from those years; most other authors of these pieces, however, paid a high price after the war, such as being blacklisted and castigated for their role in the then defunct Nazi propaganda machine. That machine also churned out collections of prose narratives like Rinser's in the blood-and-soil category. The several pieces from Rinser's pen present edifying tales of the heroic life of the Bavarian farmers and the agony of unrequited love; they revolve around the begetting and birthing of illegitimate children, their sad lives and death by drowning. Rinser's early literary output, though limited and apparently composed only in 1934–35, must cause today's reader to cringe. At best, the *Herdfeuer* pieces reflect that moral blind spot Rinser shared with so many of her German contemporaries. These incriminating articles, published in an obscure journal during the Third Reich and never re-edited, were not discovered until about 1987.[4] By that time, however, the myth with which Rinser had surrounded her past and her early history was so strong as to withstand almost any assault. Aware of her status as one of the standard bearers of antifascism in postwar Germany, Rinser has steadfastly denied authorship of these pieces, or, when directly confronted during TV appearances, she has belittled their significance and called them "harmless juvenilia."

In January 1988, another public figure, the well-known and respected telecaster Werner Höfer, was found to have published implicating materials during the Third Reich. This scandal prompted West German Radio (WDR) to air a television program entitled "Writing under the Swastika," to which it invited Höfer as well as Rinser and Axel Eggebrecht, who had directed many of the most popular films for UFA during the Nazi period. Asked about her publication record from 1935 to 1945, Rinser coyly claimed amnesia, insisting instead on her own variation on the course of events, according to which she had seen the dangers of the Nazi ideology from the start. As proof she read from a letter supposedly written in 1933 to a friend where she expressed just such doubts. Newspaper accounts of this embarrassing moment in the life of a much admired public figure varied widely. Most journalists were quite willing to downplay the significance of the aged writer's youthful indiscretions, mirroring no doubt an attitude shared by most Rinser devotees. Not so the *Deutsche National-Zeitung*, a conservative publication with whose editors Rinser has waged war since the early 1960s in suits and countersuits over the legality of the paper's terming her a Nazi writer. Rinser lost most of those suits, and her choice to live in Italy may have been partly in response to these attacks. In its account of the January 1988 talk show, the *National-Zeitung* provides a long list of writings allegedly published by Rinser in a variety of Nazi journals. I was able to confirm most of these citations in the Literatur-Archiv in Marbach, Germany. Some of the pieces mentioned in the *National-Zeitung* are innocuous, such as the narrative entitled "Die Gratulanten" (The Congratulations Line), printed in *Das Reich* of 22 December 1940, which is a mere report on the congratulatory responses the Rinsers received to their announcements of the birth of their first son.[5] Considering the long-simmering feud between Rinser and the *National-Zeitung*, it is unsurprising that the latter has inflated reports of Rinser's Nazi activities. These attempts are mean-spirited and lack journalistic ethics. However, evidence of more serious literary activity are the prose pieces and the hymn printed in *Herdfeuer* in 1934–35, and the long poem *The Voice* (Die Stimme) in *Die Neue Rundschau* of 1939, to which I will return later. The author may today disown these early works or claim to have forgotten them, but their authenticity is beyond question, and the halo that many of her devoted readers have for decades seen around Rinser's head is much tarnished by them, less for her misguided fascination with Nazi ideas than for her inability to admit her youthful transgressions. Rinser has often assumed the position of moralist, and has expressed herself with self-righteous outrage on issues such as women's rights and prison reform. These pronouncements now sound hollow and hypocritical.

Though she is silent on these issues in her autobiography *Embrace the Wolf*, Rinser there portrays herself as someone who always needed strong role models and idols and was easily swayed by the opinions of those whom she trusted. She was taught to see the error of her ways in 1935; at this point she was made to understand that her infatuation with Hitler did not sit well with the more intellectual, more left-leaning, more artistic circle of friends she had recently cultivated. A few months earlier, she had met and fallen in love with her future husband, the young conductor-apprentice Horst Günther Schnell. In a matter of months, Rinser metamorphosed into a Hitler opponent. Under Schnell's tutelage, and that of the composer Kaminski, she not only broke off all ties to the proponents of the regime, but in typical Rinser fashion, went to the other extreme.

Much later, in her diaries of the years 1972 to 1978, the author reflected, albeit in a veiled mode that leaves much leeway for interpretation, on her tendency to ideological conversions. In a diary entry of 1976, Rinser mused:

> I gave myself up to the painful grace called 'spiritual restlessness.' In concrete terms that means that I absorbed everything new, even if it did not exactly appeal to me. Though I experienced it intensely, I did not make a home in it but rather traversed through all novel realms, always enriched and wiser for having visited. In my youth and later as well, my conservative father considered me a turncoat, someone lacking in character. He never accepted the fact that a person can evolve. (*Kriegsspielzeug*, 132)

Pleasing her father may have been Luise Rinser's secret and unacknowledged ambition for much of her life; her conservative parents had lamented their only child's flirtation with the dangerous views of the Nazi regime. Yet time and again, the young teacher and aspiring author found herself incapable of reconciling their expectations with her roller-coaster politics. Her need to evolve now pointed her away from the outspoken and surely by now embarrassing adulation of a regime less and less beloved of the country's intellectuals. This is not to say that Rinser became an outspoken critic of Hitler and fascist ideology; rather, the 27-year-old withdrew from public life and devised a way to keep doing what she enjoyed most: writing. Spurred by her husband's encouragement and that of the publisher Peter Suhrkamp, Rinser started work on a childhood memoir, *The Glass Rings* (Die Gläsernen Ringe).

The novella was published in 1940 to positive reception and considerable acclaim. Since the end of the war, the author has wanted to characterize *Glass Rings* as a book of "political resistance," whose publication was consequently forbidden. These claims, reminiscent of similar demands by other authors of *inner emigration*, are, however, unsubstantiated: on the contrary, the regime-friendly illustrated *Die Woche* attests the author's "real poetic talent" in the issue of 4 June 1941. Though Rinser has told countless journalists that she was fired from her teaching position and forbidden to publish in 1941, she is still listed in the *Kürschner-Literaturkalender*, an official list of authors with permission to publish, of 1943. As it turns out, the reason that *Glass Rings* could not be printed in more editions (it had reached ten in a brief span of time) was much more mundane: reprints were prevented merely by a shortage of paper in the later war years rather than the book's allegedly controversial content.

An assessment of *Glass Rings*, applying the Brechtian epigraph at the start of this chapter, may well find the book controversial or rather problematic today, but nothing here would have troubled Nazi censors upon its publication in the second year of the war. Though Rinser had become critical of the Third Reich and the Nazis, she was not going to risk her head by speaking her mind openly. Thus, it was not so much confrontation by making an antifascist statement that was on Rinser's mind. From Jünger and the more bellicose influences of her early years, she had turned to another mentor, Hermann Hesse, in whose pacifist and apolitical message she now found the model best suited for her new project. She called Hesse, a resident of Switzerland with whom she had begun a correspondence around 1937, her "Guru ... a refuge from National Socialism." Rinser was particularly enthralled by Hesse's insistence that it was the artist's role to retreat within and overcome political difficulties through the power of the mind and spirit alone. This shift is confirmed by a closer examination of the poem mentioned above, which Rinser published in *Die Neue Rundschau* of January 1939, an issue that interestingly enough also contained a Hesse poem. Whether the older and more established writer had helped place this publication for the author-apprentice cannot be ascertained; all the more telling is the proximity of their ideas, the confluence of their minds, which met in the shared rejection of vulgar fame. In the six stanzas of *The Voice*, Rinser uses Christian imagery and a vocabulary tinted by religious fervor to outline the calling of a "lamb" to leave the flock; this persona leaves the comfort and warmth of the familiar for the wild un-known, for an unsheltered existence, with the mark on the forehead as the bloody and painful branding of the outcast. Kneeling down, the chosen one receives the oracle:

> Verwehrt ist der Pferch dir und das gewohnte
> süße Tal der Nahrung. Siehe dort
> Das Verworfene des unfruchtbaren,
> Des unaufhörlichen Gebirgs!
> Erstarrt dein But? Dort weide.
> Denn dort
> Bin Ich.

[No longer will you be allowed to dwell with the others in the corral or graze for food in the sweet dale. Turn your eyes over there to the cragged, the infer-tile realms of the endless mountain ranges! Does your blood freeze? I com-mand you to graze there. For that is where I am.]

This poem presents an exhortation to Germany's young, especially to the young author herself, to break away from the herd of those hypnotized by Hitler's slogans and ideology, is also a homage to Hermann Hesse, the mentor who issued the call prompting her to leave the stupefied masses behind and follow the mysterical dictate of the mind. Similarly, Hesse's poem a few pages later contains an appeal to the spirit of Mozart's music to serve as protector and a plea to "remain Führer and master/until the torch sinks from our hands." Starry-eyed with admiration for Hesse, Rinser appropriated for her planned memoirs the basic structural pattern as well as the apolitical message of all Hesse novels: a call for individua-tion, and a search for an inner self to be achieved solely through rebellion against society's constraints.

Rinser follows this paradigm in *Glass Rings* to a fault. *Glass Rings* is a novel of initiation, of the rites of passage, a *Bildungsroman* that could well be entitled *Luise's Lehrjahre,* with a plot whose trajectory follows the pro-tagonist from childhood through adolescence. The story lovingly paints an impressionable child's withdrawal from the ugliness of adult reality into a fairy-tale world. From the vantage point of adulthood, the universe of adolescence is celebrated as the only safe space. As such, *Glass Rings* not only follows the Hesse model, but also stands very much in the neo-Romantic tradition of other narratives written during *inner emigration* (such as Marie-Luise Kaschnitz's *Elissa* (1937), Hans Carossa's *Das Jahr der schönen Täuschungen* (The Year of the Beautiful Deceptions, 1942), and Ina Seidel's *Unser Freund Peregrin* (Our Friend Peregrin, 1940); it thus repre-sents a highly typical example of the genre predominantly produced dur-ing this era (see Denkler and Prümm).

Rinser's novella establishes in vivid images an idyllic, rural, and phys-ically remote locale, a magic realm into which the stern and forbidding grown-ups in charge of the unnamed child's care cannot intrude. This effect works particularly well in the first half of the book, set in a Bavarian monastery. This place, daunting in its austerity yet comforting in its ancient and beautiful function of sanctuary, provides the author with the opportunity for her central concern: to probe the teachings of the Catholic Church through the eyes of the child and the adolescent. The adults overseeing this education are an uncle, a high-ranking church official, and a village priest; this latter patriarch is a benevolent father figure substituting for the real one, who is off serving in the Great War of 1914. He encourages the young girl's intellectual curiosity and thus represents the only benign and nurturing force in her life. In contrast, her mother is portrayed as cold, insensitive, and hypocritical. Both the girl's mother and her father (who later reappears as a shell-shocked veteran) remain shadowy and antagonistic figures whose main educational objective is to break the girl's will and form her in their own image. Their supreme arrogance in the face of the young person's developing mind earns them scorn and rebellion. In the end, the adolescent may have emancipated herself from parental authority, but she will never feel anything but resentment for her elders' attempt to paralyze her creative urges. The secondary characters in Rinser's memoir are equally reminiscent of Hesse creatures: the gypsy vagabond, a boy who utters the stereotypical call of the wild; the religious fanatic under whose influence the child explores the existence of a stigmatized zealot with self-flagellation and asceticism; the buxom farmer's wife in whose sphere the child learns to appreciate the modest and unspoiled ways of those who till the soil. Shadows of Rinser's early "blood-and-soil" pieces fall on these scenes of a bucolic idyll, but the evocation of Bavarian country life is just one aspect of the narrative; finally, in her late adolescence there appears the protagonist's homoerotic adulation of a teacher whose readings of Hölderlin and the classics help to save her from despair.

The young girl goes through a variety of experiences tempting her to do evil, seducing her to sexual experimentation, and generally introducing her to what Rinser sees as the confusing and revolting realm of adulthood. Yet she is granted refuge in a safe haven over and again in the space alluded to in the book's title. The "glass rings" refer to the perfectly circular ripples created by pebbles thrown into the quiet dark waters of a pond that the child finds in a remote corner of the extended monastery gardens. Here, the precocious child (and later the returning young woman) finds a natural chapel, where no outside interference dims the senses and blurs reason. In the absolutely perfect circularity of the glass rings she believes to have discovered a symbol of the firm and placid structure of her future life. She envisions a life that will revolve around a religious core, defined by the image of the circle and thus by a finiteness, in stark contrast to the infinite complexity of the world outside. To quote from the concluding passages of the book, the sixteen-year-old discovers a wonderfully strict pattern that will govern her life, "not the confused and dark suffering of the physical, but the sharp and clear law of the intellect" (160).

Contemporary reviews confirm that the author's "descent into the dream-like remote realm of youth," done in descriptive passages of a "timeless, visually satiated" language met with great approval (Wehrli).[6] The narratives neoclassical form and its politically conservative message guaranteed it legality and approval by both the authorities and readers. The protagonist's quest resonated with contemporary audiences: the youth's attempt to find solace in the law of regularity signaled by the rings emanating in beautiful symmetry from a mysterious center, and "[the novella's] affirmation of the spiritual" (Hesse in 1940) must have touched some raw chords. For the readers of 1940, the lesson of *The Glass Rings* was an exhortation to turn away, to seclude themselves as best they could from the chaotic and irrational forces driving their universe and controlling their beleaguered existence. It is a simplistic yet an attractive notion, calling upon all those who were ready to listen to let themselves be hypnotized, just as the child protagonist is. The book's soothing message of affirmation in the face of devastation, lawlessness, and atrocities is plainly escapist.

If many of the neoconservative, neo-romantic works of *inner emigration* depict a regression into subjectivity and interiority, this is doubly visible in Rinser's case. The composition of *Glass Rings* constitutes Rinser's personal escape from an early infatuation with fascist ideology, but also documents the pathetic failure of *inner emigration* in general to confront and combat this reality. Its escapist gesture, expressed in the central trope of the "glass rings," thus renders it open to Walter Benjamin's bitter reproach. As early as 1930, Benjamin, who was to die en route to exile in 1941, had been alarmed by a feature he saw as typical of the works produced at the time in Germany. Framing his sense of the impending doom that threatened his home country into words of dry yet melancholy humor, Benjamin had warned of "A relentless growth of the Germans' sense of the wonders of nature which is in proportion to the totally mobilized landscape of the Nazi regime" (Benjamin, 785). A more articulate formula to capture the essentially escapist nature of *inner emigration* is neither possible nor necessary.

Notes

1. The title of one of the "Svendborger Gedichte," written in exile in Denmark and published in 1939 in Copenhagen.
2. Jünger's writings and public pronouncements have, of course, elicited a large body of critical assessments. Depending on the scholar's own viewpoint, the tenor of these analyses has ranged from ardent celebration of his oeuvre, which spans well over sixty years, to condemnation and denunciation. Even a critic as astute as Reinhold Grimm has found it difficult to pinpoint the role played by Jünger vis-à-vis the Third Reich. In his essay "In the Thicket of Inner Emigration" (included in the present volume), Grimm captures the controversial and ultimately ambiguous nature of this role in his statement that "Jünger was both a proven opponent of National Socialism while at the same time serving as a proven pacemaker for the Third Reich." On the one hand, Jünger's aestheticizing of violence and elitist disdain for the common man, an ideology pronounced with great arrogance and conviction from his earliest writing during World War I through the 1930s and 1940s, seems supportive of Nazi ideas and ideals; on the other hand, his ultimate aloofness and contempt even for the regime that tried to court him showed itself in the author's refusal to be admitted into Hitler's Academy of Arts. The paradox of Ernst Jünger's career merits attention, especially within the context of *inner emigration*.
3. The literature of the Adenauer era is another, yet unexplored, topic that merits more attention and examination by scholars. While "Germanists" have embraced the field of "Exile Literature" since the 1970s, the writings of the period following immediately upon the collapse of the Third Reich have been dealt with too gingerly. Much of what Alexander and Margarete Mitscherlich claimed to be German readers' and writers' infamous "Inability to Mourn," the inability to face up to collaborative urges with the fascistic project, could be extracted from closer scrutiny of the 1950s in Germany.
4. As I point out in "The Case of Luise Rinser," a watchful librarian in the Schiller Nationalmusem/Literaturarchiv Marbach, Germany, first drew my attention to the long-lost publications. Almost simultaneously, Rinser was confronted on German TV shows with the embarrassing discovery. That earlier article of mine was an analysis of Rinser's complete oeuvre, and as such it explored in greater depth the question of her postwar difficulty in performing *Trauerarbeit* (the work of mourning) concerning Nazi atrocities. In the context of the present volume, this chapter deals only with Rinser's writings during the prewar era and during the period of her *inner emigration* to the exclusion of all later works.
5. I failed to unearth another piece, "Anna Margarete Buxtehude," supposedly contained in *Westermann's Monathefte* of 1935. Nor have I been able to secure a copy of a book edited by Wolfgang Weyrauch in 1940 to which Rinser reportedly contributed a chapter.
6. In 1941, a review of three childhood memoirs recently published in Germany appeared in the *Neue Schweizer Rundschau*. The author, Max Wehrli, compared novellas by Hans Carossa, Luise Rinser, and Ina Seidel, detecting in all three a similar "need to descend into the lonely internal landscape of a long past youth … in order to unlock the genuine empire of poetry." (532) To legitimize these attempts, Wehrli compares his contemporaries to Jean Paul by drawing analogies between his melancholy prose narratives and the young German authors' "withdrawal into the remote realms of dream worlds." Wehrli characterizes the modern writers' style as "timeless, rich in imagery, nostalgic," but he reproaches them for taking refuge against the onslaught of the political situation. Referring to *Glass Rings*, Wehrli observes that the "*Zeitgeist* has stepped even further into the background," than in the other pieces since Rinser created "a Christian-Catholic cultural realm" within which her figures move as in a magical universe.

Works Cited

Benjamin, Walter. "Theories of German Fascism." In *Perspectives on German Cinema*, ed. Terri Ginsberg. New York: G. K. Hall, 1996.

Brecht, Bertolt. *Gedichte. Gesammelte Werke*. Frankfurt am Main: Suhrkamp, 1960–65.

Denkler, Horst, and Karl Prümm, eds. *Die Deutsche Literatur im Dritten Reich*. Stuttgart: Reclam, 1976.

Grosser, J. F. *Die Große Kontroverse. Ein Briefwechsel um Deutschland*. Hamburg, Geneva, and Paris: Nagel, 1963.

Jünger, Ernst. *Gärten und Strassen. Aus den Tagebüchern von 1939 und 1940*. 2nd ed. Paris: Zentrale der Frontbuchhandlung, 1942.

Rinser, Luise. *A Woman's Prison Journal*. Translated by Michael Hulse. New York: Pantheon Books, 1987. [Orig. *Gefängnistagebuch*. Frankfurt am Main: Fischer, 1946.]

———. *Die Gläsernen Ringe*. Berlin: Fischer, 1941.

———. *Mitte des Lebens*. Frankfurt am Main: Fischer, 1950.

———. *Den Wolf Umarmen*. Frankfurt am Main: Fischer, 1981.

———. *Kriegspielzeug*. Frankfurt am Main: Fischer, 1982.

Chapter 12

SURVIVAL WITHOUT COMPROMISE?

Reconfiguring the Past in the Works of
Hans Werner Richter and Alfred Andersch

Rhys W. Williams

In his somewhat grudging tribute to Alfred Andersch in *In the Establishment of the Butterflies: Twenty-One Portraits from the Group 47* (Im Etablissement der Schmetterlinge, 1986), Hans Werner Richter offers an illuminating insight into their shared experience of the past: "We had both survived the Third Reich without having made concessions, we had both been humiliated but had not capitulated" (44). The notion that both men had been "humiliated but had not capitulated" is, at first sight, a puzzling one, but as I shall seek to demonstrate, the cofounders of the Group 47 had made more concessions than they were prepared to admit. Moreover, they had both embarked, in a modest way, on literary careers before 1945; both were thus exponents (if only just) of a kind of *inner emigration*, which helps to explain their ambivalence toward the writing of the better known emigrants. Interestingly, both Andersch and Richter felt constrained to revisit the dilemmas of the past in their postwar creative work, reconfiguring the issues they had faced and reinterpreting their actions retrospectively. Biographical concerns inform my reading of their postwar work, because the works themselves require biographical deconstruction and formal interpretation for a proper appreciation of their wider resonance.

The values and attitudes that shaped the early direction of the Group 47 and with it the literature of the Federal Republic in the 1950s were less the product of reeducation in the American POW camps (as Volker Wehdeking has argued) than of the experience of defeat, not of the German army in 1945, but of the socialist ideals of the young generation in 1933. The failure of socialism to resist Hitler, enforced accommodation with Nazi values in the Third Reich and the sense that the complexities of their situation were not fully appreciated in the Brave New World of the Federal Republic characterized the political and literary values of the founding members of the Group 47. Both Andersch and Richter were to devote most of their own literary production to a reappraisal of their personal experiences in the Third Reich, playing out retrospectively a range of possible reactions to National Socialism, justifying and explaining their own failure to resist, and presenting themselves as psychological victims of a totalitarian regime. Refusing to accept the notion of collective guilt and retaining a belief in a demilitarized, united Germany, they were branded as nationalists (a charge they emphatically denied); holding fast to socialist values after the onset of the Cold War, they were dismissed as communist fellow-travelers (an accusation they rejected with equal vehemence). All too aware of the failure of communism to offer effective resistance to the Nazis in Germany, they harbored deep suspicions about communist policies in Eastern Europe and about ideology in general. Andersch and Richter had been socialists before 1933, they had remained in Germany in the Third Reich, and despite their literary ambitions, they had succeeded in publishing little before 1945. These facts constituted excellent credentials for both of them as spokesmen of the younger generation.

Andersch's literary and journalistic background before 1945 throws some light on his postwar attitudes. Before 1933 he had been Communist Youth Organizer for Southern Bavaria and dabbled in political journalism. After Hitler's seizure of power and the burning of the Reichstag, Andersch, like most Communist functionaries, was arrested; he emerged from Dachau after six weeks, thanks to his mother's effective intervention in drawing attention to the not insignificant contribution that his late father, Alfred Andersch senior, had made to the rise of National Socialism. Andersch himself was briefly rearrested in the autumn of 1933, and reacted—perhaps not unnaturally, in view of the threat of a return to Dachau—by breaking with his Communist Party affiliations and abandoning politics for literature. Andersch's literary beginnings were unpromising: poetry in the style of Rilke and short prose sketches evoking landscapes from which human concerns were largely excluded. In February 1942, just about the time when he was released from military service having served in France as part of the occupying force, he submitted a longer prose piece, *Sketches of a Young Man* (Skizze zu einem jungen Mann), to the literary section of the *Frankfurter Zeitung*. Early in 1943, Andersch applied for membership in the Reichsschrifttumskammer (Reich Chamber of Literature, hereafter RSK). While his application was successful, he was "freed from membership" (*von der Mitgliedschaft befreit*), the usual procedure for writers who had published little.[1] Andersch's decision to apply was the first step in his effort to gain transfer to a propaganda company (*Propaganda-Kompanie*), one of his frequent and understandable attempts to avoid a posting to front-line military service. Called up again in October 1943, Andersch was posted to Denmark, where in April 1944 he received a letter from the Suhrkamp Verlag, declining his projected volume *Remembered Figures* (Erinnerte Gestalten).[2] One of the three stories in that volume was, however, published in April 1944 in the *Kölnische Zeitung*. Although after the war, for understandable reasons, Andersch was to be silent[3] about his literary activities before 1945, he was, if only just, a writer of the *inner emigration*, and his sympathy for the writing that was published in Germany between 1933 and 1945 is, as we shall see, a salient feature of his appraisal of the postwar literary situation.

Hans Werner Richter's biography is as elusive as Alfred Andersch's. In a conversation with Hans Dieter Zimmermann in 1985 he insisted on the essentially autobiographical nature of his fiction: "I somehow experienced everything myself" (Zimmermann, 130). The qualifier "somehow" or "one way or another" clearly raises many questions. Richter's application to join the Reichsschrifttumskammer (RSK), which he submitted on 26 July 1938, contains a curriculum vitae that offers further insight into his activities in the period, as does his application for a post with the Bund Reichs-deutscher Buchhändler (Association of German Bookdealers) in Leipzig, which he appears to have held from 1 January 1936. Richter appears to have worked for intermittent periods in the Tempelhofer bookstore in Berlin (from 25 November 1927 until 24 May 1930, from 1 December 1930 until 31 March 1931, and from 1 January 1933 until 28 February 1934) and then for the Gsellius bookstore from 24 October until 24 December 1935, before his move to Leipzig. The gaps are filled in by the handwritten word, presumably inserted by Richter himself, *stellungslos* (out of work). The curriculum vitae contains the sentence: "From 1934 to 1935 I spent six months in Paris studying French language and literature," which partly explains the gap between work in Tempelhof and the Gsellius bookstore. Richter gave up his post in Leipzig on 31 August 1936 to work for the Friedrich Verlag in Berlin, a post he left on 31 July 1938. The information Richter supplied to the Information Control Division of the American Military Government in 1946, which has gained currency in biographical accounts of Richter's activities, is thus in need of significant correction. Quoting from that curriculum vitae, Vaillant notes: "Richter must therefore have left Berlin in the autumn of 1933. He moved to Paris, where he had contacts with French communists and tried to form a socialist group, which would once more take up activity in Germany. He returned to Germany in 1934 where, linked to middle-class circles in Berlin University and young literary circles around Ernst Wiechert, he became part of the resistance" (Vaillant, 16). In an interview with Graeme Cook on 22 October 1987, Richter denies any contact with Wiechert: "I never had anything to do with Ernst Wiechert. In fact, I've heard that story too. I have absolutely no idea where that comes from. I did not know him" (Cook, 36). This biographical documentation of Richter's life in the 1930s points up three problems with the accepted accounts of his activities. Firstly, there is, apart from Richter's own testimony, no corroboration of his illegal activity in the early 1930s. Secondly, his so-called flight to Paris was not, as it has been portrayed, an immediate response to National Socialism; it seems that Richter's then girl-friend was studying French and Richter merely accompanied her to Paris, not in 1933 but over a year later; and there is no supporting evidence of his contacts with French communists. Thirdly, Richter is, in all his accounts, silent both about his post with the Bund Reichsdeutscher Buchhändler in Leipzig and about his literary activity before 1945.

What did that literary activity amount to? In his application to the RSK, Richter listed five items that he had published in newspapers; it seems entirely possible that further items appeared after his application was submitted, for the very existence of an application suggests that he was keen to embark on a literary career. Stories appeared in the *Hamburger Zeitung*, the *Osnabrücker Tageblatt*, the *Görlitzer Nachrichten*, and the *Berliner Lokalanzeiger*, all between 12–13 June 1937 and 12 April 1938. Two of the stories, "Playing around the Morning Wind" (Ein Spiel um Morgenwind) and "Shooting Star" (Die Sternschnuppe), are sentimental feuilleton pieces about the pain of adolescent love. Characteristically, the stories lack any contemporary reference; they are lifted out of a political or social context. In "Playing around the Morning Wind," Jack and Marianne are becalmed in a yacht; her refusal to believe that he can conjure up a wind with his flute marks a rift in their relationship. The sense of being becalmed, of a setting remote from the city with its political pressures, evokes a timeless stasis: "Like a never-ending mirror, the sea stretched away to the bright horizon."[4] A neo-Romantic longing for the infinite, together with the suggestion of timeless calm in the midst of turmoil, characterize, as Reinhold Grimm has observed, the literature of *inner emigration*. A third story, entitled "Only a Flute" (Nur ein Flötenspiel) appeared in the *Görlitzer Nachrichten* on 12–13 March 1938, in a special supplement in honor of *Heldengedenktag* (Veterans' or Heroes' Memorial Day). Appropriately, the setting is World War I, the story of the character called Flöte is narrated by one of his comrades on the eastern front, somewhere in Galicia. The sound of the flute reminds the troops of their distant homeland: "But now and again in the exultant longing of the notes we were seized by a poignant yearning." The playing of the flute suggests "calm and forgetfulness"; the "magic of his flute-playing conjures up lost youth." Moreover, the soldiers are offered the spiritual sustenance that makes their military task easier to bear: "But whenever after such hours duty called us, our step was lighter and happier, and the war had again become a task which we had to fulfill." Richter is echoing here a tension between love of *Heimat* (homeland) and the stern duty of war, which is the staple of National Socialist literature. The language, with its fondness for terms such as "magic," "endlessness," and "mystery" (*Zauber, Unendlichkeit, Geheimnis*), is the kind of writing that Richter was to reject wholesale after 1945.

A glance at Andersch's writing under National Socialism reveals many similar hallmarks of *inner emigration*. His first published work, the short story that appeared in the *Kölnische Zeitung* on 25 April 1944 under the title "Erste Ausfahrt" (First Excursion), was republished posthumously in the volume *Erinnerte Gestalten* (Remembered Figures, hereafter *EG*) in 1986 under the title "Sechzehnjähriger allein" (Sixteen-Year-Old Alone).

The story presents a journey from the center to the periphery, away from the urban to the edge of the natural world: the young Werner (a cipher for Andersch himself) cycles south from Munich into the surrounding countryside, turning his back on the social and domestic pressures of his life in the city and losing himself in contemplation of nature, which transmits a sense of the unlimited possibilities of life opening up before him. The landscape, significantly devoid of human presence, is presented with a painter's eye:

> Close by lay stretched before him woods, fields and meadows, villages and the shining lake, and the countryside was crisscrossed by roads, but in the distance on the other side of the lake everything melted away into a dull green wave, with bright grey shadows flying above it and somewhere in the farthest distance it met an icy grey, motionless sky and then there was nothing more. Then there was space, space, space. (*EG*, 169)

Looking north, presumably back toward the city and a future adult life, Werner reflects "that there a longing for liberation would be fulfilled, for the infinity of a space in which he too with his thoughts and deeds could become infinite" (*EG*, 170). The landscape betokens intensity of experience; as a harbinger of the richness of life to come, it offers compensation for the insecurities and social compromises that Werner has fled. Leaving aside for the moment the mawkish sentimentality of the piece, one can detect that beneath the adolescent dreams lies a topography of control and restriction from which Werner seeks escape. Another early sketch, for which Andersch drew on the family of his half-Jewish wife, Angelika Albert, was entitled "The Technician" (Der Techniker), which was also part of the volume *Erinnerte Gestalten*, rejected by the Suhrkamp Verlag in 1944. The language of the text bears eloquent testimony to the values of the time: the central character, Albert, reflects, for example, on the "mysterious bonds, which chain him to the blood of his father" (geheimnisvolle Bande, die ihn an das Blut des Vaters ketten, *EG*, 64), and on "the dark blood inheritance of his father" (*EG*, 137). And Albert loves his friend Georg "for his innate industriousness, this inheritance of a healthy, unbroken race" (wegen seines eingeborenen Fleißes, dieses Erbteils einer gesunden, ungebrochenen Rasse, *EG*, 56). Uncomfortable as this language is for modern readers, it reflects as much Andersch's enthusiasm for Thomas Mann's *Buddenbrooks* as it does any conscious attempt to appeal to National Socialist values.

Both Andersch and Richter, then, underwent an apprenticeship in the literary techniques of *inner emigration*. Richter himself was explicit about his criteria for membership in the Group 47: "The rule was applied strictly: anyone who had published in the Third Reich will not be invited! Later, in fact only just recently, I discovered that some of them had indeed been published in the Third Reich. They were lyric poets who had now and again published the odd poem" (Zimmermann, 125–26). That Richter and Andersch themselves belonged in this category is not, given their literary ambitions and their age, unsurprising: Richter was thirty-seven and Andersch thirty-one when the war ended. Nevertheless, in their postwar creative work and in their theoretical pronouncements on *inner emigration* both writers were to return, time and time again, to the dilemmas that literature faced in the Third Reich. Richter's initial response to the writing of *inner emigration* was wholly negative. In the polemical essay "Literatur im Interregnum," published in *Der Ruf* on 15 March 1947, he adopted a radical position. Condemning the writing of exile as remote from the concerns of a defeated Germany, he also railed against the literature of *inner emigration*. "Formalism becomes a formula for fear, the word becomes a plaything of the fear of reality. Far from the bloody military highways of our age, aestheticism celebrated its triumph of isolation.... There is no way back from this escape. A generation has failed." In its place Richter advocated a stark realism, which he attempted to supply in his own early postwar novels.

Andersch was altogether more circumspect when he attempted to define the literary situation in 1947. His essay "Deutsche Literatur in der Entscheidung," which was read to the second meeting of the Group 47 in Herrlingen, remains one of the few theoretical texts that the Group, with its suspicion of theory and dislike of ideology, ever countenanced. Andersch purports to offer in his essay an analysis of the literary situation in 1947, but he opens his essay by emphasizing that "any investigation of the state of German literature … must therefore take as its starting point a careful analysis of the true situation of the German mind in the years of dictatorship" (*Das Alfred Andersch Lesebuch*, [*AAL*], 113). Although he is aware that the term *inner emigration* covers a multitude of different reactions to the regime, Andersch elects to adopt the term, extending it to typify all the literature produced within Germany after 1933. His argument is ingenious: since all explicitly Nazi writing is unworthy of the name literature, it may be conveniently set aside. It follows that all genuine literature produced in Nazi Germany was written in opposition to the regime. By this sleight of hand some rather dubious figures may be salvaged: Hans Grimm, Erwin Guido Kolbenheyer, Wilhelm Schäfer, Emil Strauß. These figures, for Andersch, displayed "a kind of subjective integrity" (*AAL*, 116) and could thus be regarded as opponents of the regime. In order to illustrate the tragedy of this group, Andersch helps his argument along by devoting some attention to the least problematic figure, Ernst Wiechert, whose four-month imprisonment in Buchenwald in 1938 turned him into an emblematic victim of the regime. A second, older, generation is described as belonging to a tradition of "bourgeois classicism": Gerhart Hauptmann, R. A. Schröder, Hans Carossa, Ricarda Huch, Gertrud von Le Fort. Apart from Carossa, who attempted "for very noble reasons" (*AAL*, 117) to compromise, all the others are described as opponents of the regime, driven by their humanistic values into isolation. A third and final group of writers who remained within Germany are subsumed under the category "Resistance and Calligraphy" (*Widerstand und Kalligraphie*), a group containing figures such as Stefan Andres, Horst Lange, Hans Leip, Martin Raschke, and Eugen Gottlob Winkler. The latter, Andersch insists, maintained their independence from the Reichsschrifttumskammer through the form of their work. Andersch concludes his section on those who remained in Germany with a study of Ernst Jünger, whose "conversion" is adduced as proof that genuine artistic achievement was identical with opposition to National Socialism. Andersch's admiration for Jünger, a response not shared by his left-wing colleagues, is based on a reading of Jünger's symbolic style as the only effective weapon against totalitarian control.

Andersch's attitude to the literature of exile is ambivalent: he admires those who, like Thomas Mann, went into exile, but insists that they can influence the future literature of Germany only if they return. When he turns to "Committed Realism" (*realistische Tendenzkunst*), the writing of those who expressly opposed National Socialism, including Heinrich Mann, Werfel, Arnold Zweig, and Döblin, Andersch is critical. These writers forfeit his approbation in that their realism is tainted by didacticism, by propaganda. Similarly, those in a group entitled "Satirists" (*Satiriker*: Tucholsky, Polgar, Ossietzky, Walter Mehring, Kästner) are too much satirists, for him, and not sufficiently true artists. Nor is he convinced by the "Proletarian Writers" (Oskar Maria Graf, Willi Bredel, Anna Seghers, Theodor Plivier). What inhibits their work, for him, is their Marxist values; here is an early indication of Andersch's antipathy to the cultural policy in the Soviet Zone. If Ernst Jünger encapsulated the writers of *inner emigration*, Bertolt Brecht embodies the strengths (and weaknesses) of the writers of opposition. For Andersch, Brecht's anti-German sentiments, however understandable, diminish his achievement, and Brecht's return to Germany will alone convince Andersch of his value to the new generation of German writers.

Certainly, "German Literature: The Moment of Decision" (Deutsche Literatur in der Entscheidung) was well received by the authors present, who regarded it as a statement representative of their position. Why that should have been so, is interesting: Andersch managed in his essay to rehabilitate nearly all the writing that went on in Germany in the Third Reich, to blur the distinction between those writers of an older generation who continued to write in Germany and a younger generation whose voice was first heard after 1945, to define this new possibility as anticommunist, or at least anti-Stalinist, yet as a possibility equally opposed to American control, and to argue for a realism that is ill-defined enough to permit a plurality of styles. Here in essence is the rationale for the eclecticism of the Group 47, its own blurring of distinctions between those writers who had published in Nazi Germany and those who were genuinely newcomers in the postwar era. While Richter reacted to his own early literary experiments by repudiating the aesthetic escapism they embodied, Andersch was much more indulgent toward his juvenilia, skillfully redefining his efforts as oppositional.

Both Andersch and Richter return, in their later creative works, to the unresolved questions posed by their experience under National Socialism; indeed, it would be fair to argue that these traumas resurface with growing insistence in their writing. Andersch's first major attempt at a reappraisal is *The Cherries of Freedom* (Die Kirschen der Freiheit, 1952; hereafter *KF*). He is resolutely silent in this text about his marriage and his first wife, whom he pressed for divorce in February 1943, shortly before he applied to the RSK. But he is at pains to depict his desertion in Italy in June 1944, not merely as an act of Sartrean existential choice, but also as embodying all the possibilities that faced German writers in the Third Reich: at various points in the text he manages to run the whole gamut of political reactions to dictatorship. Firstly, he depicts enforced accommodation: "I too opened my mouth and shouted: 'Heil!'" (*KF*, 33); secondly, *inner emigration*: "I reacted to the total state with total introversion" (*KF*, 46); thirdly, active resistance to dictatorship: "My private little July 20 had already happened on June 6" (*KF*, 74); and finally a kind of exile, a belated decision to choose the other side. His actual motives are more prosaic and persuasive: "because I was scared of coming under fire and having to die, meaninglessly or not" (*KF*, 82). In *Zanzibar or the Last Reason* (Sansibar oder der letzte Grund, 1957) Andersch explores, through the person of Gregor, the various possibilities of resistance, illegal activity, and active efforts to save Jewish victims of National Socialism. Andersch was closer to the question of antisemitism than has commonly been realized; not only was his first wife, Angelika, half Jewish, but at the very time when he decided to leave her, his mother-in-law, Ida Hamburger, was forced to move to the so-called Jews' Camp (*Judenlager*) in the Knorrstraße in Munich as a prelude to her deportation, in June 1942, to Theresienstadt, from where she never returned. One may speculate that Andersch is playing out in this fiction a possibility that he failed to realize in the dark days of Nazi tyranny and is casting part of himself in Gregor's role. Among Andersch's ciphers for himself is the name "Werner Gregor."[5] There is clearly a tension here between Andersch's candid exploration of the omissions and failures of the past, as part of an enlightenment project, and a sense that he is in some way rewriting the past, making good those omissions and failures retrospectively. Something of that sin of omission resurfaces in *Efraim* (1967), in which Keir Horne abandons a half-Jewish daughter. Andersch understands the legacy of responsibility that Keir Horne experiences and, moreover, delineates through Horne's alcoholism the consequences of suppressing that guilt. In *Winterspelt* (1974, hereafter *W*) Andersch is quite explicit about his literary strategy: "History reports how things happened, narration plays out a possibility" (*W*, 22). Major Dincklage's plan to desert on a grand scale, to hand himself and his division over to the Allies and thus shorten the war, is another missed historical opportunity that Andersch explores. Even in his final work, *The Father of a Murderer* (Der Vater eines Mörders, 1980), Andersch returns to the past, conflating his sense of being victimized by his authoritarian headmaster, Himmler's father, and the impending National Socialist tyranny that the headmaster's son was to embody.

If Andersch's postwar oeuvre was to explore retrospectively the pressures and missed opportunities of the Nazi years, the same could be said of Hans Werner Richter's writing. While his most celebrated novel *The Defeated* (Die Geschlagenen, 1949) sought to defend those Germans who fought for the national cause despite their disapproval of the regime, later novels treat the period of the Third Reich more ambivalently. The central character of *The Defeated*, Gühler, is captured by American troops and debriefed by an émigré Austrian in American uniform. After denying that he was a National Socialist Party member, Gühler embarks on the following attempt to demarcate his position:

> "Why do you think that Germany is losing the war?
> "Hitler is losing the war. It is Hitler's, not Germany's war."
> The interpreter, who had been standing by the window when he asked the question, swiveled around.
> "Isn't it the same thing?"
> "No," answered Gühler, "it isn't the same. For me and for lots of us."
> "So why didn't you emigrate?"
> "That would have been cowardly." (221)

There is no evidence that Richter himself ever contemplated emigration, and certainly, through Gühler, he dismisses emigration as a possibility. *The Defeated* resolutely defends those who stayed in Germany and are therefore uniquely qualified to speak of wartime German experience, unlike—and this is the unspoken implication—the émigrés. This notion that the only course of action open to non-Jewish Germans was to remain in Germany and oppose National Socialism from within became a recurrent feature of Richter's self-image in the ensuing years of the Federal Republic. His repeated desire to confront and reconfigure the possibilities open to him between 1933 and 1945 is reflected in his creative work, particularly in *White Rose, Red Rose* (Rose weiß, Rose rot, 1971) and *A July Day* (Ein Julitag, 1982; hereafter *J*). Graeme Cook has compared the sometimes wildly differing accounts Richter gave of his life in the Third Reich: the curriculum vitae attached to the RSK application, the 1946 account given to the Information Control Division, the account contained in Richter's *Letters to a Young Socialist* (Briefe an einen jungen Sozialisten, 1974), the accounts offered by Richter in several interviews, and the fictionalized versions found in his heavily autobiographical novels. The discrepancies themselves are not at issue here; there may be all manner of tactical considerations that impelled him to emphasize now this, now that aspect of his experience. What is striking, however, is that Richter is constrained to return again and again to that period of his life, as if in compulsive justification of his actions.

A brief examination of *A July Day* will illustrate the process. The central character, perhaps a little too obviously named Christian Wahl, attends as an elderly man his brother's funeral in Sweden. His brother's widow (now living in exile, as it were, in Sweden) had been Christian's partner in the 1930s. The funeral triggers memories of the past and permits Richter to address once more through Christian Wahl the choices that were then open to him. The key episode is Christian's decision to spend a period in France after Hitler's seizure of power. As noted earlier, Richter had himself spent a period in France, not from November 1933 to April 1934 (which he sometimes claimed), but a year later. Richter is drawn to present his own stay in France as both flight from Nazi oppression and as a conscious choice to emigrate, and he justifies the decision to return to Germany as a realization that the only course of action was to return to oppose National Socialism in Germany (an argument he employed against the exile writers). But he is clearly nervous about the episode, and in the fictional account ambiguities and uncertainties emerge. When Christian first impresses Karoline with his political passion he is dimly aware that he presents himself as more radical than he really is: "In her presence he felt himself as more revolutionary than he really wanted to be" (*J*, 38), which invites reflection on the extent of Christian's socialist commitment, and, by extension, of Richter's own. While it is stated categorically that Christian's brother Philip had fled the GDR for Sweden "for fear of a new dictatorship" (*J*, 65), some doubt remains about Christian's motives in leaving Nazi Germany for Paris. He crucially qualifies the expression "a flight," with the words "half a flight from the unbearable new regime, from fear of persecution" (*J*, 73), and adds "a flight and not a flight, of his own volition and yet not of his own volition" (*J*, 76). His girlfriend, a student of French, is studying for a semester at the Sorbonne; his decision to accompany her is, however, presented in a curious way: "He persuaded her to come to Paris with him. She was intending to study there" (*J*, 78), as if his decision to flee were paramount and her further study merely contingent on that flight.

Christian's reflections on the train as it approaches the border offer a version of Richter's own dilemma over the question of how to present his brief stay in Paris in 1934–35: "He didn't like the word emigration, no, he didn't want to emigrate, he was too young to do that, much too young, it was flight and he didn't want to flee" (*J*, 80). Later Christian reflects on "this journey, this flight, whatever he might call it" (*J*, 99). Christian justifies his decision to leave with some general comments about the political atmosphere in Germany, with dark references to police raids and the political persecution of his acquaintances. To the actual threat to himself there are only oblique references. When the passport inspection takes place on the train, he notes with relief: "no, they weren't looking for him, at least not here" (*J*, 93), which implies, but does not explicitly confirm, that he is under threat in Berlin. The stay in Paris is marked by a strong sense of alienation from the concerns of both the French population and the German émigrés; he is fully aware that his stay is merely a transient one and that he is not exposed to the existential pressures of those who must build a new life for themselves in exile. When he witnesses a political demonstration in Paris relating to the Stavisky scandal, he remains detached, preoccupied with personal problems. (Incidentally, the reference to the demonstration would place Richter in Paris on 6 February 1934 and would seem to confirm his flight from Germany as having been an immediate reaction to the Nazi seizure of power; his curriculum vitae to the RSK, however, places him firmly in employment in Berlin Tempelhof at this time.) Christian's decision to return to Germany is also qualified: "Perhaps his statement: 'You can only take on the enemy in your own country' is just an excuse, perhaps he is moved by other emotions, longing, perhaps, homesickness, the desire to be part of it" (*J*, 187).

As with Andersch's constant reworking of the decisions of the 1930s, Richter feels impelled to pick over the bones of what is left from his expe rience of Nazi Germany. What emerges both reinforces his original claims and systematically relativizes them, casting doubt on simple explanations, conceding mixed motives, confronting unpalatable truths. Although he confines his insight exclusively to the personal sphere of his relationship with Karoline, Christian Wahl in *Ein Julitag* reaches a conclusion that could stand as a motto for all Hans Werner Richter's postwar creative writing. He views the past "like a mistake …, an omission that can never be redeemed. It is too late for everything, corrections are no longer possible, and perhaps, he thinks, life can never be corrected" (*J*, 138).

As a result of the trauma of their years as inner emigrants there emerges in the fiction of both Alfred Andersch and Hans Werner Richter a profound unease in their portrayal of the National Socialist period. Both writers are continually drawn back to that period, repeatedly impelled to justify or to reappraise their own attitudes. In their early public pronouncements after 1945 both lay claim to the position of outright opponents of the Nazi regime, legitimizing their literary activities after 1945 as a radical break with the past. But in their fictional works more ambivalent attitudes emerge, attitudes that are, moreover, supported by the biographical evidence currently available. The origins of postwar West German literature lie less in the American experience of reeducation than in the experience of enforced accommodation with the Nazi regime. The myth that the Group 47 marked a radical break with the past could not be sustained even by its founders, who sought in their fiction to address complex and uncomfortable questions that their public pronouncements seemed to avoid.

Notes

1. Applications to the Reichsschrifttumskammer are preserved in the American Document Centre, now part of the Bundesarchiv, in Berlin.
2. See Winfried Stephan. For the references to the "Propaganda-Kompanie," see 21; for the letter of rejection, see 37–38.
3. Andersch first broke his silence in 1977 in "Der Seesack."
4. "Ein Spiel um Morgenwind," *Osnabrücker Tageblatt*, 22 May 1938.
5. Werner Gregor was the pseudonym Andersch adopted for a two-part feature on the Normandy landings, broadcast by the Süddeutscher Rundfunk in May and June 1957.

Works Cited

Andersch, Alfred. *Das Alfred Andersch Lesebuch.* Zurich: Diogenes, 1979.

⸺. "… einmal wirklich leben." In *Ein Tagebuch in Briefen an Hedwig Andersch 1943 bis 1975*, ed. Winfried Stephan. Zurich: Diogenes, 1986.

⸺. "Der Seesack." In *Literaturmagazin 7*, ed. Nicolas Born and Jürgen Manthey, 128–29. Reinbek bei Hamburg: Rowohlt, 1977.

Cook, Graeme Mark. "The Fiction of Hans Werner Richter." Ph.D. diss., University of Wales-Swansea, 1989.

Grimm, Reinhold. "Im Dickicht der inneren Emigration." In *Die deutsche Literatur im Dritten Reich: Themen, Traditionen, Wirkungen*, ed. Horst Denkler and Karl Prümm, 406–26. Stuttgart: Reclam, 1976.

Richter, Hans Werner. *Die Geschlagenen.* Munich: Kurt Desch, 1949.

⸺. *Ein Julitag.* Munich: dtv, 1984.

⸺. "Ein Spiel um Morgenwind." *Osnabrücker Tageblatt*, 22 May 1938.

⸺. *Im Etablissement der Schmetterlinge. Einundzwanzig Portraits aus der Gruppe 47.* Munich: Hanser, 1986.

Stephan, Winfried, ed. *Ein Tagebuch in Briefen an Hedwig Andersch 1943 bis 1975.* Zurich: Diogenes, 1986.

Vaillant, Jérôme. *Der Ruf. Unabhängige Blätter der jungen Generation (1945–1949).* Munich, New York, and Paris: Saur, 1978.

Wehdeking, Volker Christian. *Der Nullpunkt. Über die Konstituierung der deutschen Nachkriegsliteratur (1945–1948) in den amerikanischen Kriegsgefangenenlagern.* Stuttgart: Metzler, 1971.

Zimmermann, Hans Dieter. "Mit ihm ist Literatur über sich hinausgewachsen." *Neue Rundschau* 96, no. 2 (1985): 117–32.

Chapter 13

EXILE HONORIS CAUSA

The Image of Erich Kästner among
Writers in Exile

Guy Stern

Almost from the beginning, the field of exile studies also focused on
oppositional writers who remained in Germany, Austria, or Hitler-occu-
pied countries. The question that remains open concerned both the term
and the reality of an *inner emigration*. It was readily conceded that there
had been oppositional literature within the Third Reich, but did this
minority group really constitute a parallel phenomenon to exile literature? Several conferences were dedicated relatively early to this basic
question.[1] However, it was Walter Berendsohn, the Nestor of exile research, who immediately validated such a parallel: "In the Third Reich
there was something like a literary 'Marquis.'" Further, he asserted in volume II of his *Humanist Front* (Humanistische Front, for many years attain-
able only in manuscript form): "I never gave up my faith in the other
Germany and never doubted that there were literary works of inner
resistance, that writers were living in the Third Reich who were not
swayed by temptations or threats to deviate in any respect whatever from
their inner convictions" (26).[2] That faith, however, had to be tested against
historical reality.

To Berendsohn, Erich Kästner presented a prime example for his thesis.
Because Kästner has so often been held up as prima facie evidence by both
advocates and opponents of the concept of *inner emigration*, especially
upon the testimony of the exiles themselves, his attitudes and actions
make for a fascinating touchstone for general investigation into the phenomenon. To Berendsohn, to continue with him, Erich Kästner presented
a prime example for his thesis. Kästner's verses, known to have been circulated surreptitiously during the Nazi years, formed, Berendsohn argued,
"an invisible bond in the struggle against the common opponent" (22). He

also noted that an underground poetry anthology in occupied France, *Edition de minuit*, also contained Kästner texts (37). Similarly, Michael Kater, an American musicologist working from city police and Gestapo records, discovered that the Swings, a clandestine jazz-oriented group in the Third Reich, took its direction from Erich Kästner's pacifist works: "Swings listened to the BBC routinely, for news and for the jazz, and a few meticulously copied, multiplied, and distributed among each other British news items or pacifist prose such as that by the outlawed writer Erich Kästner" (Kater, 157).

The American Germanist Charles Hoffmann also lauded Kästner's stance during the Third Reich: "Erich Kästner's silence [and] that of Wolfgang Koeppen's was, in effect also a form of emigration" (131, fn. 1). The exile Wilhelm Sternfeld came to a similar conclusion when, in an early exile bibliography edited by Eva Tiedemann and himself, he argued that "the bibliography, though confined to exiles, had to allow for a few valid exceptions of genuine exile literature, even though the author himself had not been in exile" (15). The few exceptions, conceded by the two collaborators, included Erich Kästner, listed there with the explanatory codicil: "K. did not emigrate, but his works could neither be published nor cited in Germany" (247). The exiled author and resistance fighter Alfred Kantorowicz accorded him similar recognition right after the war, when he, in collaboration with Richard Drews, published the important anthology *Verboten und verbrannt* (Forbidden and Burned). Like Sternfeld and Tiedemann, he included a few authors who had remained in Germany and singled out a poem by Erich Kästner as part of the foreword to the Kästner entry (90), explaining that "His book of verses ... earned him the hate of the Nazis, who burned his books" (3). His inclusion in these and similar exile bibliographies received the stamp of approval of Marcel Reich-Ranicki: "If [Kästner] is mentioned in various reference books of German exile literature, that is quite proper. No, he did not emigrate, but his books did; they had to be published in Switzerland. Kästner was Germany's exile author honoris causa" (23). His membership in this honorable club is implicitly suggested as well by Robert E. Cazden (91) and by Wulf Koepke (II: 1412, 1423, 1431) when they stress that the author, unsuccessful in Germany, continued to be published in America, the country of refuge of so many of his contemporaries.

In his essay "Emil and the Émigrés: German Children's Literature in Exile, 1933–1945," Thomas Hansen gave his opinion on Kästner's contributions in postwar Germany: "The humanitarian project [of establishing the International Youth Library] found enthusiastic support from all sides. Erich Kästner, Kurt Kläber, Luise Rinser and Walter Trier were among the many individuals who participated" (Hansen, 6). The exile researchers also appreciated that Kästner had immediately welcomed the exiles' dispatches to Germany, once the war ended, and indeed had done all that he could to have their contribution published in the *Neue Zeitung*, which he edited in the postwar years.[3]

Beyond the critics, many of the exile literary figures themselves joined in this favorable assessment of Kästner. Hilde Spiel talks of the "revered Erich Kästner" (Spiel, 40), and Max Krell paid tribute to him in his autobiography:

> Everything about him was rather dainty, but never foppish—and he had a big heart. It stayed that way when the brownshirts descended on us. He did not retreat; he was prohibited from writing, but he wrote nonetheless. Friends labeled him "the last exile remaining in Germany." Far removed from Germany we never ceased to fear for his life. It could have been choked off at any moment in a concentration camp. (Krell, 200)

Robert Neumann echoed these sentiments:

> Let's concede that he stayed in Germany because of his mother, or was it, after all, because of Germany? But in doing so he gave the lie, through the way he lived, to all who maintained that one had to howl with the wolves, at least *sotto voce*, to avoid being fed to the wolves. Kästner did not howl. (Neumann, 422)

Marcel Reich-Ranicki, writing an appreciative essay about Kästner, found himself writing—as his title reflects—a "declaration of love" to him. As he explains:

> While in the Warsaw [Ghetto] someone lent me, though for a few days only, *Die lyrische Hausapotheke*. And since I had to return the book in a few days—the selection contained both old and new Kästner lyrics—I read the poems quickly and repeatedly. A few weeks later, as my twentieth birthday was drawing near, I received from my girlfriend, who would later become my wife, one of the most beautiful gifts that I've ever gotten in my entire life. She had copied for me, by hand, Kästner's entire *Lyrical Home Pharmacy* [lyrische Hausapotheke] and illustrated it.
>
> Unlike the other books that I had possessed [until World War II] this book weathered the years. When I met Kästner for the first time in 1957—that was in Munich—I showed him that copy, meanwhile somewhat faded, of his *Lyrische Hausapotheke*. With tears in his eyes he responded that the thought never would have occurred to him that someone in the Warsaw Ghetto, as in Medieval monasteries, would transcribe his poems by hand. (Reich-Ranicki, 23)

Hermann Kesten brings once more to mind that Kästner "wrote nothing for the Third Reich," and he tells of his last encounter with Kästner shortly before his emigration as evidence of Kästner's integrity:

> Shortly before leaving Germany in 1933, I told Kästner that I planned to take my apéritifs in the Café des "Deux Magots" opposite the Church of St. Germain des Prés instead of at Mampe's on the Kurfürstendamm. If I recall correctly I even suggested that we rendezvous in Paris.
>
> He replied that he meant to stay, because of his mother and in order to be a witness to the coming horrors. He wanted to write the great postwar novel and he wanted to have been present to appear as their accuser.

Erich Kästner, from 1933 to 1945, was an eyewitness to Germany's greatest self-abasement. That experience turned him into a writer of epigrams and of outraged pamphlets. (Kesten, 230)

Kesten is equally appreciative of Kästner's meritorious service in the years immediately following World War II, counting him among the handful of writers, in addition to Hermann Kasack and Kasimir Edschmidt, who championed the revival of the German PEN Club and the founding of the German Academy of Language and Literature in Darmstadt.

Precisely these "grand old men," together with Hermann Hesse in Switzerland, were the ones who, as autonomous teachers of their people and as moralists, cleansed the popular mind and buttressed the dignity of the literary profession in Germany, at a time when the Communist dictatorship in the GDR exerted pressures on writers' dignity and dismal excesses of literary and political servility often resulted.

In contrast, however, Erika and Klaus Mann did not challenge the rather equivocal judgment of a mutual friend of Kästner's and theirs:

"And what about Erich Kästner?" we wanted to know.... The answer, by now almost anticipated by us, went as follows: "He, too, has fallen silent. He no longer writes satiric verses, but petite novels, which are so fangless, that their effect borders almost on malice. It seems as though the author wanted to alert his public [by implying]: Don't you see, I now have to write such nonsense; they have reduced me to this. And surely you all remember, that I was very talented and witty at one time." (126)

Other exile authors, for example Annette Kolb, continued to think of Kästner as part of an imaginary close-knit circle ("Annette Kolb lived in Munich [as of 1961] in a large circle of old and new friends. Among them were the writer Erich Kästner ... and his companion Luiselotte Enderle" [Bauschinger, 191]) based on reciprocal friendship. Carl Zuckmayer harbored exactly those feelings when he visited Germany after the war:

We knew the murderers were among us. Therefore, all those who were good friends drew all the more closely together. In [postwar] Munich I encountered Erich Kästner, who was in charge of the feuilleton of the *Neue Zeitung*. (553)

Hans Habe, who in 1945 was in charge of eighteen German newspapers licensed by American authorities, frequently published Kästner and worked in close collaboration with him in the editing of the *Neue Zeitung* (Habe, 355).

But by way of contrast there were also a number of exile writers who interpreted Kästner's continued presence in Nazi Germany as a kind of moral failure. Franz Schoenberner was among them:

Many of the young writers—whom I introduced to the German reading public via the magazines *Jugend* and *Simplicissimus*—went astray in the war zone between the fronts; for example Erich Kästner, who after his first books, with their brilliantly aggressive verses, lost his courage. Preferring to stay in Germany he wrote innocuous children's books. (216)

A much more direct confrontation ensued between Erich Kästner and Thomas Mann, who for many émigrés was their representative-in-exile par excellence. Mann had given a resoundingly negative answer to the blandished invitations to return to Germany floated by such worthies as Walter von Molo (Grosser, 18–21) and Frank Thieß (Grosser, 22–26), who with rather questionable justification had declared themselves spokespersons for an *inner emigration* (see Stephen Brockmann's discussion in chapter 1 of this volume—NHD). Thomas Mann, avowing his undiminished attachment to his German roots, also explained that his new and primary loyalty was that of an American citizen. He also feared, he added, attacks by unreconstructed German enemies and admitted that he would find it difficult to face the throng of feckless bystanders and Nazi collaborators (Grosser, 30, 32).

A disharmonious choir of German voices responded to Thomas Mann's rejoinder to Walter von Molo's unwelcome invitation. As one commentator, a partisan of Thomas Mann's, put it: "Almost unnoticed a widespread controversy, a national dispute with and around Thomas Mann has sprung up, has erupted" (Grosser, 37). Erich Kästner jumped into the controversy with both feet. On 14 January 1946 he published a short essay, "Observations of an Apolitical Person" (Betrachtungen eines Unpolitischen, 50–54), in which he reproached Thomas Mann for his unwillingness to assume the role "of a field marshal for peace and dignity" (52) in this, Germany's hour of greatest need.

Kästner's title was, of course, both disingenuous and surreptitious. On the one hand, "Observations of an Apolitical Person" prepared the reader for a deceptively naïve and seemingly apolitical approach. By outward appearance the essay is a homiletic, informing children about the ongoing controversy. The article begins with the stylized children's language so typical of Kästner: "When I was a small boy, I liked to go shopping." While it ostensibly addresses itself solely to those "dear children," it lapses time and again, probably quite intentionally, into the sophisticated vocabulary of adults.

But beneath this persiflage there is also a hidden subtext embedded in the title, one that capitalized upon a vulnerable point in Mann's literary past. The title, borrowed from Mann's aberrant nationalistic essay of long ago, brought him, Mann, again face-to-face with an earlier text, "an underbrush of verbiage" (*Schreibgestrüpp*), as he later called it, from which he had long distanced himself without outrightly disavowing it.[4] Kästner's attack upon Mann, a biting broadside, to be sure, left Mann's standing as a towering figure of German literature unimpaired. But it rejected him as an exemplary model for a new Germany, especially if measured against such figures as Albert Bassermann, who stood ready to return to Germany. It culminated in the following polemic:

We must not blame the other man, Thomas Mann, for the fact that we stand in need of one German author, who unbeckoned, would suddenly appear among us without a special invitation, in fact still out of breath from racing home. That kind of man we don't have.

The other man, he will and should stay in America. He would just be wasted as a substitute for the former. (Grosser, 54)

As for the rest, Kästner with a good bit of irony, traces the entire controversy back to a near tragic misunderstanding (Grosser, 62).

Even though Thomas Mann did not react to the attack in public, he was quite outraged by Kästner's polemic. His outrage surfaced in a letter of 9 June 1946 to Anna Jacobson, who, missing the irony and venom in Kästner's text, had thought fit to call Mann's attention to it. Mann's reply was unambiguous: "As chance would have it, Erika owns a copy of the text and recited it for us. It is the most infamous act which the Germans have yet perpetrated against me and a classic example of Saxonian underhandedness [*Heemdicke*]" (*Briefe*, 491). Mann's resentment against Kästner still resonates four years later in a letter to Alfred Neumann of 18 February 1950, protesting the inclusion of Kästner as a potential member of the award panel that was to choose the recipient of the René-Schickele prize.

I would not be particularly pleased, if the representative from inside Germany were to be Erich Kästner. On the basis of his entire attitude he appears completely unsuited to me. He has made statements, not only about me, but quite recently about emigrant writers, which should disqualify him from participation." (*Briefwechsel*, 84)

But Thomas Mann, who here comes close to lumping Kästner with such spurious inner emigrants as von Molo and Thieß, would not live up to his reputation as a master of ambiguity and ambivalence if he had not, completely reversing himself, resoundingly supported Erich Kästner as the president of the resurrected PEN club in 1947, only a year after his indignant letter to Anna Jacobson. Not only was his advocacy reported by the *Zürcher Zeitung* (5 June 1947; in Schröter, 519), but it is further authenticated by Erika Mann, who was herself obviously surprised by this turnabout. While editing her father's letters, she glosses the word *Heemdicke*:

As honorary president of the International PEN-Club (Zurich 1947) Mann emphatically championed the admission of a [reestablished] German PEN-Club. The president, elected by his colleagues, was presciently present in Zurich, and Thomas Mann vouched for his integrity. His name: Erich Kästner. (*Briefe* 4; 52)

I was unable to find an explanation for this contradiction, all the more glaring in the light of the subsequent letter to Alfred Neumann. It is possible, of course, that Thomas Mann, for the sake of a cause as important as the founding of the postwar German PEN club, was willing to put aside, at least for the moment, the not entirely ephemeral quarrel with Kästner.

Several examples of such largesse in the life and work of that most ambivalent of all Germans—as witness his positive turnabout in his assessment of Wilhelm Herzog—can readily be cited, but the motivation of such reversals can only be guessed at (see Stern, "Thomas Mann," 65).

The attitude of the Marxist exile authors to Erich Kästner was quite different, yet no less complex. It can be distilled, as the American exile scholar Ulrich Weisstein has demonstrated,[5] from the views held by the author of juvenile literature, Alex Wedding, the wife of F. C. Weiskopf, in an article printed in *Das Wort*, the Soviet exile magazine:

> Only the prevailing lack [in children's literature] can explain how works such as those by Erich Kästner can exert such a potent influence even upon groups that ought to be rejecting Kästner's bromides about decent cops.… They should reject them together with such views, expressed in Kästner's book, that social conflicts can be solved on an individual basis and that they constitute problems of [personal] character and the presence or absence of good will. Our own writers ought to acquire those literary abilities, by means of which Kästner and people like him can write such successful children's literature. Part of that ability stems from a precise knowledge of child psychology, an avoidance of "father-knows-best" [*Onkelhaftigkeit*] attitude, of didacticism with an extended forefinger, having recourse to a spontaneous imagination, narrative art, puns and situational comedy, suspense, and not least of all, a language that is understandable.[6]

Wedding's polemic, as yet another American exile scholar maintains (Hansen, 9), fed on the exiles' resentment against the stay-at-homes, despite the prohibitions and suppression of Kästner's writings, but also contains, of course, some involuntary high praise of him.

By way of contrast, the suppression in Germany of Kästner's books was, with the exception of one state-commissioned film script, unrelenting and unmitigated.[7] And Kästner's spiritual proximity to the exiles was, of course, in part predicated on his and their mutual hatred of the vile Nazi dictatorship and on the heavy price both had to pay for their steadfast opposition. The pyres of the Nazi book-burners reduced his books to ashes, together with those of the exiled authors. The notorious slogans accompanying the book burnings defamed him, together with the exile Heinrich Mann, as examples of "decadence and moral decay" (Haarmann et al., 196). On the very night of the book burning, 10 May 1933, Eugen Lüthgens, professor of both philosophy and of law, spewed out the denunciatory linking of the names of Heinrich Mann and Erich Kästner: "Down into the flames with the poison of the class struggle and materialism, with the relics of decadence and decay, down into the flames with the works of Karl Marx and [Karl] Kautsky, of Heinrich Mann, [Ernst] Glaeser and Kästner" (204). The Gestapo in years to come linked Kästner even more closely to the exiles when it mistakenly added him to their ranks. An "urgent" teletype of 19 September 1936 from Gestapo headquarters to its branch in Hanover ordered: "Erich Kästner is a cultural bolshevik of the most nefarious kind. Previously a resident of Berlin he now resides in

Prague and is reputed to be a contributor to various emigrant newspapers. Previously he wrote for *Die Weltbühne*. All texts by Kästner are hereby prohibited" (Haarmann et al., 301).[8]

Kästner, had he known of this lapse in Gestapo intelligence (he had never emigrated to Czechoslovakia), would not have minded; at the occasion of the book burning in Berlin, Kästner went to witness the torching of his own books: he strongly identified with the exiled Magnus Hirschfeld, one of the pioneering scholars in the field of human sexuality:

> In the year 1933 my books were burned on the large plaza next to the State Opera House by a certain Mr. Goebbels, with accompanying somber ceremonial pomposity.... I was standing in front of the university, wedged in between students in stormtrooper uniforms, the flower of our nation, as I witnessed our books sailing into the flickering flames and heard the unctuous tirades of the puny insidious liar. Funeral weather hung over the city. The head of a shattered statue of Magnus Hirschfeld was impaled on a long pole, which swayed back and forth high above the mute crowd. It was disgusting. ("Durchsicht," 198)

When, after the war, on 10 May 1947, a "day of free books" was being celebrated, Erich Kästner, as a member of the honorary presidential council of the event, stood in the forecourt of Humboldt University together with representatives of the *inner emigration* and former exiles from East and West. On this precise spot fourteen years before, that act of barbarism had taken place as a prelude to much worse. Ten years later, during an address to the PEN Centre, he again commemorated the book burning and the burnt books of the exiles.[9]

Allow me to add two personal reminiscences. In 1960 I collaborated with Lotte Lenya, the voluntary exile, when she recorded the poetry anthology compiled by Gustave Mathieu and myself. After recording the poem "The Development of Mankind," she mentally paused for a moment and then uttered spontaneously: "He was a hell of a guy."

My only encounter with Erich Kästner was in the year 1964 during the opening of an exhibit of his children's books at the Children's and Juvenilia Library then located in the Kaulbachstraße in Munich. I, at that time a guest professor at the Goethe-Institut, then just down the street from the library, listened to his brief remarks, which officially opened the exhibit. Erich Kästner, Germany's most famous author of children's books —as late as 1998 the American film *The Parent Trap*, based on Kästner's *Das doppelte Lottchen*, received critical acclaim—closed with a short tribute to Jella Lepman, the exiled author of children's books whose untiring efforts had led to the founding of the, at first modest, library in the Kaulbachstraße (today it occupies splendid facilities in a Munich suburb).[10] The two authors knew each other from times long past and in 1949–50 she had proposed to him the idea for his subsequently realized children's book *The Conference of the Animals* (see Weil, 241–42). The creation of the library was a work-in-collaboration. The scholar Richard Bamberger has characterized their friendship: "The relationship between Kästner and Lepman was most cordial. He thought a great deal of her and supported her time and again. Talking with the two of them meant a great deal to me and provided me with support for my work in Austria" (37).

On this particular day of the opening Kästner stood at the lectern and when champagne was served, he lifted his glass and said "for Jella." Here, in short, was one more token of the mutual admiration between a representative of the exile writers and of Erich Kästner, a representative of *inner emigration*. But is that what he was? Opinion remains divided, with testimonials pro and con, demonstrating in sum a fascinatingly complex relationship between Kästner and his exiled contemporaries. Because of this ambivalence, the case of Erich Kästner raises a wealth of questions, going beyond his personal conduct—and this despite the fact—or because of it—that he never curried favor with the Nazis and never compromised his integrity. I should like to summarize them as a companion piece to our current inquiry.

1. What constitutes *inner emigration*?
2. Who can fairly be included in this honorific group: someone like Kästner, who stayed silent and whose few writings during the Nazi period were apolitical or even innocuous? Max Krell, Hermann Kesten, and Marcel Reich-Ranicki resoundingly said yes; Franz Schoenberner and the Manns as resoundingly said no. Should only the voices of resistance and defiance, such as that of Ernst Wiechert, be included? Or should only the subtle voices whispering surreptitious antifascist declarations within the camouflage of their plots, such as those by Ricarda Huch, be included? If so, when does subtlety become inaudible, as with Ernst Jünger? And what about writers hiding oppositional text in their desk drawers, such as Werner Bergengrün, hoping for the fall of a hated regime?

But let me return to Erich Kästner, adding now my own judgement. I am convinced that further research will tend to support my own conclusion that Kästner, living in the compression chamber of the Third Reich, erred occasionally in his judgement of the exiles or of a particular exile such as Thomas Mann, but that on balance he was all but one with them.

Notes

1. See the proceedings of the conferences in Madison, Wisconsin, and St. Louis, Missouri: Reinhold Grimm and Jost Hermand, eds. *Exil und innere Emigration, Third Wisconsin Workshop, 1971* (1972); Peter Uwe Hohendahl and Egon Schwarz, eds., *Exil und Innere Emigration II: Internationale Tagung in St. Louis* (1973) [1972].
2. That Berendsohn's opinion is still widely held, is shown by the fact that the magazine *Mit der Ziehharmonika* (dedicated to Theodor Kramer), devoted its September 1995 issue

to *inner emigration*, and raised the rhetorical question (2): "Is it still really necessary to discover the authentic literature of the *innere Emigration*?"

3. See Sigrid Kellenter, 811; also, Schneider: "Under the leadership of Erich Kästner the *Neue Zeitung* stood in no small measure for an appreciative and open access of exile literature" (1288).

4. Hans Wysling (ed., *Dichter über ihre Dichtungen*) has numerous examples of Mann's self-criticism. Characteristic is his essay "Meine Zeit" of 1950 (730): "No sooner than it [*Betrachtungen* ...] was finished, I detached myself from it." The wording "Schreibgestrüpp" appears in his letter to Jonas Lesser of 10 February 1952 (732).

5. Weisstein (43) portrays Wedding's polemic as a reflection of an abstract ideal, established by editorial policy.

6. Wedding, "Kinderliteratur," *Das Wort* 2, no. 4 (1937): 52.

7. An excellent documentation of individual measures carried out against Kästner can be found in Hermann Haarmann, Walter Huder, and Klaus Siebenhaar, eds., *"Das war ein Vorspiel nur,"* 297–302 and *passim*.

8. The catalog contains a facsimile of the original.

9. A complete rendering of the program as well as the participating members is in Haarmann, Huder and Siebenhaar, 438–40; Kästner's speech of 1958, "Über das Verbrennen von Büchern," is in *Gesammelte Schriften für Erwachsene*, VIII, 277–85. He mentions, among the exiles, Heinrich and Thomas Mann, Alfred Döblin, Leonhard Frank, Franz Werfel, Jakob Wassermann, Bertolt Brecht, Ludwig Renn, Alfred Neumann, Alfred Polgar, Stefan Zweig, and Sigmund Freud.

10. For the development of the library, see Eva-Maria Ledig, *Eine Idee für Kinder. Die Internationale Jugendbibliothek* (1988); also Jella Lepman, *A Bridge of Children's Books* (1969). At the opening a piece by Erich Kästner was read "Ein Brief an die Kinder in aller Welt"; it included the sentence: "It took Jella Lepman, an untiring woman, from 1946 until 1949 to make her plan a reality" (Ledig, 86).

Works Cited

Bamberger, Richard. "Über Jella Lepman." In *Mrs. Lepman. Gebt uns Bücher, gebt uns Flügel*, ed. Lioba Betten. Munich: Roman Kovar, 1992.

Bauschinger, Sigrid, ed. *Ich habe etwas zu sagen. Annette Kolb. 1870–1967. Ausstellung der Münchner Stadtbibliothek*. Munich: Diederichs, 1993.

Berendsohn, Walter. *Die humanistische Front*. Vol. 2. *Vom Kriegsausbruch 1939 bis Ende 1946*. Worms: Verlag G. Heintz, 1976.

Cazden, Robert E. *German Exile Literature in America 1933–1950: A History of the Free German Press and Book Trade*. Chicago: American History Association, 1970.

Grimm, Reinhold, and Jost Hermand, eds. *Exil und innere Emigration, Third Wisconsin Workshop, 1971*. Frankfurt am Main: Athenäum, 1972.

Grosser, J[ohannes] F[ranz] G[ottlieb], ed. *Die große Kontroverse. Ein Briefwechsel um Deutschland*. Hamburg, Geneva, and Paris: Nagel, 1963.

Habe, Hans. *All My Sins: An Autobiography*. Translated by E. Osers. London and Toronto: George G. Harrap, 1957.

Haarmann, Hermann, Walter Huder, and Klaus Siebenhaar, eds. *"Das war ein Vorspiel nur" Bücherverbrennung Deutschland 1933: Voraussetzungen und Folgen. [Katalog der] Ausstellung der Akademie der Künste vom 8. Mai bis 3. Juli 1983*. Berlin: Medusa, 1983.

Hansen, Thomas. "Emil and the Émigres: German Children's Literature in Exile, 1933–1945." *Phaedrus* 11 (1985): 6–12.

Hoffmann, Charles W. "Opposition und innere Emigration. Zwei Aspekte des 'Anderen' Deutschlands." In *Exil und Innere Emigration II: Internationale Tagung in St. Louis,* ed. Peter Uwe Hohendahl and Egon Schwarz. Frankfurt am Main: Athenäum, 1973 [1972].

Hohendahl, Peter Uwe, and Egon Schwarz, eds. *Exil und Innere Emigration II: Internationale Tagung in St. Louis.* Frankfurt am Main: Athenäum, 1973 [1972].

Kästner, Erich. "Bei Durchsicht meiner Bücher." In Erich Kästner, *Gesammelte Schriften für Erwachsene,* 198–200. Vol. 8. Zürich: Atrium, 1969.

———. "Betrachtungen eines Unpolitischen." In Erich Kästner, *Gesammelte Schriften für Erwachsene,* 50–54. Vol. 8. Zürich: Atrium, 1969.

———. "Über das Verbrennen von Büchern." In Erich Kästner, *Gesammelte Schriften für Erwachsene,* 277–85. Vol. 8. Zürich: Atrium, 1969.

Kantorowicz, Alfred, and Richard Drews. *Verboten und verbrannt. Deutsche Literatur 12 Jahre unterdrückt.* Berlin: Ullstein, 1947.

Kellenter, Sigrid. "Hans Sahl." In *Deutschsprachige Exilliteratur seit 1933,* ed. John Spalek and Joseph Strelka, 811. Vol. 2. Berne: Francke, 1989.

Kesten, Hermann. *Lauter Literaten: Portraits/Erinnerungen.* Munich and Zürich: Droemersche Verlagsanstalt, 1966.

Koepke, Wulf. "Exilautoren und ihre deutschen und amerikanischen Verlage in New York." In *Deutschsprachige Exilliteratur seit 1933,* ed. John Spalek and Joseph Strelka, 1409–45. Vol. 2. Berne: Francke, 1989.

Krell, Max. *Das alles gab es einmal.* Frankfurt am Main: Heinrich Scheffler, 1961.

Ledig, Eva-Maria. *Eine Idee für Kinder. Die Internationale Jugendbibliothek.* Munich: Erasmus-Graser, 1988.

Lepman, Jella. *A Bridge of Children's Books.* Translated by Edith McCormack. Leicester: Brockingham Press and Chicago: American Library Association, 1969.

Mann, Erika, and Klaus Mann. *Escape to Life. Deutsche Kultur im Exil.* Munich: Edition Spangenberg, 1991 [new printing].

Mann, Thomas. *Briefe 1937–1947.* Ed. Erika Mann. Frankfurt am Main: Fischer, 1963.

———. *Thomas Mann-Alfred Neumann Briefwechsel.* Ed. Peter de Mendelssohn. Heidelberg: Lambert Schneider, 1977.

———. "Warum ich nicht zurückkehre." In *Die große Kontroverse. Ein Briefwechsel um Deutschland,* ed. J. F. G. Grosser. Hamburg, Geneva, and Paris: Nagel, 1963.

Neumann, Robert. *Ein leichtes Leben. Bericht über mich und Zeitgenossen.* Vienna, Munich, and Basel: Kurt Desch, 1965.

Reich-Ranicki, Marcel. "Eine Liebeserklärung." In *Erich Kästner, 1899–1989: Zum 90. Geburtstag Erich Kästners zeigt die Stadt- und Universitätsbibliothek Frankfurt am Main die Sammlung Georg Sauer: Begleitheft,* 23–26. Frankfurt am Main: Die Stadt- und Universitätsbibliothek, 1989.

Schoenberner, Franz. *Der Weg der Vernunft und andere Aufsätze.* Icking and Munich: Kreisselmeier, 1969.

Schneider, Sigrid. "Deutschsprachige Journalisten und Publizisten im New Yorker Exil." In *Deutschsprachige Exilliteratur seit 1933,* ed. John Spalek and Joseph Strelka, 1257–99. Vol. 2. Berne: Francke, 1989.

Schröter, Klaus, ed. *Thomas Mann im Urteil seiner Zeit. Dokumente 1891–1955.* Hamburg: Christian Wegener, 1969.

Spiel, Hilde. *Welche Welt ist meine Welt? Erinnerungen 1946–1989.* Munich and Leipzig: List, 1990.

Stern, Guy. "Thomas Mann und die jüdische Welt." In *Thomas Mann – Handbuch,* ed. Helmut Koopmann, 54–67. Stuttgart: Kröner, 1990.

Stern, Guy, and Gustave Mathieu. *Invitation to German Poetry*. New York: Dover Publications, 1960.

Sternfeld, Wilhelm, and Eva Tiedemann, eds. *Deutsche Exil-Literatur, 1933–1945. Eine Bio-Bibliographie*. 2nd ed. Heidelberg: Lambert Schneider, 1962.

Wedding, Alex. "Kinderliteratur." *Das Wort* 2, no. 4 (1937): 52.

Weil, Renate. *Lexikon der deutschsprachigen Schrifstellerinnen im Exil*. Freiburg im Breisgau: Kore, 1995.

Weisstein, Ulrich. "Literaturkritik in deutschen Exilschriften. Der Fall *Das Wort*." In *Exil und Innere Emigration II: Internationale Tagung in St. Louis*, ed. Peter Uwe Hohendahl and Egon Schwarz, 19–46. Frankfurt am Main: Athenäum, 1973 [1972].

Wysling, Hans, ed. *Dichter über ihre Dichtungen. Volume 14, Ch. I–III: Thomas Mann*, ed. Rudolf Hirsch and Werner Vordtriede, 627–736. Frankfurt am Main: Fischer, 1975–81.

Zuckmayer, Carl. *Als wär's ein Stück von mir. Horen der Freundschaft*. Frankfurt am Main: Fischer, 1966.

Chapter 14

GÜNTHER WEISENBORN'S BALLAD OF HIS LIFE

Wulf Koepke

Günther Weisenborn, known before 1933 for successful antiwar plays, a novel *Barbarians* (Barbaren) satirizing right-wing students, and his collaboration with Brecht on the adaptation of Gorky's *Mother*, stayed in Germany and became an active resistance fighter, part of the large group known under its Gestapo code name "Die rote Kapelle" (The Red Band), which was uncovered by the Gestapo in 1942. Unlike most leaders of the group, Weisenborn survived, and went through the Gestapo prison, the prisons at Spandau and Moabit, and a Zuchthaus in Luckau, where he was liberated by the Red Army in May 1945. He became a leading figure in the cultural reconstruction of Berlin, sometime president of the Association of German Writers (Schutzverband deutscher Schriftsteller), creative director (*Dramaturg*) at the Hebbel-Theater, and editor of the satirical magazine *Ulenspiegel*. With the intensification of the Cold War in the1950s, Weisenborn became the exemplary outsider between East and West, marginalized on both sides, especially in the West, which had a decisive impact on his life and work as well as on the critical reception of his works, which were largely ignored, foremost by Germanistic scholars.

In the short period of hope for a peaceful world after 1945, however, he was considered a prominent writer, and his autobiographical *Memorial* as well as his drama on the German resistance, *The Illegal Ones* (Die Illegalen), kept him in the limelight, whereas the comprehensive account of the German resistance *The Silent Rebellion* (Der lautlose Aufstand), which he edited, found a very subdued echo when it finally appeared in 1953. Weisenborn did not have to justify his actions and (most of his) publications during the Nazi period,[1] and the terms *inner* and *outer* emigration hardly ever occur in his writings. He was not a person to formulate manifestoes and programs. He wrote some essays on the theater, but little on the present situation of literature and the author. One notable exception was his speech at the Sorbonne in Paris in 1949, printed under the title of *The Tasks of German Writers*" (Die Aufgaben der deutschen Schriftsteller).[2] The speech offers a perspective markedly different from others at the time. In two places, Weisenborn classifies the German writers of the Nazi and postwar periods. He declares that there was only a small group producing Nazi literature "with [rabid] foam at the mouth" (33), but that a large number of writers profited from the financial opportunities and were nothing but political opportunists. He includes the "inner emigration" (in quotation marks!) within this group, thinking no doubt of their vociferous post-1945 advocates Frank Thieß and Walter von Molo. However, he also acknowledges within the *inner emigration* a group "of powerless integrity, whose attitude deserves sympathy" (33). Weisenborn does not name names, except to praise the persecuted writers who were killed or committed suicide, or other bona fide resistance fighters. Remarkably, he does not differentiate between the exile writers and the German resistance.

The other reference to German writers during the Hitler period occurs in the book on the German resistance, *Der lautlose Aufstand*, in the chapter on the intellectuals, presumably written by Weisenborn:[3] "Besides the large groups of outer and inner emigration as well as the inner opposition, there was a group of defectors" ("Überläufer"; 219). The distinction between "inner opposition," that is, resistance, and "inner emigration" is reinforced by definitions of remarkable fairness, but underscoring the difference: "The 'inner emigration' was of a different kind than the opposition—an attitude adopted by some authors of rank and whose legitimacy can certainly be discussed" (218). Remarkably, Weisenborn singles out Frank Thieß and his *The Empire of the Demons* (Das Reich der Dämonen) as an effective document of anti-Nazi attitudes. He also states: "The 'inner emigration' has produced remarkable works that could have appeared in any free country" (219). This sounds like a late reply to Thomas Mann's famous phrase that all books printed in Germany between 1933 and 1945 were less than worthless and should be pulped (*eingestampft*). Again, Weisenborn names only the persecuted writers (except for Thieß), and his lists of writers who were incarcerated and who died of persecution and suicide make no distinction between the exiles and the opposition in Germany.

In his Sorbonne speech he also referred to the "overcoming of the past." The foremost task of the German writer of today is truth [*Wahrheit*]. Weisenborn mentions the difficulties with his then ongoing research on the German resistance for *The Silent Rebellion*, as an example of what needs to be done at present. He fights incessantly to tell the truth about the German resistance, why it failed, and its legacy of moral heroism.[4] And he laments: "In the dirty twilight of our days we see that the old powers are installing themselves all over again in spite of everything. The tepid historical forces [of conformism] are valued higher than those of good will [conscience]" (252). There are those numerous authors who wrap themselves in beautiful words and a *l'art pour l'art* attitude, such as, among many others, Gottfried Benn, whose attitude after 1945 was, in Weisenborn's eyes, as demoralizing and destructive after 1945 as in 1933.

Weisenborn's sharp words also reveal a literary program of realism, of truth for truth's sake, of a political *Kahlschlag*: a cutting away of all the pretenses and excuses in trying to be clearheaded when facing the past and the future. Weisenborn's speech in 1949, when the action for new war preparations was in full swing, as he vividly describes, may appear from today's perspective to be rearguard fight of the disappearing "peace squad," of those who wanted a truly peaceful future for Germany. Weisenborn renewed his old friendly ties with Brecht when they met during Brecht's stay in Zürich in 1947, and later in Berlin, and he kept away from any factions, games of blame, or self-justification, a refreshing case of a person without resentments and a bad conscience. It was only later, because of the Cold War and the ugly aspects of West German restoration, that a bitterness began to grow in him whose first traces are detectible in the words from *The Silent Rebellion*.[5]

In terms of *inner emigration*, two periods of Weisenborn's work are of prime interest: his publications after 1933, and the writings of the immediate postwar years, including a number of plays not directly linked to the current events, such as his play, written earlier, *Die Neuberin* (Caroline Neuber); another play, *The Good Enemies* (Die guten Feinde), published in 1937 and performed in 1938; and two novels, *The Girl from Fanø* (Das Mädchen von Fanö, 1935), which became a very popular movie, and *The Fury* (Die Furie, 1937), set in Argentina. The name of *The Fury's* protagonist, Christian Munk, served as a pseudonym for the author of *Caroline Neuber* and for his subsequent adventure stories, also mostly taking place in Argentina. Weisenborn's pre-1933 books were burned and forbidden, first of all *Barbarians*, but surprisingly, Weisenborn was a member of the Reichsschrifttumskammer (Ministry of Letters, RSK) until 1944 and must have had no problems in publishing his Christian Munk novels and short stories.[6] Beyond his work as creative director for the Schiller Theater (under Heinrich George), he was employed at the radio station *Großdeutscher Rundfunk*. He also worked in the film industry, writing scripts and translating soundtracks of American (MGM) movies. He was encouraged by his resistance group to preserve his camouflage well[7] and thus keep access to sensitive information, especially in the radio station.

It is necessary to begin with an account of Weisenborn the man and writer in order to evaluate his texts after 1933. Weisenborn's *Memorial* is structured in small segments, from one paragraph to two pages long, alternating between the present of the prison, from 1942 to 1945, and memorable moments of the past. While this mosaic structure was due, according to the author, to the conditions of writing in prison, secretly and on scraps of all kinds of paper, it remained the basic structure of his other, much later, autobiographical book, *The Divided Horizon* (Der gespaltene Horizont, 1964), dealing with the period from 1945 into the 60s. The mosaic structure resembles Max Frisch's first *Diary*, and would suggest an influence had Frisch not used the same technique already in his previous *Leaves From My Knapsack* (Blätter aus dem Brotsack). A fundamental difference separates the two writers, in spite of the seeming likeness of their approach: Frisch's diary chronicles day-to-day events while sketching ideas for new works, whereas Weisenborn looks back and wants to recall and record the truly memorable moments in life. Life is worth living with an intense emotional experience, of nature, of danger, of love and passion, of an intellectual encounter, of artistic beauty, of a religious space or event, such as cathedrals or a performance of Bach's *St. Matthew's Passion*.

Weisenborn does not come in any way close to the impulse toward grandiosity in Nazi ideology, as did Ernst Jünger. He remained a pacifist and never thought of glorifying World War I, or any war. He did not mention pagan cults nor a love for archaic life forms. There is no trace of racist ideology nor of hatred of the "other" in ethnic and cultural terms. His protagonists are loners and not community leaders who are possessed by a mission and a cause and want to convert humanity to their ideas. The closest proximity to Weisenborn's men can be found in figures of the youth movement, the *Wandervögel*, or perhaps in the American "tough guys," or Hermann Hesse's loners. Weisenborn's episodic love and adventure stories are popular, usually set in an exotic land, involving danger, portraying a poor young man hungry for life, experiencing friendship and love, containing intense love episodes not destined to last. His posture of the lone fighter, based on his own early years (cf. Hahn, 238–42), seems to defy any party discipline; Manfred Hahn notes that although Weisenborn was close to the German Communist Party (KPD) before 1933, neither his life nor his texts show any party loyalty: rather, they conform to the type of socialist autobiographies and stories popular among young workers, such as those by Jack London and B. Traven.

Weisenborn's first novel after 1933, an adventure story, is largely antipolitical and escapist in nature. With this in mind, the popularity of *The Girl from Fanø*[8] is no mystery. The story takes place among Frisian fishermen and follows the prescription of friendship, jealousy, danger, love, conflict, and escape, but the characters are by no means idealized. They are defined only in cultural, not racial terms, by their origin from this village and their occupation. Thus, while the story fits in with the dominant NS ideology, the protagonists remain outsiders. The significance of that distinction emerges by comparison to tales by Frenssen, Griese, or Blunck, to name *Blut und Boden* authors in descending order. *The Girl from Fanø* does not even condemn the evil big city life and its corruption, as Wiechert had done in *The Simple Life*, and it can be described as a mainstream nonpolitical novel, conforming to a leading trend through its avoidance of relevant social and political issues while catering to the prevailing taste.[9] In sharp contrast to the novel *Barbaren*,[10] a perhaps coerced folksiness is also characteristic of his late novels, such as *Built on Sand* (Auf Sand gebaut, 1956) and *The Pursuer* (Der Verfolger, 1961), with the fundamental difference that both novels use a "trivial" genre for a very serious story, in order to gain access to a reluctant readership. *The Girl from Fanø* conforms to the typical nonpolitical novel of the 1930s insofar also as it leaves room for ambiguities. Even this fairly simple and straightforward story is open to diverse readings. Ambiguities of this sort are not necessarily political, as they are in the case of Ernst Jünger's *On the Marble Cliffs*. In Weisenborn's novel, a pronounced "Germanic" and "Nordic" appearance of the characters and their environment would bring the story close to Gorch Fock, Hermann Löns, and assorted North Sea stories, but a more realistic reading would stress the problems and limitations of such a closed com munity as the Frisians are, and an escapist reading would see nothing but fairy-tale romance.

The Girl from Fanø does not, however, in any way hint at a political responsibility of its author to enlighten his readers about the dangerous and destructive consequences of the Nordic ideology. Its author provides entertainment and relief, and offers some interesting, largely positive, character portraits. In contrast, the novel *The Fury* (1948), set in Argentina, tells a story of a tragic passion within a highly political context with evident parallels to the German situation, a story of a senseless war between Bolivia and Paraguay and ruthless exploitation, even genocide. Weisenborn tells the hidden story of Latin America at a time when B. Traven wrote his *Caoba* novels about Chiapas in southern Mexico. The Chaco War between Bolivia and Paraguay lasted from 1932 to 1935, but the peace treaty was not signed before 1938. While the Chaco War had ostensibly geopolitical reasons, the eternal attempts of Bolivia to have at least indirect access to the sea, the social conditions, and the ensuing civil wars were of prime importance as well. In Bolivia, the struggle between the military and the unions of mine workers in the tin mines made patriotism a convenient diversion. In Paraguay as in Argentina, the growing agricultural exploitation of the Chaco and the discovery of oil demanded the subjugation, if not extermination, of the Indios, whose revolt was put down by the most brutal means, as described by Weisenborn.

The foreign scientist Munk and the North American Mary Peyton both get entangled in foreign conflicts. The fundamental transformation of Christian Munk from a detached objective scientist who studies pain but does not feel it himself, to a concerned human being who understands that the extermination of Indios in the Chaco is not a matter that a European can ignore, has obvious applications to the German, and by extension, the European situation, for instance, the war atrocities in Spain. In biographical terms, this was the time when the conviction grew in Weisenborn that it was not enough to be opposed to the Nazi regime, that one had to try to fight it—a conviction that led to his five years of underground activities. The free and self-centered adventurer had discovered responsibilities.

Weisenborn never wrote a true autobiography, and never explained the major decisions in his life, such as why he returned to Germany in 1937 when he was able to make a living as a newspaper reporter in New York and was beginning to build up a circle of friends. In biographical terms,

The Fury is an indication of Weisenborn's sense of obligation to fight the enemy at home.[11] Weisenborn published mere adventure stories, set in Argentina, under the pseudonym Christian Munk, but he always considered the stage as place for serious issues, even as Christian Munk. His two major plays of the Nazi period are remarkable in that they offer a positive counter image to the prevailing types of heroes. *Caroline Neuber* was performed 265 times in Berlin in 1934 with Agnes Straub in the lead role. Agnes Straub had performed in Weisenborn's play *The Workers from Jersey*, whose premiere in Coburg in 1930 had been violently interrupted by the SA, and also in Weisenborn's and Richard Hülsenbeck's comedy *Why Is Mrs. Balsam Laughing?* which was banned right after its tumultuous opening night in Berlin, March 1933. *Caroline Neuber* was played in theaters all over Germany, but not published until after 1945.

Caroline Neuber[12] takes place in the Leipzig of Gottsched and dramatizes the conflicts surrounding the theater reform attempts by Karoline Neuber that are usually associated with the influence of Gottsched and the banning of the harlequin, the *Hanswurst*, from the German stage. Weisenborn's version, called a *Komödiantenstück* (play of comedians), deals in large part with the condition of the actors, their hunger for instant fame, their anxiety about the fast march of time that will sweep their bodies and their fame away, and their ambiguities between stage emotions and "true" feelings. It would be tempting to find allusions to Hitler in the *Hanswurst* and his false theatricalities,[13] but the political issues in *Caroline Neuber* are of a different kind.

Caroline Neuber has a vision for the German theater that is sharply distinct both from the academic classicism of Professor Gottsched and the gross pandering to the base instincts of the audience by the *Hanswurst* Müller. In fact, the fulfillment of her dreams appears in person on the stage in the last act: the young student Lessing offers her his first play, *The Young Scholar* (Der junge Gelehrte, 1748), but unfortunately, the performance is anything but a success. Weisenborn makes his Caroline Neuber into a tragic heroine who dies after she has to close her theater in Leipzig. Historically, she lived for ten more years after she had to disband her company in Leipzig in 1750. The performance of *The Young Scholar* in 1747 was a success, and remained so to the end of the company's existence.

Weisenborn may have been attracted to her by, among other things, her maiden name Weißenborn. She becomes his mouthpiece for a dignified yet realistic and popular German theater, something Weisenborn connected with the name Lessing. Her demands for a true German theater sound nationalistic and thus opportunistic, but they take on a somewhat different meaning when considered in their historical context—meaning both that of the eighteenth century and that after 1933. *Caroline Neuber* echoes (or rather predates) the ideas of Lessing's seventeenth Letter on Literature (*Literaturbrief*), arguing against French classicism. She does not proclaim, however, the "wild" Shakespeare and Marlowe as her models, but calls for a new German theater in its own right. It sounds easy to portray Professor

Gottsched as a stubborn, conceited, and ridiculous figure; Weisenborn's twist is that Gottsched represents the establishment. Caroline Neuber needs his help, his protection, and his money. When she refuses to sign his manifesto and defines her ideas as opposed to his (as was indeed the case in the 1740s), he threatens her company with extinction. The price she pays for nonopportunism is the annihilation of her professional life and her reputation. Gottsched acts in conformity with the entire hierarchy of Saxony: the king and his court, the bourgeois establishment of Leipzig, and the cultural scene. The people (*das Volk*) do not appear on stage and are blinded by the tricks and slapstick farce of the *Hanswurst*. Caroline the outsider is dreaming of a future audience, an audience that would really appreciate Lessing.

Thus, classicism as the expression of court society and its academic servants is a mark of dictatorship. Caroline aspires to gain freedom *from* Gottsched, not *for* Gottsched. By extension, Weisenborn also rejects the state aesthetic of grandiose Nazi classicism. Caroline Neuber refuses to play along with the ruling powers; she has her own convictions and wants to stay true to them. Weisenborn targets the ubiquitous *Mitläufer* (Nazi conformists or "fellow-travelers") as the real curse of this society.

Whereas the German society of *Caroline Neuber* shows predominantly its ugly sides, *The Good Enemies* presents an example of true humanity.[14] There Weisenborn dramatizes and personalizes the nineteenth-century scientific dispute between Max von Pettenkofer and Robert Koch about hygiene and the causes of epidemics like cholera. Whereas Pettenkofer stressed the importance of environmental factors such as air, water, etc., Koch was working on discovering and identifying the bacilli in order to develop vaccines. Both physicians left an important legacy, but the immediate fame went to Robert Koch and his vaccines, which ended epidemics like cholera and showed the way to an effective treatment of most infectious diseases. In Weisenborn's play, the scientific theories are intertwined with public policy and personal drama. In the end Pettenkofer sees himself as a failure, but Koch generously explains to him that it was their sharp dispute that gave him the determination to carry on his lab tests and treatments in spite of initial failure. Thus, the victory, or success, belongs to both of them. They are "good enemies" who work for a common cause, albeit with opposing views and methods; the task of improving the condition of humankind is the scientist's uppermost duty, beyond factionalism, nationalism, and personal animosities. Scientific work demands high ethical standards, especially where human health is concerned. Here, remarkably, the representatives of the government are enlightened officials who want to do the best for their people: the play offers an example of what should be, as opposed to the real world in Germany in 1937. Books and films celebrating great men of the German past were not uncommon during these years, including a film on Robert Koch that centered on his conflicts with Rudolf Virchow. In contrast, Weisenborn's play does not celebrate German science, but rather the general advance of science for the sake of humanity; the adversary Pettenkofer appears as an equally up-right and courageous person, and Robert Koch, as a hero of German science, a humanist and supporter of an enlightened government, instead of an unrecognized outsider and prophet of the true Germany. The play provided a counterimage that would have been recognized immediately by audiences in 1937.

Accordingly, when Weisenborn returned to Berlin in 1945, after so many trials and tribulations, he considered the reconstruction of a cultural life in the city an ethical imperative. *The Illegal Ones* (1946; in *Dramatische Balladen* 165–239), on the work of the German resistance, depicts a resist-ance group in Berlin trying to post leaflets at night and dramatizes both the danger of their work and the human conflicts and sacrifices involved. It focuses on several people: Lil, a waitress who wants to live a normal life with a man she loves; Walter, a man with a secret radio station who com-mits suicide when he is arrested; his mother, who has lost her husband to political assassination and does not want to lose her last son; Bulle, a member of the group who is arrested and faces torture and certain death; and the others who risk their lives for the cause. Two main political points emerge: that the resistance comes from the entire political spectrum with unity as the model for the future; and that its goal is freedom (*Freiheit*), the word repeated in all climactic situations: "We survivors have as an instru-ment of the dead the very concrete obligation to erect monuments in the present for those who have passed away. We have the obligation to make known their deeds to the German people and especially to its youth" (165). *The Illegal Ones* is a very personal document: "This play was written with deep emotion by a surviving witness during the nights of this win-ter of desperation as a monument to an illegal group" (165).

The Illegal Ones is also a well-built dramatic play, with enough emo-tional scenes and conflicts to give color and conviction to the political message; it presents real conflicts and abjures any political propagandiz-ing. "The Song of the Illegal Ones" deserves to be a classic. The play was much performed in the years after 1945, but has since been shelved and forgotten as a merely topical text, except for some reprinting in the GDR. *The Illegal Ones* is a document of German opposition, in contrast to mere *inner emigration*. The play shows that this distinction did not disappear after 1945, but rather remained.

Weisenborn wrote the play *Babel* in two weeks on scraps of paper in the *Gestapo-Keller* and managed to preserve it in the suitcase that he found after his liberation from prison in 1945 (*Memorial*, 124f.). Presumably, he reworked it and then offered it as his first new play for performance (*Historien der Zeit*, 9–125; cf. bibliography, 42). *Babel* returns to South America and the year 1918. But the city Babel is a fictitious place, the name allowing various connotations. The (almost) tragic fate of Gamboa is that of a hubris, extending the control over the stock market to a political dictatorship, and thus building a tower to a point where it has to collapse. It is not common language that is lost, as in the Bible, but rather the brutal capitalist system that allows for only one winner against many losers. Though his depiction of capitalism could be called "simplistic" or even "primitive," like Brecht's *Saint Joan of the Stockyards*, Weisenborn, while maintaining the self-destructive nature of capitalism, only portrays an early variant of stock market speculation. His real purpose is the portrayal of the human passions and emotions, the suffering, the addictions, the hectic climate of brutal speculation, and the close proximity of this type of gangsterism to fascist dictatorships. *Babel* is a play about destructive hubris as the characteristic trait of the twentieth century, with its gigantic projects of construction and destruction, of reinventing nature and human identity. The implications of the parable are far reaching and very much relevant today.[15]

Weisenborn's *Memorial*, arguably his best work and certainly one of the really impressive accounts of political imprisonment under the Nazi regime, is structured by the polarities of freedom and imprisonment, of *joie de vivre* and suffering, of human development and the destruction of human dignity. The short, episodic pieces offer extremes of human existence, without a narrative thread and without mediation between the opposing poles. Taken together they present an individual trying to survive the utmost of degradation and fear by remembering the intensity of life's enjoyments. The prison experience is characterized by the sadism of the "enemy" on all levels and in all forms, from the isolated cell and the interrogations to the trial and the inhumane labor. The three forces keeping the prisoner alive are the memory of the moments of life worth living, the solidarity and mutual help among the prisoners, and the hope for a better tomorrow. The brief description of the first months after liberation offers a glimpse of such a possible future: the political prisoners put in charge of the surrounding towns try to bring reason to the existing chaos, in as even-handed and fair-minded a way as possible. The Soviet administration in these first months seems interested only in the practical needs of the population and the choice of genuine anti-Nazis as their collaborators. *Memorial* stresses traits of general humanity, not ideological correctness. Weisenborn's political creed is the "popular front" of all people of good will, based on freedom, peace, and solidarity, and thus intent on social justice rather than the economic opportunities praised by the postwar market ideology. In these months after May 1945, the voluntary cooperation and participation of everybody were needed; directives had to be practical and reasonable to make sense and to be followed. It was a brief interlude of liberation from fear and a call to volunteer for the great renewal. *Memorial* has no real conclusion; it ends with a beginning, which is Weisenborn's attempt to rebuild Berlin's cultural life. It does not have a real beginning either, other than Weisenborn's arrest by the Gestapo in 1942. Though the chronological sequence of the prison events is maintained, the text stresses the transitory moments and the passage of time, and consists of isolated moments. *Memorial* is anything but apolitical.

His most successful postwar play, the *Ballad of Owlglass, Federle and the Fat Pompanne* (Ballade vom Eulenspiegel, vom Federle und von der dicken

Pompanne, 1949), in its subject matter and tone, bears unmistakable similarities to Brecht's *Mother Courage and Her Children*,[16] one of the most frequently performed plays at that time. While Weisenborn and Brecht were personal friends, Weisenborn's conception of theater and drama was much too close for comfort to Brecht. Since Brecht's "epic Theater" was a dominant topic, Weisenborn defined his stage as *ortlose Bühne*, "displaced stages" or the empty stage (like Thornton Wilder's), which would be filled by the words of the actors and whose *Ortlosigkeit* (placelessness) indicates a general, transhistorical human nature as such.

But the *Ballad of Owlglass* presents nonetheless a pessimistic view of human nature. The forces of freedom, represented by Eulenspiegel, can never win. The Peasants' War (of 1524–25), which is the historical backdrop of the play, ends with the suppression and mass killing of the peasants who fought for their freedom. The really tragic figure is Federle, a defenseless woman who feels constrained to work for the ruling powers embodied by the *Truchsess* but then follows the wake-up call for freedom by Eulenspiegel, whom she begins to love. She pays dearly after the defeat of the peasants, although Eulenspiegel succeeds in killing her to spare her more humiliation and torture before her hanging; he then uses her knife to kill the *Truchsess*. The ending sounds like a variation of Lessing's *Emilia Galotti*, where Odoardo kills his daughter Emilia instead of the prince. Federle is denounced by the fat Pompanne, a war survivor who is reminiscent of Brecht's Mother Courage but plays a very different role. Here, the peasants are greedy for new shoes, for loot and gains, instead of pursuing the enemy and fighting for their freedom. In spite of the hopeful-sounding last line of the chorus, "since darkness will not last forever!" (84), it is hard to see how Eulenspiegel's quest for freedom can ever reach its goal. He survives, but the *Truchsess* will be replaced by another ruler, and the people (*das Volk*) will never learn. Weisenborn's view contrasts sharply with GDR historians' view of the Great Peasants' War as a prelude to all modern proletarian revolutions.

Life is a ballad of great moments of enjoyment and suffering, but modern civilization, characterized by capitalism and technology, leads to a fatal alienation from real life, and an alienation of man from man. Weisenborn's critique transcends the issues of fascism, capitalism, and socialism, however. His vitalistic views conform to a deep concern for humanity and the environment. His novel *Built on Sand* (1956) is a radical indictment of the political and business establishment in Bonn that hinges on environmental issues long before these became a common concern.[17]

Weisenborn represents the case of a writer whose political position before 1933 was among the independent socialists, whose books were banned after 1933, but who was admitted to the Reichsschrifttumskammer and was able to publish (and earn his living by publishing) after 1933, who made the conscious decision not to emigrate, and who in 1937 became active in resistance groups in Berlin, continuing until he was arrested in 1942. Weisenborn considered it one of his foremost responsibilities to preserve the memory of the German resistance fighters. He carried on their legacy of political unity, solidarity, and struggle for freedom in the ideologized political climate of the Cold War, which marginalized him as a public figure and severely limited the distribution and impact of his writings. Weisenborn was not a great writer but a brave and talented author. Writers of *inner emigration*—like Weisenborn, largely nonpolitical, passive, and humanistically oriented—remained in Germany and never lost their audience with its increasing need for visions of escape and gratification. Weisenborn's writings are very personal, but rarely give insight into his intimate feelings and thoughts. Fortunately, his widow published a collection of their illegally exchanged communications (*Kassiber*) after their arrest in 1942, called *Let Me Be Sad for a Change* (Einmal laß mich traurig sein, 1976), a truly intimate portrait of the author under extreme conditions. This modest exchange of notes, poems, and news as an expression of love and a means of survival may be worth more than the entire literary output of comfortable *inner emigrants* as a reminder of the terror of the Nazi years and the legacy of those who dared to fight.

Notes

1. Hahn points out that there are, however, discrepancies between Weisenborn's accounts of his publications made before 1945 and these made later, as well as discrepancies between accounts and documented facts, especially the statement that he stopped publishing after 1937, which has to be twisted to come close to the truth (264).
2. See *Günther Weisenborn*, by Ilse Brauer and Werner Kayser. This very useful bibliography, the only one so far, also includes essays by Ingeborg Drewitz and Walter Huder.
3. The idea for this book came originally from Ricarda Huch, who collected some materials Weisenborn continued the research and wrote or edited the text; co-editors were Walter Hammer and Guntram Prüfer.
4. When discussing in *Der lautlose Aufstand* the verdict of the world on the German resistance, he comes back to a fundamental fact, "Die Deutschen haben sich nicht selbst befreit," as a basic reason for ignoring the resistance fighters, and gives these three points explaining their failure: "1. Ihr Gegner war der gewaltigste und beste Polizeiapparat der Welt. 2. Der Krieg kam, weil so viele Deutsche der Widerstandsbewegung fernblieben. 3. Die Widerstandsbewegung war zersplittert. Ihren Aktionen fehlte die Einheitlichkeit" (249).
5. However, in his interview with Josef Hermann Sauter in 1968, a year before his death, Weisenborn remains remarkably objective in his assessment of the postwar situation. The interview is most illuminating on his relations to Brecht and Hanns Eisler, as well as on his views on literature and society; see Sauter, *Interviews mit Schriftstellern*.
6. The question of Weisenborn's membership apparently came up when the Korrespondenzverlag Zarges, Rosenhof, wanted to reprint short stories by Munk/Weisenborn and asked in a letter dated 23 August 1943 if there was an objection, since Weisenborn was "im Gewahrsam der Gestapo" at that time, but the stories in question had been published long before. Zarges wrote again on 14 October 1943, since the Reichsschrifttumskammer had not yet resolved the matter. The permission must have been denied, and subsequently, after a communication from the SD dated 22 March 1944, the expulsion from the RSK was formally pronounced with a *Bekanntmachung* from 1 November

1944. Remarkably, the *Kürschner* of 1943 includes most of Weisenborn's works: *U-Boot S 4, Barbaren, Die Neuberin, Die Furie, Die guten Feinde,* and even *Babel,* but with the designation *R.,* Roman, 1941, referring to the aborted novel about Manhattan, and certainly not to the play written in prison in 1943. *Barbaren* was the work that was most frequently mentioned on the various index lists. I owe this information to Glenn A. Cuomo, and wish to express my sincere thanks for his help. Manfred Hahn offers detailed documentation, based on the materials at the archive of the Akademie der Künste der DDR, Berlin, but he did also other research on Weisenborn and his biography. This seems to be the most exact account of Weisenborn's earlier years. Since Hahn's topic is the novel *Die Furie,* he deals mainly with the years before 1937. Josef-Hermann Sauter's interview offers a few further points of information, but jumps from 1933 to the months in New York and Weisenborn's return in 1937. The texts mentioned, apparently of special importance to Weisenborn as well, are *Memorial, Die Illegalen, Der Verfolger, Die Furie,* and the documentary *Der lautlose Aufstand.*

7. Hahn offers other intriguing evidence of a meeting with Johannes R. Becher in Prague, and his "Auftrag" to observe and collect evidence for later. In a letter to Becher, back in Berlin, from 22 June 1945, Weisenborn "meldet sich zurück" and speaks of his plan of a "großen Berichtroman" (Hahn, 231) on the Nazi period.

8. Edition used: *Das Mädchen von Fanö,* Bremen: Friedrich Trüjen, 1949. *Das Mädchen von Fanö* continued to be popular reading after 1945 and was repeatedly reprinted in East and West Germany, in the GDR by the Aufbau-Verlag. Although the sales during the 1930s may have been influenced by the film with the popular star Brigitte Horney, the postwar editions demonstrate simply the hunger of the readers for this kind of stories.

9. Manfred Hahn (270–72) sees more antifascism in the novel than I do.

10. *Barbaren* can be seen as a satire on the cult of manliness leading into the Nazi ideology and war mania. The students portrayed make a show of a manly strength that they do not possess. In the process they turn the members of German society into barbarians.

11. Hahn characterizes *Die Furie* as a "Schlüsselbuch vom Widerstehen" (268) and offers a detailed analysis (268–97). *Widerstehen,* to resist, is his key word for the problematic of a successful and popular writer, involved in the "Kulturbetrieb," but trying to resist, and also to resist the temptation of opportunism and easy money requiring political compromises. One might say that Weisenborn's schizophrenic existence as a popular writer and editor during the day and a resistance fighter at night was necessary for him, not only to accommodate his adventurous nature, but also to justify both his conscience and his love of the good life. In the interview with Josef-Hermann Sauter, Weisenborn mentions as a specific reason for his return the opinion among emigrants in New York that one had to *do* something about the situation in Germany, and secondly, that he wanted to remain a *German* writer (Sauter, 70).

12. I used the text in Günther Weisenborn, *Dramatische Balladen,* Berlin: Aufbau-Verlag, 1955. The other plays in this volume are *Ballade vom Eulenspiegel* and *Die Illegalen.* The first publication of the *Caroline Neuber* was in 1950; apparently Weisenborn was more concerned about his later, and more topical plays. In 1937, *Die Neuberin* was made into a movie with Käthe Dorsch in the lead role, without Weisenborn's participation. Manfred Hahn (272) considers *Die Neuberin* a nonpolitical work of compromise; he does not discuss *Die guten Feinde.*

13. There is a short episode in the *Memorial* (212–14) where Weisenborn witnesses the last night of the "Tag der deutschen Kunst" in Munich in 1939, and sits close to Hitler, observing him for most of the night: "Es war ein sonderbares Schauspiel." However, Hitler is portrayed as imitating a ruler giving an audience to the cultural elite of Munich and presenting himself in the aura of a great man to his paladins and a large audience of artists. Weisenborn sees Hitler as a bad actor playing a role and calls him "ein häßlicher tückischer Pascha" and "ein orientalischer Götze im Smoking, mit jener bescheidenen Brutalität, die unser Volk so an ihm liebte."

14. In *Historien der Zeit,* 127–193, together with *Babel* and *Die Illegalen.* There is a notice at the end of the play, "written in Opladen, Fischerhude, Berlin in 1937."

15. *Babel* goes back to the plan for a novel set in Manhattan that Weisenborn started to write after his return from New York in 1937, sometimes called "Schwamm und Galle" or "Scham," but was unable to complete (see Hahn, 264–66); the play was designed "den Spätkapitalismus anzugreifen" (Hahn, 266).
16. On their discussions at the time of the writing of *Eulenspiegel*, and their differing conceptions of the theater, see Sauter, 73–74.
17. In the same year another novel appeared on the corrupt and corrupting world of West Berlin and the separation of Germany, *Der dritte Blick*, also with Desch.

Works Cited

Hahn, Manfred. "Ein Linker im Widerstand. Günther Weisenborn: *Die Furie.*" In *Erfahrung Nazideutschland. Romane in Deutschland 1933–1945*, ed. Sigrid Bock and Manfred Hahn, 231–97. Berlin and Weimar: Aufbau, 1987.

Brauer, Ilse, and Werner Kayser. *Günther Weisenborn*. Vol. 10. *Hamburger Bibliographien*. Hamburg: Hans Christians, 1972.

Sauter, Josef Hermann. *Interviews mit Schriftstellern. Texte und Selbstaussagen*. Leipzig and Weimar: Gustav Kiepenheuer, 1982.

Weisenborn, Günther. *Auf Sand gebaut*. Vienna, Munich, and Basel: Kurt Desch, 1956.

———. *Ballade vom Eulenspiegel, vom Federle und von der dicken Pompanne*. Hamburg: 1949.

———. *Das Mädchen von Fanö*. Bremen: Friedrich Trüjen, 1949.

———. *Dramatische Balladen*. Berlin: Aufbau-Verlag, 1955.

———. *Historien der Zeit*. Berlin: Aufbau, 1947.

———. *Memorial*. Munich: Kurt Desch, 1947.

———, ed. *Der lautlose Aufstand. Bericht über die Widerstandsbewegung des deutschen Volkes 1933–1945*. Hamburg: Rowohlt, 1953.

Weisenborn, Günther, with Joy Weisenborn. *Einmal laß mich traurig sein. Briefe Lieder Kassiber 1942–1943*. Ed. Elisabeth Raabe with the cooperation of Joy Weisenborn. Zürich: Arche, 1984.

Chapter 15

BETWEEN APOCALYPSE AND ARCADIA

Horst Lange's Visionary Imagination
during the Third Reich

Gerald Funk

With more composure than outrage, Horst Lange writes on 29 July 1943 the following dark sentences in his diary: "The apocalypse has already existed for a long time next to our bourgeois coziness, the plush sofa. Fire falls from the skies and the disorder which man has caused is growing to infinity" (*Tagebücher*, 115). More than a year later, on 8 October 1944, he notes, this time with a few more degrees of anxiety: "The hysteria is increasing from hour to hour. The madness festers behind every normal expression of life. The apocalyptic beasts are ready to devour us all" (166). On 5 March 1945 he finally sounds full of resignation and disdain: "Nothing more can be hoped and nothing can ever be put right. That has to be eradicated" (206). Lange refers with these last words to a speech he has just heard from Himmler, whose "washerwoman-superstition" and "low-down manner of deprivation of man" (205f.) he takes to task, but the general diagnosis, which he delivers with increasing personal engagement—clearly inspired by biblical iconography—is that of the apocalypse, the last days of the world that precede the Last Judgement and that are brought about by the "middle-class antichrist" Hitler.[1]

History takes on an eschatological dimension in Horst Lange's work. Barbarism (*Barbarei*) and Decline (*Niedergang*) are the concepts he uses to state the decay of all civilized and cultural norms.[2] "Sinking worlds" (24), he calls it. His perception—this is again and again clear from his diaries and letters—is determined by faith in the disastrous presence of demons,[3] characterized by his conviction about the enduring absence of God,[4] and influenced by dualisms of light and darkness, spirit and body, love and sexuality, in which context he feels, as he writes, that he himself belongs to "the dark and gloomy" (56).

Guilt and atonement, good and evil are Lange's moral categories. "No message of love could save this world any more," he notes on Christmas Eve, 1943.

> Today no gods are visible. And if they were visible, one would not believe in them any more. This mankind is therefore so helpless and so abandoned that it falls prey to its seducers without resistance, because they are no longer capable of separating good from evil. (132)

The present that he perceives—these are the years of the Third Reich, one needs to keep in mind—is plunged into darkness (see Funk). The *deus absconditus* has left mankind to its own devices, and now, without hope of redemption, chased by evil demons, it lives like lemurs in the cities, first on the surface of the earth, but finally—increasingly, with each year of the war—damned to a shadow-like existence in catacombs underground. In the passages from Lange's diaries entitled "Shadows from a night in the big city," (9–11) and also in later descriptions of night bombings of Berlin (129ff.), one finds already what Hermann Kasack and Hans Erich Nossack later bring into polished narrative form *after* the war in their works *The City beyond the Stream* (Die Stadt hinter dem Strom, 1947) and *Nekyia* (1947): cities of death full of ghostly figures, visions of Hades.

Such dark visions of the present are reinforced by Lange's pronounced fatalism. Early on in his diaries he speaks of the "inescapable" (15) and yields to a sequence of events decreed by nameless forces of fate. "I ... submit to whatever may happen," he says laconically on 22 May 1940, shortly before beginning his military service (23). In his most important work, *Black Willow* (Schwarze Weide, 1937), he speaks—entirely in keeping with Schopenhauer's philosophy of fate,[5] but without his faith in a *harmonia praestabilitata*—of an "invisible net" (370) with which all men are bound. He expresses his deep conviction "that all their hands and feet are tied" (370). Three years later in his second novel, *Ulans' Patrol* (Ulanenpatrouille, 1940), "one had to be exposed to whatever the ... dark and formless powers had decided, one could not free oneself, and one was obligated to accept it, even if it meant death itself, which would thrive upon it" (214). Even though Lange carefully avoids using the Christian concepts of predestination and providence, and speaks of "dark and formless powers" instead of the Old Testament god, Jehovah, such subjugation to social and historical circumstances is not foreign to Christianity.

If one considers all the confessional utterances of those years, it appears only logical that many themes, motifs, and figures in Lange's poetic works can also be derived from an iconography dominated by Christian traditions, above all in his *opus magnum*, the novel *Black Willow* of 1937. Even if the complicated and not always successful ramifications of a plot stretched over generations make difficult an exact recapitulation of events, at the same time it does make clear how much Lange is impressed by the genealogical sequences of the Old Testament. Apparently he was so spellbound by the many pages listing acts of procreation that he adopted a similarly convoluted genealogy for his own work. Even after several readings of the novel one cannot trace back with certainty in each case who begat whom and who became whose husband or wife. Family relations remain obscure, but nonetheless bind the protagonists to the generations of their ancestors.

The story begins with the adolescent first-person narrator, plagued by his awakening sexuality, who while spending his holidays as a guest on a country estate, predicts but cannot prevent a murder he has seen in a vision. He finally returns after many years, tortured by a restless conscience, in order to atone for his guilt in some way. This story ends—here the biblical model is immediately recognizable—with a veritable deluge. Horst Lange pulls out all the stops. Already at the beginning of Part Two, the events are bathed in an apocalyptic light. A sect dominates the local population of the area, which the protagonist left as a youth. Led by the former murderer (a "recruiter from hell," *Black Willow*, 266), in whose place an innocent man had been sentenced, people are whipped into a hysterical frenzy and end-of-the-world mood. Terror and panic grip the masses, and omens—snow the color of blood—point to the end of time. Finally the culprit hangs himself in fear of the revelation of his crime, and in the wild culmination of the novel, many others who were partly to blame, but also many others who were innocent, drown in the rising waters of the *Black Willow*, the river on whose shores love and murder have taken place: "in order that the remains of the unclean are flushed away" (445). The deluge-like flood sweeps away man and cattle. Swelled cadavers float around; corpses are flushed out of their graves:

> The blessed earth showed gaping cracks, it exposed the buried to daylight, which was without color, as if it had been filtered through a veil of mourning, illuminating the boards of the coffins, the bones and faded lace of the shrouds. The ribs, the vertebrae, the bones and the skull were torn apart and expelled into the unholy landscape. (490)

The world, so radically swept clean, was—and this is a second set of motifs influenced by Lange's Christian values—a world in decline. A symbol of this world is the eccentric collection of the farmer Starkloff, who preserves particularly repulsive examples of plants in various stages of decay, deformity, and disease. Personal relationships also appear infected by such morbidity. If one looks a little deeper, the origin of all guilt is often enough the characters' sexual "deformity." If one sorts out the deliberate genealogical confusion of the novel, one is confronted with adultery, incest, faithlessness, lust, rape, and at the same time feelings of guilt and self-incrimination, all of which reaches far back into the past.

Nietzsche once said: "Christianity gave Eros poison to drink—he did not die from it but degenerated into vice" (91). This statement goes to the heart of *Black Willow*, but at the same time it could serve as the motto for Horst Lange's second novel *Ulans' Patrol* (1940). Here as well one finds adultery, faithlessness, brute lust and finally—as its consequence—the pathetic and rather unheroic end of the protagonist during a maneuver: everywhere signs of decay. Similar to Alexander Lernet-Holenia's *Baron Bagge* of 1936, but indebted above all to Hofmannsthal's *Story of a Rider* (1898), Lange sketches here an oppressively dark realm between fate and providence, in which the path of the protagonist can only lead to death. This undoing is anticipated by images and scenes of inescapable doom—for example, the description of a rapacious insect that lies in wait for its prey in the depths of a sand crater (*Ulans' Patrol*, 87f.). Likewise, these developments are prepared atmospherically by the narrator's repeated fixation on things in decay: rust corrodes the iron of weapons, verdigris covers the surface of a formerly shiny metal, leather gets moldy. The figures move as if in a trance. The imagination of the narrator seems to be in the grip of an all-encompassing aesthetic of decline and doom.

It is not surprising, then, that the National Socialist critique accused the novel of "defeatism" and "ridiculing the *Wehrmacht*" (Schaefer, *Auch wenn Du träumst*, 286). Reactions to *Black Willow* were even more censorious, condemning the "ugliness" and "vulgarity" of the novel and speaking with great disgust of the author's image of mankind, dominated by putrefaction, sexual license, greed, lechery, alcoholism, and "repugnant lasciviousness" (*Schwüle*), which placed him in the tradition of Dostoyevsky, Huysmans, and Strindberg (see Ter Nedden, 82f.).

This criticism was not entirely incorrect. The figures emerge in constellations of violence and sexuality, guilt and atonement, bound by symbolic topographies on the verge of decay—for example, the landscapes of marsh and bog in "Will o' the Wisp" or in "Son of the Captain's Widow" (both first published in 1939)—and indicate directly the aesthetic preferences of the author, which differ provocatively from official cultural and educational policy. Beyond that, they have deep-seated soteriological dimensions, i.e., relating to the history of salvation. As becomes clear at the end of *Black Willow* a new race may emerge from the cataclysm—in the form of two surviving children, one of whom is the daughter of the suspected murderer, the other the son of the actual murderer—that can distance itself from the guilt-ridden entanglements of the previous generation. Guilt seems atoned for and the world cleansed of corruption.

If one believes the biographic statements of Oda Schaefer, Lange's wife since 1931, her husband was "a profound believer" ("Lebensbild," 268) and had an intensive relationship with Catholicism. However, one cannot verify this from his own documented statements. Horst Lange thinks metaphysically in high dualisms such as guilt and atonement, light and darkness, body and spirit; in this respect, he is clearly marked by a gnostically influenced Christianity but does not think theologically in the classical sense. Jesus Christ does not figure prominently in his thinking; the singular god of the Old Testament at times gets translated into the plural in his diaries; and though Lange's apocalypse is clearly catastrophic, it does not introduce any condition of radical otherness or transcendence, but at best a catharsis. Here an intellectual, but primarily also an aesthetic counterweight, the classical tradition of antiquity, comes into play not to level the scale that was tipped so heavily to the one side by the Christian tradition, but at least to hold it in balance.

In her memoir of Horst Lange, Oda Schaefer reports that a reproduction of a painting by Mantegna hung over the bed in her husband's study. It showed the Latin poet Virgil, crowned with a garland of laurel, his face raised, seemingly to listen to the words of an invisible god. His hand holds a quill, poised to write, as if he were waiting for the command to record a statement. Her husband wanted to keep this image in front of him, she writes, "in order to exorcise the evil spirits and elemental forces" ("Lebensbild," 276) that set upon him repeatedly during his work on his first novel *Black Willow*.

Presumably not by coincidence, Lange held in high esteem the figure of Virgil, whom Dante had chosen as guide through the Inferno and Purgatory of the Christian middle ages, since in Virgil's fourth eclogue the appearance of a son of god born by a "Holy Maid" had been prophesied and he therefore could be regarded as a communicator between pagan antiquity and Christianity. Whereas the Christian tradition offered Horst Lange the images that were necessary in order to sit in judgement on a society in decline and to prophecy the end, like the prophets of the Old Testament, he hoped to gain from classical antiquity, while excluding Nietzsche's Dionysian god, the power to impose order. Moderation and the golden mean were key concepts for him, which he used again and again for what he once described in his diaries as the "rebirth of antiquity" (Lange, *Tagebücher*, 129). It was Lange's conviction that the corrosive powers of the dark and demonic, of decay and disintegration, can become productive forces when they are bound to the time-honored perdurability of classical forms, that is, when the contemporary shadows of (cultural) twilight are set in a framework of timelessness.

Therefore, it is only logical that most of Lange's works reveal a texture of classical mythology. An imposing example is the nymph Daphne from *Black Willow*. The very beginning of the novel depicts the destruction of a statue of this nymph, who for centuries belonged to the standard inventory of Arcadia, representing the classical gods of Greece and reflecting happier and more beautiful times. The statue is pushed from her pedestal and breaks. Only after the fatal flood has receded can the head of the statue resurface after being lost for years and the individual pieces be joined together again as a further symbol of hope, of "rebirth," in the final pages of the novel.

The foreground action in Lange's *Ulans' Patrol*, especially the condition of the male protagonist, is also set in relation to a classical myth. On the ceiling of the pavilion in which the protagonist and his former lover meet again and pass a fateful night, there hangs a painting. It represents the rape of the beautiful boy Ganymede, whom Zeus, consumed with longing, has kidnapped and brought by his eagle from the world of the mortals to

Olympus. For the young lieutenant of the novel the bird of Zeus becomes a symbol of the danger in which he finds himself. In his imagination the bird of prey hovers over him and seems to want to descend upon him to pluck out his heart. The eagle of Zeus transforms into a threatening harpy.

Such suggestive but isolated motifs, symbols and images from antiquity, as found in the first two novels, broaden later increasingly to encompass at times the whole fable. The short story "Farewell to an Apple Tree" (Abschied von einem Apfelbaum, 1940) makes that clear, though the presence of classical antiquity in this case is exclusively linked to the narrator's experience of an epiphany, seeing illuminated the figures of Philemon and Baucis behind acting individuals, almost like a double exposure of banal everyday events, as if the dimension of myth were something absent in these times, though still it generates the primordial image against which, as background, even the present gains dignity.

In the story "The Flares" (Die Leuchtkugeln, 1944), based on experiences of war at the eastern front, just the name of the mysterious protagonist, Hermes, makes clear the centrality of classical antiquity to Lange. He occasionally lets Mediterranean light illuminate the snow-covered expanses of the Russian steppes. An air of Arcadia—despite the events of war—hovers over the prose, though even in this case with a melancholic note: Hermes, the messenger of the gods, perishes at the end of the story. "I could," the first-person narrator reflects,

> not remember clearly that Olympian world, but did they [the gods] remember me, did they think only for one minute of this country, this war, these glowing golden shadows, whose rule had not quite ended, who were nourished by our memories and who were almost physically present? (98)

The narrator leaves this question unanswered here. Only after the end of the war, it seems, did Horst Lange as author find an answer.

The structured power of myth, because it crystallized ancient images in single motifs, in moments of epiphany or mysterious intimation, could at best only weaken that fatal pessimism born of Christianity and counteract visions of decay,[6] but after 1945 the desire for order becomes so pronounced in Lange that the myths of antiquity now dominate his imagination almost exclusively. As paradoxical as it may seem, whereas he had perceived the historical events as apocalyptic while living through them, he could come to terms with them retroactively in an interpretive framework provided now no longer by Christian eschatology, but by the meta-historical classical narratives of Greece. They also apparently provided him with the templates he needed for less infernal material, so that plays and comedies that had been left undone during the war years, such as *The Woman Who Imagined Herself Helen of Troy* (Die Frau, die sich Helena wähnte, 1946) and *Kephalos and Prokris* (1948), could now appear.

During the postwar years, however, there was one myth that was more than just a literary model for his own work or an abstract parable. The story of Odysseus, the hero whom the gods hinder in his return home from the Trojan War, became the quintessential mirror of existence, the screen on which Lange's generation projected its own experience. Wolfgang Schadewaldt (*The Return of Odysseus*, 1946), Emil Barth (*Grandson of Odysseus*, 1951), Werner Warsinsky (*Voyage to Kimmeria*, 1953), Ernst Schnabel (*The Sixth Canto*, 1956), and Walter Jens (*The Testament of Odysseus*, 1957), to name just a few, interpreted their experience in literary form as a reflection of the Odyssey.[7]

In Horst Lange's work, the story of the homecoming to Attica turns up as background to the title story of the volume *On the Beach of Kimmeria* (Am kimmerischen Strand, 1948). Not only do the mottoes of all four chapters come from this Homeric epic, but his protagonist, Odysseus, appears as partner in dialogue with the narrator and reports on his experiences in Kimmeria, the land of the shades of death. Tying into mythic events, the story is told of a "Return to a Foreign Homeland" (Heimkehr in die Fremde), a return that can only become reality after a visit to the realm of shades, to Hades, and after the remembrance of the dead and of the horror and misery of war. This model of classical antiquity reinforces for Lange the possibility of return, of homecoming.

With images from Gnostic-Christian iconography, and convictions determined by these images, Lange has composed in diverse literary variations a swan song, a warning sign on the wall, for his present day, which is, as he puts it in *Black Willow*, the "darkest of all time" (247). In the luminous myths of classical antiquity he has found forms of allegorical reflection that allow him to recuperate dignity and meaning from the actual horror and terror of World War II and the postwar era. As long as he hoped that the specter of Nazism and war would soon pass or at least not be too ruinous—perhaps the most egregious assumption of the many authors who did not emigrate—Horst Lange chastised his times, literally sat in judgement and prophesied the end. When the end could no longer be averted, he committed himself to order—often against his own temperamental nature—and countered the Christian furies and demons that he saw at work with the didactic Eros of ascribing coherent meaning to events. With works that try to do justice to this Eros—mainly the stories and comedies of the postwar era—he dissociated himself from the legacies of literary modernism. They lack the tension that arises from the polarity of two antagonistic forces, which had determined his works from 1933 to 1945.

"The only way to avenge oneself is not to resemble them!" So goes a maxim of Marcus Aurelius that Lange noted on 5 March 1945 (*Tagebücher*, 205). Christianity and classical antiquity each offered, with different focus, the intellectual and imaginative models for a literary mode of taking distance. Alfred Döblin once used the concept of the "imaginary revenge" on the hated [Nazi] system of coercion in order to characterize the predominant tendency of emigrant literature of those years.[8] Not coincidentally, he uses the same concept (revenge) as Horst Lange. Anything more than this abstract form of aesthetic opposition was impossible for most of the authors, who had remained in Germany and dissociated themselves as far as was possible from National Socialism. At best one made efforts to counter the brutalization of sensibility with stylistic refinement, the military heroism with an idyll, or else one set visions of collapse and destruction against the reigning euphoria for a Pan-Germanic Empire. Exemplary here is—besides Horst Lange—the work, which has been undervalued to this day, of Alexander Lernet-Holenia, especially his novels *The Man with a Hat* (1937), *A Dream in Red* (1939), and *Mars in Aries* (1941). Ernst Jünger and Werner Bergengruen ought also to be named in this context, although Jünger's apocalyptic scenario in *On the Marble Cliffs* (1939) originates not in unsentimental acts of nature, as in Lange, but with social groups that turn out in the end to be mere pawns of transhistorical forces. These endeavor, in turn, to remain in Jünger's terminology, to baptize the world from time to time with fire.[9]

But here, in the literary simulation of extreme circumstances, the rhetoric of horror, mannerism, and decadence can be understood as an attack directed at the central nerve of National Socialism, which had originated in a distorted petty bourgeois deformation of an aesthetics of the sublime.[10] That such a form of keeping his distance was not an act of political resistance does not need further emphasis. But is active resistance or socially relevant opposition the only or even the central category in the evaluation of aesthetic obsessions? Is it a sufficient characteristic of literary works? Even during the years of the Third Reich?

While working on the comedy *Kephalos and Prokris*, Horst Lange noted in his diary on 4 June 1940: "I continue to write my play as if I were sitting in Greece ... and had goddesses at my bedside. Sometimes it seems as an escape, a flight of fantasy; at other times, as a counterattack" (*Tagebücher*, 24). It is time to recognize the significance of such aesthetic options, to take them seriously, and to perceive them as *active* choices, even when their decoding does not always offer unambiguous answers.

Translated by Renata Lefcourt

Notes

1. This concise characterization originates in the diary entries of Friedrich Reck-Malleczewen (58), which were begun in 1936, but only published in 1947.
2. See Lange: *Tagebücher*, 24 (4 June 1940); 79 (26 October 1941); and 156f. (20 August 1944).
3. "The demons are gone again! There was much darkness and sorrow" (166), he writes with relief after one of his frequently repeated bouts with alcoholism, during which he had fallen asleep rolled into a carpet of an—often unknown—companion.
4. "The saving God is hiding, as usual," he writes on 29 July 1943 (*Tagebücher*, 115).
5. Schopenhauer uses the image of infinitely connected chains of causes and effects, whose interconnections form a "net entwined many times" that moves "in the direction with the time" (262) and into which man is bound.

6. It is significant that Lange was unable to complete his idyllic novel *The Song of the Oriole* (Das Lied des Pirol, begun in 1938). Even immediately after the war a planned novel about, as he writes in a comment on the first edition, "the possibility of happiness," could only appear as a fragment. Despite the awareness that there is no enduring certainty of happiness in this world, the protagonist of the novel was supposed to be "privy to the lawful order, which always resists all chaotic clamor of the external world and tries to fill it … with harmony" (125).
7. Horst Denkler, in his essay, "Hellas as Mirror of the Present in the Literature of the 'Third Reich,'" points out the fact that many authors of the *inner emigration* had already tried between the years 1933 and 1945 to interpret the present by mirroring classical antiquity. See Delabar, Denkler, and Schütz, 11–27. Denkler emphasizes that National Socialist spokespersons all the way to Hitler made an effort to "Melt the Germanic-Nordic with the Old Greek Southern" (12).
8. Alfred Döblin emphasizes in his essay "The Historical Novel and Us" (Der Historische Roman und wir, 1936) that many authors of the emigration tried to at least "take imaginary revenge" (314).
9. It says *On the Marble Cliffs*: "The order of man resembles cosmos in that it, from time to time, in order to be reborn anew, has to plunge into fire" (62).
10. Horst Lange writes in a letter to Ernst Kreuder of 12 December 1938: "Whom I was talking about as Smorczak and his sect, you can work out for yourself with some imagination and logic." Here it is important to relativize a thesis of the editors of the first supplement to the *Zeitschrift für Germanistik* (see Delabar, Denkler and Schütz: *Banality in Style*). In their preface they speak—in relation to the entire literary work between 1933 and 1945—of a literature "of synthesis, appeasement, temperance, and moderation." This literature stands, they write, "so much under the self imposed precept of moderation, that one were tempted to speak of a modern age of moderation" (9). Later one reaches for terms such as "mediocrity" and "dwarfism" (10). That this is only half the truth, I hope to have demonstrated, at least to some extent, with my remarks about Horst Lange.

Works Cited

Delabar, Walter, Horst Denkler, and Erhard Schütz, eds. *Banalität mit Stil. Zur Widersprüchlichkeit der Literaturproduktion im Nationalsozialismus*. Special Issue 1, *Zeitschrift für Germanistik* (1999).

Denkler, Horst. "Hellas als Spiegel der Gegenwart in der Literatur des 'Dritten Reiches.'" In *Banalität mit Stil. Zur Widersprüchlichkeit der Literaturproduktion im Nationalsozialismus*, ed. Walter Delabar, Horst Denkler, and Erhard Schütz. Special Issue 1, *Zeitschrift für Germanistik* (1999): 11–27.

Döblin, Alfred. "Der historische Roman und wir." In Alfred Döblin, *Schriften zur Ästhetik, Poetik und Literatur*, 291–316. Olten und Freiburg im Breisgau: Walter, 1989 [1936].

Funk, Gerald. "In dieser dunkelsten aller Zeiten. Aspekte ästhetischer Opposition im Werk Horst Langes." In *Deutsche Autoren des Ostens als Gegner und Opfer des Nationalsozialismus: Beiträge zur Widerstandsproblematik*, ed. Frank-Lothar Kroll, 127–47. Berlin: Duncker und Humblot, 2000.

Jünger, Ernst. *Auf den Marmorklippen*. Hamburg: Hanseatische Verlagsanstalt, 1939.

Lange, Horst. *Die Leuchtkugeln. Drei Erzählungen*. Hamburg: H. Goverts, 1944.

———. *Das Lied des Pirols*. Munich: Desch, 1946.

———. *Schwarze Weide*. Hamburg and Leipzig: H. Goverts, 1937.

———. *Tagebücher aus dem Zweiten Weltkrieg*. Ed. Hans Dieter Schäfer. Die Mainzer Reihe. Vol. 46. Mainz: von Hase und Koehler, 1979.

———. *Ulanenpatrouille.* Hamburg: H. Goverts, 1940.

Nietzsche, Friedrich. *Jenseits von Gut und Böse. Zur Genealogie der Moral.* Stuttgart: A. Kröner, 1953.

Reck-Malleczewen, Friedrich. *Tagebuch eines Verzweifelten.* Frankfurt am Main: Eichborn, 1994.

Schaefer, Oda. *Auch wenn Du träumst, gehen die Uhren. Lebenserinnerungen.* Munich: Piper, 1970.

———. "Horst Lange: Ein Lebensbild." In Horst Lange, *Tagebücher aus dem Zweiten Weltkrieg,* ed. Hans Dieter Schäfer, 261–89. Die Mainzer Reihe. Vol. 46. Mainz: von Hase und Koehler, 1979.

Schopenhauer, Arthur. *"Transzendente Spekulation über die anscheinende Absichtlichkeit im Schicksale des einzelnen."* In Arthur Schopenhauer, *Sämtliche Werke,* critically annotated and edited by Wolfgang von Löhneysen. Vol. 4: *Parerga and Paralipomena I,* 243–72. Stuttgart and Frankfurt am Main: Cotta and Insel, 1978.

Ter Nedden, Eberhard. "Zerrbilder aus Schlesien: Horst Lange – August Scholtis." *Die Weltliteratur* 3 (1941): 82f.

Chapter 16

"I MOUNTED RESISTANCE, THOUGH I HID THE FACT"

Versions of Wolfgang Koeppen's Early Biography

David Basker

Wolfgang Koeppen belongs to the generation of writers whose early careers coincided with the National Socialist dictatorship. However, only after World War II did Koeppen establish his literary reputation, with the publication of three novels in the early 1950s: *Pigeons on the Grass* (Tauben im Gras, 1951), *The Greenhouse* (Das Treibhaus, 1953), and *Death in Rome* (Der Tod in Rom, 1954). These works stand out as the earliest novels in the Federal Republic to deal directly and critically with contemporary life in the new state. While some critics were outraged by Koeppen's uncompromising confrontation with some of the continuities from the immediate past, the so-called postwar trilogy of novels soon came to be regarded as early high points of a specifically West German literature. Subsequently, a series of travelogues in the late 1950s and early 1960s sold well, but there followed a lengthy period during which Koeppen apparently suffered from writer's block. With the notable exception of *Youth* (Jugend, 1976), he was unable to produce any lengthy piece of fiction for his indulgent publisher.

At this stage, Koeppen began to use his career before 1950 as a source of material. The republication of works that predated the postwar trilogy was accompanied in each case by an author's foreword explaining the circumstances under which the text was written, and publication coincided with a series of interviews in newspapers and journals, in which Koeppen gave an account of his experiences in the Third Reich. In this way, Koeppen himself brought to the fore his own early biography as a means of interpreting his work; as a result, questions arise about the selectivity of his memory of this period. In fact, the image of Koeppen's life in the period from 1933 to 1945 that emerges from these retrospective accounts is at odds on a number of points with extant documentary evidence, particularly relating to his membership of the Reichsschrifttumskammer (Reich Chamber of Literature, hereafter RSK).

Koeppen began his writing career in the town of his birth some ten years before Hitler came to power, with the publication of an article in the *Greifs-walder Zeitung* in 1923. In 1926 Koeppen worked at the City Theater in Würzburg for a year, during which he published an article in the *Pages of the City Theater* (Blätter des Stadttheaters) against censorship. Subsequently, he recounts in interview, he was able to survive the economic hardship of the late Weimar period by taking a variety of temporary jobs, even as a ship's cook. Around 1928 Koeppen had moved to Berlin, and here his career as a writer began to unfold more rapidly: two short stories appeared under his name in *The Red Flag* (Die Rote Fahne) in 1928, and an article was published in *The World Stage* (Die Weltbühne) in 1930. In January 1931 Koeppen secured a job as a journalist with the liberal, Jewish-owned *Berliner Börsen-Courier*, a post he held until the newspaper was closed down by the Nazis in December 1933. This was a particularly productive period in Koeppen's life as a writer: in all, over two hundred articles for the *Börsen-Courier* have survived in his name. He was employed primarily as an art critic, in the widest sense of the term, although he also contributed a number of articles on life in Berlin and its surroundings, traveled on assignments on a few occasions, and wrote for the newspaper's *Nebenbei* (Asides) column, which featured humorous anecdotes from everyday life. As far as can be ascertained, Koeppen published only two works of fiction in the *Börsen-Courier*.

In the present context, two specific aspects of Koeppen's work as a contributor to newspapers and periodicals are worthy of note: in the first place, the variety of Koeppen's experience as a journalist was wide. Through the *Börsen-Courier* he traveled and got to know Berlin very well. Moreover, he was able to attend premieres of leading films and theater performances, make the acquaintance of writers such as Heinrich Mann, Alfred Döblin, and Else Lasker-Schüler through readings and meetings of literary circles, and establish excellent—not to say vital—contacts with the film industry. In an interview with Karl Prümm and Erhart Schütz for *Schreibheft* in 1983, Koeppen recalled the important part that the film industry played in his career in the 1940s, a time when he needed employment: "In a certain sense, film saved my life. From earlier I knew a lot of actors and was friends with two of them, and with the director Erich Engel. We gave each other advice. In the meantime, Herbert Ihering had got himself into a silly position, he was the head of personnel at Tobis" (Oehlenschläger, 377). Koeppen came into regular contact with these figures in the film industry through his reports for the *Börsen-Courier* in the early 1930s (see, for example, the article "Blutauffrischung bei der Ufa" [1933]); indeed, Herbert Ihering was head of the review section of the newspaper during Koeppen's period of employment.

The second notable aspect of Koeppen's journalism in the late Weimar and early Nazi years is a not entirely surprising development in his political stance. The early stories for *Die Rote Fahne* express the type of working-class solidarity one would expect in view of the journal's communist sympathies, and the article for *Die Weltbühne* continues in an antiauthoritarian, antinationalist vein. The first articles for the *Berliner Börsen-Courier* show few signs of such obvious left-wing commitment, although on a number of occasions Koeppen addresses issues surrounding the economic hardship of the late Weimar years with sensitivity and sympathy for the ordinary working person (see, for example, the article "Jugend, die nie schreiben würde" [1932]). Where his attention is drawn to the rise in nationalist feeling, he is openly critical. In the morning edition of 29 June 1932, for example, under the heading *Political Books* (Politische Bücher), Koeppen reviews Wolfgang Ertel-Breithaupt's history *France, the Scourge of the World*, a text that attempts to lay the blame for all of Europe's woes over the past four hundred years firmly at the door of the French. For Koeppen, this is nothing more than "a hate-filled representation of history," especially unwelcome in these "times of greatest national tensions."

However, the political victory of the Nazis brought about a rapid change in the tone of Koeppen's articles. Koeppen's own criticism of the French now surfaces on a number of occasions in the articles that appeared after Hitler's accession to power. On a trip to the Saarland in the early summer of 1933, Koeppen describes the European boundaries set up by the Treaty of Versailles as "becoming entirely senseless" (*GW*, 5:69). The trip ends in Paris, where, he claims in another article from June 1933, he hears exiles from Hitler's new regime speaking about the possibility of returning to Germany, which "in most cases, is prevented only by a misunderstanding" (*GW*, 5:75–76). At the same time, Koeppen's journalism shows a sudden conversion to the type of openly nationalist art that he had been quick to condemn before 1933. He reviews two unmistakably nationalist studies of Stefan George's life and works, and his conclusion is that this kind of *Blut und Boden* (Blood and Soil) approach to literary criticism is "fruitful" (*GW*, 6:44); indeed, in 1933 he had already published a similar appreciation of the (deservedly forgotten) dramatist Emil Gött to mark the twenty-fifth anniversary of his death: "He was a German writer, a poet of the homeland and the earth, a pure opponent of the spirit of the big cities." As Koeppen describes it, Gött's work should be part of any good German's home library in 1933, and he offers further guidance in this area in an article entitled "The Home Library in our Time" (Die Hausbibliothek unserer Zeit, *Berliner Börsen-Courier*, 24 October 1933):

> To a large extent the library has become a political library in the widest sense. Publications about the particular questions of the present, the Jewish question for example or the national idea of eugenics are, as bookshop owners confirm to us, being bought and discussed. In this sense philosophy is no longer just a matter for academics, but a concern of the whole nation. (6)

In fact, his work for the *Berliner Börsen-Courier* suggests that in all areas of artistic activity, Koeppen saw the early stages of the new regime as an opportunity to inject new life. The Italian model, in which the fascist movement and futurism go hand in hand, inspired Koeppen to support attempts to associate artistic advance with the political rise of National Socialism.[1] At this early stage in the regime, Koeppen can find similar views being expressed in public by members of the Party, views that, for the time being at least, reconcile his own interest in artistic modernism with National Socialism:

> That young people are fighting back against the misuse of their influence is proved by a very recent announcement by the National Socialist German Student Association in the Auditorium Maximum of Berlin University, which, under the slogan Young People Fight for German Art, turned with refreshing openness against any reactionary attitude, any stagnation. Artists such as Barlach, Kolbe, Schmidt-Rotluff and Emil Nolde were spoken of with enthusiasm and genuine youthful exuberance, and at the same time, with an openness of a sort we have not heard for a while, an attack was launched against the petty-bourgeois opportunists ... who ... use the words "cultural Bolshevism" ... against any work of art that goes beyond their microcephalic intellectual horizons. (*GW*, 5:87)

The evidence of a change in Koeppen's political stance over this period—from left-wing support in the late 1920s, through antinationalism, to an appreciation of what the new regime might offer—is overwhelming. This is not to claim, of course, that Koeppen was ever a committed supporter of National Socialism in private. The development in his views appears to be the attempt of a young writer to adapt his work to the dominant ideology in a newspaper that was in any case under the huge pressure of *Gleichschaltung* (ideological coordination). Nevertheless, his equivocal stance toward the early stages of the regime in his published work of the period remains unmentioned in his own accounts of his life.

Indeed, Koeppen has repeatedly presented the next stage in his experience of the Third Reich in a way that has stressed his oppositional stance toward National Socialism. Despite, he claims, having been offered a number of jobs with other newspapers following the enforced closure of the *Berliner Börsen-Courier*, he took the decision to leave Germany in 1934 for Holland, apparently to stay with Jewish friends. In an interview with *Sinn und Form* in 1986, Koeppen explained his position following the publication of his first novel: "In 1934, after I had written the book *An Unhappy Affair* [Eine unglückliche Liebe], I went into exile voluntarily, because I found National Socialism terrible and repugnant. In fact I had no reason to take flight. My life was not under threat. I was not Jewish and I was not considered to be a communist.... I went abroad out of feelings of pure abhorrence" (Sauter, 544). In the absence of corroborating evidence, one can only take the author's word for the reasons behind his decision to emigrate. It is perhaps worth noting, however, that the only publication that has survived from this period is the novel *The Wall Is Swaying* (Die Mauer schwankt), which appeared in Germany in 1935. This text is not an unequivocal expression of Koeppen's distaste for the regime; in fact, it was republished with Nazi approval under the title *The Duty* (Die Pflicht) in 1939.

In retrospect Koeppen has described his period in exile as a mistake, on the grounds that his literary reputation was not sufficiently well established for his career to flourish outside Germany. In 1938 he was able to return without arousing suspicion, he claims, on the basis of a bureaucratic oversight that meant that he was already registered with the police in a small town in Schleswig-Holstein. For the period following this clandestine return, a number of documents have survived in the Berlin Document Center relating to Koeppen's involvement with Nazi writers' organizations. This material throws a somewhat different light on his position in Germany in the 1940s than emerges from his recollections in interview.

To begin with Koeppen's own version of events, it seems that in the years following his return from Holland, he was able to return to Berlin and, through the contacts he had made earlier, secure employment in the flourishing Nazi film industry. He was apparently successful in walking the tightrope between benefiting from the privileges of his post (financial survival and exemption from military service) and compromise with the regime:

> I wrote scripts for a few film companies, never anything of my own. And I wrote these scripts in such a way that the film people, the directors had to say: Oh, he's actually a very gifted person. He can certainly write films. But we can't make any of them. It's just not possible. We'll never get them past the "Promi" —as the Ministry of Propaganda was called. (Durzak, 96)

Koeppen survived for some time in this way (the precise chronology is unclear from such anecdotes), until the head of the Bavaria film company in Munich forced his hand by demanding the completion of a usable film script within two weeks. This ultimatum coincided with the destruction of the author's flat in Berlin, probably in 1942, during an Allied bombing raid. Together, these two events persuaded Koeppen to leave Berlin and go into hiding. With the help of an acquaintance in the Bavaria offices in Munich, he apparently secured a letter that allowed him, as an employee of the film industry, to use the train system without restriction. This enabled him to reach the village of Feldafing on the Starnberger See, where the owner of the Golf-Hotel agreed to offer him shelter, "because I had the protection of a famous actor" (Wehdeking, 49). Bribery, it seems, played a part too, for once he ran short of money, Koeppen found the hotel owner less accommodating. He was able, he claims, to prevent his host from reporting him to the authorities by pointing out that the man had already committed a crime himself by sheltering Koeppen in the first place. Nevertheless, the situation as Koeppen describes it was precarious, and the conditions in which he was forced to live were particularly disagreeable: "For six months I lived on raw potatoes in his cellar" (Durzak, 98). It was under these circumstances, Koeppen recalls, that he lived out the final years of World War II.

From this evidence, then, Koeppen's life in the Third Reich was marked by dangerous adventure at every turn, willingly recounted in interview in anecdotal form. Koeppen appears as someone whose attitudes were fundamentally anti-Nazi; this opposition was mitigated, however, by a deep attachment to his homeland and by considerations of financial survival. This pattern explains his departure for Holland in 1934, his decision to return to Germany in 1938, and his duplicitous involvement with the film industry. Above all, Koeppen claims he was never prepared to fight in the name of the Nazis; of his uncomfortable time in Feldafing he modestly concludes: "Why did I do that? I'm no hero, absolutely not, I'm the opposite. But I did not want to do this one thing: become a soldier for Hitler" (Durzak, 98).

The evidence concerning this period in Koeppen's life that has survived in the Berlin Document Center consists of twenty-three items: forms and letters broadly concerning his membership in Nazi writers' organizations. The earliest documents, from December 1933, consist of the author's application to join the Reichsverband Deutscher Schriftsteller (Reich Association of German Writers). One might speculate that this application, coming as it did toward the end of the life of the *Berliner Börsen-Courier*, was an attempt by Koeppen to explore another career path; he was presumably working on *An Unhappy Affair* by this time and would have required membership in the Reichsverband in order to publish the novel. The remaining documents relate to the period after the author's return from Holland in 1938. These include: a successful application to join the RSK in 1939, attached to which is a *curriculum vitae*; a number of letters concerning specific incidents in Koeppen's life in the late 1930s and early 1940s; and a series of declarations of income for the years 1940, 1941, and 1942.

This material serves in the first place to establish a much clearer chronological sequence than is possible from the interviews, and some of the evidence supports Koeppen's recollections. Particularly as far as his overriding desire to avoid military service is concerned, the documentation shows that he did indeed go to considerable lengths in these years. What he has neglected to mention in interview, however, is that (his oppositional stance toward the regime notwithstanding) he was closely enough involved with Nazi writers' organizations to enlist their support in avoiding the army draft. A letter dated 17 April 1940 from Koeppen's publishers, the Universitas Verlag, to the RSK contains a request on Koeppen's behalf to delay his conscription on the grounds that he was near completion of a novel. On the same day, Koeppen himself visited the offices of the RSK in Charlottenburg. The speed with which the RSK then took up the case is remarkable. An immediate and urgent memorandum was sent from the RSK to the Propaganda Ministry, in which the details of the novel *Advent*, including its plot and the amount of money he could expect to make from it, are set out. Beyond the questions as to what became of the novel *Advent* and why Koeppen makes no mention of it elsewhere, these documents point to the fact that Koeppen was far more active in the literary field at that time than he has acknowledged in interview. The declarations of income support this thesis, showing that Koeppen was earning money from a wide variety of literary activity: from book publications, publications in newspapers and periodicals, from *Aufführungen* (performances— presumably his work for the film industry), and "from work as an editor." Koeppen's total earnings from literary work for the period from 1940 to 1942 amounted to some 12,000 reichsmarks, a relatively comfortable financial position. One might also note that the permanent address given on each of the three declarations is that of the Universitas Verlag, again pointing to a close association with that organization.[2]

It is possible to account for only some of Koeppen's earnings in the early 1940s through surviving publications. Two short stories and one book review are the only publications by Koeppen to be identified from this period, and all three appeared in 1941: the two stories were published in the *Kölnische Zeitung*, while *Das Reich* carried Koeppen's review of *Introduction to Zen Buddhism* (Die Einführung in den Zen-Buddhismus). Once again, Koeppen's writing seems to indicate a political metamorphosis. Of course, the left-wing enthusiasm of the *Rote Fahne* stories has no place in Hitler's Germany, but there are no signs of any attempt by Koeppen to engage in any other way with the dominant ideology. Rather, by 1941, he has adopted the stance of the *inner emigrant* who prefers to withdraw from a consideration of the public world, in order to concentrate on the inner life of his characters. His story "Early in the Morning" (Am frühen Morgen), published on 30 March 1941, recounts the bizarre mental images that haunt the mind of a bank employee as he makes his way to work one morning. The visions are so intense that they threaten to plunge Herr Herbert into a psychological abyss; only by concentrating on the mundane routine of his life in the bank can he banish this mental turmoil and return to the "track of sensible order" (*GW*, 3:137).[3] Likewise, in the story "The Engagement" (Die Verlobung), which appeared in the *Kölnische Zeitung* on New Year's Day of 1941, the narrator focuses on the inner life of a protagonist who is only slowly realizing the consequences of committing the rest of his life to one woman. Explicitly, Paul's problems here in respect of his fiancée Christine Keetenheuwe are not part of the external world, but are located in his own mind: "Rather, it angered him much more to see Keetenheuwe's young daughter possessed of so much power and mystery; power and mystery which only had their roots in his imagination, only drew their force from his thoughts and unfolded solely in his heart" (*GW*, 3:125). When mention is made of Christine's father's visit to Amsterdam, there is no reference to political events. Indeed, characters' emotional concerns dominate to the extent that in both stories it is impossible to be certain when the events take place. One might even interpret Koeppen's book review in *Das Reich* in terms of a similar punctilious avoidance of the political in favor of transcendent, affective values. His account of *Introduction to Zen Buddhism* concludes: "And Zen is perhaps nothing more (or nothing less) than inner experience with a Buddhist interpretation" (*Das Reich*, 9

March 1941). The preoccupation with subjective experience that Koeppen identifies in Buddhism could equally stand as a characterization of his own literary approach in the 1940s.

The available evidence of irregular but not inconsiderable earnings from his writing in this period suggests Koeppen's much more active involvement in the literary world of the 1940s than emerges from his statements in interview. Far from maintaining an oppositional stance toward Nazi organizations, he was prepared to involve himself with official bodies—the RSK and the officially sanctioned Universitas Verlag—if only to maintain his income and remain as a civilian. The literary corollary of this pragmatic approach to his career is the complete withdrawal from political issues in his two surviving short stories in favor of introspection. These observations do not constitute a moral judgement of Koeppen's actions at the time, but rather an attempt to clarify the historical record; they must, however, make us wary of Koeppen's own retrospective accounts of his life when it comes to the postwar period.

Of course, Wolfgang Koeppen is certainly not alone in recalling the episodes of his life under the Third Reich in a way that glosses over anything that might smack of compromise with the regime. There are obvious and understandable reasons why an author should wish to represent his life in this way, not the least of which are the demands that the victorious Allies made of German writers before they were allowed to publish in the immediate postwar years. What is perhaps unusual about Koeppen's case is that he subsequently used this partial view of his career as a way of bringing missing texts back into the public domain several decades after the end of the Nazi dictatorship. The most obvious cases in point here are the novel *Die Mauer schwankt*, which was first published in 1935 and then reissued as *Die Pflicht* in 1939, but effectively remained a missing text in the postwar period until its reappearance in 1983; and in 1992 the first text in Suhrkamp's Jüdischer Verlag, *Jakob Littner's Notes from Underground* (Jakob Littners Aufzeichnungen aus einem Erdloch), a work which, it was revealed, Koeppen had published as *Jakob Littner's Notes from Underground* by Jakob Littner in 1948. As is clear from the peculiar history of the publication of *The Wall Is Swaying*, at the very least it is susceptible to a reading that would have corresponded with Nazi ideals of duty toward the state. Yet, in the foreword to the 1983 edition, Koeppen argues that his protagonist is a proto-resistance fighter, that in *Die Mauer schwankt* as a whole: "I mounted resistance, though I hid the fact" (Ich leistete Widerstand, wenn auch versteckt; *GW*, 1:164). Of course, there are textual arguments for and against Koeppen's claim, but of more direct relevance in our context is the question of how Koeppen was able to square this partial view of his life in the Third Reich with the rather equivocal attitudes and changing political stances that he held, as is clear from the documentary evidence. Similar questions emerge as a result of the re-presentation of the Littner text. In the 1991 foreword, Koeppen indicates that the story of the horrendous suffering of a Jew in the ghetto of Zbaraz is based simply on a few notes given to him by the real Littner, which he turned into a piece of creative writing of his own, a *Roman*, as Suhrkamp chose to call it. If this is the case, one must ask, how can the Littner character in the book absolve the Germans of collective guilt, as he does in its conclusion? Recent research has revealed that Koeppen was in fact supplied with a complete manuscript by the real Littner, and that his creative input was far more modest (see the fascinating articles by Reinhard Zachau and Roland Ulrich). How then could he possibly claim to be speaking on behalf of Jewish victims of Nazi persecution?

In conclusion, the answers to these questions lie not, I would argue, in any dishonesty on Koeppen's part (although he clearly lied in the foreword to *Jakob Littner*), but in the way in which he came to perceive his own career in the Third Reich. To make a cautious return to his evidence in interview, it seems that he came to regard himself as a victim of National Socialism, as a result of the disruption to his career that the regime brought about. His interview with Volker Wehdeking in 1988 is entitled *The Burden of the Lost Years* (Die Last der verlorenen Jahre), for example, and here, as elsewhere, he regards the Hitler dictatorship as a period in which his own career suffered serious setbacks. In conversation with Alfred and Monika Estermann in the *Frankfurter Allgemeine Zeitung* in 1982, he comments: "If the Weimar Republic had lasted longer and cultural life had continued to flourish in Berlin and the whole of Germany as it had done before Hitler, then I imagine that for a time at least I probably would have brought out a new novel every other year, I think I would have made a name for myself and things would have gone very well" (see Estermann). This confident assessment stands in obvious contrast to his view of his own position immediately after World War II: "I published a few things in the *Neue Zeitung* too, but things were going badly for me again and I really did not know how I would survive. I had enough to do just keeping myself alive,... was disappointed by the postwar period" (Estermann). Even more striking is his assertion in an interview in 1983 with the *Süddeutsche Zeitung* that anyone who had lived through the Third Reich as he had should be regarded as its victim: "National Socialism, its period of rule and the war were a gigantic machine of destruction and even those who survived carry with them, invisibly burnt into the skin the blue stamp of the victim" (interview with Jurczyk).

Further evidence to suggest that Koeppen regards his own life story in the same light as someone like Littner's comes through a number of remarkably close parallels between Littner's story as retold by Koeppen and Koeppen's autobiography as recounted in interview. There are obvious points of contact, for example, between the account of his time in Feldafing, as he describes it, and his reworking of Littner's story: both men find themselves forced to live out the regime in a cellar, entirely dependent for survival on the good will of an avaricious Nazi. One might even note that Littner and his companion Janina also survive on "the daily potatoes" (*JL*, 132).

What emerges from a comparison of Wolfgang Koeppen's own statements about his life under National Socialism with documentary evidence and his published works is a complex picture of a young writer attempting to make progress in his chosen career under inauspicious circumstances. His desire to make a living from writing and to avoid military conscription meant that, despite the *Abscheu* (disgust) that apparently drove him to Holland, he was prepared to engage in a certain degree of compromise with the regime, if only in manipulating official organizations to his own ends. In the early 1940s, he was able to make a reasonable living from such involvement. His pragmatic position toward the regime is full of contradictions that are glossed over in interview, in favor of incidents that tend to stress an oppositional attitude to National Socialism. Koeppen is, of course, not alone in this. What makes his case so interesting, however, is that this unbalanced version of events acquired such a powerful dynamic in the postwar years that he felt comfortable using it as a publishing tool on more than one occasion and comparing his own experience to that of more obvious victims of Hitler's tyranny. The controversy surrounding *Jakob Littner's Notes from Underground* continues; it typifies the moral minefield into which Koeppen repeatedly strayed after 1945 by presenting his period of *inner emigration* before 1945 in such a partial way.

Notes

1. Koeppen was, of course, not alone in hoping that the new regime would promote modernist art. Gottfried Benn, whose work had a considerable influence on Koeppen, is perhaps the most notable literary figure to find his hopes for the new regime dashed.
2. It seems likely that Hans Georg Brenner was Koeppen's close contact with Universitas. Koeppen states that it was Brenner who persuaded him to allow the republication of *Die Mauer schwankt* under the title *Die Pflicht*. See the "*Schreibheft*-Gespräch" in Oehlenschläger, 381.
3. From the description of the plot of *Advent* submitted to the Reichsschrifttumskammer, it seems likely that "Am frühen Morgen" is all that remains of the missing novel.

Works Cited

Estermann, Alfred, and Monika Estermann. "Ich bin ein Mensch ohne Lebensplan. Gespräch mit Wolfgang Koeppen." *Frankfurter Allgemeine Zeitung*, 13 November 1982.
Durzak, Manfred. "Überleben im Dritten Reich: Gespräch mit Wolfgang Koeppen." *Die Neue Rundschau* 95, no. 4 (1984): 88–98.
Jurczyk, Günter. "Zeit des Steppenwolfs. Junge Schriftsteller im Dritten Reich – ein Gespräch mit Wolfgang Koeppen." *Süddeutsche Zeitung*, 19 May 1983.
Koeppen, Wolfgang. "Blutauffrischung bei der Ufa." *Berliner Börsen-Courier*, 10 January 1933.

————. "Die große Befreiung: Zu einer Einführung in den Zen-Buddhismus." *Das Reich* 9 (March 1941).

————. "Die Hausbibliothek unserer Zeit." *Berliner Börsen-Courier*, 24 October 1933, 6.

————. "Emil Gött." *Berliner Börsen-Courier*, 13 April 1933.

————. "*Frankreich, die Geißel der Welt* von Wolfgang Ertel-Bretihaupt." *Berliner Börsen-Courier*, 29 June 1932.

————. "Jugend, die nie schreiben würde: Zwei Bücher zwischen Reportage und Sozial-pädagogik." *Berliner Börsen-Courier*, 20 October 1932.

————. *Gesammelte Werke in sechs Bänden* [*GW* in text]. Ed. Marcel Reich-Ranicki. Frankfurt am Main: Suhrkamp, 1990.

————. *Jakob Littners Aufzeichnungen aus einem Erdloch* [*JL* in text]. Orig. Munich: Kluger, 1948; Frankfurt am Main: Jüdischer Verlag, 1992.

Oehlenschläger, Eckart, ed. *Wolfgang Koeppen.* Frankfurt: Suhrkamp, 1987.

Prümm, Karl, and Erhart Schütz. "'Die Situation war schizophren': *Schreibheft*-Gespräch mit Wolfgang Koeppen über seinen Roman *Die Mauer schwankt.*" *Schreibheft* 21 (1983). [Reprinted in *Wolfgang Koeppen*, ed. Eckart Oehlenschläger, 370–82. Frankfurt: Suhrkamp, 1987.]

Sauter, Josef-Hermann. "Gespräch mit Wolfgang Koeppen." *Sinn und Form* 3 (May/June 1986): 543–55.

Ulrich, Roland. "Vom Report zum Roman. Zur Textwelt von Wofang Koeppens Roman *Jakob Littners Aufzeichnungen aus einem Erdloch.*" *Colloquia Germanica* 32, no. 2 (1999): 135–50.

Wehdeking, Volker. "Die Last der verlorenen Jahre: Gespräch mit Wolfgang Koeppen." *Literatur in Bayern* 11 (1988): 47–51.

Zachau, Reinhard. "Das Originalmanuskript zu Wolfgang Koeppens *Jakob Littners Aufzeich-nungen aus einem Erdloch.*" *Colloquia Germanica* 32, no. 2 (1999): 115–33.

Chapter 17

ELISABETH LANGGÄSSER AND THE QUESTION OF *INNER EMIGRATION*

Cathy S. Gelbin

During the brief period of her postwar fame, Elisabeth Langgässer (1899–1950) was not considered only one of the greatest contemporary German women writers, but also one of the few non-exiled authors untainted by Nazism. Due to her paternal Jewish descent, Langgässer had been expelled from the Nazi writers' organization in 1936 and placed under a complete writing ban until the defeat of the Third Reich. Her postwar reception as a nonfascist writer resulted from her racial persecution under the Nazis and from the publication of her novel *The Indelible Seal* (Das unauslöschliche Siegel, 1946). Thomas Mann, for example, considered this novel one of the few noteworthy works of contemporary literature in Germany and "a masterpiece of internalized prose" (ein Meisterwerk verinnerlichter Prosa).[1]

As one of the representatives of *inner emigration* and as an international icon of the democratic traditions of German literature during and after the Nazi period, Langgässer spoke in 1947 at the first all-German writers' conference on the role of the "writer under the Hitler dictatorship" ("Schriftsteller," 26–30). Her talk was surprisingly critical of writers who had remained in Germany between 1933 and 1945. She particularly condemned those authors who had cultivated inwardness (*Innerlichkeit*) without making reference to the horrors of the Nazi period. According to Langgässer, however, even the most accomplished writers had sometimes employed esoteric evasions in their writings or taken an ambiguous stance toward the Nazi rulers. As she put it, "esotericism and the juggling of meanings" (die Esoterik und das Spiel mit sechserlei Bällen: "Schriftsteller," 28) had been the two major dangers to the moral integrity of writers during that time. Furthermore, Langgässer hinted at the possibility that her own role as a writer during the Third Reich had been far more complicated than now publicly perceived. As she remarked, she did not know offhand

> what gives me the right to tell you anything.... I really have nothing, absolutely nothing, I could boast of.... [26] It was a great, undeserved mercy when God stayed a mortal's arm; put more soberly, when He ordained that due to unqualifiable forebears ... she was thrown out of the so-called Reichsschrifttumskammer in time, before she could be tempted to make pacts with that rabble. (30)

As a matter of fact, Langgässer's political attitudes and her literary works before her expulsion from the Reichsschrifttumskammer (The Reich Chamber of Letters, or RSK) in 1936 were marked by at least a certain extent of co-optation toward Nazism.[2] In 1933, Langgässer even voted for Hitler (see Fliedl). Like other national-conservative intellectuals of her time, she initially had greeted the Nazis' rise to power as a long-necessary national transformation of Germany while, however, disagreeing with the Nazis' excessive persecution of their political and "racial" enemies. In 1933, for example, when Langgässer's own Jewish background was not yet publicly known, she co-published an anthology of women's poetry, *Heart to Harbor* (Herz zum Hafen, with Ina Seidel), which included the works of Jewish poets Gertrud Kolmar and Else Lasker-Schüler. At the same time, some of her successive publications prior to her definition as a "first degree Jewish *Mischling* [person of mixed race]" in 1936 must be viewed as a deliberate, yet—due to her particular biographical constellation— necessarily ambivalent attempt to situate herself within the Nazis' literary canon. In the following pages, I will sketch out some aspects of Langgässer's complex endeavor to configure political, racial, and gender identity in the context of writing during the Third Reich.

Langgässer's 1934 article "Paths of Women's Poetry Today" (Wege heutiger Frauendichtung) in the periodical *Die literarische Welt* again included Kolmar and Lasker-Schüler in the concept of German history and culture as symbolized in the image of "the forest of history, the German forest " (2). According to Langgässer, German women's poetry was fueled by a mystical knowledge of the origins of human cultural history; its path ran "wherever the earth is very old and mindful of her graves, where alien cultures have fought and fused, where the landscape and its currents are more important than human community, or else where they lay down the community's formation" (2). German literature accordingly arose from a soil that embodied the clashing and merging of different cultures, and that in turn shaped the nature of the human community living on it today. Langgässer's universalizing concept of German women's writing thus portrayed cultural and ethnic "hybridity" as an essential source of German culture—a move that allowed her to explicitly include Jewish writers, and thus implicitly also herself, in the body of a German national literature. While Langgässer sought to undermine racial notions of the German *Volk*, her article at the same time conformed to some of the ideological postulates and aesthetic particularities common to Nazi literature. According to Ernst Loewy, Nazi literature is commonly marked by an amalgamation of mystical considerations and sacralizing metaphors with regard to topics such as maternity, the German nation and military images, as well as an overuse of imperatives, superlatives, and florid adjectives. Of course, these characteristics are also found in, for example, the much older genre of *Heimatdichtung* (regional poetry), but they became markers of Nazi art in their specific amalgamation with Nazi ideology.[3]

Langgässer's article sometimes employs similar metaphors, stylistic elements, and expressions, such as the term *Umbruch* (revolution, sudden change) for the Nazis' rise to power without, however, ever making explicit reference to the Nazi movement or even to Hitler. But the reference is, of course, clear, since the term was popularly employed in precisely that ideological context. As Victor Klemperer observed, the Nazis had adopted this already existing expression (literally translated as "plowing up") "because it fits so well the notion of blood and soil, the glorification of soil, of being firmly rooted" (*LTI*, 204). Langgässer's strategy of referring to the new language and ideology in a both affirmative and aberrant way becomes especially apparent in her reading of Ina Seidel and her simultaneous rejection of the genre of *Blut-und-Boden* literature. According to Langgässer, Seidel's representation of the holy mother and her child in her 1930 epic *The Longed-for Child* (Das Wunschkind) provided a parable to German national resurrection and the sacrificial myth, images also mobilized in the military rhetoric of Nazi Germany. In Langgässer's words, this child becomes

> the spiritual child of a yearning which, rushing into being from the mighty oppositions of the German character, builds in that child's body the historical dream of the perfect human being; and now it is Germany herself that becomes its mother, shapes her son, raises him up above herself until he is more powerful than she and, as the final gift of life, is permitted to wish for death, to take his sacrificial death with him into the blossoming ring of the desires. (2)

This passage portrays the conjunction of sacralizing metaphors with maternal and military images, which I have already mentioned among the essential features of Nazi literature.[4]

At the same time, Langgässer's article explicitly rejected *Blut-und-Boden* ideology as inauthentic and instead conceived women's poetry as outside these politically enforced modes of writing:

> To watch over this "inner space" of destiny's determination is given to woman by the biological conditions of her nature, and while the thinking man—and precisely the heroic, lonely and isolated man that is the poet—is coerced and enslaved by the slogan "blood and soil" as Heracles was enslaved to the distaffs of Omphale, the woman may express it, she alone; she may invoke the earth, her mother, and this invocation is ... far removed from the so-called poetry of the soil, which neither knows the soil nor is true poetry. (2)

Although this passage constructs women's poetry as a space of resistance against *Blut-und-Boden* literature as an inauthentic mode of writing, Langgässer by no means escapes its construction of a mystical relationship between poetic language and the soil. She continues to construct a supposedly authentic relationship to literature as biologically determined, even though her version privileges gender over race. Furthermore, her already cited assertion that German women's writing arose from a soil imprinted by cultural "hybridity" precisely repeats the presupposition of a correlation between the soil, character, and writing in *Blut-und-Boden* literature. The uneasy relationship between Langgässer's criticism of certain modes of Nazi literature and her simultaneous adoption of some its motifs may indicate her own ambivalent stance toward the Third Reich, i.e., her willingness to adapt to the new political system, her partial agreement with aspects of its ideology, and her simultaneous attempt to subvert some of its premises.

Langgässer repeated this ambiguous textual strategy and many of its themes in her first major novel, *The passage through the marsh* (Der gang durch das ried), written between 1933 and 1935, and published in early 1936. Like Langgässer's previously cited article, this novel must be read as an example of both Langgässer's conformist attitudes as a writer during the Third Reich, and the simultaneously existing subversive dimension of her writing in this political context. On the one hand, the novel utilizes nationalistic and racist concepts of Blacks, Arabs, Jews, and the French as Germans' absolute Others. On the other hand, the text destabilizes the notion of a homogenous cultural and racial heritage of Germany and instead represents the German population itself as inherently mixed. Owing to the mixed nature of this population, a local community of right-wing farmers glorifying the slain Nazi hero Schlageter accepts into its ranks descendants of such illegitimate relationships with foreigners, including Jews. Langgässer's representation of the integration of Jean-Marie Aladin, the protagonist whose name already inscribes his racial and cultural "hybridity," into a proto-fascist concept of the German *Volk* can be read as symbolic of Langgässer's own attempt to reinscribe herself as a "German" writer.

Mainly for aesthetic, not ideological reasons, the novel was forthrightly condemned by Nazi critics, among other reasons for its vivid representations of "decadent" sexuality and its undermining of traditional narrative forms.[5] The noncapitalized nouns in the book title *The passage through the marsh* already signified the work's link to modernism. Other influences of modernist writing can be found in the novel's undermining and fracturing of a coherent narrative voice; instead, for example, the text casts representations of a repulsive physicality in a kaleidoscope of seemingly incoherent, yet nonetheless extremely vivid images.[6] At the same time, the modernist allusions in *The passage through the marsh* do not necessarily signify a radical critique of the Nazis' cultural politics. Instead, they constitute an attempt by Langgässer to fuse aesthetic elements of literary modernism with certain aspects of the current ideology. This maneuver was not automatically doomed to fail; in fact the Nazi state embraced some modernist writers, such as Arnolt Bronnen, Gottfried Benn, and Hanns Johst (the latter even became president of the RSK, at least temporarily).

Drawing on Walter Benjamin's postulate of a convergence between futurism and the ritualization of art in Italian fascist propaganda, some recent critics have challenged the postwar idealization of modernism as inherently resistant to fascist ideologies. This view drew largely on the Nazis' purge of *entartete Kunst* (degenerate art) from German culture. In contrast, Andrew Hewitt traces the ways in which the self-construction of the two movements as both the high point and termination of historical sequentiality converge in Italian fascist modernism and its images of totalized fragmentation (Hewitt, 7). With regard to the German context, Peter Ulrich Hein observes similar ideological linkages. Hein sees certain parallels between Nazi ideology and the avant-garde's investment with cultural and spiritual purification, including its tendency to posit artistic abstraction as a totalizing order. Superfluous "material," including humans, became dispensable. Furthermore, German avant-garde artists and writers, such as Emil Nolde and Stefan George, conveyed notions of *völkisch* (racial) thinking in their search for a particular German essence in art (see Hein).

Although Langgässer cannot be considered an avant-garde writer, she certainly figures among the "classical modernists," i.e., those authors who still participated in the aesthetic innovations of the avant-garde while realigning themselves with bourgeois high culture (Hesse, 486). For the period of National Socialism, Hans Dieter Schäfer has developed the inverted term of modern classicism. The term connotes those authors of *inner emigration* who attempted to remain connected to modernism despite the growing hostility of the Nazi regime (Schäfer, 11). However, Schäfer's assertion that these writers constituted a supposedly nonfascist, i.e., neutral sphere leaves one uneasy in its foregrounding of aesthetic commonalities alongside its near neglecting of positional and political differences among the writers. The notion of nonfascist writing includes "racially" persecuted authors, such as Gertrud Kolmar and Elisabeth Langgässer, as well as those who had ingratiated themselves at least temporarily, such as Gottfried Benn and Ernst Jünger. At the same time, Schäfer's reliance on aesthetic criteria has certain benefits in pointing out the aesthetic similarities among exiled, "nonfascist" and Nazi writers, who commonly drew on premodern styles and ahistorical subjects. If, then, a particular Nazi aesthetic becomes increasingly difficult to pinpoint, the question of a supposedly nonfascist realm of artistic production also becomes far blurrier than Schäfer admits.

Even Langgässer's follow-up novel *The Indelible Seal*, widely considered a "masterwork of inner emigration" (PWF) exemplifies the flawed nature of the concepts discussed above. In May 1936, only two months after the publication of *The passage through the marsh*, Langgässer had been expelled from the RSK due to her inability to prove her "non-Aryan" descent. Although this resulted in a complete publication ban within Nazi Germany, she secretly worked on *The Indelible Seal* between 1936 and 1945. Although the novel allegorizes National Socialism as satanic and destructive, its evocation of the French as miscegenational and morally corrupt reflects certain strands of Nazi ideology.[7]

The baptized German Jew Lazarus Belfontaine, with his inherently rationalistic and split nature, stands symbolic of Langgässer's construction of France as the epitome of the enlightenment and miscegenation. This conflation between the Jew and France is already signified by Belfontaine's French last name and his move from Germany to the French town of Senlis in the course of the novel. As in *The passage through the marsh*, Langgässer casts France as a racial melting pot enhancing sexually transgressive relationships of all kinds—from morbid fantasies of incest to lesbian liaisons and cross-racial relationships between French women and North African soldiers. Belfontaine's adoption of a black child, a French-Moroccan "bastard" (*Siegel*, 488), exemplifies the allegedly hybrid nature of both the Jew and France as his host nation.

Langgässer's representation of the novel's French protagonists as physically, sexually, and mentally corrupt seems to parallel racial theorists' construction of "hybridity" as inherently degenerate. "The rabbit-like brain bent on fornication of the distinguished gentleman Mr. Bonmarché" (Das hasenhaft geile Gehirn des ehrenwerten Herrn Bonmarché, 427), for example, betrays the quintessential French bourgeoisie's alleged obsession with abnormal sexuality. Through his sadistic nature and small mustache, together with his trembling hands, the external signifier of his degenerate nature, Bonmarché ultimately appears as a caricature of Hitler. At the same time, the text implicitly links Bonmarché with images of the Jew and the hybrid, since the Frenchman Bonmarché and the Jew Belfontaine, his future son-in-law, function as interchangeable characters through their trade and through their split nature. While Belfontaine is a store owner in the first book of *Das unauslöschliche Siegel*, Bonmarché's last name points to the Bon Marché department store in Paris. Both protagonists are thus associated with the essentially Jewish trait of dealing and a preoccupation with material values. Like Belfontaine, Bonmarché's mode of discourse is marked by the split mentality attributed to the racial hybrid. These themes illustrate Langgässer's construction of France as the epitome of Jewish rationalism and racial hybridity. In the novel, fascism ultimately arises from this constellation.

Having been forced into silence during the Nazi period on "racial" grounds rather than retreating voluntarily, Langgässer came to represent an idealized image of writers of *inner emigration*, thus lending herself to the frequent self-construction of postwar Germans as Nazi victims.[8] However, the combination of Langgässer's status as a racially persecuted writer and her own literary employment of ideologically tainted metaphors raises questions about the accuracy of terms such as *inner emigration* or nonfascist writing, which tend normally to suppress or euphemize the different shades, circumstances, and conditions of co-optation (a practice that this volume now reverses). Individual case studies accounting for the particular circumstances of authors and their literary productions will now contribute to a more complex understanding of the cultural sphere as a microcosm of German society during the Nazi period.

Notes

1. PWF, "Gespräch mit Thomas Mann," *Heute* 87 (June 1949): 10, 24.
2. As early as 1955, Karl Storz pointed out that "the young Elisabeth Langgässer shared in what in Germany or perhaps in all of Europe at the end of the Twenties, was, as the saying goes, in the air." According to Storz, even the most sensitive and aware writers turned "at that time from form to the formlessness, away from people toward terrifying demons.... The secret underground attracted not only poets, but rather had already become the object of other research as a mystical vision." For a further analysis of Elisabeth Langgässer's writings, see Cathy Gelbin, *An Indelible Seal: Race, Hybridity and Identity in Elisabeth Langgässer's Writings*. Essen: Blaue Eule, 2001.
3. Loewy outlines (111–14) the basic themes of "Blood-and-Soil" literature as follows: (1) the restoration of the German people through return to the soil; (2) the centrality of the peasantry in the struggle against modernity; (3) the linking of notions of blood, tradition, and geography in constructions of German nationhood; (4) the focus on racial purity; (5) the essentializing of woman with regard to her reproductive functions, and her simultaneous asexualization.
4. This passage also portrays the ways in which Langgässer's general employment of religiously infused images of maternity partially converged with the focus on maternity and fertility in Nazi ideology.
5. As one critic wrote: "This seems to us to be something very, very different, not to say, completely contrary to what we would call a great German novel.... Everything is dull, gray, it smells of rot, it swells with urges.... Many traits, no image, no clear line [of plot], no [clear] thought, no true ethos, there is nothing in this book that would offer anything to the reader's own inner self, that would speak to him" (*Bücherkunde Bayreuth*, September 1936).
6. For an overview of aspects of modernist writing, see for example Rolf Grimmiger.
7. In *Mein Kampf*, Hitler characterized the Rhineland takeover by Germany's "mortal enemy" as a scheme of "the cool calculating Jew who would use this means of introducing a process of bastardization in the very centre of the European Continent" (508). According to him, France itself had already become an "African state on European soil" (525). The French thus represented a "threatening menace to the existence of the white race in Europe, because they are bound up with the Jewish campaign for world domination" (508).
8. As Schäfer himself points out, some authors, such as Günter Eich, left works actually published during the Nazi period unmentioned after the war in order to detract from the actual ambiguity of their situation. See Schäfer, 87f.

Works Cited

Benjamin, Walter. *Das Kunstwerk im Zeitalter seiner technischen Reproduzierbarkeit*. Frankfurt am Main: Suhrkamp, 1963.

Gelbin, Cathy. *An Indelible Seal: Race, Hybridity and Identity in Elisabeth Langgässer's Writings*. Essen: Blaue Eule, 2001.

Grimmiger, Rolf. "Aufstand der Dinge und der Schreibweisen über Literatur und Kultur der Moderne." In *Literarische Moderne. Europäische Literatur im 19. und 20. Jahrhundert*, ed. Rolf Grimmiger et al., 12–40. Reinbek bei Hamburg: rororo, 1995.

Fliedl, Konstanze. *Zeitroman und Heilsgeschichte. Elisabeth Langgässers Märkische Argonautenfahrt*. Vienna: Wilhelm Braumüller, 1986.

Hein, Peter Ulrich. *Die Brücke ins Geisterreich. Künstlerische Avantgarde zwischen Kulturkritik und Faschismus*. Reinbek bei Hamburg: rororo, 1992.

———. "Völkische und konservative Motive im Denken der künstlerischen Avantgarde. Von der Jahrhundertwende zum Dritten Reich." In *Kunst und Faschismus. Politik und Ästhetik im Nationalsozialismus und im italienischen Faschismus. Gesprächsforum Mathildenhöhe 3*, ed. Klaus Wolbert, 63–103. Darmstadt: Institut Mathildenhöhe, 1995.

Hesse, Eva. "Die literarische Reproduktion des Führerprinzips." In *Literarische Moderne. Europäische Literatur im 19. und 20. Jahrhundert*, ed. Rolf Grimmiger et al. Reinbek bei Hamburg: rororo, 1995.

Hewitt, Andrew. *Fascist Modernism. Aesthetics, Politics, and the Avant-Garde*. Stanford: Stanford University Press, 1993.

Hitler, Adolf. *Mein Kampf*. Unexpurgated edition. London: Blackett Ltd., 1939.

Klemperer, Victor. *LTI. Notizbuch eines Philologen*. Leipzig: Reclam, 1985.

Langgässer, Elisabeth. *Das unauslöschliche Siegel*. Munich: dtv, 1989.

———. *Der gang durch das ried*. Leipzig: Jakob Hegner, 1936.

———. "Schriftsteller unter der Hitler-Diktatur." In *Der erste gesamtdeutsche Schriftstellerkongreß nach dem Zweiten Weltkrieg im Ostsektor Berlins vom 4. bis 8. Oktober 1947*, ed. Waltraud Wende-Hohenberger, 26–30. Frankfurt am Main: Peter Lang, 1988.

———. "Wege heutiger Frauendichtung." *Die literarische Welt. Unabhängiges Organ für das deutsche Schrifttum* 20/21 (19 May 1933): 1–2.

Langgässer, Elisabeth, and Ina Seidel, eds. *Herz zum Hafen. Frauengedichte der Gegenwart*. Leipzig: R. Voigtländers, 1933.

Loewy, Ernst. *Literatur unterm Hakenkreuz. Das Dritte Reich und seine Dichtung*. Frankfurt am Main: Fischer Taschenbuch, 1987.

PWF. "Gespräch mit Thomas Mann." *Heute* 87 (June 1949).

Schäfer, Hans Dieter. *Am Rande der Nacht. Moderne Klassik im Dritten Reich*. Berlin: Ullstein Verlag, 1984.

Storz, Gerhard. "Elisabeth Langgässer." In *Christliche Dichtung der Gegenwart. Beiträge zur Europäischen Literatur*, ed. Hermann Friedemann and Otto Mann, 359–74. Heidelberg: n.p., 1955.

Wende-Hohenberger, Waltraud, ed. *Der erste gesamtdeutsche Schriftstellerkongreß nach dem Zweiten Weltkrieg im Ostsektor Berlins vom 4. bis 8. Oktober 1947*. Frankfurt am Main: Peter Lang, 1988.

Chapter 18

THE UNSETTLING HISTORY OF GERMAN HISTORIANS IN THE THIRD REICH

Amy R. Sims

In the years after 1945, German historians did not spend much time analyzing the role of their profession during the Hitler period. In September 1998, Johannes Fried, president of the German Historical Association, publicly challenged historians for their reticence. At the opening meeting of the German *Historikertag* at Frankfurt University, Fried wanted to know: "Why has the German historical profession kept quiet about the National Socialist past of its leading representatives? Why have we lived with sanitized biographies?" (Fried, 873). At issue was newly uncovered evidence of some leading historians' complicity with the Nazi regime, and their stubborn silence about it during their subsequent academic careers in the 1960s and 1970s. The time had finally come for historians to engage in critical self-examination of their own discipline.

The role of German historians under National Socialism generated hot debate at the historians' 1998 conference. At the heart of the controversy was the contention by a group of younger historians, including Götz Aly, Peter Schöttler, and Michael Fahlbusch, that many historians freely and willingly served the Hitler regime. Specifically implicated were three leading figures and past presidents of the German Historical Association, Theodor Schieder, Werner Conze, and Karl-Dietrich Erdmann, who were accused of helping to prepare for resettlement and the Holocaust with their research on the East (Jarausch). When Hans Mommsen joined the discussion to question the "Faustian pact between research on the East and National Socialism" (Hettling, 43), many present felt that "the ice was conclusively broken" (Ullrich, 53) and the way opened for broader discussions about different degrees of collaboration on the part of nationalist historians. While Hans Mommsen asserted that "the radical nationalism of many historians was identical with National Socialism," his twin brother

Wolfgang disagreed and countered that "both were parallel projects that ultimately diverged" (Jarausch, 5). The Mommsens' argument tested the generally held view that because most prominent historians were nationalist conservatives, they already agreed with Nazi foreign policy aims and therefore did not require further Nazification. Secure in their ardent nationalism, they remained unhampered by the Nazis and untainted by Nazism. A conclusive answer did not emerge, and the debate about historians' role during the Nazi period continues (see Hohls and Jarausch), as the general picture gains clarification from new research. That research into a recent generation of historians also raises questions about prior generations.

If some of the most prominent members of the profession during the 1960s and 1970s had been more seriously associated with National Socialism than previously thought, then what about the older generation of historians who were the leading figures when Hitler came to power? Did they recognize the dangers of National Socialism as it emerged? Is the traditional view that many historians entered into *inner emigration* still valid?

The total *Gleichschaltung* or "ideological coordination" of the German historical profession by November 1935 made clear to historians the dangers of National Socialism. Some had been naïve about the nature of Nazism at the outset. Friedrich Meinecke, for example, wrote in a newspaper article ("Von Schleicher zu Hitler," *Berliner Volkszeitung*, 22 February 1933) one month after the Nazis achieved power: "We wish to confront these men at the voting table without hate, for they are our national comrades and we hate only the destructive ideas with which they are intoxicated." That Meinecke pinned his hopes on voting the Nazis out of office, demonstrates the vast misperception of Nazism in university circles. The corruption of their own discipline, however, was something that historians could not fail to understand.

The most prominent historians of the Weimar period, Hermann Oncken, Friedrich Meinecke, and Walter Goetz, were dismissed from their teaching and editorial positions, and attacked in newspaper articles. The two most important organs of the profession, the Historische Reichskommission (the preeminent research institute), and the *Historische Zeitschrift* (the leading journal) were transformed into Nazified institutions, while the remaining historical institutes of the various states were saturated with politically reliable historians. To oversee all research, a new institute named Reichsinstitut für Geschichte des neuen Deutschlands was created and placed under the leadership of the Nazi zealot Walter Frank. The universities were purged (in April 1933) of professors who were non-Aryan or politically unreliable, including over sixty historians. They were transformed from independent entities into compliant institutions organized around the *Führer* principle. All new appointments were made on the basis of political reliability, and those who retained their old positions found it in their best interest to exhibit enthusiasm for the new order. The regime did not just violate academic freedom, but rather eliminated it.

Books were burned, scholars attacked, and concentration camps created to serve as warnings to all of the regime's abrogation of freedom of speech.

German historians had a long tradition of interest in the state, in foreign policy, and in power politics. In a country without a well-developed discipline of political science, historians of the modern period were the most astute observers of state policy. They were the German academicians most likely to understand the nature of Nazism and to recognize its dangers. Gerhard Ritter made precisely this critical point to fellow historian Wilhelm Mommsen in a letter of 21 December 1945: "We modern historians must have known, and for us there is no alibi" (Schwabe and Reichardt, 406). Moreover, unlike scholars in most other disciplines, historians had a public role. They were the scholars to whom the general public traditionally turned for interpretation of political events. It was quite customary, then as now, for historians to write articles for the major newspapers in which they gave the historical context for major political and cultural events. They wielded additional public influence because virtually all prominent historians were university professors. Many students and scholars have attested to the deep-seated reverence and esteem accorded to university professors in Germany.[1] Because of their prestigious position, they were well positioned to influence the population at large, in addition to their own students. When they published their books and articles, lectured outside of the university, or taught their classes, they became commentators on and participants in the general political culture, i.e., in public life. They could legitimize and fortify government actions, if they so desired, by placing the full weight of history behind them. Without necessarily accepting the Nazi demand for an ideological scholarship, they could further the regime's goals with their interpretations of history. They could help shape the general public attitude by the way they interpreted contemporary political events. For these reasons, the historians' collective response to the Nazi regime was crucial; just as their criticism might have encouraged resistance, their passivity in fact facilitated Nazi aims and actions.

Even though historians in general understood the dangers of Nazism, they nonetheless rejected emigration. Although the tradition of exile was an established one among scholars, virtually all of the tenured, Aryan professors of history remained in Germany. Those who were defined by Nazi law as Jewish, whether or not they were practicing Jews, faced danger and emigrated; Germany lost the talents of a generation of gifted historians such as Hans Baron, Fritz Epstein, Felix Gilbert, Felix Hirsch, Ernst Kantorowicz, Hans Kohn, Hans Rosenberg, Hans Rothfels, Dietrich Gerhard, Georg Hallgarten, Gerhard Masur, and Ernst Simon. Hajo Holborn, whose wife was Jewish, also left Germany and went on to become one of America's most prominent historians at Yale University. A 1936 list published by the *Notgemeinschaft Deutscher Wissenschaftler im Ausland* indicated that fifty-three historians had been displaced. But for most members of the historical profession, the question of emigration did not crystallize into an ethical dilemma. They pragmatically analyzed their possibility of being able to pursue an uninterrupted career in Germany and decided to stay. Even renowned historians who could have obtained positions elsewhere, such as Hermann Oncken, Gerhard Ritter, and Friedrich Meinecke, remained in Germany. The vast majority of refugee historians were young lecturers who were directly affected by the Civil Service Law of 7 April 1933, or the Nuremberg Racial Laws of 1935. They had not chosen to leave the country in principled protest against Nazism, but were forced to flee from imminent danger. As Georg Iggers has pointed out, this was not an emigration of activists or resisters (102).

Those historians remaining behind had to decide, however, to what extent they should cooperate with the regime in order to remain active in their profession. The most ordinary questions about historical method (hitherto considered strictly an academic matter) became ethical dilemmas as the Nazis demanded total cooperation with the regime in all scholarly matters. The various reactions of historians to Nazi demands for cooperation reflected intensely personal decisions. The options they had were few; one was, of course, collaboration with the Nazis by joining Walter Frank's institute, adapting scholarship to Nazi ideology, and contributing articles and reviews to the *Historische Zeitschrift* and the other Nazified journals of the profession.[2] Many conservative, nationalist historians took this approach. Karl Alexander von Müller had joined the Nazi party before 1933, and other (younger) historians now joined as well, including Adolf Rein, Willy Hoppe, and Walter Recke. Also, Richard Fester, Fritz Hartung, Heinrich von Srbik, Erich Marcks, Arnold Oskar Meyer, Karl Alexander von Müller, Otto Westphal, and Albert Brackmann all became members of Frank's Nazi history institute.[3] Karl Alexander von Müller, Erich Marcks, and Heinrich von Srbik agreed to become editors of the *Historische Zeitschrift* after Meinecke's forced resignation. Von Müller promised that "the marching steps of the soldiers and the masses have not only seeped into each scholar's study, our work itself, in its innermost essence, has swung into march with the times" ("Zum Geleit," 1). Those historians who became Nazi sympathizers readily adapted their works to Nazi ideology. Fritz Hartung wrote two books on the Nazi themes of *Volk* and *Reich*; Richard Fester tackled several Nazi favorites—the Versailles Peace Treaty, the glories of the German army, and "The Jewish Question." Erich Marcks and K. A. von Müller wrote numerous books on the *Volk*, the *Reich*, Bismarck, and Germany's rivalry with England for world power.

Outspoken dissent and active resistance was another option open to historians, but this path was taken by almost no one. Among the prominent historians, Gerhard Ritter's name alone appears in connection with the resistance movement. Active in the Protestant Confessional Church, Ritter was implicated in the 20 July 1944 plot against Hitler's life, and the Gestapo imprisoned him in November 1944. Prior to his arrest, Ritter had published several works in which he courageously interpreted the lives of both Martin Luther and Frederick the Great[4] (both of whom the Nazis admired as heroic Germans) in direct contradiction to the official Nazi line. In another bold work written during World War II (*Machtstaat und Utopie*, 1940), Ritter emphasized the essential differences between the Prussian concept of the rational use of power and Hitler's willful and immoral use of it.

Only a very few historians chose even milder forms of resistance. Hermann Oncken, for example, wrote books and articles about revolutionary leaders that skillfully depicted their leadership so as to resemble Hitler's actions, and then he severely criticized them.[5] Historical parallels were effective forms of resistance because the Nazi professors and students who served as spies and informers lacked scholarly talent and sophistication. Chosen for their political reliability rather than their intelligence, many simply did not comprehend the subtleties of this form of resistance (see Ritter, "The German Professor in the Third Reich," 1946). Unfortunately for Oncken, his parallels were too clearly drawn in his lecture to the German Philosophical Society, "Revisions of History in Revolutionary Epochs" (Wandlungen des Geschichtsbildes in Revolutionären Epochen), as was his warning about the destructive effects of the Nazi attempt to rewrite the past.[6] It led, ultimately, to his forced "retirement" from his university position.

Gerhard Ritter's and Hermann Oncken's mild resistance in their publications and lectures were notable exceptions: the historical profession as a whole did not resist the Nazi regime. The majority of the prominent non-Nazi historians saw their most viable alternative as keeping quiet about political issues and attempting to minimize the extent of their own complicity with the regime. As long as they avoided controversy and outspoken dissent, and as long as they did not collaborate with the Nazis on any of the federally funded historical commissions, they were free to pursue their scholarly interests relatively unhampered. The fact that many of the most prominent historians were in their sixties and approaching retirement age also undoubtedly affected their decisions. As university professors, historians were also *Staatsbeamte* (civil servants), because German universities were owned and operated by the state. Professors held the rank of Councilor of State, third class (Ringer, 36) and were guaranteed life tenure with full pension rights. When they retired (*emeritiert*), they received full salary and retained the right to give seminars at the university, and to use its facilities. For the many historians approaching retirement, or already retired, avoiding action that would jeopardize their pensions was an important consideration.[7] They were familiar with the case of their colleague, Walter Goetz, who was dismissed from his position at Leipzig because of political unreliability. Although Aryan, he had represented the unacceptably liberal German Democratic Party (DDP) in the Reichstag for eight years, and had supported the Weimar Republic in numerous articles for the liberal journal *Hilfe*. Eager to discredit such a prominent republican sympathizer, the Nazis took away all his emeritus rights, including his pension, when they forced him to retire in 1933.[8]

The safest choice for many historians, therefore, was to go into *inner emigration* and eschew politics while immersing oneself in scholarship.

The goal was to write apolitical, esoteric monographs on subjects of limited popular appeal, about which the Nazis had no interest. Friedrich Meinecke's *Die Entstehung des Historismus* (1936) was probably the best known example. The American ambassador to Germany, William Dodd, confirmed in his diary that *inner emigration* was, in fact, the chosen precaution some historians took to veil other attitudes. He wrote, "eminent German professors of the old order come to me in all confidence to tell me facts and attitudes that would cause their deaths if known" (Dodd, 127). Two years later he wrote, "they all submit, though they are much opposed to what they have to submit to" (358).

Historians such as Goetz and Meinecke, who were forced from their positions, lived quiet lives of scholarly research. At times, they even described their lives as pleasant. Goetz lived in a garden home near his sons in Munich. "Naturally I had to withdraw from all political activity," he wrote. But this did not trouble him, he said, because "I could devote myself entirely to the work, which I had left unfinished in the earlier periods of my life" (Goetz, 79). Meinecke too mentioned in several letters that he led a pleasant existence in another world. To his friend Srbik, Meinecke maintained that he had no hard feelings about his forced resignation. "I am not embittered, of that you can be sure," Meinecke assured him (letter of 8 November 1935; *Briefwechsel*, 164). He insisted that he was calm and content because he lived "as the most private of private men." Meinecke said that he enjoyed living that way "because the greatest comfort of scholarly production is not yet denied me." As long as Meinecke could write and conduct research, life was bearable. His scholarship was his greatest interest, and he wrote, "I would go on working even if I couldn't any longer find a publisher."

The Nazi period, in fact, was a fairly prolific one for both Goetz and Meinecke. Goetz completed the *Propyläen Weltgeschichte* and published several other books, including two volumes of essays on Italy during the Middle Ages: *Italien im Mittelalter* (1942) and *Geschichte der deutschen Dante-Gesellschaft* (1940), as well as his 1944 book *Die Entstehung der Italienischen Kommunen im Frühen Mittelalter*. Meinecke published one of his most influential books, *Die Entstehung des Historismus*, in 1936, as well as no fewer than five other books, fifteen articles, and two book reviews during this twelve-year period.[9] The inwardness of research and reflection coincided almost naturally, it seemed, even when imposed by threats of persecution, with these scholars' inveterate inclinations and professional training. The distinction, however, between choice and lack of choice remained, particularly with regard to their topics of research.

Other historians used their enforced retreat from political and administrative concerns to spend more time on their scholarship as well. Franz Schnabel, compelled in 1936 to resign from his position in Karlsruhe at the age of forty-nine, was in the middle of his career and, unlike Meinecke, Oncken, and Goetz, was not yet eligible for a pension. Unable to teach or give public lectures, Schnabel, too, continued his scholarly career by focusing on his publications. In 1933 and 1937, he completed two volumes in his four-volume series *German History in the Nineteenth Century* (Deutsche Geschichte im 19. Jahrhundert), in addition to his volume *Recent History* (Geschichte der neuesten Zeit, 1935). These works contained no concessions to the ideology of the Third Reich, and tried to emphasize earlier, more humane values. In his foreword to volume two of his *Deutsche Geschichte* (1933), Schnabel wrote, "The genuine values of the past can be temporarily eclipsed but never extinguished" (Gall, 162). His 1937 volume of *German History* so pointedly avoided Nazi ideology that the Nazis considered banning it. But the report on the book concluded that it was "neither National Socialist nor a direct attack on the Nazi world view." Because it was held to be "solid and well known to the scholarly public," the report read, "if it were banned then we must also ban a thousand other books."[10] In a newspaper article written shortly after the fall of France ("Zwischen den Zeiten," 22 June 1941), Schnabel evoked the image of the humanism of a gentler period. In his 1942 essay, "Humanism and Bourgeois Thought" (Humanismus und Bürgerliches Denken), Schnabel wistfully stressed the central role that humanism had played in German thought, even during periods of intense nationalism such as the uprisings against Napoleon (182). Pensive, longing for more humanistic periods, and firm in his resolve to avoid any political concessions, Schnabel's work during the Nazi period could still be read and respected after 1945.

Publication was the last aspect of their former public roles still open to historians. Non Nazi historians were not permitted to give public lectures or to represent Germany in any official capacity. According to Nazi interpretation, this included lecturing abroad. The archives give ample evidence of the regime's attempts to keep its historians safely at home. The Education Ministry refused permission to Hermann Oncken to give three lectures in Holland (Heiber, 238), for example. Similarly, Ritter declined invitations to lecture in Rome and Basel because the ministry denied him permission ("The German Professor," 244), and Otto Hoetzsch could not accept an invitation to lecture at the University of Chicago because the Foreign Office did not approve of his proposed topic (Dodd, 298). With their activities carefully circumscribed by the regime, historians immersed themselves in their publications. They were able to write outside of a Nazi ideological rubric and still have their works published if they avoided topics on the Modern Period. As Gerhard Ritter has demonstrated, it was impossible for historians of the modern period to write objective history about World War I, the Treaty of Versailles, the Weimar period, or the origins of Hitler's Reich because they were confined by Nazi "official historical legends" ("The German Professor," 251). Similarly, Nazi ideology transformed history into official myth regarding several favorite historical figures. Charlemagne became idealized as the Saxon slaughterer (*Sachsen-schlächter*) (Werner, 39); Luther was transformed from a religious leader into a zealous nationalist who forged the national consciousness of the German nation (see Ritter, "Die Fälschung des deutschen Geschichtsbildes im Hitlerreich"); and Bismarck was revered as Hitler's predecessor and model in nation building, in whom the origins of Hitler's Reich could be found (see Frank, "Zunft und Nation"). The case of Wilhelm Mommsen, father of Hans and Wolfgang, illustrates the issues involved in research on favored Nazi topics.

Mommsen, full professor in Marburg, exercised more caution than Meinecke, Goetz, and the other "retired" professors because he had his position to protect. At age forty-three (in 1935), he had many more years left in his university career before he became eligible for a pension. Mommsen's 1935 book *Political History from Bismarck to the Present* (Politische Geschichte von Bismarck bis zur Gegenwart), therefore, made several concessions to Nazism. He acknowledged that the new period required a new view of history, he compared Hitler's accession to power to the English Glorious Revolution of 1688 because both had been peaceful, and he lauded Hitler's accomplishments in reducing unemployment and reawakening the *Volk* community (5–8). Mommsen had been a known democrat. He supported the Weimar republic and had founded a democratic student association during his own university years. His book, therefore, pleased no one. On the one hand, Frank and his fellow Nazis scorned it as opportunistic and claimed that the author only made small concessions because he had been surprised by the success of the Nazi revolution in the midst of writing (Heiber, 764); on the other hand, non-Nazi historians found his accommodations to Nazism distasteful. Felix Hirsch, in exile in the United States, wrote, "it is painful to observe how Mommsen, a former democrat, tries to coordinate himself without convincing anybody" (Hirsch, 7). Mommsen's book illustrates the dilemmas of historians who wished to continue publishing in Nazi Germany, and helps to explain why historians sought refuge in esoteric, apolitical topics for their publications. During the denazification process in the postwar period, Mommsen wrote to Gerhard Ritter asking for assistance in maintaining his university position. But Ritter replied (letter to W. Mommsen of 21 December 1945; in Schwabe and Reichardt, 406) that "to vouch for you in any way that you wrote a brave book, or that you had in any way a particularly brave position, that I cannot do with good will," adding that he personally would have ceased publishing rather than betray his conscience.

The point has frequently been made that historians' devotion to their work, and the large number of books they published during this period constituted an *inner emigration* or a flight in a psychological rather than a physical sense. This is not entirely true for a number of the prominent non-Nazi historians. For example, Otto Hintze's bad health and failing eyesight made it impossible for him to do sustained research. Hermann Oncken was so depressed over his fall from power and esteem, and over being shunned by former colleagues, that his health suffered.[11] He no longer had patience for scholarly work, and published few books after his dismissal from his teaching position. His 1937 volume *The Security of India* (Die Sicherheit Indiens) was a cautious and uncontroversial treatment of British foreign policy.

But for a good part of the time after his dismissal, Oncken sat at his desk in deep depression, doing nothing. Gerhard Ritter, far from immersing himself in his work as a refuge, used his many publications to counter official party interpretations of events and historical heroes.

Nonetheless, *inner emigration* was the reality for a group of non-Nazi historians in the years prior to the outbreak of World War II, and the most prominent case was that of Friedrich Meinecke. Throughout the Nazi period, Meinecke mentioned in his personal letters that he occupied himself with a far more pleasant world than the one raging around him. He sought to escape from the Third Reich by turning inward toward a timeless, aesthetic realm where he felt freer and more peaceful. In a poignant 1938 letter discussing the problems of the period, Meinecke wrote that he did have one small comfort: "For two hours every day I read Greek" (letter to Gustav Mayer of 25 February 1938; *Briefwechsel*, 178). In 1942 Meinecke characterized his research as his own "small island of the most private joy in the middle of the storming ocean of world events" (393).

None of the fifteen articles or six books that Meinecke published during the Nazi period contained compromises with Nazism; three of them were clear rejections of the ideological scholarship and the new view of history that Walter Frank and his Nazi institute continually demanded.[12] Meinecke's most important work was his book on the *Origins of Historicism*. In his introduction, Meinecke wrote that this book was an account of historicism written in an affirmative attitude, and he considered historicism to be "one of the greatest intellectual revolutions ever experienced in Western thought" (*Entstehung*, 1). Meinecke's firm statement of belief in historicism was a direct defense of the basic principles of historical scholarship that Walter Frank had attacked. In 1934, even before the Nazis had completed the *Gleichschaltung* of the historical profession, Frank unveiled the Nazi view of history. Entitled "Fighting Scholarship" (Kämpfende Wissenschaft), the lecture was the first warning of what the Nazis expected from historians. As the most basic component of the Nazi view of history, Frank stressed the role of the historian as a political activist. He made Heinrich von Treitschke into an ideal type of the politically engaged scholar, and demanded that historians emulate his example. He approvingly quoted Treitschke's belief that "great political passion is a precious treasure," and instructed historians to write history suitable for a great nation (5). Just as Treitschke had served the cause of Germany in his time, so must historians serve the ideas of the National Socialist Revolution. History must not be impartial, but didactic and ideological because its main purpose was to validate the Nazi world view. In stressing the political, activist nature of history, Frank repudiated the most basic assumption of historicism (traditional historians' method and view of history). Historicists firmly believed that history must be nonpartisan. What traditional historians regarded as their noblest ideal, the search for pure, apolitical truth, elicited Frank's greatest scorn. He called historicists men of "petty cleverness" because their work lacked a central idea, or what

Frank called an "Archimedean point." Frank believed that "without a governing belief, historical writing is only pure pedantry" (18). According to Frank, historians' ultimate responsibility was not to objective truth, but to the National Socialist Revolution.

In his *Origins of Historicism*, Meinecke reaffirmed the idea of pure objective history. He dared not criticize Frank directly, but did so circuitously. He criticized enlightenment thinkers for placing history in service to their worldview (which was of course precisely what Frank demanded). Meinecke warned that "historical truth is not something given from the start which has only to be freed from certain accidental veils" (*Entstehung*, 85). This ruled out writing history from the starting point of Frank's basic ideological precepts of racial struggle, Aryan supremacy, and the *Führer* principle. Meinecke also rejected the view that Jews must be depicted only in terms of their harmful influence, when he boldly praised Jacob Bernays as an "important Jewish philologist" while extolling his work on Gibbon (235). Meinecke even attached as an appendix his memorial address to the Prussian Academy on Leopold von Ranke (23 January 1936), in which Meinecke acclaims Ranke as the exemplar and great culmination of the German historicist tradition. His praise for Ranke constituted a fundamental statement in support of historicism because Ranke and Treitschke had been made into two opposing ideal types: the objective scholar and the political soldier. Their names became slogans for worldviews. Yet as firmly as Meinecke himself embraced the non-Nazi view, he had no desire to become embroiled in controversy. While he chose to keep his own work free from Nazi ideology, he did not assume a public role in opposition. At the end of the appendix, he advised that "it is proper on this occasion to avoid dispute" and to "withdraw into the peace of pure contemplation" (599).

Nonetheless, the book elicited sharp Nazi criticism in the form of an article by Erich Seeberg in the 1938 issue of the *Historische Zeitschrift*. Entitled "The Rise of Historicism" (Zur Entstehung des Historismus), Seeberg's article repeated many of Walter Frank's criticisms about the inadequacy of the traditional *Geschichtsbild* for the present period. He claimed that Meinecke had not succeeded in overcoming relativism or the anarchy of values, or finding an Archimedean point. He argued that the new Germany needed a new history. But Meinecke avoided confrontation by retreating into his inner world of timeless, aesthetic concerns. To Gustav Mayer he wrote, "Let us both hold ourselves to that which is called eternal" (25 February 1938; *Briefwechsel*, 178), while later, he ended a letter to W. Steffens with Max Planck's quotation, "the metaphysical world is the truly real world" (7 November 1941; *Briefwechsel*, 200). In his private thought and correspondence, and in his publications, Meinecke focused on gentler values and nonideological concerns. He devoted his energy to two essays in 1937 on eighteenth-century topics ("Schiller and the Concept of Individualism" [Schiller und der Individualitätsgedanke] and "Classicism, Romanticism and Historical Thought in the Eighteenth Century" [Klassizismus, Romantizismus, und Historisches Denken im 18 Jahrhundert]), because he believed that the eighteenth century, in contrast to his present period, was an age "which united basically and practically, great thought and great, rich and harmonious beauty" (*Schaffender Spiegel*, 143).

The German army's stunning early victories in World War II changed the nature of Meinecke's private thought and correspondence (although in his public role as author, he continued to show evidence of his *inner emigration*). Historians such as Meinecke had opposed Nazi war actions in scope and method, but not in principle. They feared Hitler as an adventurer whose ruthlessness would bring Germany to ruin. Yet Hitler appeared to be achieving only success. The goal of a powerful, unified Germany encompassing all German nationals was accomplished for the first time in German history. "Imperceptibly one feels oneself landed on shores which one earlier had considered completely impassable" Meinecke wrote in 1942 (letter to Goetz of 1 October 1942; *Briefwechsel*, 206). About the atrocities of the war, Meinecke remained silent. He did not criticize the war in the east, but exulted over the victories in the west. Although Walter Frank publicly defined the war as a battle against the pernicious influence of world Jewry (in his "Deutsche Wissenschaft im Kampf gegen das Weltjudentum"), Meinecke continued to view the war in traditional, power-political, or military terms. Each victory brought him closer to acquiescence to Nazism, and he finally ended his confused musings with the admission to his friend Srbik: "[Y]ou see that I am ready to readjust my ideas on many things, but not all, and above all not in the innermost. But one must always learn more and distinguish the peripheral from the central" (letter to Srbik of 8 July 1940; *Briefwechsel*, 193). He also wrote to Kaehler of his willingness to adjust his views, and in 1943, as the worst atrocities in the east were becoming known, Meinecke wrote to Goetz: "I would have no objections to the merging of certain elements of National Socialist ideology, provided only that the golden threads of the German spirit come into acceptance" (18 May 1943; *Briefwechsel*, 216). Yet at the same time that he envisioned a possible, constructive future for Nazism in Germany, he continued to resist the Nazi view of history. In his 1942 collection of essays, *Aphorismen und Skizzen zur Geschichte*, he openly disapproved of the Nazis' revision of history and accused them of encroaching on true historical scholarship when they attempted to elevate *Volkstum* and race in history as the firm guiding principles of historical understanding. In the midst of the raging world war, Meinecke reminded historians not to surrender objectivity in the face of political pressures: "The historian must attempt to define his own course in the winds and streams of the period, no matter how strongly he may feel their power and his own dependence on them" (*Aphorismen*, 114). In another, more private way, Meinecke appeared distant from the reality of the war. In response to his friend Wilhelm Steffens, who had written to inquire about Meinecke's safety during air raids, Meinecke wrote about the psychology and sociology of air raid shelters as a possible research topic for a book on the history of this war (12 November 1940; *Briefwechsel*, 196).

While most prominent, non-Nazi historians sought to minimize the impact of the war on their personal lives, and to continue with their scholarly interests, Gerhard Ritter wrestled with significant questions about the legitimate use of power that were raised by the war. In his *Machtstaat und Utopie* (1940), he presented both a general discussion of power politics and a critical commentary on the war surrounding him. Under the guise of a philosophical discussion of the ideas of Machiavelli and More, Ritter severely criticized Hitler for his abuse of power. "The fog of success of the ruler blinds him and drives him on beyond the boundaries of the humanly bearable" (33), Ritter wrote. Even Machiavelli feared, hated, and condemned tyranny and arbitrary actions, Ritter declared. "He knew that nations and princes were secure from excesses only if laws created barriers" (44). The themes in *Machtstaat und Utopie* clarify Ritter's reaction to the war and provide both a significant exception to historians' attitudes (it was the most critical book on the war written by a prominent historian during the course of the war) and a vision of other possibilities, if historians had so chosen. Ritter showed that traditional statecraft and the legitimate use of power as practiced by Frederick the Great and Bismarck had nothing in common with Hitler's designs on Europe. As openly as he dared in 1940, Ritter drew parallels between Machiavelli and Hitler in order to goad his readers with his own moral indignation. "Somewhere a point is reached when political and moral repugnance become stronger than natural cowardice," he wrote boldly. Even Machiavelli realized this, "which was why he warned his prince not to cause the rest of the world to resist him as would happen if he indulged in unlimited wars of conquest" (33).

In his publicly expressed concern about Hitler's abuse of power, however, Ritter remained alone. When news of German defeats in Russia reached historians, they intensified their support because defeat frightened them more than continued Nazi success. As the tide of war turned against Germany, Meinecke did not find relief in the thought that Hitler soon would be gone, but worried about the future of Germany and became severely depressed. In March 1945, on the day after American forces crossed over the Rhine, making German defeat an absolute certainty, Meinecke showed a despair deeper and blacker than he had ever experienced at any time during the Hitler regime. "Living and dying both have certain ambivalences," he wrote. "One lets oneself prefer to remain living, but dying and being carried away from all the terrible things that are coming to Germany is also good and acceptable" (letter to Kaehler of 8 March 1945: *Briefwechsel*, 492).

Oncken and Meinecke both evacuated their homes during the heavy bombing raids over Berlin, and they spent the last days of the war in close proximity at relatives' homes in Göttingen. There they commiserated over Germany's defeat. Shortly before his death (on 28 December 1945), Oncken confided sadly to Meinecke, "I no longer understand this period" (Heiber, 214). As if they literally gave up, many historians died of natural causes at the end of the war: Erich Brandenburg, Karl Brandi, Otto Hoetsch, and

Hermann Oncken all died within a short time of each other (Gilbert, 58). Walter Frank committed suicide in May 1945. Many of the young Nazi historians who had turned history into ideology were killed in the war. One exception was Karl Alexander von Müller, who, despite Ritter's forceful protests, was eventually restored to his teaching position at the University of Munich and lived out his life as an integral member of the German historical profession until his death in 1964, although he did have to resign from his positions as editor of the *Historische Zeitschrift* and president of the Bavarian Academy.[13]

Meinecke lived to the age of 91 and became rector of the newly constructed Free University of Berlin, erected by the Allies to replace the old university that fell under Soviet domination. In his old age, he tried mightily to understand what had befallen him and Germany in the Third Reich. In his book *The German Catastrophe* (Die Deutsche Katastrophe, 1946), Meinecke again affirmed the aesthetic and timeless qualities in the German past, not from the point of view of *inner emigration*, but from the perspective of maintaining a certain and firm belief in the value of the best aspects of German culture and history. Like the other non-Nazi historians who sought refuge in *inner emigration*, Meinecke believed that it had allowed him to safeguard the autonomy and objectivity of his historical writing. He believed that by refusing active cooperation in scholarly matters, he had effectively distanced himself from the Nazi regime. But his attitude during World War II, typical of his colleagues, demonstrated that historians could maintain a posture of dissent toward the Nazi view of history even while applauding the military successes of the Nazi regime. Their earlier passivity during the *Gleichschaltung* indicated that they could tolerate Nazi encroachment on political and administrative affairs even though they abhorred the regime's intrusion into scholarly matters. The scholarly objectivity permitted by their *inner emigration* differed from political opposition or dissent, although many chose to view them as the same. In their publications, non-Nazi historians found the strength to remain guardians of the purity of their scholarship. But in their public role as the commentators on and participants in general political culture, they could not provide the guidance and leadership the German public needed to retain their civilized values and their humanity.

Notes

1. Ralf Dahrendorf discovered in 1951 that this reverence still existed: *Society and Democracy in Germany*, 81.
2. The discussion of historians' options is drawn from my article "Intellectuals in Crisis: Historians under Hitler."
3. "Liste der Mitglieder des Reichsinstituts für Geschichte des neuen Deutschlands" (Membership List of the Reich's Institute for the History of the New Germany). Geheimes

Staatsarchiv Preussischer Kulturbesitz/Secret Central Archive. Archivstrasse 12–14, 14195 Berlin/Dahlem.

4. Gerhard Ritter, *"Luther und der deutsche Geist." Die Weltwirkung der Reformation.* Ritter claims in this essay, originally published in 1941, that far from being a revolutionary nationalist, Luther was a modest, godly man who was nothing other than a truth seeker. In *Friedrich der Grosse: Ein historisches Profil* (1936), Ritter stresses Frederick's caution rather than his boldness, his rationality rather than his will, and his sense of the natural limits of power.

5. Hermann Oncken, *Cromwell: Vier Essays über die Führung einer Nation* (Berlin: Grotesche Verlag, 1935) and *"Wandlungen des Geschichsbildes in Revolutionären Epochen" Historische Zeitschrift* 189 (1959) are the two best examples.

6. In 1937, Felix Hirsch wrote: "[T]his speech was Oncken's swan-song, as some of us felt at the very moment" (3).

7. Albert Brackmann, Erich Brandenburg, Karl Brandi, Walter Goetz, Karl Hampe, Gustav Mayer, Hermann Oncken, and Adalbert Wahl were all in their sixties when Hitler came to power. Johannes Ziekursch was almost sixty. Richard Fester, Otto Hintze, Paul Kehr, Erich Marcks, Friedrich Meinecke, and Konrad Bornhak were all in their seventies.

8. Helmut Heiber relates the story of Goetz's dismissal (181–82).

9. Friedrich Meinecke, *Staat und Personlichkeit* (Berlin, 1933); *Vom Geschichtlichen Sinn und vom Sinn der Geschichte* (Leipzig, 1939); *Preussisch-deutsche Gestalten und Probleme* (Leipzig, 1940); *Erlebtes* (Leipzig, 1941); *Aphorismen und Skizzen zur Geschichte* (Leipzig, 1942).

10. Unsigned letter to Party member Dr. Payr, 2 November 1939. *Institut für Zeitgeschichte, Archiv.* MA/10 microfilm.

11. Oncken's son, Onno Oncken, to author, fall 1975, New York City.

12. Friedrich Meinecke, *Die Entstehung des Historismus* (1936); idem, *Vom Geschichtlichen Sinn und vom Sinn der Geschichte* (1939); idem, *Aphorismen und Skizzen zur Geschichte* (1942).

13. Von Müller was a full professor of history at the University of Munich and became emeritus in 1956. The topics of his post-1945 published works changed significantly as he assiduously avoided modern topics or political considerations. They included a two-volume memoir that excluded the period after 1919—*Mars und Venus: Erinnerungen 1914–1919* (1954), and *Aus dem Garten der Vergangenheit: Erinnerungen 1882–1914* (1958)—as well as a light *Landtagesbuch, Unterm Weissblauen Himmel.*

Works Cited

Dahrendorf, Ralf. *Society and Democracy in Germany.* New York: Doubleday, 1969.

Dodd, William. *Ambassador Dodd's Diary 1933–1938.* Ed. William Dodd, Jr. New York: Harcourt Brace, 1941.

Faulenbach, Bernd. "Die deutschen Historiker in der Emigration." In *Geschichtswissenschaft in Deutschland,* ed. Bernd Faulenbach. Munich: Beck, 1974.

Fried, Johannes. "Eröffnungsrede zum 42. Deutschen Historikertag." *Zeitschrift für Geschichtswissenschaft* 46 (1998): 869–74.

Frank, Walter. "Deutsche Wissenschaft im Kampf gegen das Weltjudentum." *Münchner Neueste Nachrichten,* 13 January 1939.

———. *Kämpfende Wissenschaft.* Hamburg: Hanseatische Verlagsanstalt, 1934.

———. "Zunft und Nation." *Historische Zeitschrift* 153, no. 1 (1936): 6–23.

Gall, Lothar. "Franz Schnabel 1887–1966." In *Paths of Continuity: Central European Historiography from the 1930s to the 1950s,* ed. Hartmut Lehmann and James Van Horn Melton, 155–65. Washington, D.C.: Cambridge Press, 1994.

Gilbert, Felix. "German Historiography during the Second World War." *American Historical Review* 53, no. 1 (1947): 50–58.

Goetz, Walter. *Historiker in Meiner Zeit.* Cologne: Bohlau, 1957.

Heiber, Helmut. *Walter Frank und sein Reichsinstitut für Geschichte des neuen Deutschlands.* Stuttgart: Deutsche-Verlagsanstalt, 1966.

Hettling, Manfred. "Schweigen im Konsens." *Die Zeit* 31 (27 July 2000): 43.

Hirsch, Felix. "Recent Historical Writing in Germany." *Books Abroad* (1937): 3–7.

Hohls, Rüdiger, and Konrad Jarausch. *Versäumte Fragen: Deutsche Historiker im Schatten des Nationalsozialismus.* Stuttgart: Deutsche Verlags-Anstalt, 2000.

Iggers, Georg. "Die deutschen Historiker in der Emigration." In *Geschichtswissenschaft in Deutschland,* ed. Bernd Faulenbach, 97–111. Munich: Beck, 1974.

Jarausch, Konrad. "Unasked Questions: The Controversy About Nazi Collaboration Among German Historians." Ms. Evanston: n.p., 2000.

Meinecke, Friedrich. *Aphorismen und Skizzen zur Geschichte.* Leipzig: Koehler & Amelang, 1942.

———. *Ausgewählter Briefwechsel.* Ed. Ludwig Dehio and Peter Classen. Stuttgart: Koehler, 1962.

———. *Die Entstehung des Historismus. Werke.* Vol. 3. Munich: Oldenbourg, 1936.

———. *Klassizismus, Romantizismus, und Historisches Denken im 18 Jahrhundert.* Cambridge: Harvard Tercentary Publications, 1937.

———. *Preussisch-deutsche Gestalten und Probleme.* Leipzig: Koehler & Amelang, 1940.

———. *Schaffender Spiegel.* Stuttgart: Koehler, 1948.

———. "Schiller und der Individualitätsgedanke." *Wissenschaft und Zeitgeist* 8 (1937).

———. *Staat und Personlichkeit.* Berlin: E. S. Mittler & Sohn, 1933.

———. *Vom Geschichtlichen Sinn und vom Sinn der Geschichte.* Leipzig: Koehler & Amelang, 1939.

———. "Von Schleicher zu Hitler." *Berliner Volkszeitung* 89 (22 February 1933).

———. "Von der Krisis des Historismus." In Friedrich Meinecke, *Aphorismen und Skizzen zur Geschichte,* 114–26. Leipzig: Koehler & Amelang, 1942.

Mommsen, Wilhelm. *Politische Geschichte von Bismarck bis zur Gegenwart.* Frankfurt am Main: Moritz Diesterweg, 1935.

Müller, Karl Alexander von. *Mars und Venus: Erinnerungen, 1914–1919.* Stuttgart: Klipper, 1954.

———. *Unterm weissblauen Himmel.* Stuttgart: Klipper, 1952.

———. "Zum Geleit." *Historische Zeitschrift* 153, no. 1 (1936): 1–5.

Oncken, Hermann. *Cromwell: Vier Essays über die Führung einer Nation.* Berlin: Grotesche Verlag, 1935.

———. "Wandlungen des Geschichtsbildes in Revolutionären Epochen." *Historische Zeitschrift* 189, no. 1 (1959): 124–38.

Ringer, Fritz. *The Decline of the German Mandarins.* Cambridge: Harvard University Press, 1969.

Ritter, Gerhard. "Die Falschung des deutschen Geschichtsbildes im Hitlerreich." *Deutsche Rundschau* 70, no. 4 (1947): 11–20.

———. "Luther und der deutsche Geist." In Gerhard Ritter, *Die Weltwirkung der Reformation,* 66–80. Munich: Oldenbourg, 1959.

———. *Friedrich der Grosse: Ein Historisches Profil.* Leipzig: Verlag von Quelle & Meyer, 1936.

———. *Machtstaat und Utopie.* Munich: Oldenbourg, 1940.

———. "The German Professor in the Third Reich." *Review of Politics* 8, no. 2 (1946): 242–54.

Schnabel, Franz. "Humanismus und bürgerliches Denken." In *Abhandlungen und Vorträge 1914–1965,* ed. Heinrich Lutz, 174–83. Freiburg: Herder, 1970.

———. "Zwischen den Zeiten." *Stuttgarter Neues Tagblatt,* 22 June 1941.

Schwabe, Klaus, and Rolf Reichardt, eds. *Gerhard Ritter: Ein Politischer in seinen Briefen.* Boppard: Harald Boldt, 1984.

Seeberg, Erich. "Zur Entstehung des Historismus." *Historische Zeitschrift* 157 (1938): 241–66.

Sims, Amy R. "Intellectuals in Crisis: Historians Under Hitler." *Virginia Quarterly Review* 54, no. 2 (1978): 246–62.

Ullrich, Volker. "Späte Reue der Zunft." *Die Zeit* 39 (17 September 1998).

Werner, Karl, F. *Das NS Geschichtsbild und die deutsche Geschichtswissenschaft.* Stuttgart: Kohlhammer, 1967.

Chapter 19

STATE OF THE ART AS ART OF THE NAZI STATE

The Limits of Cinematic Resistance

David Bathrick

Much of what has been written about German cinema in the Third Reich has understandably concerned itself with questions revolving around the medium's relation to official Nazi policies between 1933 and 1945. Social historians dealing with its immediate impact as a tool of totalitarian persuasion have often narrowed in on what they perceived to be the overtly political propaganda value of certain films from that era. The Nazi youth films *Hitler Youth Quex* (Hitlerjunge Quex, 1934), *SA-Mann Brand* (1934), and *Hans Westmar* (1934); Leni Riefenstahl's spectacular tribute to Hitler and the Nazi Party in *Triumph of the Will* (Triumph des Willens, 1935); the antisemitic films *Jud Süß* (1940) and *The Eternal Jew* (Der ewige Jude, 1940); or the *Durchhaltefilme* (films encouraging viewers to struggle through the increasingly hard times) *Kolberg* (1945) and *The Great King* (Der große König, 1944) often served to mark Nazi cinema for posterity as a "systematic abuse of film's formative powers in the name of mass manipulation, state terror, and worldwide destruction" (Rentschler, 2).

While such an emphasis appropriately highlighted the extensive use of media by the Nazi regime to reshape the values and social imagination of the German people in the cause of war and ethnic genocide, its propaganda-driven methodological approach, together with its strong emphasis upon an ideological canon, led to some misunderstanding concerning the nature of Third Reich cinema in its entirety. Of the approximately 1,100 feature films produced between 1933 and 1945, 86 percent of them were not officially coded as political by the regime. In addition to melodramas and detective stories, almost half of all films made in Germany at this time were comedies and musicals, many of them similar in genre if not in quality to movies coming out of Hollywood during the same period. One should also mention that after the war a vast number of these were gradually cleared for showing in East and West Germany.

Since 1970, there has been a gradual "normalization" in the view of Third Reich cinema, fueled in part by its growing acceptance as a part of programming inside and outside of Germany. The word "normalization" should not be construed here to mean exculpation; nor do I suggest that there has been a shift toward ignoring the role that cinema played in the political and socio-economic life of Nazi Germany. On the contrary, the increased acknowledgment of Third Reich film as an ongoing source of entertainment has brought about intensified scholarly and critical efforts to understand the complex ways that the Nazi culture industry itself evolved in relation to cultural traditions and socio-economic contingencies both within and beyond the historical and geopolitical situation in which it was produced. Thus, normalization in this regard would mean historicization and contextualization in its broadest aesthetic and thematic sense.

The increased emphasis on entertainment comes in the wake of a growing interest among scholars in rethinking the question of Nazi cinema in light of the already extensive historical work that has been done on everyday life in the Third Reich.[1] One result of this focus on social life has been to demonstrate the similarity of cultural and industrial policies under Hitler to forms of modernization and mass culture in other advanced industrial societies of this period, in particular the United States. Among these are the building of the *Autobahnen*; the further development and application of the most modern industrial and technological design in the areas of machine technology, factory organization, and the communication industries; the continuation of the *Bauhaus* and art deco movements in home design and as a part of international expositions; and, particularly important for the film industry, the building in Germany of the same kind of consumer and leisure industries that were transforming the very self-understanding of class and national identities in Europe and the United States during that period.

Thus, the focus by historians on forms of modernization and the rhythms of everyday life does not diminish the gravity of Nazi criminality or relativize the horror of Auschwitz. Rather, these scholars argue that the programmatic effort to complete the project of modernity as the specific variant of a racist order enabled the Nazi elite to reconcile and thus facilitate the development of technological rationalization in the name of a spiritual and racial superiority. "By identifying technology with form, production, use value, creative (German or Aryan) labor, and German Romanticism, rather than with formlessness, circulation, exchange value, and parasitic (Jewish) finance capital," writes Jeffrey Herf in *Reactionary Modernism*, "they incorporated technology into the 'anti-capitalistic yearnings' that National Socialism exploited" (224). Moreover, their alignment of the war machine and what Goebbels called *stählerne Romantik* (steel-like romanticism) with the fulfillment of a "good" German modernization also made it possible to link policies of exterminationist antisemitism and the militaristic realization of a pan German Reich with the fulfillment of the *promesse de bonheur* (promise of happiness) lying at the heart of the advertising and entertainment industries. Nazi modernization, the argument went, can provide its citizens with everything: private, autonomous need-fulfillment within the larger security net of a contemporary, forward-looking, and ultimately triumphant *Volksgemeinschaft*.

What is significant about the evolution of film from the end of the Weimar period to the collapse of the Nazi regime in 1945 is above all the role it played in helping negotiate these seeming contradictions within the Nazi program. The formal, structural, aesthetic, and entertainment values of individual films were often just as important as their thematic and ideological content, if not more so. In regard to the question of propaganda, both Goebbels and Hitler became increasingly opposed to the overly heavy-handed methods that had been employed so successfully by the NSDAP in their rise to power in the 1920s. "Whatever you do, don't be boring," Goebbels told a group of directors from leading radio networks shortly after the Nazi takeover in 1933, "fantasy must employ all means in order to present our new message in a modern, contemporary, and interesting manner—interesting, instructive but not didactic" (Heiber, 1: 81–82, my translation). The increasing number of "non-political" films, many of which had little or no direct discursive or even visual reference to the contemporary political scene, emerged out of a belief that the politics of entertainment had as much to do with state-of-the-art production values, creative cinematography, and sophisticated performance as with any explicit programmatic message. This did not mean that conservative values were abandoned or that ideology was ever not of primary importance to the Nazis. What was recognized, however, was the extent to which the style of a film, beyond suggesting something about one's mastery of the medium, also expressed the power and vision of those who produced it and controlled its distribution.

Goebbels's emphasis upon professional craft as a not-so-hidden larger political message of Nazi cinema anticipated in interesting ways Marshall McLuhan's later mantra "the medium is the message." As a statement about films being made in the Third Reich, such an insight has as much to say about the nature of their intended impact upon German audiences as it does about how we should be viewing them in the contemporary context. Whereas purely ideological or propagandistic treatments have tended to isolate Third Reich cinema within a framework inscribed primarily along the overdetermined lines of its antisemitism and its glorification of nation, *Volk*, and war, more culturally and historically grounded readings have sought to establish specific parallels and continuities between these films and other cinematic and political traditions inside and outside Germany.[2] This extraction of Nazi cinema out of the realm of pure demonology and its insertion into the coordinates of mass and high culture as they have developed both nationally and as a part of a global economic system allows comparative analysis of influence and evaluation in terms of the often contradictory manner in which it appropriates and takes issue with these traditions within the Nazi context.

Such cultural contextualization can also shed light on the classical propaganda films in Nazi Germany, such as Hans Steinhoff's *Hitlerjunge Quex*, which premiered in 1933. While often viewed simply as another SA film from the early days of the Third Reich, a closer look at its cinematic technique reveals the ways in which it knowingly or unwittingly recycled topoi and stylistic devices from Weimar cinema. Such an analysis demonstrates, for example, not only that a film like *Hitlerjunge Quex* is indeed a reply to Slatan Dudow's 1932 film *Kuhle Wampe*, sponsored by the German Communist Party, but that the very similarity of these two party-initiated, prerevolutionary youth films—in political gesture and even at the level of cinematic style—mark this Nazi film itself as more a last breath of Weimar in transition than anything indigenous to the cinematic world of the Third Reich that began to emerge in 1936. Both *Quex* and *Kuhle Wampe* are agit-prop films that direct their appeal to youth at a time of massive unemployment, proffering very similar utopian solutions to the problems at hand. This, of course, did not prevent *Hitlerjunge Quex* from having an important function in the Third Reich, above all as a martyr film replayed often within the ghetto of youth culture; but it was also popular because of its star signature. The renowned formerly left-wing actor Heinrich George—who had starred as Franz Biberkopf in the first film version of *Berlin Alexanderplatz* in 1931 and who later became a director of the Schiller Theater and a major UFA luminary through 1945—literally performed in *Hitlerjunge Quex* his own conversion to Nazism: that turning point for him also marks metonymically a moment of transition and continuity for many others. Like other UFA stars such as Werner Krauss, Emil Jannings, Paul Wegener, Gustav Fröhlich, Sybille Schmidt, Fritz Rasp, Gustaf Gründgens, Jenny Jugo, Hans Albers, Lilian Harvey, and Lil Dagover, George's embodiment of the Weimar cinematic heritage in the Nazi present lent a cultural familiarity that helped create its own kind of cultural legitimation.

Thus, references to the cinematic German past in the Nazi present often came in the form of familiar faces as well as through thematic and stylistic citations from well known films of the 1920s. But as Linda Schulte-Sasse has demonstrated, these films drew from a reservoir of familiar "underlying literary paradigms" (11). Richard Rundell has recently given us a reading of Veit Harlan's 1943 film *Immensee* that marks it as typical of a vast number of literary films that seemingly have no underlying political function other than to provide entertainment at a time of crisis, in this case the defeat at Stalingrad and the increased bombing of major cities. The dazzling Afgacolor, the high quality of the production values, and the star allure of Kristina Söderbaum and Carl Raddatz, along with the sheltered world of Theodor Storm's novel, offered in their congruence little more than a nineteenth-century idyll (despite the film's twentieth-century setting) at a time of very contemporary industrial devastation.

In Helmut Käutner's extraordinary *Romanze in Moll* (1943) the literary antecedents multiply in direct relation to the film's distancing itself from the Guy de Maupassant story on which it was based. Recent studies have traced its myriad other formal borrowings from the eighteenth-century bourgeois tragedy, which came to serve as a kind of *Urschrift* for the Nazi imaginary in films such as Veit Harlan's *Jud Süß* and *Der große König*, or G. W. Pabst's *Komödianten* (1941), to considerably more realist and therefore less tragic epigonic incarnations of nineteenth-century literary sources. *Romanze in Moll*'s refusal to be reduced, finally, to any one generic code, be it a literary or cinematic one, is as steadfast as the film's refusal to be pressed into a single ideological mold. Indeed, its pessimism upset Goebbels, who, ever on the lookout for gloomy attitudes, initially banned it, though its fascination with death (particularly that of a sacrificing woman) reproduces a metaphysics that lies at the heart of the Nazi death wish. However, the film's Chinese box of enigmas, its unresolved contradictions, are indeed what explain the critical success of this aesthetically intricate work, so resistant to easy interpretation. Thus, its richness of formal complexity, laced with ambiguities, repudiates the simplistic, ideologically straightforward reading required by the Nazi propaganda machine.

Romanze in Moll's recalcitrance at a formal level has led some critics to mark its creator Helmut Käutner as one of a select group of Third Reich filmmakers who have managed, through the creation of the "art film," to carve out a kind a "space of reflection" within the Nazi film industry. Filmmakers such as Käutner, Wolfgang Staudte, Rolf Hansen, Werner Hochbaum, and Detlev Sierck are said to develop a critique of the cinematic world around them, less at a conceptual level by means of dialogue and screenplay than cinematically, through their subtle employment of lighting, sound, framing, and camera movement.

Two sequences from the beginning of the film illustrate well the aesthetic nuances of *Romanze in Moll*. This melodrama tells the story of Madeleine, the wife of a low-level French bureaucrat at the turn of the century, who falls in love with a successful composer named Michael. After a clandestine affair, the liaison is discovered by the husband's employer, who blackmails Madeleine into submitting to him sexually. Caught in a trap, she commits suicide. The opening sequence provides the frame for the story. The husband returns home from an evening of gambling to discover his wife lying in bed, having poisoned herself. Finding a pearl necklace whose extremely high value suggests that Madeleine could not have bought it herself, he is propelled into uncovering the story of her final days. The second sequence is a flashback to the seduction scene at the beginning of the romance. Madeleine has come to the house of Michael to end the relationship before it has really begun.

Several stylistic characteristics mark these clips as a variation from the classical Babelsberg style: the use of light and shadow to create dramatic and psychological inner space in contrast to the excessive idealization of UFA's front-lighting effects; the employment of a highly mobile camera, searching into the claustrophobic inner sanctum that makes up the world of Madeleine and her husband, or into Michael's darkened parlor, which will be the locus of their love affair; the haunting, continual presence of a dissonant music, indeed "in a minor key," which occupies the diegetic and nondiegetic sound space of this film; the long takes extending time to an unbearable degree and violating the shot-reverse-shot, cross-cutting efficiency of the Babelsberg system. The world of *Romanze in Moll* is interior, foreboding, hopeless. At a time in 1943 when the propaganda machine was calling for optimism, Käutner delivered a powerful melodrama, which turned out to be a popular hit.

Carl Frölich's 1936 film *Heimat*, starring the highest earning star in the Third Reich, Zarah Leander, is also marked by narrative and semiotic indeterminacy, qualities that appear as symptoms of the social forces the film seeks to negotiate and resolve. Leander's character remains trapped between the old and the new, as do the characters she plays in most of her Nazi films. On the one hand, the film offers the extraordinary allure of a modern, independent woman, blessed with a surfeit of love and feeling, who brings reinvigoration and the forbidden flavor of America into a tired, late nineteenth-century German provincial town. At the same time, in part with the help of the forbidden, the film offers the ultimate restabilization of that very "Heimat" as the precursor of a modern Germany capable of respecting and harmonizing seemingly contradictory social values.

In the war film *Die große Liebe*, one of the genuine box-office blockbusters of the period, the inevitable antinomies generated by the "Leander effect" work themselves out in the battle between love and duty, rather than between Germany and the allied nations, which in turn becomes the principle conflict of the film and, by extension, the times. As in earlier films of Leander's such as *Heimat, Zu neuen Ufern* (1937), and *La Habanera* (1937), this conflict entails the taming of a shrew whose desire for both love and career, home and the exotic Other, must be folded into the realities of what is presented as a viable compromise. And what *does* love have to do with it? Boguslaw Drewniak (239) and Robert Reimer ("Turning Inward," 214) are right in reminding us that love indeed plays a commanding role in many of the Reich's officially touted films, particularly, I would add, those that were made during the war. What love means, of course, is anybody's guess, or better perhaps anybody's projection. What love in fact quite often ends up *doing* is driving the narratives it motivates into closures that in some way seem inadequate to the utopian longings they initially release. This was as true for *Romanze in Moll* as it was for *Die große Liebe*.

Assessing the official attitudes of the Nazi leadership toward the United States is one further means by which to explore the question of cultural modernity and modernization in the Third Reich. On the one hand, the discourse of "Americanism" as it emerged in the Weimar Republic was often employed by the far right as synonymous with the metropolitan alienation and racial decadence against which a national culture must immunize itself; on the other hand, particularly subsequent to the *Machtergreifung* in

January of 1933, the Nazi elite show an increasing tendency, more obvious in their practice than in explicit policy statements, to identify the Party and its rule with an Americanism represented generally by glamour and consumerism, and specifically by its explicit acknowledgement of Hollywood production values and stylistic conventions as the norm. Actors from Babelsberg were given to modeling themselves on internationally renowned Hollywood stars: Marianne Hoppe aspired to be a local Barbara Stanwyck; Zarah Leander consciously and obviously imitated Marlene Dietrich, right down to the sultry voice; Brigitte Horney aimed to be known as the German Joan Crawford; and the little Hungarian Marika Rökk did everything in her power to emulate the dancing majesty of Eleanor Powell. Similarly, German directors of the time sought to copy the generic conventions of Hollywood, a cinematic system that continued to hold enormous attraction for German audiences of the period. Hans Dieter Schäfer has described the schizophrenic attitude of the Nazi powers in this regard as an example of *gespaltenes Bewußtsein* (split consciousness). Schäfer's term expresses the seemingly two-sided nature of a policy apparatus that officially denigrated the materialist, "Jewish" values of American culture while it simultaneously promoted them for its own benefit and self-aggrandizement.

A film like *Glückskinder* (Lucky Kids), the extremely successful German remake in 1936 of the American film *It Happened One Night*, successfully synthesizes its German values with its eager adoption of a Hollywood look (see Rentschler's particularly illuminating analysis, 99–122). Here there is nothing split or schizophrenic in the way the lightness and comedic *joie de vivre* of these seemingly nonphallic representatives of American maleness are narratively and visually made to line up with the paradigms of a now "modernized" but also Germanized form of the reconstructed male. "American" here means slapstick figures as happy-go-lucky, pre-oedipal anarchy; the German realignment thereof is a man who has to be taught how to desire. Karsten Witte labeled this kind of national recoding of certain stylistic conventions from American cinema in German films of the Third Reich *"eingedeutschter Amerikanismus"* (Americanism writ German) (Witte 1995, 102). Its unconscious claim, of course, is to have it both ways, which is really the dream of reactionary modernism from the very beginning. The ultimate message of *Glückskinder* remains necessarily ambiguous. What narrative closure could possibly obliterate the still resonating comic-book mayhem represented by those three momentarily prepubescent adults screaming in a wild frenzy of song and dance "I wish I were a chicken!"

Luis Trenker's lifelong dialogue with American culture offers another, somewhat inverted and considerably more ponderous version of "Americanism writ German." This time it is not the cinematography that bears the American side of the equation, but the mise en scène itself: in *Der verlorene Sohn* (1934), the city of Manhattan reflects the values of an alienated, debilitating form of modernity that stands in contrast to the pristine beauty of the South Tyrolean mountains, from whence the hero comes and to which he will return; in *Der Kaiser von Kalifornien* (1936) the American West represents the promise of nature itself, whose meaning hovers as a floating signifier somewhere between the dreamed-of *Lebensraum* and an alternative space in which to carve out a better life. One should be cautious here about reducing Trenker's work to one-sided critiques of ideology. The filmmaker's confusions about his relation to Hitler, Germany, fascism, and, finally, his own identity were often translated into double messages that resist the either/or of Nazi inscription. This double figuration makes Trenker a model figure for understanding the continuities from Weimar into the Third Reich (*Der Rebell*) and from the Third Reich into postwar Germany.

Wolfgang Liebeneiner, the filmmaker who in the 1950s went on to make the German version of *The Sound of Music*, is another paradigmatic transitional figure in this regard. Like Albert Speer, he was a successful bureaucrat, respected intellectual (Hitler anointed him a "professor" in 1943), and renowned artist (as actor and director). Having established himself with such successful films as *Versprich mir nichts* (1937), *Der Mustergatte* (1937), *Ich klage an* (1941), and his two Bismarck films, he was made head of production at UFA. Also like Speer, Liebeneiner seems to have survived his professional commitment to the Third Reich with his personal and artistic image unsullied, despite the fact that he worked closely with Goebbels on the euthanasia project and was deeply implicated in the day-to-day socioeconomic and aesthetic operations of the Reich's major studio. In fact, the continuity of Liebeneiner's aura as a sophisticated professional artist in its varying incarnations, in his work as well as in his person, demonstrate the necessity of careful historical inquiry to untangle the complicated threads of complicity and continuity in the afterlife of Nazi cinema within the Federal Republic.

Afterlife and continuity also mark Leni Riefenstahl's undiminished efforts to stage her life and work as outside or beyond the conventions of the Third Reich. In her biography, Riefenstahl claims outsider status by asserting that her success as the creator of the acclaimed documentaries *Triumph des Willens* and *Olympia* (1938) allowed her to withdraw from public life in the Third Reich into an *inner emigration* in the production of her film *Tiefland* (1954). But Riefenstahl also sees herself as outside political complicity on the basis of her role and vision as an artist. Ignoring the use to which this artistry was put or the impact that it had, Riefenstahl maintains her steadfast insistence on the transcendent powers of her own artistic professionalism as the redeeming final word (or image, as it were).

Like the Third Reich directors Veit Harlan, Wolfgang Liebeneiner, Helmut Käutner, Detlev Sierck, and Arthur Maria Rabenalt, Leni Riefenstahl has been recognized for her artistry, but, unlike them, she has never been able to escape her past, although not for lack of effort. Her unremitting postwar efforts to exonerate herself of the ever-recurring charges of Nazi collusion were rooted in a notion of art as well as *state of the art* that would seal the genius-artist off from the entanglements of a real-world society in which she or he will inevitably have to produce. Paradoxically, this is a notion that all these artists would share with none other than Joseph Goebbels himself. It is not that Goebbels was ultimately nonpolitical or nonideological; rather, he realized from early on the political potential of the state of the art itself and its considerable drawing power for talented and ambitious filmmakers eager to practice their trade.

Whether these cinematic artists ever used the means that this devil's pact provided them in order to produce subversive film or even a place of creative refuge is a question that has become increasingly debated in recent years. For most critics, the term *inner emigration* has seemed woefully inadequate, even as a metaphor, for grasping the institutional role of a film artist in the Third Reich. The suggestion of a withdrawal to the periphery of public life or even of self-imposed silence seems particularly inadequate for describing an industry where virtually all those involved in its operations found themselves firmly imbedded in the ruling system and its highly integrated or coordinated (*gleichgeschaltet*) cultural public sphere. Given such institutional constraints, one must be equally skeptical about any notion of conscious political resistance, subversion, or opposition to describe the activities of filmmakers during this period. Wolfgang Staudte tells of his attempts in the late 1930s and early 1940s to "hide" from military conscription by working within the interstices of the film industry, where at one point, in order to guarantee his survival, he was compelled to accept a minor role in Veit Harlan's antisemitic film *Jud Süß*.

Yet it was this same Wolfgang Staudte who as a director in 1943 made what has been considered by many to be one of the classic alternative films of the period, *Acrobat schö-ö-ö-n*.[3] I use the term "alternative" film to designate a small body of cinematic work within Nazi Germany, which on the basis of its textual richness and conscious or unconscious ignoring of the prevailing aesthetic and even thematic norms, lent itself to alternative readings. The late Karsten Witte characterized the work of just such a select group of filmmakers (Käutner, Hochbaum, Sierck, and Carl Junghans) as belonging to an "aesthetic opposition":

> Films of the aesthetic opposition are characterized by an absence of violence, a lack of visual grandiosity, a dearth of ideological impact, and a failure of ethereal obeisance to the System.... Their focus is not on the "Grand Totality" [das Große Ganze], but rather the traces of destruction that the "Grand Totality" has left in its wake. They peer into the everyday, gather up the shards and splice together in fragmented fashion a physical reality, which because of their fixation on mere content has long since been absent from the official films. (1980, 113–14)

Significantly, in Witte's formulation, that opposition is defined in terms of "absence" or "lack," not on the basis of explicitly critical articulation; it entails one's conscious or unconscious refusal to participate in a cinematic discourse.

For Witte, the directorial career of Helmut Käutner fits the norms of an "aesthetic opposition." The first such norm had to do with one's institutional relation to the system as a whole. Although a prominent member of the Nazi film industry, Käutner situated himself (or was situated) as an outsider. Except for his final film, *Unter den Brücken* (Under the Bridges), which was made in 1945 for UFA shortly before capitulation, he worked with smaller companies (Terra, Tobis) and made for the most part cheaper films that were clearly at odds with the official cinematic "look," and were therefore occasionally banned. Käutner's differences with the officials were not ideological in nature, nor did he in any way consider himself part of a political opposition. What was particularly unsettling about Käutner for the Propaganda Ministry was the former's refusal to take up thematic concerns of a given hour. When, in the late 1930s, Goebbels called for more overtly propagandistic films in support of approaching war on the eastern and western fronts and as a part of the stepped-up campaign against the Jews, Käutner made light cabaret comedies dealing ironically with role switching and gender instability (*Marguerite 3* [1939]; *Kitty und die Weltkonferenz* [1939]; *Frau nach Maß* [1940]; *Kleider machen machen Leute* [1940]). If the perceived social need for *light* entertainment during the time of increased bombing assaults in 1942–43 led the regime to encourage the making of films of flight and fancy, Käutner delivered fatalistic melodramas (*Auf Wiedersehen Franziska* [1941] and *Romanze in Moll*), whose morose messages were those of renunciation and death.

But more important than his refusal to conform to the thematic lines of a changing *Kulturpolitik* was Käutner's assertion of aesthetic complexity in the face of increasing demands for monumentality of spectacle and monolithic meaning. This was the case even when a film's narrative message happened to please Nazi critics because it conformed to the ideological guidelines of the status quo, as was the case with *Auf Wiedersehen Franziska*. Regardless or even despite the dictates of the screenplay, Käutner's use of light and shadow seemingly lent to objects and characters a symbolic and transcendent power, suggesting something profoundly at odds with the reductiveness (of plot, image, mise en scène, etc.) found in the existing semiotic system. In Käutner's visual spaces meaning seemed to hover— self-contained, impenetrable, and sovereign—in a world that could not entirely be deciphered.

Thus, the "aesthetic" in Witte's sense of opposition refers primarily, although not exclusively, to the visual dimension and the extent to which in the translation from word to picture a nondiscursive space is created where the audience is encouraged to produce meaning. In her essay entitled "Douglas Sirk's *Schlußakkord* and the Question of Aesthetic Resistance," Linda Schulte-Sasse raises a question about Sierk similar to the one Witte has raised regarding Käutner: "Can cinematic form operate 'in competition' with narrative content to constitute resistance?" (18). Schulte-Sasse's answer to this query involves disposing with the term "resistance" in favor of "reflexive space," by which she means "the operations with which a given text forces its audiences to move away from a seamless identification with narrative figures and a linear absorption by the plot's trajectory and which encourage an awareness of the text as form" (18).[4] A number of recent reevaluations of Sierck's work in the Third Reich have scorned his own claim (and that of some of his supportive critics)[5] to have been in a kind of *inner emigration* (read "noncomplicity"), stressing instead his affiliation with the institutions within which he worked, the themes he chose to illustrate, and the sentimental, melodramatic, ultimately non-Brechtian nature of his aesthetic (see Trumpener). Citing the validity of such historical and institutional accounts, Schulte-Sasse (like Witte) assiduously avoids any sweeping claim of institutional noncomplicity or even neutrality vis-à-vis the status quo on the part of Sierck in the Third Reich. What she argues instead is that Sierck created reflexive spaces within the narrative flow of individual films in which meanings could be reversed or destabilized and audiences encouraged to read such texts against the grain of the official horizon of expectancy. Although the term "aesthetic" in her account does not take on the clearly non-narrative function it had for Witte's more subtle cinematic analysis, reading both authors together does help us sum up the limits and possibilities of artistic agency within the medial (film, radio, television) structures of the Nazi public sphere.

With regard to the institutional framework of the industry as a whole, filmmakers in Nazi Germany functioned throughout the system as integrated members of a highly modernized, state-of-the-art film industry. Whereas some may have realized their art as committed purveyors of the prevailing ideological policies and others sought to express themselves as practitioners of aesthetic excellence, all ultimately participated in and thereby contributed toward the image of a modern, German mass culture. There could be no involvement in this highly centralized and visible operation without some form of compromise. Thus, at the level of participation, which also meant legitimation, these artists were all complicit, regardless of what they thought they were doing.

However, within this structure of professional complicity and compromise there were moments of choice involving one's integrity to the material at hand. This may have involved finding a way to extend an image, sustain a mood, minimalize or personalize a style, and in so doing create, if only momentarily and for specific audiences, a sensibility that pointed beyond the world of violence and sycophancy from which it emerged. That such creative achievements have occasionally resulted in disproportionate critical excitement on the part of later scholars looking for something beyond the norm is a sad but historically grounded statement of just how abnormal the normal had become in the film world of Nazi Germany.

Notes

A shorter version of this essay appeared in *Cultural History through a National Socialist Lens: Essays on the Cinema of the Third Reich*, ed. Robert C. Reimer (Rochester, N.Y.: Camden House, 2000), 1–10. The author and editors thank Camden House for their generous permission to reprint an expanded version of that essay.

1. Of particular importance has been the work of Ralf Dahrendorf, *Gesellschaft und Demokratie in Deutschland* (1965); Detlev J. K. Peukert, *Inside Nazi Germany: Conformity, Opposition, and Racism in Everyday Life* (1987); Peter Reichel, *Der schöne Schein des Dritten Reiches: Faszination und Gewalt des Faschismus* (1991); Hans Dieter Schäfer, *Das gespaltene Bewußtsein: Über deutsche Kultur und Lebenswirklichkeit 1933–1945* (1987); David Schoenbaum, *Hitler's Social Revolution: Class and Status in Nazi Germany, 1933–1939* (1966); and Rainer Zittelmann, "Die totalitäre Seite der Moderne" (1991).
2. The work of the following scholars has been particularly important within recent scholarly developments in the area of Third Reich cinema: Klaus Kreimeier, *Die Ufa Story: Geschichte eines Filmkonzerns* (1992): Stephen Lowry, *Pathos und Politik: Ideologie in Spielfilmen des Nationalsozialismus* (1991); Eric Rentschler, *The Ministry of Illusion*; Linda Schulte-Sasse, *Entertaining the Third Reich: Illusions of Wholeness in Nazi Cinema* (1996); Karsten Witte, *Lachende Erben, Toller Tag: Filmkomödien im Dritten Reich* (1995).
3. Staudte went on to make a number of significant antifascist films for DEFA after the war, notably *The Murderers Are Among Us* (1946) and *Rotation* (1949).
4. Surprisingly, Schulte-Sasse does not cite Witte's article, which in choice of terminology and critical approach seems very close to her own.
5. Paul Willemen makes the strongest argument in this regard in his "Towards an Analysis of the Sirkean System."

Works Cited

Dahrendorf, Ralf. *Gesellschaft und Demokratie in Deutschland*. Munich: Piper, 1965.

Drewniak, Boguslaw. *Der deutsche Film 1938–1945: Ein Gesamtüberblick*. Düsseldorf: Institute, 1987.

Fischer, Lucy, ed. *Imitation of Life*. New Brunswick, N.J.: Rutgers University Press, 1991.

Heiber, Helmut, ed. *Goebbels-Reden*. 2 vols. Düsseldorf: Droste Verlag, 1971.

Herf, Jeffrey. *Reactionary Modernism: Technology, Culture and Politics in Weimar and the Third Reich*. Cambridge: Cambridge University Press, 1984.

Kreimeier, Klaus. *Die Ufa Story: Geschichte eines Filmkonzerns*. Munich: Hanser, 1992.

Lowry, Stephen. *Pathos und Politik: Ideologie in Spielfilmen des Nationalsozialismus*. Tübingen: Niemeyer, 1991.

Peukert, Detlev J. K. *Inside Nazi Germany: Conformity, Opposition, and Racism in Everyday Life*. Translated by Richard Deveson. New Haven: Yale University Press, 1987.

Reichel, Peter. *Der schöne Schein des Dritten Reiches: Faszination und Gewalt des Faschismus*. Munich: Hanser, 1991.

Reimer, Robert C., ed. *Cultural History through a National Socialist Lens: Essays on the Cinema in the Third Reich*. Rochester, N.Y.: Camden House, 2000.

———. "Turning Inward: An Analysis of Helmut Käutner's *Auf Wiedersehen Franziska; Romanze in Moll*; and *Unter den Brücken*." In *Cultural History through a National Socialist Lens*, ed. Robert C. Reimer. Rochester, N.Y.: Camden House, 2000.

Rentschler, Eric. *The Ministry of Illusion: Nazi Cinema and Its Afterlife*. Cambridge: Harvard University Press, 1996.

Rundell, Richard. "Literary Nazis? Adapting Nineteenth-Century German Novellas for the Screen: *Der Schimmelreiter, Kleider Machen Leute,* and *Immensee.*" In *Cultural History through a National Socialist Lens,* ed. Robert C. Reimer. Rochester, N.Y.: Camden House, 2000.

Schäfer, Hans Dieter. *Das gespaltene Bewußtsein: Über deutsche Kultur und Lebenswirklichkeit 1933–1945.* Munich: Carl Hanser Verlag, 1987.

Schoenbaum, David. *Hitler's Social Revolution: Class and Status in Nazi Germany, 1933–1939.* Garden City, N.Y.: Doubleday, 1966.

Schulte-Sasse, Linda. "Douglas Sirk's *Schlußakkord* and the Question of Aesthetic Resistance." *Germanic Review* 73, no. 1 (winter, 1998).

———. *Entertaining the Third Reich: Illusions of Wholeness in Nazi Cinema.* Durham, N.C.: Duke University Press, 1996.

Trumpener, Katie. "Puerto Rico Fever: Douglas Sirk, *La Habanera* (1937) and the Epistemology of Exoticism." In *"Neue Welt/Dritte Welt": Interkulturelle Beziehungen Deutschlands zu Lateinamerika und der Karibik,* ed. Sigrid Bauschinger and Susan Cocalis, 115–39. Tübingen and Basel: Franke Verlag, 1994.

Willemen, Paul. "Towards an Analysis of the Sirkean System." In *Imitation of Life,* ed. Lucy Fischer, 268–78. New Brunswick, N.J.: Rutgers University Press, 1991.

Witte, Karsten. *Lachende Erben, Toller Tag: Filmkomödien im Dritten Reich.* Berlin: Vorweg 8, 1995.

———. "Ästhetische Opposition? Käutners Filme im Faschismus." *Sammlung: Jahrbuch für antifaschistische Literatur und Kunst* 4 (1980): 110–123.

Zittelmann, Rainer. "Die totalitäre Seite der Moderne." In *Nationalsozialismus und Modernisierung,* ed. by Michael Prinz and Rainer Zittelmann, 1–20. Darmstadt: Wissenschaftliche Buchgesellschaft, 1991.

SELECTED BIBLIOGRAPHY

Adorno, T. *Minima Moralia. Reflexionen aus dem beschädigten Leben (Gesammelte Schriften 4)*. Ed. R. Tiedemann. Frankfurt am Main: Suhrkamp, 1997.

Arntzen, H., ed. *Ursprung der Gegenwart: Zur Bewusstseinsgeschichte der Dreissiger Jahre in Deutschland*. Weinheim: Beltz Athenäum, 1995.

Assmann, M., and H. Heckmann, eds. *Zwischen Kritik und Zuversicht: 50 Jahre Deutsche Akademie für Sprache und Dichtung*. Göttingen: Wallstein, 1999.

Barbian, J.-P. *Literaturpolitik im'Dritten Reich': Institutionen, Kompetenzen, Betätigungsfelder*. Munich: Deutscher Taschenbuchverlag, 1995.

Basker, David. *Chaos, Control and Consistency: The Narrative Vision of Wolfgang Koeppen*. Bern and New York: P. Lang, 1993.

Berendsohn, W. *Die humanistische Front*. Vol. 2, *"Vom Kriegsausbruch 1939 bis Ende 1946."* Worms: Heintz, 1976.

Berglund, G. *Der Kampf um den Leser im Dritten Reich: Die Literaturpolitik der "Neuen Literatur" (Will Vesper) und der "Nationalsozialistischen Monatshefte."* Worms: Heintz, 1980.

Bluhm, L. *Das Tagebuch zum Dritten Reich: Zeugnisse der Inneren Emigration von Jochen Klepper bis Ernst Jünger*. Bonn: Bouvier, 1991.

Bock. S., and M. Hahn, eds. *Erfahrung Nazideutschland. Romane in Deutschland 1933–1945*. Berlin and Weimar: Aufbau Verlag, 1987.

Brekle, W. *Schriftsteller im antifaschistischen Widerstand 1933–1945 in Deutschland*. Berlin and Weimar: Aufbau Verlag, 1985.

Caemmerer, C., and W. Delabar, eds. *Dichtung im Dritten Reich? Zur Literatur in Deutschland 1933–1945*. Opladen: Westdeutscher Verlag, 1996.

Cuomo, G. *National Socialist Cultural Policy*. New York: St. Martin's Press, 1995.

———. *Career at the Cost of Compromise: Günter Eich's Life and Work in the Years 1933–1945*. Amsterdam and Atlanta: Rodopi, 1989.

Dahm, V. "Anfänge und Ideologie der Reichskulturkammer. Die "Berufsgemeinschaft" als Instrument kulturpolitischer Steuerung und sozialer Reglementierung." *Vierteljahreshefte für Zeitgeschichte* 34, no. 1 (1986): 53–84.

Denk, F. *Die Zensur der Nachgeborenen: Zur regimekritischen Literatur im Dritten Reich*. Weilheim: Denk-Verlag, 1996.

Denkler, H. "Hellas als Spiegel der Gegenwart in der Literatur des 'Dritten Reichs.'" *Zeitschrift für Germanistik* (1999): 11–27.

———. "Janusköpfig: Zur ideologischen Physiognomie der Zeitschrift *Das Innere Reich* (1934–1944)." In *Die deutsche Literatur im Dritten Reich*, ed. H. Denkler and K. Prümm. Stuttgart: Reclam, 1976.

Dirks, W. "Die restaurativen Charakter der Epoche." *Frankfurter Hefte* 5 (1950): 942–54.

Dolan, J. P. "Die Rolle der *Kolonne* in der Entwicklung der modernen deutschen Naturlyrik." Ph.D. diss., University of Pennsylvania, 1976.

———. "The Theory and Practice of Apolitical Literature: *Die Kolonne, 1929–1932.*" *Studies in Twentieth-Century Literature* 19, no. 1 (1977): 157–71.

Donahue, N. H. *Karl Krolow and the Poetics of Amnesia in Postwar Germany.* Rochester, N.Y.: Camden House/Boydell & Brewer, Inc., 2002.

Erke-Rotermund, H., and E. Rotermund. *Zwischenreiche und Gegenwelten: Texte und Vorstudien zur 'Verdeckten Schreibweise' im "Dritten Reich."* Munich: Fink, 1999.

Grimm, R., and J. Hermand, eds. *Exil und Innere Emigration: Third Wisconsin Workshop.* Frankfurt am Main: Athenäum, 1972.

Grosser, J. F., ed. *Die grosse Kontroverse: Ein Briefwechsel um Deutschland.* Hamburg, Genf, and Paris: Nagel, 1963.

Haarmann, H., W. Huderer, and K. Siebenhaar, eds. *"Das war ein Vorspiel nur" Bücherverbrennung Deutschland 1933: Voraussetzungen und Folgen.* [Katalog der] *Ausstellung der Adademie der Künste vom 8. Mai bis 3. Juli 1983.* Berlin: Medusa, 1983.

Hein, P. U. *Die Brücke ins Geistreich. Künstlerische Avantgarde zwischen Kulturkritik und Faschismus.* Reinbek bei Hamburg: rororo, 1992.

Hewitt, A. *Fascist Modernism: Aesthetics, Politics, and the Avant-Garde.* Stanford: Stanford University Press, 1993.

Hoffmann, C. W. *Opposition Poetry in Nazi Germany.* Berkeley and Los Angeles: University of California Press, 1962.

Hopster, N. "Literatur und 'Leben' in der Ästhetik des Nationalsozialismus." *Wirkendes Wort* 43 (1993): 99–115.

Horst, K. A. "Epitaph auf eine Epoche." *Merkur* 16 (1962): 1162–69.

Kantorowicz, A., and R. Drews. *Verboten und verbrannt. Deutsche Literatur 12 Jahre unterdrückt.* Berlin: Ullstein, 1947.

Kater, M. *Different Drummers: Jazz in the Culture of Nazi Germany.* New York: Oxford, 1992.

Kesten, H. *Lauter Literaten: Portraits/Erinnerungen.* Munich and Zurich: Droemersche Verlagsanstalt, 1966.

Ketelsen, U.-K. *Literatur und Drittes Reich.* Schernfeld: SH-Verlag, 1992.

Kirchner, D. *Doppelbödige Wirklichkeit: Magischer Realismus und nicht-faschistische Literatur.* Tübingen: Stauffenburg, 1993.

Klemperer, V. *I Will Bear Witness: A Diary of the Nazi Years 1933–1941.* New York: The Modern Library/Random House, 1998.

———. *LTI. Notizbuch eines Philologen.* Leipzig: Aufbau, 1975 [1946].

Klieneberger, H. R. *The Christian Writers of the Inner Emigration.* The Hague: Mouton, 1968.

Krenzlin, L. "Grosse Kontroverse oder kleiner Dialog? Gesprächsbemühungen und Kontaktbruchstellen zwischen 'inneren' und 'äusseren' literarischen Emigranten." *Galerie: Revue culturelle et pedagogique* 15, no. 1 (1997): 7–25.

Kretschmer, M. "Die Dichterrolle als Reflexionsmedium literarischer Praxis in Deutschland 1945–1950." *Poetica* 11 (1979): 207–32.

Krohn, Claus Dieter, Erwin Rotermund, Lutz Winckler, and Wulf Koepke, eds. *Aspekte der künstlerischen Inneren Emigration 1933–1945.* Vol. 12, *Exilforschung: Ein internationales Jahrbuch.* Munich: text + kritik, 1994.

Kroll, Frank-Lothar, ed. *Deutschsprachige Autoren des Ostens als Gegner und Opfer des Nationalsozialismus. Beiträge zur Problematik des kulturellen Widerstandes im Dritten Reich*. Berlin: Duncker & Humblot, 1999.

Loewy, E. *Literatur unterm Hakenkreuz. Das Dritte Reich und seine Dichtung. Eine Dokumentation*. Frankfurt am Main: Fischer, 1987.

Mallmann, M. *'Das Innere Reich': Analyse einer konservativen Kulturzeitschrift im Dritten Reich*. Bonn: Bouvier, 1978.

Mitscherlich A., and M. Mitscherlich. *Die Unfähigkeit zu trauern: Grundlagen kollektiven Verhaltens*. Munich: Piper, 1967.

Natter, W. *Literature at War, 1914–1940: Representing the "Time of Greatness" in Germany*. New Haven and London: Yale University Press, 1999.

Niven, B. "Ernst Wiechert and His Role Between 1933 and 1945." *New German Studies* 16 (1990–91): 1–20.

Paetel, K. O. *Deutsche Innere Emigration: Antinationalsozialistische Zeugnisse aus Deutschland*. New York: Friedrich Krause, 1946.

Parker, S. "Visions, Revisions and Divisions: The Critical Legacy of Peter Huchel." *German Life and Letters* 41, no. 2 (1988): 184–211.

Paulsen, R. "Der Dichter und die Zeit." *Der Schriftsteller* 18 (1930).

Perels, C., ed. *Lyrik verlegen in dunkler Zeit: Aus Heinrich Ellermanns Reihe Das Gedicht: Blätter für die Dichtung, 1934–1944*. Munich: Ellermann, 1984.

Peukert, D. *Inside Nazi Germany: Conformity, Opposition, and Racism in Everyday Life*. New Haven: Yale University Press, 1987.

Philip, M. "Distanz und Anpassung: Sozialgeschichtliche Aspekte der *Inneren Emigration*." *Aspekte der künstlerischen Inneren Emigration 1933-1945*, ed. Claus Dieter Krohn, Erwin Rotermund, Lutz Winckler, and Wulf Koepke, 11–30. Vol. 12, *Exilforschung: Ein internationales Jahrbuch*. Munich: text + kritik, 1994.

———. "Auswahlbibliographie Innere Emigration." In *Aspekte der künstlerischen Inneren Emigration 1933–1945*, ed. Claus Dieter Krohn, Erwin Rotermund, Lutz Winckler, and Wulf Koepke, 200–216. Vol. 12, *Exilforschung: Ein internationales Jahrbuch*. Munich: text + kritik, 1994.

Reichel, P. *Der schöne Schein des Dritten Reiches: Faszination und Gewalt des Faschismus*. Munich: Hanser, 1991.

Rüther, G., ed. *Literatur in der Diktatur: Schreiben im Nationalsozialismus und DDR-Sozialismus*. Paderborn: Schöningh, 1997.

Sarkowicz, H., and A. Mentzer. *Literatur in Nazi-Deutschland: Ein biografisches Lexikon*. Hamburg and Vienna: Europa Verlag, 2000.

Schäfer, H. D. *Am Rande der Nacht. Moderne Klassik im Dritten Reich*. Berlin: Ullstein, 1984.

———. *Das gespaltene Bewusstsein: Über deutsche Kultur und Lebenswirklichkeit, 1933–1945*. Frankfurt am Main: Ullstein, 1981.

———. "Kultur als Simulation: Das Dritte Reich und die Postmoderne." In *Literatur in der Diktatur: Schreiben im Nationalsozialismus und DDR-Sozialismus*, ed. G. Rüther, 215–45. Paderborn: Schöningh, 1997.

———. "Naturdichtung und Neue Sachlichkeit." In *Die deutsche Literatur in der Weimarer Republik*, ed. W. Rothe. Stuttgart: Reclam, 1974.

———. "Die nichtfaschistische Literatur der 'jungen Generation' im nationalsozialistischen Deutschland." In *Die deutsche Literatur im Dritten Reich: Themen, Traditionen, Wirkungen*, ed. H. Denkler and K. Prümm. Stuttgart: Reclam, 1977.

———. "Zur Periodisierung der deutschen Literatur seit 1930." *Literaturmagazin* 7 (1977): 95–115.

Scheffel, M. *Magischer Realismus. Die Geschichte eines Begriffes und ein Versuch seiner Bestimmung*. Stauffenburg Colloquium. Vol. 16. Tübingen: Stauffenburg, 1990.

Schnell, R. *Dichtung in finsteren Zeiten: Deutsche Literatur und Faschismus*. Reinbeck bei Hamburg: Rowohlt, 1999.

———. *Literarische Innere Emigration, 1933–1945*. Stuttgart: Metzler, 1976.

Schoeps, K.-H. *Deutsche Literatur zwischen den Weltkriegen: Literatur im Dritten Reich*. Frankfurt am Main: P. Lang, 1992.

Schonauer, F. *Deutsche Literatur im Dritten Reich: Versuch einer Darstellung in polemisch-didaktischer Absicht*. Olten und Freiburg im Breisgrau: Walter, 1961.

Schröter, K., ed. *Thomas Mann im Urteil seiner Zeit: Dokumente 1891–1955*. Hamburg: Christian Wegener, 1969.

Schwarz, E., ed. *Exil und Innere Emigration II: Internationale Tagung in St. Louis*. Frankfurt am Main: Athenäum, 1973.

Sontheimer, K. *Thomas Mann und die Deutschen*. Munich: Nymphenburger Verlagsanstalt, 1961.

Steinweis, A. *Art, Ideology and Economics in Nazi Germany: The Reich Chambers of Music, Theater, and the Visual Arts*. Chapel Hill: University of North Carolina Press, 1993.

Sternberger, D. *Aus dem Wörterbuch des Unmenschen*. Hamburg: Claassen, 1957.

Sternfeld, W., and E. Tiedemann, eds. *Deutsche Exil-Literatur, 1933–1945. Eine Bio-Bibliographie*. Heidelberg: Lambert Schneider, 1962.

Thuneke, J., ed. *Leid der Worte: Panorama des literarischen Nationalsozialismus*. Bonn: Bouvier, 1987.

Trommler, F. "Die nachgeholte Resistance: Politik und Gruppenethos im historischen Zusammenhang." In *Die Gruppe 47 in der Geschichte der Bundesrepublik*, ed. Justus Fetscher, 9–22. Würzburg: Koenigshausen & Neumann, 1991.

———. "Emigration und Nachkriegsliteratur: Zum Problem der geschichtlichen Kontinuität." In *Exil und Innere Emigration: Third Wisconsin Workshop*, ed. H. Grimm and J. Hermand. Frankfurt am Main: Athenäum, 1972.

Vaillant, J. *Der Ruf. Unabhängige Blätter der jungen Generation (1945–1949)*. Munich, New York, and Paris: Saur, 1978.

Vieregg, A. "The Truth about Peter Huchel." *German Life and Letters* 41, no. 2 (1988): 159–83.

Walter, D., H. Denkler, and E. Schütz, eds. *Banalität mit Stil. Zur Widersprüchlichkeit der Literaturproduktion im Nationalsozialismus*. Special Issue 1. *Zeitschrift für Germanistik*, 1999.

Ziolkowski, T. "Form als Protest: Das Sonett in der Literatur des Exils und der inneren Emigration." In *Exil und Innere Emigration: Third Wisconsin Workshop*, ed. R. Grimm and J. Hermand. Frankfurt am Main: Athenäum, 1972.

INDEX